RISK, ENVIRONMENT
AND MODERNITY

Theory, Culture & Society

Theory, Culture & Society caters for the resurgence of interest in culture within contemporary social science and the humanities. Building on the heritage of classical social theory, the book series examines ways in which this tradition has been reshaped by a new generation of theorists. It will also publish theoretically informed analyses of everyday life, popular culture, and new intellectual movements.

EDITOR: Mike Featherstone, *University of Teesside*

Recent volumes include:

The Consuming Body
Pasi Falk

Cultural Identity and Global Process
Jonathan Friedman

The Established and the Outsiders
Norbert Elias and John L. Scotson

The Cinematic Society
The Voyeur's Gaze
Norman K. Denzin

Decentring Leisure
Rethinking Leisure Theory
Chris Rojek

Global Modernities
Mike Featherstone, Scott Lash and Roland Robertson

The Masque of Femininity
The Presentation of Woman in Everyday Life
Efrat Tseëlon

The Arena of Racism
Michel Wieviorka

Undoing Culture
Globalization, Postmodernism and Identity
Mike Featherstone

RISK, ENVIRONMENT AND MODERNITY

Towards a New Ecology

edited by
Scott Lash, Bronislaw Szerszynski
and Brian Wynne

SAGE Publications
London • Thousand Oaks • New Delhi

First published 1996

Published in association with *Theory, Culture & Society*,
School of Human Studies, University of Teesside

SAGE Publications Ltd
6 Bonhill Street
London EC2A 4PU

SAGE Publications Inc
2455 Teller Road
Thousand Oaks, California 91320

SAGE Publications India Pvt Ltd
32, M-Block Market
Greater Kailash – I
New Delhi 110 048

British Library Cataloguing in Publication data

A catalogue record for this book is
available from the British Library

ISBN 0 8039 7937 1
ISBN 0 8039 7938 X (pbk)

Library of Congress catalog card number   95–074765

Typeset by Photoprint, Torquay, Devon
Printed in Great Britain by The Cromwell Press Ltd,
Broughton Gifford, Melksham, Wiltshire

Contents

Preface

This book arose out of an international symposium – 'The Risk Society: Modernity and the Environment' – organised at Lancaster University in May 1992 by the Centre for the Study of Environmental Change (CSEC) and the Department of Sociology. The symposium was founded on a critical examination of the perspectives of Ulrich Beck and Anthony Giddens, focusing on modernity, risk and the cultural dimensions of contemporary environmental issues. It occurred at a time when dominant understandings of risk and environmental issues were undergoing what many at the symposium felt to be an unreflexive shift towards a highly globalised, scientised and universalistic idiom.

The Lancaster meeting brought together for the first time a range of European social theorists and scholars interested in these issues, not only as academic fare but also in terms of their profound importance to late-modern society, and to the turbulent debate over the meaning of European Union. The book is inspired by a shared conviction that more creative intellectual work is needed if we are to engage fully with the social, cultural and political dimensions of these issues, dimensions whose complexities are being obscured by the dominant modes of thought in policy and academic circles.

We are grateful to our authors for the work and commitment they have shown in responding to our editorial efforts to offer a more coherent framework of debate than would be offered by a simple collection of papers. We are also grateful to those many symposium participants from all parts of Europe whose ideas and contributions do not appear as chapters. Thanks are also due to Anne Stubbins for her highly effective organisational support, and to Robert Rojek at Sage for his continued interest and calm reassurance. The UK's Economic and Social Research Council provided funding for the symposium, as well as for CSEC's ongoing research programme on Science, Culture and the Environment. This and the continuing intellectual support of Robin Grove-White and other colleagues in CSEC, together with that of members of the Department of Sociology, and the Lancaster Cultural Change Network have played a crucial role in making this volume possible.

Contributors

Barbara Adam is a social theorist working at the University of Wales, Cardiff. She has published widely on the social analysis of time. She is the author of *Time and Social Theory* (Polity, 1990) and *Timewatch* (Polity, 1995), and editor of the Sage journal *Time and Society*.

Ulrich Beck is Professor of Sociology at the University of Munich. He is the author of *Risk Society* (Sage, 1992), *Ecological Politics in an Age of Risk* (Polity, 1995), *Ecological Enlightenment* (Humanities Press, 1995), *The Renaissance of Politics* (Polity, 1996) and co-author of *Reflexive Modernization* (Polity, 1994) and *The Normal Chaos of Love* (Blackwell, 1995).

Elisabeth Beck-Gernsheim is Professor of Sociology at the Friedrich Alexander University of Erlangen-Nürnberg. She is the author of *Techno-Health* (Humanities Press International, 1995) and co-author of *The Normal Chaos of Love* (Blackwell, 1995).

Helmuth Berking is Visiting Associate Professor of Political Science at Northwestern University, Illinois. He is the author of *Masse und Geist: Studien zur Soziologie in der Weimarer Republik* (1984), and has written extensively on lifestyle, new social movements and politics in East and West Germany.

Marco Diani is Research Professor and Senior Research Fellow at the Centre National de la Recherche Scientifique, and Director of the Institut de Recherches sur le Moderne, at the Université de Savoie, Chambéry, France. His publications include *The Immaterial Society* (Prentice Hall, 1992), and the edited collections *Restructuring Architectural Theory* (Northwestern University Press, 1989) and *L'Intelligenza dell'Automazione* (Franco Angeli, 1991).

Klaus Eder is Professor of Sociology at the Humboldt University, Berlin, and at the European University Institute, Florence. His publications include *Geschichte als Lernprozess* (Suhrkamp, 1985), *Der Vergesellschaftung der Natur* (Suhrkamp, 1988) and *The New Politics of Class* (Sage, 1993).

Robin Grove-White is Director of the Centre for the Study of Environmental Change, Lancaster University. He was Director of the Council for the Protection of Rural England from 1981 to 1987, has served as Specialist Adviser (Environment) to the House of Lords Select Committee on the European Communities, and is still actively involved in environmental politics. He has written widely on the social and cultural aspects of environmental conflicts.

Maarten Hajer teaches sociology at the University of Munich, specialising in environment, risk and technology in the context of theories of modernisation. He is the author of *The Politics of Environmental Discourse: Ecological Modernisation and the Policy Process* (Clarendon Press, 1995).

Andrew Jamison is Associate Professor of Science and Technology Policy and Director of Studies at the Research Policy Institute, University of Lund. He is the co-author of *The Making of the New Environmental Consciousness* (Edinburgh University Press, 1990), and, with Ron Eyerman, of *Social Movements: A Cognitive Approach* (Polity, 1991).

Scott Lash is Professor of Sociology at Lancaster University. He is the author of *Sociology of Postmodernism* (Routledge, 1990) and co-author of *The End of Organized Capitalism* (Polity, 1987), *Economies of Signs and Space* (Sage, 1993) and *Reflexive Modernization* (Polity, 1994).

John Maguire is Professor of Sociology at University College, Cork, and the author of *Marx's Paris Writings* (Gill and Macmillan, 1972) and *Marx's Theory of Politics* (Cambridge University Press, 1979). His current research interests are in emotional and cultural critiques of organisations and policymaking. He is the author, with Joe Noonan, of *Maastricht and Neutrality: Ireland's Neutrality and the Future of Europe* (People First / Meitheal, 1992).

Bronislaw Szerszynski is Research Fellow at the Centre for the Study of Environmental Change, Lancaster University. He has published a number of articles on ethics and environmentalism, and is currently engaged in a research project on sustainable development, cultural movements and identity.

Brian Wynne is Professor of Science Studies and Research Director at the Centre for the Study of Environmental Change, Lancaster University. He has published widely in the field of science studies, most notably in the areas of risk and public understanding. He is the author of *Rationality and Ritual* (British Society for the History of Science, 1982) and co-editor of *Misunderstanding Science* (Cambridge University Press, 1995).

INTRODUCTION: ECOLOGY, REALISM AND THE SOCIAL SCIENCES

Bronislaw Szerszynski, Scott Lash and Brian Wynne

Journalists and other commentators on environmental matters never cease, it seems, to bemoan our ignorance of the needs of nature. This is indeed ironic because the last decade or so has, much to the contrary, witnessed an unprecedented outbreak of environmental discourse. We hear of benign – and not-so-benign – ecological neglect, but never before has the environment been the object of so much knowledge. We hear of silent watching while seals fade into extinction and rainforests are despoliated, yet never has there been such a cacophony of voices taking ecology as their thematic – a cacophony led by a multitude of disparate expert voices.

This book thus begins not from the presupposition of too much silence about the environment, but from that of perhaps an overproduction of expertise on green issues. How, amidst the rising clamour, to tell signal from noise? More specifically, it begins not so much from the volume, the overload of noise generated on things environmental, but rather from the mode in which such 'greentalk' has been enunciated. It contends that the translation of things 'environmental' into authoritative scientific and policy vocabularies occurs in ways which could be described as, amongst other things, epistemologically 'realist', positivistic, disembedded, technological and cognitivist, and that it thus tends to mask important cultural, social and existential dimensions of the contemporary 'environmental crisis'.

This is all the more serious because widespread public concern over the effects of human activity on the natural world has produced a broad consensus between scientists, policymakers and other 'authoritative' commentators about the need for more reliable information about the present condition of the environment, the status of current threats, and the imperative for appropriate responses. From such a consensus has emerged a number of large-scale intergovernmental research programmes, global conventions and national policy commitments, all too often orientated around overwhelmingly realist accounts of the environment. Even the social sciences, in their embryonic grapplings with the environmental agenda, have hitherto largely proceeded uncritically on the basis that the environment exists simply as a material substrate of the social, defined by scientific inquiry. The increasing role of social science in environmental policy knowledge generation has been attended by an intensification of the dominant idiom of social scientific knowledge – positivistic, rational-choice, economistic, behaviourist even – thus obliterating the possibility that the human conceptions reproduced in such 'scientific' discourses may well be part of that which has come to be crystallised as the modern environmental problem.

This book constitutes a sort of 'slow manifesto' against such tendencies in the social sciences more broadly, presenting a number of different accounts of the environmental phenomenon in late modernity which are in different degrees constructivist rather than realist, hermeneutic rather than positivist, poetic rather than technological, situated rather than disembedded. These accounts are organised under three broad themes. Part I addresses issues of science, technology and expert systems, exploring in different ways the exhaustion of the very modernist ideas of technical prediction and control which are being reinvoked in responses to the global environmental crisis. Part II explores questions of subjectivity and individualisation: at a time of rapid environmental, technological and cultural change how are our identities, and hence the modes in which we might engage with our predicament, being transformed – and at what cost? Finally, Part III points to emerging problems with the ways in which environmental considerations are being incorporated at the level of political institutions.

An important catalyst for the arguments presented here has been the work of the German sociologist Ulrich Beck. Beck's *Risikogesellschaft*, published originally in 1986 and then in English by TCS/Sage in 1992, has had an enormous impact on the understanding of the environment, sociological theory and political debates in general, first in Germany and now in the UK and elsewhere in Europe. Beck argued that an older industrial society, whose axial principle was the distribution of 'goods', was being displaced by an emergent 'risk society', structured, so to speak, around the distribution of 'bads'. In risk society the distribution of hazards seems blind to inequalities; they flow easily across national and class boundaries; they are not delimited by metanarratives of temporal closure.

Risk society is recognisable not only by the problematisation of objective physical-biological dangers, but also fundamentally by a principle of individualisation, in which agents become ever more free from the normative expectations of social institutions. This was thematised in, for example, his and Elisabeth Beck-Gernsheim's *Das ganz normale Chaos der Liebe* (The Normal Chaos of Love), which examined the self-construction of love- and life-narratives resulting from the institutional shake-up of the modern family. Addressing the risk problematique, other books like *Gegengifte* (Antidotes) and *Der feindlose Staat* (The State without Enemies), all translated or in the process of being translated into English, examine ecological danger in the context of *de facto*, *de jure* and possible institutionalisations and move directly into the political realm.

The authors of this Introduction and a number of the contributors to the book are fundamentally sympathetic to the thrust of Beck's thesis. They all share the perspective that reifiying environmental problems as if they are shaped by real processes in nature alone, and as if the range of possible societal responses is also thus determined, is self-defeatingly reductionistic. However, the occasional sociological tendency to criticise such scientific reification by advancing the alternative view that all such problems are 'mere' social constructions, and hence (it is implied) not real, is equally misleading. Both such positions simply reproduce the cultural categories of modernity, nature versus culture, which are rightly problematised as part and parcel of the environmental problem. An aim of this collection is to help transcend such sterile reductionisms. Most of us will thus argue that Beck has not gone far enough in his break with the dominant 'technological' paradigm in environmental analysis. However, whatever the pros and cons of Beck's particular approach, his creative drawing together of the problems around environmental risk (and especially its globalisation) with those of modernity at large is a valuable and lasting contribution. In this collection we use Beck's contributions to illuminating this modern environmental problematique as a starting place for critical reflection on the state of social science and dominant 'social paradigms', using Europe as an arena. In particular, the main themes addressed by Beck – (1) environmental discourse as technology, (2) individualisation and (3) the transformation and cultural renewal of the political – give at the same time a basis and a structure to this book.

Part I   Environment, Knowledge and Indeterminacy: Beyond Modernist Ecology?

With the disintegration of the external threat from the East, Ernst Bloch's dictum concerning 'technology as the enemy within' is today, as never before, apposite. And indeed Horkheimer and Adorno's dire warnings of a dialectic of enlightenment in which reason would metamorphose into technology is nowhere more profoundly confirmed than in 'man's' domination and instrumentalisation of nature – including human nature. The instrumentalist epistemic shift of mainstream science from the 1920s onwards – a shift that coincides intriguingly with the rapid growth of big bureaucracies of public administration – has occasioned surprisingly little critical observation from the social sciences, which have instead anxiously sought to follow the road so mapped by their more confident and prestigious 'natural' cousins. Humanity's colonisation of nature through technology has taken place through a whole apparatus of material resources, such as machinery and computers, as well as through a range of expert-systems – especially capitalist management and the administrative apparatus of the state. Instrumentalist social science has only aided and abetted these trends and transformations. And it is as a challenge to the subjugation of the natural lifeworld by the ravages of state and technology that environmentalism began as a critical discourse, rich in cultural resources and resonances.

The shift of register in environmental discourses around the 1987 Brundtland Report, from environmental threat to sustainable development, offered the promise of overcoming the usual opposition of nature to society – the idea that we could only achieve environmental protection at the expense of human economic and social development. Sustainable development insisted that notions of global equity, justice and basic human rights were intrinsic aspects of the environmental issue. In principle, this resonated with the constructivist, culturalist insistence that the environmental issue is fundamentally an issue of human relations, and thus of culture and politics. However, these politically enlarging ideas – which it has to be noted implied more complex challenges in integrating multiple and even contradictory dimensions – were met not by cultural recognition and revolution but by grandiose ideas of 'Managing Planet Earth' by technocratic expertise (Clark, 1989; Sachs, 1993). Significantly, these managerial resources included the new resource of *social* science, conceived in identical epistemic clothing to the natural sciences – instrumental prediction and control. Thus, for example, the Intergovernmental Panel on Climate Change, set up in 1988 to advise governments and international bodies on the threats of human-induced global warming, and built around a natural-scientific working group of climate modellers, called unselfconsciously for deterministic social-scientific predictions of human inputs to the climate system for up to centuries ahead, and assumed that equally deterministic predictions could be made of human impacts of thus-predicted climate changes. Human society and culture was thus in effect reduced to a behavioural stimulus–response mechanism, and international social science was largely cultivated within this idiom, often quite determinedly and anxiously enforced (for example, in the Human Dimensions of Global Change programme of the International Social Science Council and the US National Science Foundation). The representation of environmental factors in decisions by economic monetary valuation, often operating as an alternative to considering more lasting, participatory and deliberate institutional and procedural changes, further intensifies this dominant social science paradigm and its culturally self-defeating epistemology.

Within the European context, analysts such as Jachtenfuchs and Huber (1993) have shown how environmental policy concerns have repeatedly been 'technologised', for example by translating the diverse complex social and lifestyle challenges of energy efficiency and energy demand reduction into technological programmes of new energy sources. This 'path of least resistance' syndrome is not, of course, unusual. However, an extra dimension appears to prevail at European level, one which takes on particular significance. The European Union (EU) response to environmental challenges like global warming has been, as noted, to evacuate them of any social or cultural meanings and to construe them instead in terms of new technologies of energy supply, or standard Europe-wide measures (like an energy tax) whose hugely different meanings, impacts and ramifications across the social and cultural heterogeneity of Europe are ignored. This standardises the problem and the human agents it encompasses. Yet whatever the universals of the issue may be, cursory examination underlines the most intense if diffuse and variable cultural energies fuelling recognition of and engagement with environmental issues. Several sociological critics have proposed that the sense of environmental threat is rooted in just those alienated culturally disembedded and humanly unsatisfactory models of the human and social embodied in dominant discourses of response to environmental problems – the individualistic, instrumental, non-relational models framing the economistic social science paradigms which have monopolised official and wider reactions, even (as we shall see in Part III of this volume) amongst non-governmental organisations (NGOs). Thus the dominant discourses of 'solution' at the European level may perversely be laying the foundations, not only of their own ineffectuality in environmental policy, but also of a much deeper – and, we believe, reactionary – antagonism to the idea of Europe as such, captured as it has been by this culturally arid technocratic modernism.

European institutions have run scared of acknowledging the cultural dimensions of difference which pervade and shadow all emergent European practices and formal frameworks, of legal and regulatory rules, technical definitions supporting the single market, and the like. In truth, this has been an understandable denial, given the extreme regressive forces of nationalism, sentimentality and naked racialism which seem to haunt the modern European project. But this instinctive denial of cultural (and even institutional) variation, depth and difference on the part of policy officials and their social science handmaidens only fuels the fires of parochial fear and retrenchment to which it attempts to deny air. Rather than grasp the nettle of recognising the culturally rooted, human relational dimensions of environmental sensibilities, European policy culture and its institutions have been at the forefront of articulating and imposing an acultural, standardised, unreconstructed modernist conception of the problematique. This resonates all too easily with the familiar shibboleth of the nationalist right – a federalist bureaucratic superstate. Thus the germ of a culturally attuned environmental sensibility in Europe is pincered between on the one side a dominant instrumentalist managerial standardising paradigm, emptied of human meanings, and on the other a set of populist, all too humanly meaningful, parochialist, sentimentalist and antimodern cultural defence movements. Transcending this barren modernist/antimodernist, culture/nature dichotomy requires us to find a new set of terms which reflect the co-construction of nature and culture, and which in so doing may provide the grounds for a renewal of public agency and identification with environmental and related public policies. Thus far, the dominant idioms of social science giving identity to European environmental research and development have shown not the remotest awareness of these deep currents washing over the environmental issue, seen as it is in largely literal, realist terms. The scientific and policy discursive communities implicated in this sterile 'discourse-coalition' thus seem about to be joined by the sociological experts. And it is this particular actor-network, this alliance-in-truth, to which this volume lays down the gauntlet, in the name of the deleted dimensions of culture and of human commitment.

This environment-as-technology coalition not only presents us with a set of constructed and violently imposed truths, but also gives us an attached metadiscursive epistemology – an objectivist, physicalist and fully naive realism. It is objectivist in its insistence that the scientific observer is somehow separate and not irreducibly embedded in the 'object' he/she is studying. It is physicalist in its construction of risks and dangers through the symbolic prism of biological extinction, thus at the same time strategically maximising affective impact on the public. It is naively realist in its assumption of the brute fact – determined solely by nature, and only revealed by science – of global warming as the central environmental hazard, and in its neglect to mention that a number of such 'brute facts' were with us before the mid-1980s, yet have been constructed as pivotal environmental dangers only in the past few years. Within this paradigm, the fact that *globalised* dangers have become the axial principle of environmental threat at this point in historical time can only be explained by invoking supposed exogenous factors, such as a lag in institutional learning (Hajer, this volume). The complex social and cultural changes that have brought about the constitution of the environmental threat in these terms are completely overlooked.

It is at this point that the account put forward by Beck, whose contribution forms the first chapter of this volume, begins. Beck starts from the premise that the environmental crisis is primarily not a natural but a *social* crisis. The hazards produced by society can no longer be contained within conventionally modernist systems of prediction and control. In the face of nuclear, chemical and biotechnological dangers it is no longer possible for authoritative decisions to be made by groups of experts. Because of this, epistemic authority no longer rests with particular groups of scientists, politicians and industrialists, but has fragmented across a huge range of social groups, the incessant interaction of which is potentially raising society to a qualitatively new level of self-critique. As Beck emphasises, this is not a critical theory of society, but a theory of critical society – critique is endemic to the risk society, and does not have to be introduced from outside by the sociologist.

But what Beck usefully spells out here, as he indicated for the first time for English readers in his collaboration with Anthony Giddens and Scott Lash (Beck et al., 1994), is that reflexive modernisation is characterised as much by 'reflex' as it is by 'reflection'. The publication of *Risk Society* itself had raised worries for many readers that Beck seemed to be offering a vision of a kind of hyper-Enlightenment, where individuals and institutions were becoming increasingly able consciously to reflect on the premises of their own and others' commitments and knowledge claims. In his more recent work, however, it is possible to detect a move towards seeing reflexive modernisation as in most part propelled by blind social processes – a shift, crudely, from one where risk society produces reflection which in turn produces reflexivity and critique, to one where risk society automatically produces reflexivity, and then – perhaps – reflection (indeed his work can be seen as a *call* to reflection on our changed social condition). This shift has largely met concerns that he had illegitimately treated forms of knowledge as floating free from culture, institutions and practices – and thus as enabling subjects to reflect on society from outside, as it were (though the 'individualisation' strand of his analysis does indeed tend to imply such a picture, as should become clear from our discussion of the papers of Part II below).

However, despite our characterisation above of Beck as being perhaps excessively social constructionist with respect to the ontological status of environmental problems, at another level there is a curious realism in his analysis. For Beck it appears to be the genuine, real, physical riskiness of, for example, large-scale nuclear and chemical technologies, that has taken industrial society beyond its own limits of calculability. In Chapter 2, Brian Wynne takes Beck – and Anthony Giddens – to task for this realism, and for the asymmetry of their treatment of expert and lay knowledge, in a lengthy critique of the politics of the risk society thesis. Wynne, drawing on some fifteen years of his own research into risk and the environment, and his own background in the sociology of science, presents perhaps the most sustained effort to date to provide a radical alternative to the Beck thesis. The thrust of his case is a challenge to the strict division between scientific and lay knowledge that 'neo-modernist' analysts such as Beck and Giddens put forward in their juxtaposition of the 'propositional' and determinate knowledge of science on the one hand and the 'formulaic', indeterminate knowledge of the lay public on the other. But rationalists such as Beck and Giddens who privilege (social-) scientific over lay knowledge are not the only ones guilty of this flaw. So are more 'post'- or 'anti'-modernist writers such as Lash or Zimmerman who would seem to privilege the hermeneutic truths of lay actors over the propositional truths of the scientists in the understanding of the natural environment. Again the same dichotomy is invoked; the hierarchy is merely stood on its head.

Wynne's claim is that scientific knowledge itself is pervaded with a quite indeterminate and formulaic set of communications and practices, whilst the logos of practical and theoretical reason is always, already and also present in the language and truths of lay social actors. Wynne's idea of 'indeterminacy' here goes well beyond Giddens's allusions to the unanticipated consequences of scientific knowledge for the environment: the very woof and warp of scientific practices are irretrievably hermeneutic and indeterminate. Not only does scientific knowledge produce unanticipated consequences, but the knowledge *itself* is indeterminate and uncertain.

Furthermore, the claims of scientists for determinacy is first and foremost a legitimating rhetoric which helps constitute the 'actor-networks' of which they are the key members, but which stretch far beyond science to materially order society. Perhaps the worst problem in this is that scientists believe in the validity of this rhetoric, thus preventing their solutions from taking into account the local knowledge of lay actors involved in ecological crisis points. Wynne illustrates this with his research on the effects of radioactivity and struggles between scientists from various agencies and sheep farmers in the north of England. Here the experts' systematically bracketed inattention to the practical and contextual knowledge of the sheep farmers made their predictions on the time span of radioactive danger catastrophically inaccurate.

Wynne's argument – illustrated through the examples of the sheep farmers and of the 'craft-based' knowledge of Andean potato farmers – is that this science-serving dichotomy between propositional and formulaic knowledge, along with the necessarily flawed nature of the scientists' predictions, puts the lay public in a double bind. On the one hand they are made to be dependent on the knowledge of the experts, and, on the other, they have a basic mistrust of them. The result of this very constructed (rather than ontological) insecurity is fear – the sort of fear explicated by John Maguire in Chapter 7 below. This anxiety is, often, only exacerbated by social-scientific surveys of public perceptions of risk, surveys that share the epistemological assumptions of the natural scientists, effectively joining them, along with government and various business interests, in an actor-network of literally overwhelming proportions and power.

Wynne's position is in many ways closely aligned to that of Bruno Latour. Like Latour, Wynne in effect argues, against both moderns and postmoderns, that 'we have never been modern' (Latour, 1993). For both of them, the supposed fundamental qualitative differences between pre-modernity and modernity, and between 'simple' and 'reflexive' modernity, on which modernisation theories like those of Beck and Giddens rest, just do not exist. Thus lay actors, well before the onset of reflexive modernity and the risk society, fundamentally distrusted scientific opinion. Thus even scientific knowledge is also irreducibly pre-modern, indeterminate, uncer-tain and formulaic. Furthermore, not just the craft-based wisdom of potato farmers but also 'laboratory life' itself involves local knowledge – the main difference being that the 'discoveries' of laboratories are presented as being universalistic in character. Wynne, however, does part with Latour in respect of the latter's antihumanistic reduction of human beings, institutions, non-humans and inanimate objects to 'actants'. In so far as there is a 'realist' element in Wynne's own position it consists in a refusal to see human beings as malleable without remainder. For Wynne, what propels public reactions to technocratic projects is resistance to the inadequate models of the human person and the social which institutions attempt to impose on the public. Compared to Beck, then, Wynne's account is much more 'social', in that it is not physical but 'identity' risks that propel reflexivity. But compared to Latour, it is a lot more 'realist' – but this in the sense of moral, not scientific, realism.

The need for an explicit moral dimension is also a strong theme in the recent work of Barbara Adam, who, in Chapter 3, takes up this volume's challenge head-on by insisting on, and providing pointers for, the 'revisioning' of the assumptions about *time* held by the social sciences. Time, she reminds us, is not just an abstract backdrop for social and cultural change, but something which is itself understood differently in different cultures and different social contexts. The social sciences, she argues, have tended unthinkingly to reproduce Enlightenment notions of linear, one-dimensional, ordered time which are no longer appropriate under the conditions of late modernity, and which prevent us from adequately engaging with the environmental crisis. In describing these new conditions, she closely follows the accounts of Beck and Giddens: globalisation processes, particularly the diffusion of telecommunications technology, have created a 'global present', compressing decision-making processes and fostering a sense of global connectedness; the acceleration of the innovation process has rendered the future *in principle* unknowable; contemporary technologies are generating dangers (often invisible and unprovable) on timescales, from the infinitesimal to the millennial, which are completely dislocated from those of their benefits and control systems; and the bringing of nature under increasing human control has rendered obsolete distinctions between the social and the natural, and thus between social and natural time. These conditions demand of us that we develop a different framework for the conceptualisation of the environmental crisis. We must move from an emphasis on the material, the quantifiable, and linear causality to one on the immaterial, the unquantifiable and the unpredictable; and we must abandon individualism, Eurocentrism and anthropocentrism in order to embrace the not-like-us, the not-human, and the not-yet-born.

Time is an extraordinary difficult – perhaps impossible – area to theorise without paradox. In this case, we might perhaps wonder whether Adam's account fails to be self-exemplifying – whether, despite her persuasive argument that our experience and concepts of time are always socially and historically situated, she herself has produced yet another desituated account of time with her classically sociological narrative of the emergence of globalised time. Is there something qualitatively different about the present epoch? Or is such a notion a more nuanced version of ethnocentrism? Is it not always the case that technologies – from gunpowder, through the printing press, to eighteenth and nineteenth century industrialisation – have had invisible effects on multiple, dislocated timescales? But Adam's core insight about time – that we need to *morally* engage with the future – remains robust and vitally important for any endeavour to revision the social sciences in an age of ecological crisis. Perhaps because the world has become more complex and unpredictable than it was, or perhaps simply because it has *always* been more complex and unpredictable than we thought, the social – and natural – sciences need to move away from an orientation to the future based on naively modernist ideas of prediction and control. The future is not a pre-existing land towards which we are all moving, and which it is our task to discern through the mist and prepare for, but something which is created and shaped through all the decisions we make. A simultaneous recognition of the intrinsic indeterminacy of the future, and of all our roles in shaping that future, impose on us all the duty to take responsibility for the future that we are creating.

Just as with that of Beck, a crucial element within Adam's account is the real physical risks – however intangible – produced by the new technologies. For Wynne, as we saw, it is the *social* risk produced by the institutions within which the technologies are embedded which is the driving force behind public anxiety and dissent. In particular, such phenomena are reactions to the risks to identity engendered by relationships of dependency to untrustworthy institutions, and by the imposition on the public of impoverished technocratic notions of human beings. In this more thoroughgoingly social explanation, whether the risks 'actually', physically exist is irrelevant to this dynamic. In Adam's account, by contrast, despite her critique of 'materialist/empiricist epistemologies', physical risks are often invoked as an intervening variable – technologies produce physical risks, which then produce social risks as they impact on society. This emphasis on materiality can perhaps be linked to Adam's ecofeminist commitment to recalling our biophysical nature – that we are, after all, flesh and blood beings, and what happens to nature happens to us. But does the way that Adam sometimes seems to objectify risks in this way, representing them as, however invisibly, existing 'out there', indicate that she has not completely broken with the modernist dichotomy of nature and culture – that she is conceiving our corporeality in purely scientific terms? Or is it Wynne who is too modernist in his all but erasure of the physicality of environmental problems, reproducing what ecofeminists would regard as the patriarchal error of seeing culture as floating free of nature?

It is this kind of tangle between realism and constructionism that Bronislaw Szerszynski tries to overcome in Chapter 4 by uncovering their common historical roots. Whereas in Adam's chapter it is modern ideas of *time* that have to be problematised if we are to think our way out of the environmental crisis, here it is our very understanding of the relationship between language and the world. Szerszynski points out the complex ways in which attempts to think about the ecological crisis, and thus to orientate our actions in respect of it, are mired within the very splitting of language and world that, in the form of gnostic denials of our essential embodiment, gave rise to that crisis in the first place. Prior to the seventeenth century, he argues, epistemological and ethical meanings were to be read as already in the texture of the things and practices of everyday life. Natural meaning was not determined in the laboratory, but instead a matter of interpreting signs in nature and the world. Language, culture and the order of things were part and parcel of the world. The dawn of modernity in the seventeenth and eighteenth centuries brought a differentiation and autonomy of cultural spheres – of religion, the ethical, the religious, both from the *Sittlichkeit* of everyday life, and from one another. Language now was no longer embedded in the world but became separate from and a mirror of the world in the guise of self-certain, apodictic knowledge. Discourse was something that could produce knowledge of what now was an *extra-discursive* reality.

To the extent that this idiom of the Enlightenment presumed subsumption of the object under the weight of the subject, it also legitimated man's domination of nature, itself conceived as apodictically knowable object. The ecology movement is born in the *crisis* of these discourses of identity and technology – in the legitimation crisis of determinate and propositional knowledge. There have been in this context, observes Szerszynski, two main reactions. The first is best understood as a 'neo-modernism', exemplified in the thought of such analysts as Karl Popper, Jürgen Habermas, Giddens and Beck. This neo- (or 'reflexive') modernism has a more flexible view of knowledge than the Cartesian determinacy of the earlier and 'simpler' modernity. The new thinkers reject assumptions of correspondence between language and nature, their epistemology instead being based on specified procedures of argumentation and evidence to decide what will be valid knowledge, which is now never certain but only possible. This proceduralising shift is also true, Szerszynski argues, of neo-modernist ethics, which rejects the cosmic authority of the Kantian imperative for a much more discursively decidable and flexible notion of how to arrive at the good. In the environmental arena this shift from 'content' to 'form' is captured in the contrast between the positions of Barry Commoner and of Beck. Both argue that the problem with the environment is not one of too much modernity, but instead of *not enough* modernity. Both urge the 'modernisation of modernisation' in order to counteract the natural damages of the earlier modernity's excesses. Yet, while Commoner's vision is one of a planned society based on the content of a certain knowledge about the 'laws' of nature, Beck's solution is purely procedural in nature, merely specifying the form of society – necessarily pluralistic and dynamic in character – which is needed for an ecological modernity.

The second and polar opposite reaction would seem to be 'deep green' romanticism. But here, Szerszynski tells us, our stereotypes belie an underlying complexity. He breaks this down analytically into phenomena of, on the one hand, an individualistic deep ecology and, on the other, a more collectivist response which he understands as communitarian. Both of these seem prima facie to be a throwback to pre-modern and traditional conceptions, yet both, Szerszynski shows, only reproduce the problematique of modernity. Deep ecology thus proffers a separation and hypostatisation of nature as separate from social practices. And communitarianism, for its part, replicates modernity's subject–object thinking through its positing of a transcendental and substanceless 'community' above the brute reality of an alien, unknowable nature. As an alternative to these two dominant reactions, Szerszynski attempts to open up a third ecological space, one neither of hypermodernisation nor of nostalgic roots. He points instead to an understanding of the environment in which social practices and nature are conceived as interwoven and ongoing forms of life: forms of life which are at the same time both incessantly interpreted and ever already given.

Szerszynski's chapter, like that of Adam, engages creatively with elements of 'deep green' thinking, incorporating them into a sociologically informed account. But beyond that he also gives us a vocabulary for understanding the continuous 'flip-flop' between realism and construction-ism which is so apparent in theorising about the environment and elsewhere. For Szerszynski, both the idea of language as referring to a physical reality outside itself, and that of a language that *doesn't* refer to reality so is merely a human construction, are simply two aspects of the same problematic, a dyad that cannot be separated. In realism, the nihilism of a language whose correspondence to reality can never be secured is always there in the background, as the fate which awaits us if correspondence is not maintained. In constructionism, likewise, realism is always the suppressed supplement; the 'real' asserts itself by its very absence as that to which language can be secured. Whether or not one accepts Szerszynski's closing call for what is almost – but not quite – a return to a pre-modern ontology, the observation that both realism and constructionism have at their hearts a very similar and deeply modern idea of language is one we would do well to recall.

Part II   Risk and the Self: Encounters and Responses

The idiom of risk presupposes ideas of choice, calculation and responsi-bility, so that whether the risk attitude prevails or even makes sense in a given area of life depends on the degree to which that area is regarded as fixed and inevitable, or as subject to human agency. In the process of modernisation, as Beck points out, more and more areas of life have moved from the former category to the latter – have been taken from the sphere of the natural and inevitable and made the objects of choice and responsibility. The riskiness of contemporary life owes much to this dynamic, irrespective of any increase of real, physical risks – in earlier, 'simple' modernity, risk-taking affected only a limited number of spheres of life simply because so few of them were constructed in terms of choice at all.

One socio-historical process which has been importantly implicated in this shift has clearly been that of individualisation. Risk and individualis-ation have been closely intertwined since the origins of modern society, when the language of 'risk' first appeared on any significant scale among merchants in Early Modern Italian city-states. It is in this context of market transactions – in the isolated social act of buying and selling – that we can discern at least one of the roots of the desituated language of means–ends rationality, and thus of the idioms of preference schedules, of rational choices and of risks. But in the context of increasing individualisation the idiom of risk has come to have purchase not just in buying and selling on the market, but also in child-rearing, marriage, friendship and in much of the lifeworld itself. This shift derives more, in Beck's terms, from the *Freisetzung* (setting-free) of agents from normative institutional constraints than from the proliferation of new dangers *per se*.

The language of 'setting-free' is one not without its problems. Paralleling Foucault's (1979) account of the role of the confessional in the constitution of the inner, psychological life of modern individuals, we might want to see the shift Beck describes not so much as the liberation of an already-existing self to express its wants and preferences in more and more realms of life, but a complexification of the self, as we are forced to *have* wants and opinions in respect of radically new topics. From such an analysis, discourses of risk – in relation to, say, food or ionising radiation – would operate as 'technologies of the self' which do not just allow and help us to decide but actually constitute and transform our inner lives. But, whether we understand this process in terms of self-liberation or of self-construction – as an erosion of cultural constraints or as a reconstitution of our souls by technique (Ellul, 1964) – it is one which produces a condition where modern individuals are prone to states of heightened uncertainty and anxiety, as decisions proliferate and the cultural codes used to negotiate those decisions become more and more complex and variegated. Existence becomes risky, as more and more of what happens to the individual and his or her loved ones are understood as a product not of impersonal social and natural forces, but of earlier decisions he or she has taken.

Individualisation, then, is one side of the problem of subjectivity in late modernity, as the self is burdened with more and more responsibilities, and thus with a sense of risk and uncertainty. But, as we suggested in the discussion of Part I above, the other side is surely that of objectification – the stripping away of human meanings on both inner and outer reality, and their replacement by alien ones, through the ever-expanding reach of science and technology. As modern science has expanded its social authority and its social reach, its formalised and reductionist vocabularies have delegitimated and displaced many of the more situated understandings that people have of the world and their place in it. Again, the technologisation of environmental policy in the EU has been a striking and ironic example of this dynamic, given that its vocabularies of standardisation and objectification threaten the very lifeworld out of which environmental concern can be said to have sprung. Social science, which might have been expected to be particularly alert to these dangers, has to date been more prone to exacerbate them. Although it has not been *directly*

responsible for these culturally alienating articulations of European identity, the dominant ethos of social science has *indirectly* validated and
encouraged them. Thus we here lay down a criticism of much of the social
science which has enthusiastically entered the environmental arena, and
whose orientation has been unduly shaped by uncritical deference to the
realist and instrumentalist epistemic commitments and expectations of
natural science.

But one might question whether these two dynamics – individualisation
and objectification – are totally separable. Is not individualisation and risk
simply the other side of technology? Is not the internalisation within the
self – inner nature – of more and more functions which were once taken
care of at the social level (or did not exist at all) not linked to the
progressive objectification of outer nature (Barfield, 1954: 166)? Is not the
subjective experience of the contemporary world as full of risk and
uncertainty, and of ourselves as needy of expert knowledges to guide us
through that risk and uncertainty, not itself produced by the instrumentalisation of lifeworlds to the extent that they are emptied of familiar
meanings, and are hence fearful, barren places? These questions raise a
particular challenge to critics such as those authors represented here. For if
we identify an important element of the modern environmental problem as
lying in the epistemic temper of modernist approaches *per se* – the
alienation and dichotomisation of nature and culture, and the artificial
deletion of the human subject in our knowledge, replacing it with an
implicit and overarching instrumental 'superagent' – how much a part of
the problem are the dimensions of individual choice and planning which
are also a part of modern freedom and responsibility? Such questions arise
especially in relation to the chapters in Part II.

At first glance, Elisabeth Beck-Gernsheim in Chapter 5 seems to gives us
a 'setting-free' narrative in respect of the effects of individualisation
processes on parenting. Whereas the family previously functioned primarily to promote normative integration into social institutions, in the socially
mobile world of today it has increasingly shifted its attention to the
securing of achievement and status mobility. In the case of children, where
once they were accepted more or less as they were, nowadays their talents
and capabilities have to be nurtured and developed, thus extending the
modernist dynamics of rationalisation and planning to the biographical
narrative itself – both one's own and one's offspring's. But Beck-
Gernsheim wonders whether the increasing availability and use of genetic
technologies are creating a tendency for this planning to extend ever
backwards – before birth, and even before conception – in the form of
securing the best genetic starting point for one's children. This shift from a
concern for cultural capital to one of genetic capital, she suggests, could be
yet another Habermasian colonisation of the lifeworld. Note that for Beck-
Gernsheim the problem is not the extension of planning and choice to
parenthood *per se*, but simply its transposition from cultural and educational terms into biological ones. There is no nostalgia here for older

styles of parenting, just a concern that the modernising process might be taking an unwelcome turn – one, indeed, that might threaten the advances made in respect of the social provision of education.

But there is a subtly different theme to Beck-Gernsheim's chapter, one that is more consistent with our Foucauldian reading of individualisation above – in terms not of setting-free but of technologies of the self. Her analysis of the way that the very possibility of diagnostic tests and medical intervention rapidly becomes an obligation to do so, on pain of being seen as a negligent parent, is a chillingly clear example of the dynamic whereby modern freedoms subtly metamorphose into obligations. From a Habermasian perspective, this could be seen as an invasion of the richer, communicative rationality of the lifeworld by instrumental technologies. From a Foucauldian perspective, by contrast, it is the technologies themselves – understood broadly, as including the institutions and discourses in which the 'physical' technologies are embedded – which constitute us as choosing, planning subjects in the first place. As Beck-Gernsheim reminds us, the space occupied by modern subjects, and within which they move, is filled by the 'regulatory density' of contemporary society. But whether this density should be seen as invading a pure space of unconditioned choice, or as constituting that space in the first place, is not a purely scholastic issue, since it bears crucially on whether our modern freedoms can be disentangled from their dystopic manifestations.

In Chapter 6 Marco Diani looks at another, increasingly pervasive, context within which technological changes are altering the very internal economy of our subjectivity – office work. Echoing Adam's account of the unanticipated consequences for decision-making of telecommunications technology such as the telephone, Diani argues that the new information technologies are having dramatic effects on the cultural dimensions of work. There is an interesting comparison that can be made with Beck-Gernsheim's chapter here. In the context of the family, Beck-Gernsheim noted the modern shift away from an emphasis on normative integration to the nurturing of generic competences and health in order to equip the child for success in a socially mobile society. In the new paperless office, Diani observes a parallel shift in occupational identity. Firstly, the accelerating tempo of change in the actual tasks performed in office work is leading to a situation where work has become 'virtual'. Training that simply integrates the worker into existing tasks and competences is already out of date as soon as it is started. Instead, there is a shift towards the acquiring of generic competences in the handling of novel situations.

Secondly, Diani describes how under conditions of office automation the institutional 'weight' of the organisation tends to evaporate. Despite differentials in job categories and status, there is a marked levelling out of tasks between supervisors and supervised. Increasingly, the tasks they are both actually doing are almost indistinguishable. But this does not mean that the organisational functions of the supervisor–supervised relationship have just disappeared; instead, they have migrated in two directions – into objects and subjects, into the machines and their software on one hand, and into the subjectivities of the machines' operators on the other. Information technology systems, as they are typically designed, are not capable of supporting the complex negotiative dimensions of the life of organisations, and particularly those of aligning the self-image of individual office-workers and that of the company. This burden thus has to be taken up by the individuals themselves, who have to invest a disproportionate amount of their work time in actually trying to align their own goals and identity with those of the organisation as a whole.

This, then, is a story about individualisation – of increasing isolation, of the levelling-out of social structure, of increased competition through peer-group assessment, and of a general weakening of integrative cultural processes. But, once again, this is not necessarily a straightforward 'setting-free' narrative, one where anxiety and uncertainty are produced by the releasing of a pre-existent, agoraphobic self from external but necessary social constraints. What is striking about Diani's account is the way that this expanded but lonely decisional space occupied by the individual in the modern office is one which is always already structured by the technology involved. It is alienating not because it is unstructured, giving the individual no guidance, as Szerszynski would say, in 'knowing what to do' – *or* because it is colonised after-the-fact by technological constraints. It is alienating because of the *particular* ways it structures our subjectivity in relation to the wider organization of which we are a part. It is this insight which lies at the heart of Diani's insistence that we must be neither temperamentally optimistic nor pessimistic about technological change. If, as is the case for Diani, we accept that there is no pure, untechnological space which we can retreat to and preserve in contemporary society, then we have a duty to ensure that technology is designed in ways that preserve the human qualities we value.

John Maguire, in Chapter 7, directly addresses the consequences of the twin processes of individualisation and objectification through an exploration of the labyrinthine dynamics of fear in our contemporary predicament. For Maguire, these dynamics involve both the production and the suppression of fear, and operate at both the individual and the social levels. There is an improper fear that engenders, and is in turn reinforced by, the gnostic denial of our nature as embodied, dependent beings. There is a proper acknowledgement of the impossibility of certainty and control which is fearfully suppressed by modernist institutions such as the EU. There is a tragic fearfulness instilled in us as children if we deny our neediness in order to be loved and honoured by the adults in our lives. There is an all-too-appropriate fearfulness in the public response to the cruel fate of being dependent for our environmental well-being on institutions which are undependable and hubristic.

Maguire holds back from giving us any clear pointers to the breaking of these cycles of fearfulness. Indeed, he at times seems to link the suppression of fear to the suppression of a saving wildness which inhabits the margins of civilised existence. Like Wynne, Maguire seems to be operating with an implicit realism about human nature – a human nature which reasserts itself or is pathologised if denied by the structures of modern existence. But whereas Wynne's humanity is conceived as having an intrinsic sociality and incompleteness, Maguire's is a more conventionally romantic notion of the individual's recovery of an original wholeness which has been wounded by social forces. This psychoanalytically recoverable wholeness is one in which a kind of natural uncivilizedness plays an essential part. Thus, in a way that has ironic parallels with Diani's more technophilic exploration of contemporary individualisation, it is not that we should seek to eradicate the 'howls' that disturb our civilized 'decorum', but that we need a different, more healthy economy of wildness, which would then be manifest not as the denial but the expression of our createdness and creativity.

In Chapter 8 Helmuth Berking offers an altogether more optimistic account of the process of individualisation in late modern society. Rather than demanding a radical transformation of the character of contemporary subjectivity, Berking argues that contemporary individualism *itself* contains the seeds of a deeper moral engagement with the global environmental problematique. And rather than seeing those seeds as lying in the healing of the individual psyche, Berking suggests that it is in the movement from self to other, from solitary to *solidary* individualism, that moral engagement becomes possible. For Berking, the very character ideals of the modern, reflexively self-constituting individual has led not to a decline but to an intensification of solidary social practices such as gift-giving, social protest and voluntary work. Although the language of utilitarian individualism remains the dominant vocabulary through which people describe their moral lives, rather than this vocabulary expelling solidary relationships in favour of purely self-regarding actions, it is *itself* increasingly used to justify and describe these relationships – in terms of their contribution to individual self-realisation.

The crucial thing to note about Berking's argument is the way that it frames the widespread other-regarding actions of contemporary society not as survivals from earlier, more collectively orientated times, but as the products of a distinctive kind of solidary individualism which is actually generated by modern cultural conditions. A central role in this process is played by the same 'lifestyle coalitions' – typified by but also a far broader social phenomenon than the 'new social movements' – which Giddens saw as the site of his 'life politics' (1991). For Berking, such coalitions provide, through their substantive cultural content, the character-ideals which propel the utilitarian individual towards solidary relations. While this might be thought to produce a merely 'sectoral' morality, which diminishes as closeness diminishes and otherness grows, in fact, Berking argues, the reflexive personality-ideals nurtured within such lifestyle coalitions serve to maintain a momentum towards universality.

In many ways this is an account of the modern individual which curiously echoes that of Beck-Gernsheim, but with a far more optimistic twist. Like Beck-Gernsheim, Berking sees the modern individual as progressively freed from institutional constraints, and engaging in the self-narrating processes described by Beck and Giddens. Again, like Beck-Gernsheim, he argues that in specific cultural contexts freedom and responsibility transform into an obligation to choose in a particular way. But the distinctiveness of Berking's position is the way that the cultural specificity of the course of individualisation results in a new kind of collectivity, on the hinge of individualism and group affiliation. For Berking as for Beck-Gernsheim, the moral-decisional space in which the modern reflexive individual finds him or herself, once he or she is supposedly 'set-free' from normative constraints, is one that is *already structured*, in ways that constrain and impel the individual towards new normative obligations. Whereas obligations were once spoken of in terms of institutional conformity, they are now justified by reference to the duty to be reflexive; but they are normative constraints nonetheless. But whereas for Beck-Gernsheim these new obligations are taking regrettable, technocratic forms which are steering individual choice inexorably down the road of genetic essentialism, for Berking they are the bulwarks against the slide into pure egoism, and form the foundation for a new collective politics. Perhaps the reason for this different emphasis lies in Berking's focus on lay cultural formations, rather than on the affordances of new technologies, as the arena within which our choices are structured. This alone should reinforce Wynne's reminder of the epistemic value of such lay formations (a point perhaps overlooked by Beck-Gernsheim, whose public seem merely to be individuals who react to and choose between technologies made available by experts). As Berking suggests, perhaps it is in such non-expert networks that much of the cultural work necessary for an adequate collective ethical response to the ecological crisis is going on. Environmentalism, after all, was given birth by such networks.

Part III   The Politics of the Environment: Exhaustion or Renewal?

But if the impulse of environmentalism has its roots in such 'lifeworld' phenomena and their alienation from institutions, what happens when it succeeds in getting its concerns incorporated into the 'system'? For ecological politics does not always manifest itself as expressive, subcultural experimentation; increasingly, it takes the form of complex coalitions of actors and institutions, many of which lie at the very heart of contemporary society. The next three chapters in different ways all explore the rich and complex ironies which have followed the success of the environmental movement in getting its voice heard, and the migration of its concerns from the margins to the centre of modern life.

Environmental politics as we know it today grew largely out of the counterculture of the 1960s, focusing on – indeed constituting – different issues at different times in its development – the proliferation of chemicals in the 1960s, resource depletion in the early 1970s, nuclear power in the later 1970s and acid rain in the early 1980s. Initially, the assumption behind environmental politics was that environmental issues involved a zero-sum game of social and natural limits to growth. A symbiotic harmony of self- and inter-regulating social and natural systems was regarded as a precondition for an ecological society; at this time the dominant term for such a harmony was 'equilibrium', implying a homeostatically regulated, stable society.

Starting in the the mid-1980s, however, there was a striking change in environmental politics. Pundits came to speak increasingly of *global* environmental problems, and at the same time multinational and multi-divisional firms began to take on 'green' issues. By the late 1980s in most industrial societies environment had been adopted as an 'official' agenda of big business, government and international institutions such as the OECD and the EC. Global commitments were seen to be urgently needed, to mitigate global risks. This conjuncture seems to have created conditions for a paradigm shift in environmental discourse. In the new dominant 'greenspeak' of sustainable development following the 1992 Rio Earth Summit, eternally expanding technological-economic systems (of course correctly designed) are assumed to be compatible with environmental 'sustainability' – a term which accommodates ideas of growth, change and development much more easily than the earlier term of 'equilibrium'. Now the assumption is more of a positive-sum game, with environmental discourse proferring optimistic technological solutions. No human, *cultural* challenge is recognised as integral to the environmental problematique. Serious discussion about the environment is ever more monopolised by a dispositive of what Maarten Hajer (this volume) calls 'ecological modernis-ation', where technical solutions are found for even the most potentially apocalyptic of natural issues, and where, crucially, the instrumental social sciences are harnessed as a key resource for 'optimising' societal responses to the environmental costs and benefits in an intensifying commodification of nature – ironically in the name of its own protection.

In such ecological modernisation what has been constructed is a new dominant paradigm in the politics of environment – that is, a new truth of growth *and* sustainability. An entire 'actor-network' of institutions, organ-isations, resources, machines, ideas, noxious substances and practices has mobilised itself in order to underpin and ensure the validity of the sustainable growth truth-claim. The institutionalised expertise of (now substantially funded) environmental science, and of well-funded bureau-cratic multinational NGOs, may well now have joined forces with enlightened global business interests and with the administrative systems of the major Western states. It is this alliance whose symbolic violence has constructed the social reality of global environmental risk.

What have been the moral costs of environmentalism's apparent enrol-
ment into this discourse coalition of ecological modernisation? Beck in
Gegengifte argues that for such coalitions to present risks as real is
simultaneously for them to deny the responsibility for the creation of those
dangers of these very technological interests themselves (Beck, 1988). The
very title of *Gegengifte* states the problem well. '*Gift*' in German means
poison; *Gegengift* is counterpoison or antidote. If originally capitalist
technology in alliance with state administrators were responsible for the
Gift, for the poison, then the *Gegengift*, the antidote, was environmental
critique itself. But what happens when the *Gegengift* takes on naturalistic
and hence realist assumptions? What happens when the critique of
technocracy and industry itself becomes instrumental and technocratic? Is
this a question of *Gegengift* – the antidote which is now environmentalism-
as-expert-system – or is it a matter of merely different and sometimes less
noxious varieties of *Gift*? Has the institutionalisation of ecological politics
led to a neutralisation of the critical impulse which gave it birth? Or,
conversely, has environmental discourse so firmly established itself as a
commonplace of public life that the movement that spawned it is all but
redundant?

It is such questions that Klaus Eder considers in Chapter 9. Like Beck,
his starting point is the proliferation in knowledge claims about the
environment. But whereas Beck represents this proliferation in terms of
the ending of the exclusive right of established experts to make such
knowledge claims, for Eder it is the *environmental movement* whose
monopoly – the monopoly on 'ecological discourse' – has ended. And,
whereas for Beck this development should be seen as a *de*structuring of the
public sphere, so that its very unspoken rules become a topic for discussion
and contestation, Eder argues that the public sphere is best understood as
being *re*structured, due to the emergence of *new* rules – rules supplied by
an emergent discourse of ecology. Eder argues that this discourse is
becoming a new *masterframe* in the public sphere, bringing together
cognitive, normative and aesthetic elements in highly resonant ways. As a
masterframe, it becomes the common ground on which agreement and
disagreement between actors has to be formed. Eder goes as far as to
suggest that the emergence of this ecological masterframe constitutes a
second transformation of the public sphere. Whereas the first such
transformation – the colonisation of the eighteenth and nineteenth century
public sphere of open discourse by powerful institutional actors – resulted
in a contraction of the free flow of communication, this second transformation is one where communication proliferates, as actors increasingly turn to
the mass media in order to present a 'green' identity and thus legitimate
themselves and their actions.

What happens to the environmental movement under such conditions?
Firstly, it become just one voice amongst many, and has to compete with a
range of other actors if it wants to try to shape a discourse over which it no
longer has exclusive control. Gone are the days of protest actions over the

environment – this is an era of 'post-environmentalism', where ecological discourse is normalised and belongs to everybody. Secondly, Eder argues, it is a particular *kind* of environmentalism that has achieved masterframe status. Neither conservationism (which emphasises the protection of a nature defined as *a*social, over against the human and the artificial) nor deep ecology (which attempts to reimmerse the social in that asocial nature) but only what he calls 'political ecology' (which thematises the complex causal and political relationships which shape the natural and social environment) is capable of mediating the broad range of institutional relationships obtaining in the modern public sphere. Because it is the 'political ecology package' which is structuring the rule regime of the public sphere, environmental groups have either to embrace *this* kind of environmentalism, or they can no longer survive in the public sphere; they have to adapt, die, or operate purely in subcultural realms outside public life. Thirdly, the structuring of the public sphere around a discourse of ecological public goods, and the consequent intensification of media use to legitimate actors within that discourse, creates an *identity market*. Environmental groups are drawn into this market, and thus have to expend an increasing amount of their resources on self-presentation and the building of symbolic resources. This turns them into 'cultural pressure groups', whose goal is not so much to achieve concrete political objectives as to secure their survival in the identity market.

In Chapter 10 Andrew Jamison constructs a similar account from rather different materials. In a narrative which supplies more depth than the brief account at the beginning of this section, he tracks the development of environmental politics from the isolated intellectuals and writers of the post-war period, through the emergence of a popular movement in the 1960s and 1970s, to the rise over the last decade of professionalised transnational environmental NGOs such as WWF and Greenpeace. For Jamison as for Eder, this 'coming in from the cold' spells the demise of radicalism in environmental politics. The organisational success of the large NGOs has created both internal and external pressures on them to present themselves in certain ways in order to ensure their continued viability as organisations. Specifically, this has led to a convergence of interests between international NGOs and multinational corporations in presenting the environmental crisis as global in scope and requiring technical expertise to solve – the 'alliance-in-truth' we referred to above. But Jamison parts with Eder on the topic of 'post-environmentalism'. Rather than seeing the normalisation of ecological discourse as a positive development, allowing the further rationalisation of modernity's public sphere, Jamison sees it as a regrettable sidelining of environmentalism's capacity as a medium for critical reflection about society. And rather than seeing radical environmental protest as something that has been outgrown, he awaits the emergence of new critical currents in society, taking up the causes of the increasingly disregarded South, and given a voice by new partisan intellectuals.

In constructing his account, Jamison also adds weight to Brian Wynne's point about the neglected epistemic value of lay knowledge. The 'truth' of the environmental crisis, he points out, is one that has not sprung directly from nature, or even from the purely technical activities of scientists whose role it might be to 'represent' that nature. It has crucially depended on the creative cognitive and symbolic activity of social movements. Such movements do not just passively react to technological developments presented to them by experts, either rejecting them or accepting them in accordance with pre-existent values. They themselves have played a central role in creating the 'symbolic packages' (Eder) or 'story lines' (Hajer) through which the notion of environmental crisis is given identity and achieves social purchase. But in other ways the denouement of Jamison's narrative also tends to confirm Beck's account of reflexivity. Firstly, although his social movements start out as lay actors, by the end of his narrative they have clearly transformed themselves into professionalised counterexperts. Secondly, Jamison's explanation for the converging representations of the environmental crisis of NGOs and industrial actors tends to reinforce Beck's estimation of the importance of blind, reflex-like institutional dynamics – though the fact that there *is* a convergence might not sit so easily with Beck's emphasis on the 'organic' generation of contestation and conflict.

It could be argued that both Eder's and Jamison's accounts involve excessively stark oppositions between the past and the present. Firstly, their convergence narratives rely to different degrees on perhaps overly simple pictures of the earlier environmental movement as a pure, critical space insulated from the realities of wider society, whereas the discourse of that movement was always one that was shaped by dominant discourses and political opportunities. Secondly, Eder and Jamison both imply that the movement's contemporary reliance on symbolic and identity politics represents a qualitative departure, as if an earlier purity of ideological commitment has been displaced by an institutionally driven need for careful, but ultimately instrumental, media self-presentation. Yet surely environmental groups always were 'cultural pressure groups', as much concerned with the iconic and the mythic as with propositional or narrowly normative statements, and with the construction of themselves as authoritative social actors – but through complex processes of self-invention that cannot be reduced to the narrowly strategic. Thirdly, both writers perhaps overstate the degree to which environmental radicalism is a thing of the past. Not only are significant environmental groups such as Greenpeace maintaining a highly critical stance towards the conciliatory rhetorics of government and industry, but in many European nations vibrant new grass-roots movements are emerging to occupy the arena of radical local protest at least as rapidly as any of the older groups might be abandoning it. These concerns notwithstanding, we would not want to deny that there are important choices facing the environmental movement today, choices that may involve the redefinition of its central goals and identity. Eder and

Jamison provide us with theoretical and descriptive materials which are an invaluable aid to comprehending the movement's predicament.

Maarten Hajer also addresses this issue in Chapter 11, this time through a critical consideration of the discourse coalition of 'ecological modernisation' which embraces many movement, industrial and policy actors. Hajer puts forward three different readings of this phenomenon. The first is the 'institutional learning' reading held by its proponents, one which sees industrial and administrative organisations as having learnt from the critiques of earlier industrial society by the environmental movement, and as developing paths of further economic development which are compatible with or even enhance environmental quality. The second is the harshly critical reading offered by radical environmentalists, which attempts to expose ecomodernism as another 'technocratic project'. From this perspective, environmentalism should be about the creation of a radically different kind of society; ecological modernisation is a betrayal of this spirit of environmentalism in the name of a further strengthening of technocracy and hierarchy. Hajer elegantly pits the proponents of ecological modernisation against their green critics in order to point towards a third political option – a 'cultural politics' reading of ecological modernisation.

Finding intellectual resources for this in the cultural theory of Mary Douglas and Michael Thompson, as well as in his own discourse-analytic tradition, Hajer argues that all framings of the environment are social constructions which at once express and disguise preferences about the kind of society we ought to have. He thus refuses to take any account of the environmental crisis at face-value – either the *natura naturans* to be preserved at all cost offered by the radical greens, or the technological optimism offered by the ecomodernists – but sees them all as 'story lines'. But this does not mean they are to be discarded, just that they need to be unpacked. They may not in reality be assertions about objective 'truth', but they still have a value as expressions of preferred future scenarios for society. Here he echoes Barbara Adam in his insistence that we engage with the future politically, rather than through specious objectivist ideas of prediction and certainty. A cultural politics which revealed the social and cultural consequences of adopting any given story line would enable an open and undeluded debate to commence about the sort of society and nature we want. This, for Hajer, would be a real ecological modernisation – one where the environmental problematic became the arena for a reflexive debate about modern society and its direction.

It is interesting to contrast the contributions to this Part in terms of the role they allocate for the academic community – and particularly social scientists – in the politics of the environment. Klaus Eder's approach implies a fairly conventional role for the social scientist as a neutral observer of society, whose systematic analyses can then contribute to the learning process of administrative institutions in respect of the formation of policy. Andrew Jamison, as we saw, called for social scientists to take up positions of advocacy in respect of radical environmental politics, recalling the engaged intellectuals of the post-war era. Maarten Hajer's account involves a different role again for social scientists – neither neutral description, nor partisanship, but the deconstruction of *all* positions taken up in society, in the name of open discussion about our collective future.

The concluding contribution, from Robin Grove-White, takes a position that has elements of all three of these. Grove-White askes what *kind* of knowledge policymakers need in modern societies, in the context of proliferating cultural tensions. For Grove-White, these tensions increasingly cluster around the problem of the citizen's relationship with the state, and with the other social institutions which have hitherto been, more or less, the focus of public identification and assent. Against this background, the question of the kind of 'intelligence' that governments need to steer through these choppy waters takes on a particular significance. Arguably, these increased cultural tensions make the largely positivistic and reductionistic nature of government-funded social science research and policy analysis even less suited to the task of adequately grasping contemporary social realities. Furthermore, the unthinking application of such approaches could well exacerbate these tensions, as the public react against having identities imposed on them which fail to capture their own senses of themselves and their world (Wynne, this volume).

Drawing on his wide experience of environmental campaigning, Grove-White uses three examples to illustrate the kinds of problems that can occur when governments rely on social science research which pays inadequate attention to the cultural dimensions of environmental conflicts. The first example, that of disputes over the capital costs of nuclear electricity generation, is particularly strong because of its counterintuitive nature. Surely here, if anywhere, we are dealing with hard, technical facts. But, as Grove-White shows convincingly, it was largely because official cost projections neglected to incorporate the economic impacts, felt through increased regulation, of enduring public anxiety about the plant, that they were so inaccurate. With Grove-White's second example, that of biotechnology, he points to the dangers of the overwhelmingly physical way in which the risks of this technology have been understood and communicated. He argues that a potential public reaction against biotechnology developments may well be being temporarily masked by the tendency of the public not to express strong opinions where they feel little agency, and by the fact that ethical and more conventionally cultural tensions about biotechnology are being occluded by the restricted, physicalist terms of the debate. By analogy with the dynamics of public protest and resistance in other areas, the apparent assent or indifference of the public to developments in this area may well turn out to be highly misleading, since apparent quietude may conceal far greater ambivalence and alienation than institutions with their realist orientations are able to recognise. Grove-White's third example, that of sustainable development, illustrates the ways in which a policy initiative which at first glance seems to represent an opening-up to new voices and vocabularies can start to lose momentum if framed in narrow ways. What is striking here, especially in the light of the other contributions in this Part, is the way that the language of sustainable development fails to resonate with the subcultural and other lifeworld contexts in which it arguably has its roots. In the post-Rio environmental problematique it is recognised – even officially, for example in the EU 5th Action Plan on the Environment – that policy can no longer be seen as an expert matter alone, but has to engage the commitments of social partners in all sectors of lay society. Yet so far this recognition has not been reflected in the institutional practices, relationships and discourses of mainstream policy culture, once again revealing the inadequacy of governments' understanding of the complex dynamics of people's relationships with institutions and their actions, and underlining the urgent need for a different kind of social science to be given a greater role.

This final contribution neatly returns us to the issue raised in the discussion of the chapters of Part I above – that of the politics of knowledge. How can the social sciences contribute to an opening, rather than a closing, of the environmental agenda? Grove-White usefully warns that any change in the dominant ethos of social scientific research cannot be brought about in isolation. He argues that the dominant positivism of both the natural and social sciences has been fed by the particular relationship that has been routinised between political institutions and research establishments. If we are to produce accounts of environmental problems that are sensitive to culture and indeterminacy we will need different institutions, and different knowledge cultures. But these are not likely to come about while researchers are under pressure to produce short-term 'policy-useful' knowledge, in the kind of idioms that dominate in policy circles. Clearly, as well as the theoretical and methodological questions that our contributors have posed, there are urgent institutional questions as well. If this collection plays even a small part in stimulating a sustained consideration of any of these, then it will have fulfilled its role.

References

Barfield, Owen (1954) *History in English Words*. London: Faber and Faber.

Beck, Ulrich (1988) *Gegengifte*. Frankfurt am Main: Suhrkamp. Published in English as (1995) *Ecological Politics in an Age of Risk*. Cambridge: Polity Press.

Beck, Ulrich, Giddens, Anthony and Lash, Scott (1994) *Reflexive Modernization: Politics, Tradition and Aesthetics in the Modern Social Order*. Cambridge: Polity Press.

Clark, William C. (1989) 'Managing planet earth', *Scientific American*, 261 (3): 18–26.

Ellul, Jacques (1964) *The Technological Society*. New York: Vintage.

Foucault, Michel (1979) *The History of Sexuality, vol. 1: An Introduction*, tr. Robert Hurley. London: Allen Lane.

Giddens, Anthony (1991) *Modernity and Self-Identity: Self and Society in the Late Modern Age*. Oxford: Polity Press.

Jachtenfuchs, Markus and Huber, Michael (1993) 'Institutional learning in the European Community: The response to the greenhouse effect', in J.D. Liefferink, P.D. Lowe and A.P.J. Mol (eds), *European Integration and Environmental Policy*. London: Belhaven Press. pp. 36–58.

Latour, Bruno (1993) *We Have Never Been Modern*, tr. Catherine Porter. Hemel Hempstead: Harvester Wheatsheaf.

Sachs, Wolfgang (1993) 'Global ecology and the shadow of "development" ', in Wolfgang Sachs (ed.), *Global Ecology: A New Arena of Political Conflict*. London: Zed Books. pp. 3–21.

PART I

ENVIRONMENT, KNOWLEDGE AND INDETERMINACY: BEYOND MODERNIST ECOLOGY?

1

RISK SOCIETY AND THE PROVIDENT STATE

Ulrich Beck

Translated by Martin Chalmers

If modernisation is understood as a process of innovation which has become autonomous, then it must also be accepted that modernity itself ages. The other aspect of this ageing of industrial modernity is the emergence of risk society. This concept describes a phase of development of modern society in which the social, political, ecological and individual risks created by the momentum of innovation increasingly elude the control and protective institutions of industrial society.

Between Industrial Society and Risk Society

Two phases may be distinguished. The first is a stage in which conse-quences and self-endangerment are systematically produced, but are *not* the subject of public debate or at the centre of political conflict. This phase is dominated by the self-identity of industrial society, which simultaneously both intensifies and 'legitimates', as 'residual risks', hazards resulting from decisions made ('residual risk society').

A completely different situation arises when the hazards of industrial society dominate public, political and private debates. Now the institutions of industrial society produce and legitimate hazards which they cannot control. During this transition, property and power relationships remain *constant*. Industrial society sees and criticizes itself *as* risk society. On the one hand, the society *still* makes decisions and acts on the pattern of the old industrial society; on the other hand, debates and conflicts which originate in the dynamic of risk society are already being superimposed on interest organisations, the legal system and politics.

In view of these two stages and their sequence, the concept of 'reflexive modernisation' may be introduced.[1] This precisely does *not* mean *reflection* (as the adjective 'reflexive' seems to suggest), but above all *self-confrontation*. The transition from the industrial to the risk epoch of modernity occurs *un*intentionally, *un*seen, compulsively, in the course of a dynamic of modernisation which has made itself autonomous, on the pattern of *latent side-effects*. One can almost say that the constellations of risk society are created because the self-evident truths of industrial society (the consensus on progress, the abstraction from ecological consequences and hazards) dominate the thinking and behaviour of human beings and institutions. Risk society is *not an option* which could be chosen or rejected in the course of political debate. It arises through the automatic operation of autonomous modernisation processes which are blind and deaf to consequences and dangers. In total, and latently, these produce hazards which call into question – indeed abolish – the basis of industrial society.

This kind of self-confrontation of the consequences of modernisation with the basis of modernisation should be clearly distinguished from the increase in knowledge and the penetration of all spheres of life by science and specialisation in the sense of the self-reflection of modernisation. If we call the autonomous, unintentional and unseen, *reflex*-like transition from industrial to risk society *reflexivity* – in distinction and opposition to *reflection* – then 'reflexive modernisation' means self-confrontation with the consequences of risk society which cannot (adequately) be addressed and overcome in the system of industrial society[2] (that is, measured by industrial society's own institutionalised standards). At a second stage this constellation can, in turn, be made the object of (public, political and academic) reflection, but this must not cover up the unreflected, reflex-like 'mechanism' of the transition. This is produced and becomes real precisely through abstraction from risk society.

In risk society, conflicts over the distribution of the 'bads' produced by it are superimposed on the conflicts over the distribution of societal 'goods' (income, jobs, social security), which constituted the fundamental conflict of industrial society and led to attempts at solution in appropriate institutions. The former can be shown to be *conflicts of accountability*. They break out over the question of how the consequences of the risks accompanying commodity production – large-scale nuclear and chemical technology, genetic engineering, threats to the environment, the arms build-up and the increasing impoverishment of humanity living outside Western industrial society – can be distributed, averted, controlled and legitimated.

At any rate, the concept of risk society provides a term for this relationship of reflex and reflection. For a theory of society and for cultural diagnosis the concept describes a stage of modernity in which the hazards produced in the growth of industrial society become predominant. That both poses the question of the self-limitation of this development and sets the task of redefining previously attained standards (of responsibility, safety, control, damage limitation and distribution of the consequence of loss) with reference to potential dangers. These, however, not only elude sensory perception and the powers of the imagination, but also scientific determination. Modern societies are therefore confronted with the principles and limits of their own model precisely to the extent that they do *not* change themselves, do not reflect on the consequences, and pursue an industrial policy of more-of-the-same.

The concept of risk society takes this as its starting point, in order to articulate systemic and epochal transformation in three areas. *First of all*, the relationship of modern industrial society to the resources of nature and culture, on whose existence it depends, but whose reserves are being used up in the course of an assertive modernisation. This is true for nature external to human beings and human cultures as well as for cultural life-forms (such as the nuclear family and order of the sexes) and social labour assets (such as housewives' labour, which although it has still not been recognized as labour, nevertheless made men's paid labour possible).

Second, the relationship of society to the hazards and problems produced by it, which in turn *exceed the bases of societal conceptions of security*. As a result, they are, in so far as there is awareness of them, likely to upset the basic assumptions of the previously existing social order. This is true for all sectors of society – such as business, the law, academia – but becomes a problem above all in the area of political activity and decision-making.

Third, the exhaustion, dissolution and disenchantment of collective and group-specific sources of meaning (such as belief in progress, class consciousness) of the culture of industrial society (whose lifestyles and ideas of security have also been fundamental to the Western democracies and economic societies until well into the twentieth century) leads to all the work of definition henceforth being expected of or imposed on individuals themselves. This is what the concept of 'individualising process' means. Georg Simmel, Émile Durkheim and Max Weber shaped the theory of this process at the beginning of the century and investigated its various historical stages. The difference is that today human beings are not being 'released' from corporate, religious-transcendental securities into the world of industrial society, but *from* industrial society into the turbulence of world risk society. They are, not least, expected to live with the most diverse, contradictory global and personal risks.

At the same time, this release – at least in the highly developed welfare states of the West – occurs in the framework of the social state. It takes place, therefore, against a background of educational expansion, the high levels of mobility demanded by the labour market and an extended legal framework for working conditions. The individual is turned, however, into the bearer of rights (and duties) – but only as an individual. The opportunities, hazards and ambivalences of biography which once could be coped with in the family unit, in the village community, and by recourse to the social class or group, increasingly have to be grasped, interpreted and dealt with by the individual alone. These 'risky freedoms'[3] are now imposed on individuals, without the latter being in a position, because of the great complexity of modern society, to make unavoidable decisions in a knowledgeable and responsible way; that is, with regard to possible consequences. At the same time the question as to the *we*, that is able to bind and motivate the individualised individuals, becomes urgent. If, after the end of the Cold War, even the national friendships and enmities of the East–West conflict disappear, then individuals in the networked media world, which compels not love-thy-neighbour, but love of whoever is far away, must repeatedly discover and justify even their own personal foreign policy in rapidly changing constellations.

The Provident State and Risk Society

Risks always depend on decisions – that is, they presuppose decisions. They arise from the transformation of uncertainty and hazards into decisions (and compel the making of decisions, which in turn produce risks).[4] The incalculable threats of pre-industrial society (plague, famine, natural catastrophes, wars, but also magic, gods, demons) are transformed into calculable risks in the course of the development of instrumental rational control, which the process of modernisation promotes in all spheres of life. This characterises the situation and the conflicts in early, classical industrial and bourgeois society. In the course of its expansion it is true not only for the 'feasibility' of production capacities, tax revenues, the calculation of export risks and the consequences of war, but also for the vicissitudes of individual lives: accidents, illnesses, death, social insecurity and poverty. It leads, as François Ewald argues, to the emergence of diverse systems of insurance, to the extent that society as a whole comes to be understood as a risk group in insurers' terms – as a *provident state* and a *providing state*.[5] Consequently and simultaneously, more and more areas and concerns of society that have been considered to be natural (family size, questions of upbringing, choice of profession, mobility, relations between the sexes), are now made social and individual, are thereby held to be accountable and subject to decisions, and are so judged and condemned. This situation offers the possibility of autonomous creation and also involves the danger of wrong decisions, the risks of which are to be covered by the principle of provident after-care. For this purpose there exist accident scenarios, statistics, social research, technical planning and a great variety of safety measures.

The institutions of developing industrial society can and must also be understood from the point of view of how the self-produced consequences can be made socially calculable and accountable and their conflicts made controllable. The unpredictable is turned into something predictable; what has not-yet-occurred becomes the object of present (providential) action. The dialectic of risk and insurance calculation provides the cognitive and institutional apparatus. The process is not only theoretically, historically and philosophically of importance, but also of great political significance, because here a stage in the history of how early industrial society learned to cope with itself is opened up and investigated, and because this learning process can point the way to another modernity of self-limitation – especially at the end of the twentieth century, which is overshadowed by the ecological question.

As a result, the epochal difference that distinguishes the risks of industrial society and the bourgeois social order from the hazards and demands of risk society can also be grasped more clearly. The entry into risk society occurs at the moment when the hazards which are now decided and consequently produced by society *undermine and/or cancel the estab-lished safety systems of the provident state's existing risk calculations*. In contrast to early industrial risks, nuclear, chemical, ecological and genetic engineering risks (a) can be limited in terms of neither time nor place, (b) are not accountable according to the established rules of causality, blame and liability, and (c) cannot be compensated or insured against.[6] Or, to express it by reference to a single example: the injured of Chernobyl are today, years after the catastrophe, not even all *born* yet.

Anyone who inquires as to an operational criterion for this transition has it to hand here: *the absence of private insurance cover*. More than that, industrial technical-scientific projects are *not insurable*. This is a yardstick which no sociologist or any kind of artist needs to introduce to society from the outside. Society itself produces this standard and measures its own development by it. Industrial society, which has involuntarily mutated into risk society through its own systematically produced hazards, balances *beyond the insurance limit*. The rationality on which this judgement is based derives from the core rationality of this society: *economic* ration-ality. It is the private insurance companies which operate or mark the frontier barrier of risk society. With the logic of economic behaviour they contradict the protestations of safety made by the technicians and in the danger industries, because they say that in the case of 'low probability but high consequences risks' the technical risk may tend towards zero, while at the same time the economic risk is potentially infinite.[7] A simple mental experiment makes plain the extent of the normalised degeneration. Anyone who today demands private insurance cover – such as is taken for granted by every car owner – before an advanced and dangerous industrial production apparatus is allowed to get under way at all, simultaneously proclaims the end for large sectors, above all of so-called industries of the future and major research organisations, which all operate without any or without adequate insurance cover.

Hazards versus Providentiality: Environmental Crisis as Inner Crisis

The transformation of the unseen side-effects of industrial production into global ecological trouble spots is therefore not at all a problem of the world surrounding us – not a so-called 'environmental problem' – but a far-reaching institutional crisis of industrial society itself. As long as these developments continue to be seen within the conceptual horizon of industrial society, then, as negative side-effects of seemingly accountable and calculable actions, their system-breaking consequences go unrecognised. Their central significance only emerges in the perspective and concepts of risk society, drawing attention to the need for reflexive self-definition and redefinition. In the phase of risk society, recognition of the incalculability of the hazards produced by technical-industrial development compels self-reflection on the foundations of the social context and a review of prevailing conventions and principles of 'rationality'. In the self-conception of risk society, society becomes *reflexive* (in the narrow sense of the word) – that is, becomes an issue and a problem to itself.

Industrial society, the bourgeois social order and, especially, the provident and social state are subject to the demand that human lived relationships are made instrumentally rational, controllable, capable of being produced, available and (individually and legally) accountable. In risk society, however, unforeseeable side- and after-effects of instrumentally rational behaviour lead, in turn, into (or back to) the modernisation of whatever cannot be calculated, answered for or easily comprehended. It can correspondingly be shown that societal measures of organisation, ethical and legal principles like responsibility, blame and the 'polluter pays' principle (such as in the pursuance of damages) as well as political decision-making procedures (such as the majority rule principle) are not suitable for grasping and/or legitimating the processes thereby set in motion. Analogously, it is the case that social scientific categories and methods no longer work when confronted by the complexity and ambiguity of the state of affairs to be described and understood. It is not only a matter of making decisions; more importantly, in the face of the unforeseeable and unaccountable consequences of large-scale technologies, it is necessary to redefine the rules and principles for decision-making, for areas of application and for critique. The reflexivity and incalculability of societal development therefore spreads to all sectors of society, breaking up regional, class-specific, national, political and scientific jurisdictions and boundaries. In the extreme case of the consequences of a nuclear disaster, there are no bystanders any more. Conversely, that also means that under this threat everyone is affected and involved and accordingly can speak in their own right.

In other words, risk society is tendentially a *self-critical* society. Insurance experts contradict safety engineers. If the latter declare a zero risk, the former judge: non-insurable. Experts are relativised or dethroned by counterexperts. Politicians encounter the resistance of citizens' initiatives, industrial management that of consumer organisations. Bureaucracies are criticised by self-help groups. Ultimately, industries responsible for damage (for example, the chemical industry for marine pollution) must even expect resistance from other industries affected as a result (in this case fishing and the business dependent on coastal tourism). The former can be challenged by the latter, inspected, perhaps even corrected. Yes, the risk question even divides families and professional groups, from the skilled workers of the chemical industry right up to top management,[8] often even the individual: what the head wants, the mouth says, the hand is unable to carry out.

Reflexive Modernisation as Theory of the Self-criticism of Society

Many say that with the collapse of really existing non-socialism the ground has been cut from under every critique of society. Just the opposite is true: the prospects for critique, including radical critique, have never been so favourable in Germany and elsewhere in Europe. The petrification of critique which the predominance of Marxian theory meant for critical intellectuals in Europe for a century has gone. The father figure is dead. In fact, only now can the critique of society get its breath back and see more clearly.

The theory of risk society avoids the difficulties of a critical theory of society in which the theorists apply more or less well justified standards to society and then judge and condemn accordingly (and often counter to the self-conception of those concerned). In a risk society which identifies itself as such, critique is *democratised*, as it were; that is, there arises a reciprocal critique of sectional rationalities and groups in society (see above). Thus a critical theory of society is replaced by a theory of *societal self-critique* and/ or an analysis of the intersecting lines of conflict of a reflexive modernity. The uncovering of the immanent conflicts of institutions *still* programmed in terms of industrial society, which are *already* being reflected on and criticised from the perspective of the concept of the self-endangerment of risk society, allows norms, principles and practices in all society's fields of action to become contradictory – that is, measured by immanent rankings and claims. For example, risk calculations which are based on a (spatially, temporally and socially circumscribed) accident definition, are supposed to estimate and legitimate the potential for catastrophe of modern large-scale technologies and industries. This, however, is precisely what they fail to do and so they are falsifications, and can be criticised and reformed in accordance with their own claims to rationality.

It is worth defining with conceptual precision the perspectives and conditions of societal self-criticism which the theory of risk society opens up. This is what the concept of reflexive modernisation attempts to do. It contains two components (or dimensions of meaning). On the one hand, it refers to the automatic transition from industrial to risk society (argued with reference to this theme; the same could be demonstrated, for example, by way of the fulfilment of modernity beyond the limits of male–female duality or in the systematic self-doubt of the sciences through more and better knowledge and interrogation of the foundations and conse-quences of scientific distribution and decision-making). It is not the looking, or the looking away, which produces and accelerates the dynamic of world risk society. This 'mechanism' has its origin in the momentum of industry, which, alarmed at 'side-effects' of hazards, rescinds its own principles (of calculation).

On the other hand, it is the case that, if this is understood, seen, enters general awareness, then a whole society is set in motion . What previously appeared 'functional' and 'rational' now becomes and appears to be a threat to life, and therefore produces and legitimates dysfunctionality and irrationality. If in addition professional *alternatives of self-control and self-limitation* arise and are propagated in contexts of activity, the institutions open themselves to the *political* right down to their foundations, and become malleable, dependent on subjects and coalitions.

This means that because the transition from industrial to risk society takes place unreflectingly, automatically, on the basis of industrial modernity's 'blindness to apocalypse' (Günther Anders), situations of danger establish themselves, which – having become the theme and centre of politics and public debates – lead to the questioning, the splitting of the centres of activity and decision-making of society. Within the horizon of the opposition between old routine and new awareness of consequences and dangers, society becomes self-critical. It is therefore the combination of reflex and reflections which, as long as the catastrophe itself fails to materialise, can set industrial modernity on the path to self-criticism and self-transformation.

Reflexive modernisation contains both elements: the reflex-like threat to industrial society's own foundations through a successful further modern-isation which is blind to dangers, *and* the growth of awareness, the reflection on this situation. The difference between industrial and risk society is first of all a difference of knowledge – that is, of self-reflection on the dangers of developed industrial modernity. The political arises out of the growing awareness of the hazards dependent on decision-making, because at first property relations, social inequalities and the principles of the functioning of industrial society as a whole remain untouched by it. In this sense the theory of risk society is a *political theory of knowledge* of modernity becoming self-critical. At issue is that industrial society sees itself as risk society and how it criticises and reforms itself.

Many candidates for the subject of the critique of society have appeared on (and departed) the stage of world history and the history of ideas: the

working class, the critical intelligentsia, the public sphere, social movements of the most diverse tendencies and composition, women, subcultures, youth, lepers, self-organising psychopaths and counterexperts. In
the theory of reflexive modernisation the basis of critique is first of all
thought autonomously. Thanks to its momentum and its successes,
industrial society is stumbling into the no man's land of uninsurable
hazards. To the extent that this, briefly, is seen, fatalistic industrial
modernity can transform itself into a conflictual and self-critical risk
society. Self-criticism in this context means that lines of conflict, which can
be organised and are capable of coalitions, arise within and between the
systems and institutions (and not only at the edges and areas of overlap of
private lifeworlds).

The End of Linear Technology?

Even if the above does not allow any clear conclusions as to the nature,
course and successes of conflicts and lines of conflict, one forecast at least
seems justified: the decision-making centres and the 'objective laws' of
scientific-technological progress are becoming political issues. That gives
rise to a question: does the growing awareness of risk society coincide with
the *invalidation of the linear models of technocracy* – models which,
whether optimistic or pessimistic about progress, have fascinated society
and its science for a hundred years?

In the 1960s Helmut Schelsky (drawing on Max Weber, Veblen, Gehlen
and many others) had argued that, with ever-increasing automation and
the penetration of science into all spheres of life, the modern state must
internalise technology, as it were, in order to preserve and expand its
power. Consequently, however, it pursues normative state goals less and
less, and is determined solely by technological constraints – becomes the
'technological state'. In other words, the instrumental rationalisation and
the encroachment of technology exhaust the substance of an ever-
modernising society. It is increasingly the case that experts rule, even
where politicians are nominally in charge. 'Technical-scientific decisions
cannot be subject to any democratic informed opinion, otherwise they
would become ineffective. If the political decisions of governments are
made in accordance with scientifically determined objective laws, then the
government has become an organ of the administration of objective
necessity, the parliament a supervisory organ of the correctness of expert
opinion.'[9]

Jost Halfman points out that from a risk-sociological point of view,
Schelsky assumes 'a development of society towards zero risk'. In other
words, the explosive force of a modernity which transforms everything into
decisions and therefore into risks, remains completely unrecognised.
'(High) risk technologies directly contradict technocratic theoretical expectations . . . The central position of the state in the material support and

political regulation of technological progress has increasingly given political institutions an important role in the "liability" for the consequences of
progress, with respect to society. Technological progress and its consequences have thereby assumed the character of collective goods.' Where
society has become a laboratory (Krohn/Weyer), decisions about and
control of technological progress become a collective problem.

> Science is no longer experimental activity without consequences, and technology
> is no longer low-risk application of secure knowledge. Science and technology
> produce risks in carrying out their experiments and thereby burden society as a
> whole with managing the risks . . . Depending on the risk culture quite different
> strategic consequences follow for dealing with risk. Industrialists assess risks
> according to cost–benefit principles; failure in the marketplace becomes the most
> important focus of risk avoidance. Bureaucracies judge risks according to
> hypothetical definitions of the common good and look for redistributive
> solutions in dealing with risks; here the principal problem is the institutional
> integrity of the administrative apparatus. Social movements measure risks by the
> potential for catastrophe involved and seek to avoid risks which could lead to a
> threat to present and future quality of life. The effective irreconcilability of these
> various risk assessments turns concrete decisions over acceptable risks into
> struggles for power. 'The issue is not risk, but power'. (Charles Perrow)[10]

What is at stake in this new risk conflict, as Christoph Lau demonstrates,
is not so much risk avoidance, as the *distribution* of risk, which means that
it is about the *architecture of risk definition* in the face of the growing
competition between overlapping discourses of risk (such as nuclear power
versus ozone hole:

> Debates over risk definitions and their consequences for society take place
> essentially at the level of public (or partially public) discourses. They are
> conducted with the aid of scientific arguments and information, which serve, so
> to speak, as scarce resources of the collective actors. The scientifically pen-
> etrated public sphere then becomes the symbolic location of conflicts over
> distribution even if this is disguised by the objectified, scientistic autonomous
> logic of specialist argument about risk.

Such risk definitions impose boundaries on society, by attempting to
determine factors such as the size, location and social characteristics of
those responsible for and those affected by the risks involved. As such,
they become the focus for contestation.

> Whereas, within the framework of the 'old' distribution conflicts, the success of
> strategic behaviour can be designated and measured by distinct media (money,
> ownership of means of production, wage settlements, voting figures), such
> symbolic media which could unambiguously reflect risk gain and risk loss are
> hardly available. All attempts to establish risk yardsticks, such as probability
> estimates, threshold values and calculations of costs, founder, as far as late
> industrial risks are concerned, on the incommensurability of hazards and the
> problem of the subjective assessment of the probability of occurrence. This
> explains why conflicts essentially break out at the level of knowledge around
> problems of definition and causal relationships. Primary resources in this
> struggle over risk justice are not immediately strikes, voting figures, political
> influence, but above all information, scientific findings, assessments, argu-
> ments.[11]

Niklas Luhmann takes this pattern of risk conflict as his starting point. For him the distinction between risk and danger coincides with the opposition between the situation of those *making* a decision and those *affected* by the decision. Agreement between the two is difficult, if not out of the question. At the same time neither do any clear lines of conflict develop, because the confrontation between decision-makers and those affected varies according to theme and situation.

> We talk of risks if possible future injury is attributable to one's own decision. If one does not enter an aeroplane, one cannot crash. In the case of hazards, on the other hand, damage has an external source. If, say, to stay with the given example, one is killed by falling aircraft wreckage . . . Familiar hazards – earthquakes and volcanic eruptions, aquaplaning and marriages – become risks to the extent that the decisions by which it is possible to avoid exposing oneself to them become known. But that illuminates only one half of the situation, since with the decisions made, the hazards also increase once more, and, that is, in the form of hazards which result from the decisions of others . . . Thus today the distinction between risk and hazard cuts through the social order. One person's risk is another person's hazard. The smoker may risk cancer, but for others it is a hazard. The car driver who takes a chance when overtaking behaves in just the same way, the builder and operator of nuclear power stations, genetic engineering research – there is no lack of examples.

The impossibility or at least the sheer insurmountability of the barriers to agreement arise from the perception and assessment of catastrophes. Here the yardstick of the 'rationality' of the probability of occurrence is ineffective.

> It may indeed be true that the danger which comes from a nearby nuclear power station is no greater than the risk involved in the decision to drive an extra mile and a half per year. But who will be impressed by an argument like that? The prospect of catastrophes sets a limit to calculation. Under no circumstances whatsoever does one want it – even if it is extremely improbable. But what is the catastrophe threshold beyond which quantitative calculations are no longer convincing? Obviously, this question cannot be answered independently of other variables. It is different for rich and poor, for the independent and the dependent . . . The really interesting question is what counts as a catastrophe. And that is presumably a question which will be answered very differently by decision-makers and victims.[12]

That may be, but it neglects and underestimates the systemic yardstick of economic insurance rationality. Risk society is *uncovered* society, in which insurance protection *decreases* with scale of the danger – and this in the historic milieu of the 'provident state', which encompasses all spheres of life, and of the fully comprehensive society. Only the two together – uncovered *and* comprehensively insured society – constitute the politically explosive force of risk society.

On the Antiquatedness of Pessimism about Progress

The ancestral line of profound and pitiless critics of modernity is long and includes many respected names. The best thinkers in Europe have been among them, even in the present century. Max Weber still tries to keep a cool head in the face of the grim consequence of his linear analyses (though repressed pessimism often bursts out between the lines and in the incidental and concluding remarks). In Horkheimer and Adorno's *Dialectic of Enlightenment* the judgement veers round. Here darkest darkness prevails (so that one sometimes asks oneself how the authors themselves were able to recognise what they believed they recognised). Subsequently, Günther Anders believed that the gulf between what rules our heads and what results from the labour of our hands was so great, so irrevocable, that to him all attempts to challenge it were embarrassing, if not unbearable. Karl Jaspers, Arnold Gehlen, Jacques Ellul or Hans Jonas, to whose analyses I am deeply indebted, also have to admit, when it comes to the point, that they do not know where the forces could come from which are to bring the superpower of technological progress to its knees or at least to admit contrition.

In these overpowering analyses one can read for oneself how the authors are spellbound by the automatic process they describe. Sometimes a hopeful little chapter is tacked on at the end, which bears the same relationship to the general hopelessness as a sigh to the end of the world, and then the writer makes his exit and leaves the shattered readers behind in the vale of tears he has portrayed. (I can permit myself to banter like this, since I have already demonstrated my talent as an up and coming prophet of doom.)

Certainly, hopelessness is ennobling and the advantages of wallowing in superiority, while at the same time being relieved of all responsibility for action, are not to be underestimated. However, if the theory sketched out here is correct, then the theorists of doom can begin to rejoice, because their theories are wrong or will become so!

In a discussion of the English edition of *Risk Society* Zygmunt Bauman once again summarised with breathtaking brilliance the arguments which encourage everyone to sit back and do nothing. The problem is not only that we are facing challenges on an undreamt of scale, but, more profoundly, that all attempts at solution bear in themselves the seed of new and more difficult problems. '[T]he most fearsome of disasters are those traceable to the past or present pursuits of rational solutions. Catastrophes most horrid are born – or are likely to be born – out of the war against catastrophes . . . Dangers grow with our powers, and the one power we miss most is that which divines their arrival and sizes up their volume.'[13]

But even where risks are picked up, it is always only the symptoms that are combated, never the causes, because the fight against the risks of unrestrained business activity has itself become

> a major business, offering a new lease of life to scientific/technological dreams of unlimited expansion. In our society, risk-fighting can be nothing else but business – the bigger it is, the more impressive and reassuring. The politics of fear lubricates the wheels of consumerism and helps to 'keep the economy going' and steers away from the 'bane of recession'. Ever more resources are to be

consumed in order to repair the gruesome effects of yesterday's resource consumption. Individual fears beefed up by the exposure of yesterday's risks are deployed in the service of collective production of the unknown risks of tomorrow . . .[14]

Indeed, life and behaviour in risk society have become Kafkaesque – in the strict sense of the word.[15] Yet my principal argument comes from another angle. Even negative fatalism – it above all! – thinks of modernisation in *linear* terms and so fails to recognise the ambivalences of a modernisation of modernisation, which revokes the principles of industrial society itself.

In fact Zygmunt Bauman explicitly takes up this idea of reflexive modernisation:

> Beck has not lost hope (some would say illusion) that 'reflexivity' can accomplish what 'rationality' failed to do . . . What amounts to another *apologia* for science (now boasting reflexivity as a weapon more trustworthy than the rationality of yore and claiming the untried credentials of risk-anticipating instead of those of discredited problem-solving) can be upheld only as long as the role of science in the past and present plight of humanity is overstated and/or demonised. But it is only in the mind of the scientists and their hired or voluntary court-poets that knowledge (*their* knowledge) 'determines being'. And reflexivity, like rationality, is a double-edged sword. Servant as much as a master; healer as much as a hangman.[16]

Bauman says 'reflexivity' but fails to recognise the peculiar relationship of reflex and reflection within risk society (see above). This precisely does not mean more of the same – science, research into effects, the controls on automatic. Rather, in reflexive modernity, the forms and principles of industrial society are dissolved. With the force, and as a consequence of its momentum, there arise unforeseen and also incalculable social situations and dynamics within, but also between, systems, organisations and (apparently) private spheres of life. These present new challenges for the social sciences, since their analysis requires new categories, theories and methods.

The theory of risk society suggests, therefore, that it is what cannot be foreseen that produces previously unknown situations (which are not for that reason by any means better, or closer to saving us!). If this becomes part of general awareness, society begins to move. Whether this is a good thing or simply accelerates the general decline can be left open for the time being.

At any rate, the theory of reflexive modernisation contradicts the fundamental assumptions of negative fatalism. The proponent of the latter *knows* that which from his own assumptions he cannot know at all: the outcome, the end, the hopelessness of everything. Negative fatalism is twin brother to the belief in progress. If in the latter a momentum, thought in linear terms, becomes the source of a naive belief in progress (according to the motto 'if we can't change it, let's welcome it'), with the former the incalculable is *foreseeably* incalculable. In fact, however, it is precisely the power of fatalism which makes fatalism wrong.

For example, it is because Günther Anders is right that the diagnosis of his *Die Antiquiertheit des Menschen* (The Antiquatedness of Human Beings)[17] is antiquated. In the course of reflexive modernisation new political lines of conflict of a high-revving industrial society, which understands and criticises itself as risk society, arise. These may be better or worse, but are in any case *different*, and must first of all be perceived and decoded as such.

Similarly Zygmunt Bauman – the social theorist of ambivalence – thinks modernity in terms which are far too linear. The banal possibility that something unforeseeable emerges from the unforeseeable (and the more incalculable, the more surprising it is) is lost from sight. Yet it is with this adventure of decision-determined incalculability that the history of society begins anew at the end of the twentieth century.

Just as earlier generations lived in the age of the stagecoach, so we now and in future are living in the hazardous age of creeping catastrophe. What generations before us discovered despite resistance, and had to shout out loud at the world, we have come to take for granted: the impending 'suicide of the species' (Karl Jaspers). Perhaps fatalism is the *birth* mood of the risk epoch? Perhaps dominant yet still unspoken hopes inspire fatalism? Will the post-optimism of post-fatalism perhaps at last emerge, when the seriousness of the situation is really understood, and the situation has been accepted and understood as one's own situation? I am not playing with words. I know of no greater security and no deeper source of creativity than a pessimism which cannot be outbid. Where everything is at stake, everything can and must be rethought and re-examined.

Only the naive, ontological pessimism of certainty commits one to pessimism. Whoever cultivates doubt can and must resaddle the stallions of inquiry.

Résumé and Prospects

A completely opposite picture of the historical evolution of society is often contrasted with the succession and overlapping of industrial and risk society presented here. According to this picture, the pre-industrial epochs and cultures were societies of *catastrophe*. In the course of industrialisation these became and are becoming societies of *calculable risk*, while in the middle of Europe late industrial society has even perfected its technological and social providential and security systems as *fully* comprehensively insured societies.

Here, however, it was argued – drawing on François Ewald's systematic historical analyses – that risk society begins where industrial society's principles of calculation are submerged and annulled in the continuity of automatic and tempestuously successful modernisation. Risk society negates the principles of its rationality. It has long ago left these behind, because it operates and balances beyond the insurance limit. This is only *one* indicator which demonstrates that an enterprise which began with the extension of calculability has slipped away into what is now decision-determined incalculability. The results are concrete reciprocal possibilities of critique and politicisation within and between institutions, lifeworlds and organisations.

On the whole this represents only *one* special case of reflexive modernisation. The concept combines the reflex of modernisation threatening itself with reflection on this (self-) threat, whereby new conflicts and tensions between interests run through and split society. That, however, leads to further questions.

Does risk society already begin where the insurance limit has been crossed, but this is neither seen nor understood? How does this condition of industrial society, which by abstraction from the consequences and hazards actually exacerbates these, at the same time block out any insight into its threat to itself? Here the unsettling effects of risk society emerge and grow more significant, but they are not comprehended as such and are not at all made the object of political action and societal (self-) criticism. Are these disruptions of a modernisation annulling its own principles thereby deflected and distorted into turbulences of every kind – from violence to right-wing extremism?

Or perhaps risk society only begins when the sound barrier of in-surability has been broken *and* this has been understood, noted and made into the theme and conflict which is superimposed on everything. Do these turbulences of an industrial society which understands and criticises itself *as* risk society now present a way out from the feeling that there is no way out? Or do the 'no exits' simply fork here, leaving no perspectives for action, but only a general paralysis and blockages which accelerate the catastrophe?

A third variant, involving both, would also be conceivable – first, the crossing of the insurance limit, leaving whole industries and areas of research hovering without net and parachute in the weightless zone of non-insurability; and second, the comprehension of this situation. These are certainly necessary but not sufficient conditions of risk society. It only begins where the discussion of the repair and reformation of industrial society become clearly defined. Does, therefore, talk about risk society only start to make full sense with the ecological reform of capitalism? Or does it already become less meaningful there, because, as a result, the politicising dynamic of decision-determined hazards begins to fade away?

Are there not always first of all, and permanently, the distribution conflicts of an industrial society with a more or less encompassing welfare state? Whereas risk questions and conflicts are only superimposed on these as long as the latter appear tamed – that is, in periods of economic upturn, low unemployment, etc.?

All these questions require a new approach in order to be answered, which would be beyond the scope of this chapter. But I shall nevertheless make one point. The political confusions of risk society also arise (in contrast to the distribution conflicts of a society of lack) because institutional answers to the challenges of an uncovered (global) society of hazards in a comprehensively insured milieu have so far hardly been thought up, invented, still less tested and successfully realised. In other words, the contours of the social state are familiar. No one knows, however, how, whether and by what means it might be possible to really throttle back the self-endangering momentum of the global risk society. Talk of the nature state – by analogy with the social state – remains just as empty in this context as attempts to cure industrial society of its suicidal tendencies with more of the same: morality, technology and ecological markets. The necessary learning step still lies ahead of the global risk society on the threshold of the twenty-first century.[18]

Notes

An earlier version of this chapter was originally published in *Der Vorsorgestaat*, edited by François Ewald © Suhrkamp Verlag, Frankfurt am Main, 1993.

1. See on this: S. Lash (1992) 'Reflexive modernization: the aesthetic dimension', *Theory, Culture and Society*, 10(1): 1–23. U. Beck, A. Giddens and S. Lash (1994) *Reflexive Modernization: Politics, Tradition and Aesthetics in the Modern Social Order* (Cambridge); R. Merten and T. Olk (1992) 'Wenn Sozialarbeit sich selbst zum Problem wird – Strategien reflexiver Modernisierung', in T. Rauschenbach and H. Gängler (eds), *Soziale Arbeit und Erziehung in der Risikogesellschaft*. Berlin: Neuwied. 81–100; T. Rausenbach (1992), 'Soziale Arbeit und soziales Risiko', in ibid.: 25–60; U. Beck (1996), *The Renaissance of Politics* (Cambridge); W. Zapf (1992) 'Entwicklung und Zukunft moderner Gesellschaften seit den 70er Jahren', in H. Korte and B. Schäfers (eds), *Einführung in Hauptbegriffe der Soziologie*. Opladen, esp. p. 204.
2. U. Beck (1992) *Risk Society: Towards a New Modernity*. London; U. Beck (1995) *Ecological Politics in an Age of Risk*. Cambridge: Polity.
3. U. Beck and E. Beck-Gernsheim (eds) (1994) *Riskante Freiheiten – Individualisierung in der modernen Gesellschaft*. Frankfurt am Main.
4. There is now a consensus on this: see F. Ewald (1986) *L'État Providence*. Paris: Editions Grasset. A. Evers and H. Nowotny (1987) *Über den Umgang mit Unsicherheiten*. Frankfurt am Main; P. Lagadec (1987) *Das grosse Risiko*. Nördlingen; C. Perrow (1984) *Normal Accidents: Living with High-risk Technologies*. New York: Basic Books; C. Lau (1991) 'Neue Risiken und gesellschaftliche Konflikte', in U. Beck (ed.), *Politik in der Risikogesellschaft*. Frankfurt am Main; J. Halfmann (1990) 'Technik und soziale Organisation im Widerspruch', in J. Halfmann and K.P. Japp (eds) *Riskante Entscheidungen und Katastrophenpotentiale*. Opladen, as well as the other essays collected in this volume; V. von Prittwitz (1990) *Das Katastrophen-Paradox*. Opladen; W. Bonss (1991) 'Unsicherheit und Gesellschaft', *Soziale Welt*: 258–77; N. Luhmann (1993) *Risk: A Sociological Theory*. Berlin; A. Hahn, W.H. Eirmbter and R. Jacobs (1992) 'Aids: Risiko oder Gefahr', *Soziale Welt*: 404–21; also my own books mentioned in note 2; D. Brock (1991) 'Die Risikogesellschaft und das Risiko soziologischer Zuspitzung', *Zeitschrift für Soziologie*, 1: 12–24; K.P. Japp (1992) 'Selbstverstärkungseffekte riskanter Entscheidungen', *Zeitschrift für Soziologie*: 33–50.
5. F. Ewald (1986), op. cit.
6. U. Beck (1991) *Ecological Enlightenment: Essays on the Politics of the Risk Society*. Atlantic Highlands, NJ. p.2.
7. Recently, the insured but increasingly incalculable hazards which have driven many insurance companies to the brink of ruin have been added to what cannot be insured. The

international insurance trade is feeling the devastating consequences of the greenhouse effect. This encourages tornadoes, which, for example, in 1992 in Florida alone, caused insurance losses of 20 billion dollars. Nine insurance companies went bankrupt because of the hurricanes in Florida and Hawaii, according to Greenpeace. The result is that insurance companies drop risks. Today, new house owners in Hawaii can no longer get any insurance cover. The same could soon also be true for Florida and the US Gulf Coast, reports *Süddeutsche Zeitung* (3 February 1993: 12).

8. R. Bogun, M. Osterland and G. Warsewa (1992) 'Arbeit und Umwelt im Risiko-bewusstsein von Industriearbeitern', *Soziale Welt* 2: 237–45; H. Heine (1992) 'Das Verhältnis der Naturwissenschaftler und Ingenieure in der Grosschemie zur ökologischen Industrie-kritik', *Soziale Welt*, 2: pp. 246–55; L. Pries (1991) *Betrieblicher Wandel in der Risiko-gesellschaft*. Opladen.

9. H. Schelsky (1965) 'Der Mensch in der wissenschaftlichen Zivilisation', in Schelsky, *Auf der Suche nach Wirklichkeit*. Düsseldorf. p. 459.

10. J. Halfmann (1990) 'Technik und soziale Organisation im Widerspruch', op. cit.: 21, 26, 28 U. Beck (1995) 'The World as laboratory', in Beck, *Ecological Enlightenment*, op. cit.: 107ff.

11. C. Lau (1991) 'Neue Risiken und gesellschaftliche Konflikte', op. cit.: 254.

12. N. Luhmann (1991) 'Verständigung über Risiken und Gefahren', *Die politische Meinung*: 81, 91. See Luhmann (1993) *Soziologie des Risikos*. Berlin.

13. Z. Bauman, 'The solution as problem', *The Times Higher Education Supplement*, 13 November 1992: 25.

14. Ibid.

15. U. Beck (1995) 'We fatalists', in Beck, *Ecological Enlightenment*, op. cit.: 77ff.

16. Z. Bauman (1992) 'The solution as problem', op. cit.

17. Günther Anders (1982) *Die Antiquiertheit des Menschen* (7th edn). Munich.

18. See U. Beck (forthcoming) *The Renaissance of Politics*. Cambridge: Polity. A step in this direction was taken with the switch of the Federal German Environmental Liability Law from liability for damage caused by intentional and negligent acts to absolute liability. Under this law (changed in 1991 following the major fire in a warehouse belonging to Sandoz, the Basle chemical company) companies are liable – without proof of fault – for damage up to a level of DM160 million each for injury to persons and to property. A *suspicion of cause* is sufficient (para. 6, Environmental Commerical Code): simply, if the 'plant is likely, given the circumstances of the particular case, to cause the injuries arising, then it is presumed that the injury has been caused by this plant'. In other words, the burden of proof is no longer on the injured party, who, as a rule, cannot offer proof, but on the (potential) injurer. Para. 19, appendix 2, requires, for especially high-risk production plants, a 'cover provision', which – under given conditions – can effectively only be provided by an environmental liability insurance. According to an insurance model for environmental risks developed by the liability insurers, the 'legal liability under civil law is insured for injuries to persons and property which have been caused by an "environmental effect" on ground, air or water' (Jörrissen). Uninsured and uninsurable in principle are thereby injuries to the plant itself, and contaminated sites. Here the limit of *economically* incalculable hazards has quite evidently been reached and/or crossed, because the international reinsurance market does not make any provision for these environmental risks either. The result is that 'hundreds of thousands of companies will have to take good care' (cf. *Süddeutsche Zeitung*, 13–14 February 1993: p. 24).

2

MAY THE SHEEP SAFELY GRAZE? A REFLEXIVE VIEW OF THE EXPERT–LAY KNOWLEDGE DIVIDE

Brian Wynne

It has been a frequently remarked feature of the environmental issue that it is so strongly characterised in scientific terms, even though the modern cultural reflex to do so may be seen as part of the deeper roots of the 'environmental' problem (Yearley, 1992; Redclift and Benton, 1994). Likewise, even environmental NGOs, originally the creative cutting edge of a new cultural sensibility, are seen as selling the pass when they trade so heavily in the scientific discourse of modern officially espoused environmentalism (Jamison, this volume). It is not clear how far and in what precise ways modern environmentalism as a social movement and a historical shift of societal awareness represents a crystallisation of more complex forces and realities than straightforward physical-biological environmental threats. However, that it does so has been persuasively argued, without falling into the sterile polarisation of 'real' environmental processes versus 'unreal' social constructions (Grove-White, 1991; Wynne, forthcoming).

It is interesting to note a parallel feature of the sociological debate over the 'risk society'. Here too, Beck's (1992 [1986]) original thesis has been criticised for an overly realist account of the generation – via the growth of real risks which are now universal and unmanageable – of a new cultural consciousness which introduces modernity and its institutions to pervasive public scepticism, or 'self-refutation'. Hence the epistemologically realist underpinnings of the political edge of 'reflexive modernity'. In this light it is perhaps unsurprising that a defining feature of the sociological treatments of modernity and postmodernity, and of the risk society thesis, has been their almost exclusive focus on expert knowledge. For example, in his exchange with two of the most productive sociological analysts of modernity's transformations, Giddens and Beck (Beck et al., 1994: 200), Lash noted that:

> Beck's and Giddens's virtual neglect of the cultural/hermeneutic sources of the late modern self entails at the same time a neglect of this crucial dimension of politics and everyday life. It means further that their conceptions of sub-politics or life-politics focus on the experts with relative neglect of the grass roots. It

means for them a concentration on the formal and institutional at the expense of the increasing proportion of social, cultural, and political interaction in our increasingly disorganised capitalist world that is going on outside of institutions.

In attempting to clarify our understanding of the transformations of modernity, different authors have developed their own ideas of reflexive processes and their consequences (Giddens, 1990, 1991; Bauman, 1991; Beck 1992, and this volume). These bear different relationships to the concept of risk, and imply different characteristics of scientific knowledge or expert systems, which are agreed to be central to those transformation processes. As implied by Lash, a major dimension of these transformation processes is excluded, or at least dealt with only in unsatisfactory ways. This is the 'grass-roots' or lay public dimension.

However, I will argue that this is far more than merely an omission, because it implicitly reproduces just those fundamental dichotomies which are key parts of the problem of modernity: natural knowledge versus 'social' knowledge, nature versus society, expert versus lay knowledge. It also reflects – and reinforces – a more basic lack of recognition of the cultural/hermeneutic character of scientific knowledge itself, as well as of social interaction and cognitive construction generally. In consequence it also radically delimits our understanding of the sense of risk which may be seen as a central element of those transformation processes. In particular, I suggest that this neglect of the cultural/hermeneutic character of modern knowledge, specifically of modern scientific knowledge itself, seriously constrains the imagination of new forms of order and of how their social legitimation may be better founded. Adopting a more social constructivist epistemology than Beck and Giddens do in their conception of scientific knowledge and of the ecological wellsprings of late modernity's pervasive risks, I also thus problematise their uncritical conception of science and knowledge *per se*. It is important to distinguish here between their recognition of the (in recent years only) *contested* nature of scientific knowledge, and their uncritical reproduction of a 'realist' concept of scientific knowledge. This realist epistemology also, I argue, gives rise to an unduly one-dimensional understanding of the underlying dynamics of the nature of 'risk' in the risk society. A more constructivist perspective on scientific knowledge also problematises their conceptions of trust, and indeed of the nature of social relations generally. Here I align partly with Lash in his suggestion that their perspectives are unduly influenced by rational-choice models of the social. This seems to be another way of saying that they have understated the importance of the cultural nature of science, and especially of the implications of fundamental indeterminacies in knowledge which a cultural perspective should be able to capture.

Again, it is not that Giddens especially ignores the lay public dimension; but in his account it is exclusively concerned with the interpersonal and intimate, and even then I agree with Lash, in an overly rational-choice way. *There is never the slightest hint that there could in the public realm be the basis of alternative forms of public knowledge, and order, from those given in existing forms of instrumental expertise.* However, I also argue that Lash neglects the hermeneutic dimensions of science when he – rightly in my view – takes Beck and Giddens to task for overlooking the cultural/ hermeneutic dimensions of (reflexive) lay responses to expert intervention and disruption of everyday life.

In this chapter I therefore wish to address the reflexive processes amongst the 'grass-roots' or lay publics – those who can be thought of as outside of the expert systems which in the debate so far have been the almost exclusive focus of analysis. In doing so I will also throw a different, more thoroughly cultural, light on the prevailing conceptions of the scientific or expert, and on the concept of risk itself. Although prevailing treatments do recognise reflexivity amongst lay people, this is inadequately captured by being restricted to the intimate and interpersonal.[1] Thus alternative, more culturally rooted and legitimate forms of collective, public knowledge – and of corresponding public order – which could arise from the informal non-expert public domain are inadvertently but still systematically suppressed. There is a wide range of suggestive fieldwork on public responses to science and expertise which is a valuable resource for clarifying the issues and possibilities here (Wynne 1994), and I will use some of this to illustrate my arguments.

In their later work on reflexive processes (Beck et al., 1994) both Beck and Giddens have begun to recognise the importance of non-expert apprehensions and responses to expert systems (whether to the culture of these in general, or to specific ones such as genetic technologies). They have thus begun to redress what was previously a lacuna, or rather perhaps a taken-for-granted issue, in accounts of the complex relationships between lay publics and experts. Beck has perhaps the least deferential and subordinated model of public groups, 'non-experts', as is captured in his ideas of sub-politics. Yet both these authors tend to take the public and its knowledges for granted. This appears to be a function of the fact that to these authors, it seems, defining expert knowledge, expert, and expert system is unproblematic.

This lack of reflexive attention to the question of how the category of 'expert' is defined and bounded is somewhat surprising given the centrality of the concept to those debates and theories. One way of interpreting this state of affairs would be troubling to the whole debate, namely that the sociological categories of modernity, postmodernity and its variants can only themselves be entertained as unambiguous and 'real' by trading on a realist conception of expert knowledge. This would be an implication of Latour's more radical questioning of the very terms of this debate in *We Have Never Been Modern* (Latour, 1992). The constructivist ethos of sociology of science which has problematised what scientific knowledge means, has also suggested that there has never been any such thing as modernity in the mythic sense described in the rhetoric of scientists and the prescriptive descriptions of philosophers and epistemologists. Scientific 'modernity' has always been imbued with tradition, a point recognised and developed since Kuhn (1962) and Polanyi (1958). What is more, those elements of tradition, in the sense of received authority, dogmatic commitment and 'mechanical solidarity', have been recognised as *essential* to scientific culture, not temporary and localised *betrayals* thereof. If the so-called essence of science is the creative social tension between 'modernity' (openness) and tradition (closedness), this also opens up more complex and interesting ways of conceiving of the democratic possibilities of science, and thus of the reconstruction of politics. In this reconstruction out of the same transformations that Beck and Giddens are trying to illuminate, a central issue will still be the construction and authority of universals; but these will be universals whose human basis can also be apprehended, and negotiated.

Illusions of Trust: Recognising Dependency and Alienation

Trust has long been recognised by sociologists as an essential and somewhat taken-for-granted element of social relations (Garfinkel, 1963). In his earlier treatments of modernity, Giddens (1990) also took for granted public trust in expert systems, in which lay people simply assumed expert competence and trustworthiness. Giddens understood reflexive transformations not as being due to public questioning of expert authority but as rooted in private interpersonal responses to processes of globalisation and disembedding. Although expert systems were central to these processes, in Giddens's account public trust in experts was not an issue, and reflexive processes were driven by private responses to the interventions by expert systems in intimate microsocial worlds.

Beck's (1992) concept of the risk society, on the other hand, involved the central idea that modernity's institutions were 'self-refuting' because they could no longer live up to their claims of managing and controlling the escalating risks from modern science and technology – hence his useful notion of focusing not on knowledge and planning, but on ignorance and the unanticipated (Beck, 1994). Implicit in Beck's model is the proposal that lay people are losing their sense of trust in science and expertise because they feel betrayed by them. Note also for later reference that this notion of public mistrust is instrumental-calculative, implying a rationalistic and contractual model of the wellsprings of social response.

In his more recent work, Giddens (1994) has moved towards Beck's more political framing of the processes of transformation of modernity. Here Giddens recognises, if belatedly, that expertise is contested in public. However, the way in which this contestation is conducted and, if not resolved at least contained, is through reflexive processes *conceived by Giddens in terms of rational choice*. In the face of contestation of expert claims, publics invest active trust in expert systems – that is, trust is invested in particular experts via deliberate choice between recognised alternatives. Previously it seems, in 'simple modernity', they simply trusted and believed, as a taken-for-granted. This development of Giddens's view (from Giddens, 1990 and 1991, to Giddens, 1994) has been conflated somewhat with a descriptive account of historical change, from earlier 'simple' modernity in which automatic trust supposedly prevailed, to 'reflexive modernity' in which, it is claimed, actively calculated and chosen trust now has to be invested.

These basic theoretical conceptions deserve to be more carefully and critically examined. If we are indeed dealing with a proposed account of social change rather than a change of view encouraged by productive interchange with other theorists, it is first of all worth examining what the relationships of lay publics to expert systems is or was under 'simple modernity' conditions. Contrary to Giddens I argue that the supposed earlier conditions of unqualified public trust have never prevailed, and that Giddens has reproduced what is a widespread confusion between unreflexive trust, and reflexive dependency and private ambivalence (Wynne, 1987, 1992). He thus makes two mistaken and mutually reinforcing assumptions – that the earlier, ostensibly publicly uncontested status of expertise equalled public trust; and that the reflexive processes of late modernity in which expertise is widely and openly contested are a result of the choices that have to be deliberately made by people exposed as they are (on this view) to a new dimension of insecurity, namely the problematisation of (supposedly) previously unproblematic expert authority.

An analogous assumption to those of Giddens outlined above has been made about changes in public perceptions of nuclear expertise and nuclear power. The conventional wisdom amongst political and academic commentators is that opposition to nuclear power and public scepticism towards nuclear expertise only began in the 1970s, encouraged by the rise of environmentalism as a political force, and by immediate plans for rapid growth of the industry.[2] Before that, it is assumed, the public unambiguously believed in and trusted the experts.

Yet Welsh (Welsh, 1993, 1995; McKechnie and Welsh, 1994) has shown for example that well before the 1970s and the emergence of organised national and international political opposition to nuclear power, there was by no means a condition of automatic lay public trust in such expert systems. Well before people were confronted by nuclear experts disagreeing amongst themselves in public, they were actively challenging the expertise that they were monolithically offered as authority, and questioning their enforced dependency upon it. In the earliest years of the UK programme, Welsh found ample evidence of public mistrust and opposition to the industry, and alienation from its perceived scientistic hubris. Two elements of a dominant idea are combined in the conventional wisdom which Welsh challenges, and they also shape Giddens's perspective:

- that public mistrust only follows increasingly open expert dissent and contestation. This needs revision, perhaps even complete inversion. It may well be that expert dissent is often only encouraged and sustained by the existence of a public backcloth of scepticism or alienation.

• that an observed lack of overt public dissent or opposition means that public trust exists. As I discuss below, public alienation from and ambivalence towards expert institutions are not necessarily manifested in behaviour or overt commitments, so that observation of no dissent cannot be taken to mean that trust exists and alienation does not.

Indirect support for the more sceptical view can be drawn from other aspects of the nuclear risk debate which indicate how easily lay public authorship of knowledge is deleted from social recognition. In the 1970s local claims were made by ordinary people living near the Sellafield nuclear reprocessing complex, that excess childhood leukemias were occurring in that area. These observations persisted despite official denials not only by the operators British Nuclear Fuels but by the public health authorities. When environmental groups heard of these informal local observations and concerns they commissioned a researcher to gather proper statistics so as to test the claims, but they were refused access to the health authority data. Eventually, the issue came to the attention of TV researchers, and a national documentary programme was eventually broadcast in 1983, essentially supporting the lay public claims. This dramatic intervention brought an immediate official inquiry of blue-riband experts chaired by the Department of Health's Chief Medical Officer, Sir Douglas Black. The inquiry (Black, 1984; MacGill, 1987) confirmed a persistent cluster of excess childhood leukemias in the immediate vicinity of the plant, though it was unable to attribute it to any cause. A large investment of research was initiated into such cancers and their possible causes, and a new government standing committee of experts was established to examine and report on the medical aspects of radiation in the environment.

However, the significant point underneath all this new flurry of expert attention to this risk issue was that the excess cancers around the Sellafield plant were almost routinely referred to as having been *discovered* by the Black Committee (MacGill, 1987; McSorley, 1990). The prior authorship of the ordinary non-expert lay public, which even had to endure expert denial and refusal of access to data, was thus obliterated from social discourse. It is easy to see how non-institutional forms of experience and knowledge come to be systematically deleted from recognition, and alternative collective idioms of identity and order thus pre-empted.

Parallels can be taken from history of science too. Much of the more recent work in this field has concerned itself with the public role and authority of scientific knowledge, and the co-construction of epistemic and political order (Shapin and Schaffer, 1985; Golinski, 1992; Shapin, 1994). In this work a tension has always existed between on the one hand narrative commitments which stress the influence and sometimes imply the *automatic* power of elite discourses that entwine together particular constructs of natural and social order, and on the other those which stress the autonomy of dominated social groups. In examining the role of the discourse of Darwinian evolution in the nineteenth century workplace, Desmond (1987) counters the 'cultural dupe' model of the lay public:

> Pinpointing the scientific trade that [social elites] were plying in working class markets is different from revealing the sorts of intellectual commodities that the artisans themselves were prepared to buy – or make; for we might picture the artisan-craftsmen not as passive recipients of bourgeois wisdom, but as active makers of their own intellectual worlds, their own really useful knowledge.

I suggest that Giddens's concept of simple modernity is misconceived; and further, that the way in which it is wrong pervasively affects his concept of reflexive processes and of the relationships between expert and lay knowledge more generally. The key element of this misconception is something akin to a 'cultural dupe' model of the place of lay people in relation to expert systems in the condition of (simple) modernity. Lack of overt public dissent or opposition towards expert systems is taken too easily for public trust. Yet there is ample sociological evidence supporting a different theoretical conception of this relationship, one which recognises ambivalence and also the clustered problems of agency, identity and dependency. In other words, the reality of social dependency on expert systems should not be equated with positive trust, when it could be better characterised as 'virtual' trust, or 'as-if' trust. This has radically different implications from Giddens's concept, and it problematises his idea that public responses have changed from non-reflexive to reflexive-calculative. Indeed it suggests that public relationships with expertise and its institutions has always been reflexive, though in a more thoroughly hermeneutical sense than the rational-calculative model of Giddens. The sociological work which has identified the unrecognised sense of dependency and lack of agency which pervades public experience of and relations with expert institutions also identifies the unsuspected reflexive ways in which this is manifested as lack of overt public dissent or mistrust (Michael, 1992; Wynne, 1992, 1994; Irwin and Wynne, 1995). It shows how people informally but incessantly problematise their own relationships with expertise of all kinds, as part of their negotiation of their own identities. They are aware of their dependency, and of their lack of agency even if the boundaries of this are uncertain; and awareness of these conditions occasions anxiety, a sense of risk, and an active interest in evidence, for example about the basis of their unavoidable as-if 'trust' in those experts. These lay public processes are deeply imbued with reflexivity even though no public dissent or contestation is apparent.

Different parts of the sociological evidence for the view that public responses to scientific expertise are based in a realistic lay public appreciation of and accommodation to (even enculturation of) social dependency on expert institutions, are reviewed by Wynne (1987, 1994). Cases reviewed in the earlier work showed how the social construction of responsibility by expert institutions around accidents, risks and environmental problems worked to obscure the social structure of 'effective causes' or responsibility, so that these often appeared as Acts of God which no one could have possibly anticipated or controlled. This is closely similar to Beck's analysis of modern science's systematic denial of responsibility for creating modern risks (Beck, 1988, 1994). The expert institutions are often thus concealing their own agency and responsibility; but in doing so they are in my analysis amplifying the diffuse but powerful sense of (social) risk on the part of publics who appreciate their own dependency on expert institutions to control the (physical) risks.[3] As is now well recognised, the issue of the trustworthiness of controlling expert institutions is a crucial factor in affecting not just public risk perceptions *qua* perceptions or symbolic fears, but also the objective scale of the material risks. Institutions which can be seen to be reconstructing history so as to confirm their own blamelessness whilst attempting to manufacture public trust and legitimation are prima facie likely to be undermining public trust rather than enhancing it.

Several pieces of work indicate just how ambivalent public relationships with expertise are, and how deeply dependency relationships are enculturated into social habits and identities. Erickson's (1976) study of the 1972 Buffalo Creek dam disaster in an Appalachian mining community indicated how the community was torn apart not just by the grief inflicted on it, but by the release of a sense of chronic disaster which pre-dated the actual dam-burst and flood. This *chronic* syndrome was attributable to an unspoken but deep sense of stigma caused by the community's recognition of its complete dependence on a coal company which, they also knew, held a ruthless disregard for them. It was not at all that they had trusted the company and then been betrayed by the accident – which would be the conventional analysis consistent with the approach of Giddens. Rather, their implicit and long-standing sense of self-denigration at 'allowing' their own dependency on such an untrustworthy owner and employer had been confirmed and rendered explicit.

In another set of studies of public perception of risk information amongst residents around major hazard chemical plants in the UK, Jupp (1989) found that there were deep ambivalences about the trustworthiness of the companies. The response was given that the companies were trusted 'so long as they are well policed'. This was combined with a realistic appreciation of the public dependency on the company experts. A majority of the public ranked the company as the first source of information to which they would refer in the event of a felt need – but this was not associated with trust in the company; indeed it ranked lowest in terms of public trust, on the list of possible sources of information. It was found that the reason the companies were ranked top as a sought-after information source was not at all a reflection of trust, but was to reinforce the *prescriptive* message that industry should be made to fulfil a responsibility for providing public information, and this was one way of registering and enforcing that point. Thus an 'obvious' reading of the sociological data would have been utterly misleading.

It is notable in respect of Giddens's view of public trust and contestation that in neither of these two cases (the latter involved research at several sites) was there any contestation of the risks, either between different experts or between experts and the public. On the face of it there was nothing but public trust, and public assimilation of expert view of the risks; but more careful inspection revealed:

- extensive realism about the existence of risks nearby – the public was not living in an illusory world of belief in a risk-free environment (Wynne, 1990);
- unsuspected levels of informal mistrust and ambivalence about the expert institutions and their public claims;
- fundamentally different reasons from those conventionally assumed, for a given public disposition towards the expert institutions (in this case, industry);
- considerable unrecognised levels of resilience and adaptability to this situation of informally acknowledged dependency and ambivalence. The residents effectively had to behave *as if* they trusted the experts because it would have been socially and psychologically unviable to do anything else when they were so dependent on them.

Thus the assumption of lay public trust in expert systems under conditions of so-called simple modernity has to be replaced by a more complex notion of this relationship, in which ambivalence is central and trust is at least heavily qualified by the experience of dependency, possible alienation, and lack of agency, though there are of course many areas of experience where relationships between experts and lay publics are well integrated and non-alienated.

A key point of my argument is that this critical analysis is not only relevant to the model of 'simple modernity', but it implies a more basic challenge to the very categories of simple and reflexive modernity as advanced by Giddens. The change from simple to reflexive modernity as conceived by Giddens cannot be correct if it starts from such a false starting point. People are already more reflexive about their relationships with expert institutions than Giddens recognises. Even when people do align their identities with those of expert bodies, and do believe and trust in them (Michael, 1992), this 'trust' is much more conditional and indeed more fragile than the notion of 'simple modernity' reflects. Lay relationships with expertise are thus routinely (if informally) more sceptical, more ambivalent and more alienated from expert institutions than is recognised in Giddens's schema. It also follows from this that he is mistaken to treat the reflexive processes (of deliberatively judged and allocated trust) as brought about only by expert contestation, which then generates critical distance on the part of the lay public. It seems that there has always been more reflexive public ambivalence than this. Therefore the basis of the supposedly categorical historical transformation from simple to reflexive modernity is thrown into question.

It might well be asked, how could lay publics so successfully conceal their alienation and ambivalence, and the ferment, to which I am drawing attention, of continual reflexive self-negotiation of their relationship to expert systems? Here it is important to acknowledge the subtlety and extent of the cultural processes whereby dependency and powerlessness are rationalised into ingenious social constructions of agency and responsibility.

Erickson (1976) in his Buffalo Creek study noted how the powerless always tend to rationalise and thus consolidate their own impotence and apathy because to do otherwise is to expose themselves to the greater pain of *explicit* recognition of their own neglect and marginality. Not only withdrawal occurs, but justification of that withdrawal in *cultural* narratives, as consistent with cosmic principles. Thus beliefs about cause and effect in the experiences they encounter become integrated with their established social relationships and identities. When those relationships and experiences are highly prescribed by others, yet follow logics that are obscure and apparently capricious, this can be encapsulated and 'naturalised' in fatalistic beliefs, identities, and senses of (non-) agency. Erickson's account of the Buffalo Creek survivors' beliefs reflected this alienated human reaction, 'a sense of cultural disorientation, a feeling of powerlessness, a dulled apathy, and a generalised fear about the state of the universe'. The effective causes of their impotence and arbitrary suffering were in this case socially relatively visible (the coal owners and bosses), but the sudden dam-burst disaster was tantamount to the condensation onto a single catastrophic event of years of identity-stripping and denigration by those significant others.

A coal company and its management of a dam might be seen as a relatively transparent set of 'effective causes' of risks, with immediately identifiable lines of control and responsibility. Yet even here the impetus to wrap these up in alien and fatalistic natural idiom was overwhelmingly strong, and deeply entrenched in history. If such familiar systems as a coal company and a dam can be seen as alien and impenetrable, how much more must this be true of the complex and interconnected global systems of the modern biotechnology and information revolutions? In these the controlling human agents and relationships are far more extensive, complex, esoteric, diffuse and socially remote. It is often impossible for anyone, let alone the ordinary public encountering them, to identify or to identify with the effective causes in such socio-technological systems. Yet the pervasive and increasingly close importance of these systems requires that people construct some working rationalisations of their troubling and confusing experiences of them, even when they do not unleash dramatic interventions into their lives.

Psychiatrists have examined clinical cases involving images of technology which people have constructed and lived by. These have apparently often taken the form of spectres; that is, condensed forms of agency which short-circuit the emotionally impossible complexity of experiences of powerful but obscure forces such as those involved in modern technology and risk. Daly (1970: 420) has defined such spectres as potent, artificially created but invisible behavioural forces:

> A sense of the operation of such forces arises when men [sic] find they cannot account for emotionally significant events by ascribing them to the conventional sources of power and efficacy (e.g. human, natural, divine) which are believed to make things happen in the world. When such inexplicable events persist and are experienced by numbers of people, agencies are created to account for these events. These agencies are given names, made into realities, and adapted to as powerful things.
>
> The spectral view of technology arises from a sense of domination by mysterious forces or agencies which are, or were, linked to technological enterprises but which are now apprehended as being beyond the control of any particular [human agency] . . . [People] behave as if the spirit of meeting specifications in many discrete, limited and finite human ventures had taken flight from the hands of responsible agents and become an independent reality – a reality which has come to overhang the modern world and to enter into the dynamic processes of personality – as a spectral object.

There is in other words a kind of defence mechanism for coping with the overwhelming difficulty of living with inexplicable and uncontrollable, yet emotionally important forces, which is to convert them into identifiable agents, even superhuman ones. A central point of Daly's analysis is that these conditions are not confined to definable individuals – they are in his view mass cultural conditions. They may also be considered to be reasonable reactions of people to irrational situations in which they have been placed by expert systems. McDermott (1974) gives an example taken from the Vietnam war, in which GIs created such a technological spectre. The US GIs were operating in the jungle, constantly sniped at and ambushed by Vietcong guerrillas who could not be identified or pinned down, but who vanished into their own terrain. The GIs were regularly shelled, shot at, mined and rocketed, but were never sure whether it was the enemy or their own side; and they received orders but never explanations from their distant superiors who knew little of their situation. Their experience was terrifying, confusing, contradictory and utterly obscure as to its effective causes and dynamics. They could not find and engage a definite enemy, and they could not identify their friends. They received orders, and were attacked, in equally arbitrary fashion, and no one could tell them what was happening and why. Their very high risks were a combination of physical and social realities.

As part of their attempted rationalisation of this frightening and disorientating predicament the GIs had come to condense the potent but diffuse and invisible effective causes of their experience onto a single symbolic agent that they had discursively created – they lived a relationship with a 'huge-fucking' gun which hid in a hollowed-out mountain and which emerged unpredictably and at whim to unleash death and destruction onto them, in a manner which authentically described their actual daily experience. Thus they had obscured and 'naturalised' the social relations in which they were enmeshed – with the Vietcong enemy, the US war machine and Vietnamese villagers – into a technological spectre, a metaphor for the social relations they could not begin to identify and explain, but which controlled their fate in acute and menacing fashion.

This kind of enculturation process *normalises and consolidates* whatever dependency and lack of agency is thought to exist. It obscures the alienation and ambivalence or worse which people may feel in relation to elites and expert institutions. Thus it may help to explain why it is that ambivalence is apparently routinely overlooked, even though it is a widespread if not universal part of lay public relationships with expert systems. This may in turn help explain why lack of *expressed* public ambivalence or alienation is mistaken for unambiguous trust.

Contradicting the received view as reproduced in the canonical socio-logical treatments of modernity and its transformations, is a growing body of work which highlights the reflexive processes of lay public responses to scientific expertise, and the ways in which people construct their social identities in relation to such potent external agents which intervene so often and so multifariously in their lives. This work (for example, Michael, 1992) underlines that a reflexive public stance does not automatically mean a critical one; but equally that a deferential relationship may be based on a sense of inevitable – and perhaps socially impenetrable – dependency rather than a considered and decisive investment of trust. This in turn may engender a sense of ambivalence that is harboured in relative privacy. Furthermore, the most fundamental dimension of risk expressed in such social interactions is that of the *risk to social identity* which is felt to be involved in this kind of dependency, upon expert institutions which disseminate and impose such questionable models of the human and the social, whilst pretending to deal only with objective facts. The empirical cases described later exemplify these points.

Aided by this more multivalent reading of trust, dependency and ambivalence in lay relationships with expert systems, we can begin to develop a more thoroughgoing culturalist conceptualisation of the charac-ter of risk than that given in the risk society thesis.

Risk: The Cultural Dimensions

Both Beck and Giddens offer a similar model of the pervasive sense of risk which they argue now grips industrial society, and which is a new logic superseding that of class conflict. The features of this model are that modern science and technology now produce truly global risks from which not even the rich and powerful can escape. In addition, according to Beck, the principle of insurance wherein risk damage could be capped and controlled, allowing the further unimpeded growth of modern science, technology and their risks, has with these new global dangers ruptured itself. As identification with existing institutional structures erodes and individuals are increasingly thrown upon their own resources and networks for the negotiation and sustenance of identity, so modernity's quintessential institutions of technology and science self-refute their own enlightenment promises and programmes. In particular, the failure of those institutions to control the risks they have created, seen most acutely in the ecological crisis of industrial society, has generated a more profound and pervasive sense of risk. As the contradictions grow more frequent and intense, so the sense of risk grows, and the legitimacy of those institutions which have designated themselves the saviours erodes correspondingly. Giddens's account is essentially consistent with this, though he emphasises more the disruptions effected by expert systems and globalisation processes in private lives, and the transformations brought about by this. A key part of the sense of risk is, as in Beck's theory, seen to be the existential insecurity associated with the expansion of 'individual choice' and the erosion of traditional forms of existence.

Much of this account is persuasive and original. Despite this Lash observes, correctly in my view, that their basic ethos is too rooted in rational-choice neo-classical economistic models of human behaviour and response – that is, in modernist concepts of the human and the social. However, Lash's criticism itself invites critical development.

The basic model of reflexivity and risks in modernity is that lay people reflect critically upon the failure of modern scientific institutions to control risks such as ecological and nuclear risks adequately. Those institutions thus contradict their own self-legitimatory promises and induce further independent critique from alternative expertise and further erosion of the cultural authority of modernity and science and its formal political institutions. Included in this model of the erosion of modernity under its own intrinsic dynamics is the claim that science and technology also regularly disrupt the familiar patterns and identities of daily life and empty it of meaning, thus further encouraging 'retreat' into informal sociations and lifestyle- or sub-politics, outside the formal sphere. As Lash (1994a) has noted, this is based on a rationalistic model of social and cultural response to the experience of science, technology and modernity. In this conception, human response is rooted in an instrumental-calculative standpoint. The modern institutions and culture have failed to live up to their promise and to deeply rooted social expectations because the risks and side-effects are now unacceptably high; so the response is to disengage from and reconstruct the prevailing institutions and political culture. Behaviour and the ensuing redefinitions of identity are driven by instrumental concern about security from ecological risks, and the failure of modern expert institutions to provide that security whilst pretending to do so.

To argue that this model is too exclusively framed by the 'realist' assumption that public responses to expert institutions are based in responses to their handling of real risks, is not to imply that there are no ecological risks, nor that people do not think instrumentally and care about those risks. However, my point is that the same basic social dynamics in the transformations of modernity could be occurring whether or not those risks objectively exist 'out there'. It is likely therefore that their explanatory role is not as large as presently assumed.

My proposal instead is that much of the dynamics of the self-refutations of modernity is instead explicable by a more thoroughly hermeneutical perspective. Through their rationalist discourses, modern expert institutions and their 'natural' cultural responses to risks in the idiom of scientific risk management, *tacitly and furtively impose prescriptive models of the human and the social upon lay people, and these are implicitly found wanting in human terms*. This analysis connects closely with a non-realist conception of the basis of public risk perceptions argued in the risk field since 1980 (Wynne, 1980), and itself connected with the argument in the previous section about the importance of tacit dependency in the social and cognitive dynamics of risk issues.

Against the dominant idea that public risk perceptions relate to perceptions or evaluations of what is thought to be an objectively existent physical risk as the object of experience, I have argued that public perceptions of and responses to risks are rationally based in judgements of the behaviour and trustworthiness of expert institutions, namely those that are supposed to control the risky processes involved.[4] That is, the most germane risks are (social) *relational*. There are several parts to this thesis which are worth taking one by one:

1. Most risks are actually intellectual constructs which artificially reduce larger uncertainties to ostensibly calculable probabilities of specific harm. The tacit social assumptions which create such 'natural' frames are rarely expressed or recognised. Such expert 'natural' knowledges thus typically embody implicit models of the social and human. Risky activities are often objects of much greater commitment on the part of promoters than the scale of particular projects or plans may reflect.
2. Given these kinds of uncertainty it is rational of people not to limit themselves to assessing the magnitudes of claimed risk that exist, because such estimates will always be subject to the larger uncertainties indicated above. It is instead logical for them to ask, how trustworthy are the institutions supposedly in charge? How likely is it when faced with evidence which overturns existing understandings, or with changes of circumstances which alter the terms of the commitments involved, that they will act in a way consistent with, rather than compromising public health and environmental protection, and democratic principles of open participation?
3. As I have noted before, such institutional dimensions (trustworthiness, competence, independence, etc.) actually influence the scale of material risks anyway. If for example a regulatory body does not rigorously inspect and guarantee standards of maintenance of technical plant, the risks of physical accident will materially increase, and not

just public perceptions of the social risks of dependency upon such incompetent or non-independent institutions.

4. Thus public risk perceptions rationally involve some element of judgement both of the quality of relevant social institutions, and of their relevance, in other words of the roles of different social agents including one's own relationship to them.

5. Involved in this judgement is an assessment of the extent and implications of dependency upon those institutions, for safety or for the protection of other valued aspects of life, including valued social relationships. This returns us to the complexities of dependency and its rationalisations as briefly outlined above.

As nearly all studies of public risk perceptions and responses show, ordinary people bring more to their definitions and evaluations of risks than recognised in the reductionist framing of experts (Otway, 1992; Slovic, 1992). There are two aspects to this expert reduction: first there is the neglect of socially valued dimensions such as whether the risk is imposed unnegotiated by distant authorities, whether it is voluntarily engaged in, or whether it is reversible or irreversible. Second, there are assumptions made by the experts about the actual risk situation and the issue in hand. For example, this may be framed very narrowly if the experts take for granted the competence and trustworthiness of the controlling bodies, whereas if this is questioned the risk issue to be addressed will be wider and more indeterminate. These framing questions about what the issue is are often pre-empted by the institutionalised authority of scientific discourses which tacitly impose such evaluative social commitments embedded in the scientific knowledge, without anyone even noticing or at least being able to protest effectively that this has happened. Frequently, such framing commitments embody models of the social world and relationships of lay people which are at least open to question, but which are innocently imposed on those people as prescriptive commitments. In the course of such processes from risk analysis to regulation or policy commitment, what may have begun life as hypothetical assumptions about those social worlds (for example, whether nuclear reactor maintenance and operating personnel will always follow the rules rigorously or not) become increasingly prescriptive 'demands' to be *ordered* into existence so as to confirm the expert analysis. In this process, and well hidden in the depths of their objectivist discourse, scientists are acting in effect as naive sociologists, except that they may have the power to bring into being the implicit social assumptions or commitments that tacitly shape their knowledge.

This kind of analysis of scientific knowledge as constructed and used in risk and environmental issues opens it up to recognisable indeterminacies as to whether the controlled and artificial conditions assumed in the analytical process (perhaps the laboratory) will actually prevail in practice, so it is implied, everywhere and at all times. These indeterminacies correspond to the inevitable gap between laboratory conditions and real-world conditions in which risks are actually experienced. The resolution of the empirical question of whether the expert knowledge is correct depends partly and significantly upon the reciprocal question: can the social conditions be brought into being and maintained so as to correspond with and confirm the underlying assumptions of the expert knowledge? Hence truth depends partly upon commitment and the open-ended issue as to whether the appropriate conditions can be organised into existence. It is in this sense too that this perspective corresponds with Latour's (1987) ideas of the coproduction of intellectual and social orders, in which it is otiose to use the one to try deterministically to explain the other, in whichever direction the causal arrow is pointed.

Thus the risks from social dependency on institutions which may be supposed to be controlling the 'direct' physical risks are a dimension of the risk society which is inadequately recognised in Beck and Giddens. These risks are in essence threats to basic social identities – threats brought about by the alien and inadequate models of human nature and human relations tacitly embodied in the objectivist expert discourses. They are threats because they come not as mere assumptions or hypotheses to be tested – and perhaps revised – in practice, but as prescriptions or forms of social control. It is important also to note that many of these threatening and alienating models of the human, which general category constitutes a key dimension of the risk society not recognised by Beck, are articulated and imposed by modern institutions supposedly advancing *solutions* to modern environmental risk problems.

The vernacular, informal knowledge which lay people may well have about the validity of expert assumptions about real-world conditions – say, about the production, use or maintenance of a technology – is also an important general category of lay knowledge that is usually systematically under-recognised. This oversight is understandable, and indeed inevitable in the absence of a constructivist conception of scientific knowledge. It is therefore not surprising that both Beck and Giddens overlook this kind of lay knowledge, and misconceive its relationships with formally defined expert knowledge, since they do not understand scientific knowledge to be intrinsically cultural. I suggested above that a general reason for possible divergence between expert and public knowledges about risks is that expert knowledge embodies social assumptions and models framing its objectivist language, and that lay people have legitimate claim to debate those assumptions. I further suggested that these assumptions are much more than that – they are incipient social prescriptions, or vehicles of particular tacit forms of social order, relationships and identities. I therefore argued that a central part of the reflexive processes of lay discomfort, alienation and distance from expert knowledges and interventions is not the purely rational-calculative one which Beck and Giddens conceive as the driving force of reflexive modernity. It is the more thoroughly hermeneutic/cultural one in which alien and inadequate tacit models of the human are imposed on lay publics through the discourse of

'objective' science in such potent fields as environmental and risk management and regulation.

Here it is worth noting that Lash does recognise, *contra* Giddens and
Beck, that the responses of ordinary people to expert interventions and
disruptions of their lives are cultural/hermeneutic, not just calculative-
rationalist. But those expert interventions and the resulting public alienation and delegitimation are understood by all three of these authors in
terms of risks 'out-there', and responses to them. In my view they should
be seen more as responses to the identity-risks arising from the fundamentally impoverished and morally-emotionally threatening models of the
human which are silently embodied in the objectivist science of those
modernist expert institutions, ironically intervening increasingly in the
name of 'public protection' from risks. Thus whereas all three authors talk
of the interventions of expert systems as 'emptying their lives of meaning'
(that is, the public's) I would argue that far from *emptying* indigenous lives
of meaning, the expert knowledges are typically *importing dense but
inadequate* meanings. Thus, contrary to Giddens and Lash, science is not
meaning-free or meaning-neutral, but dripping with impoverished and
expropriated meanings, and ones in which there is no longer ordinary
participation and access. It is just because people know these to be
indeterminate that they also intuitively recognise the depth and importance
of what has been expropriated by expertise here. Just because those
meanings and identities are open and indeterminate, a whole lifetime of
relations and negotiation is involved; yet the interventions of expert
systems would often exchange this for a one-off response – say, to a
consumer survey or a contingent valuation questionnaire.

Thus essentialist and deterministic concepts, including a non-
constructivist concept of science, also delete the extent of cultural devas-
tation and moral provocation wielded by modernistic decision approaches
and expert systems. To claim that science is objective propositional truth as
Giddens does is to sell the pass here by thinking of science as meaning-
neutral, thus only emptying lives of meaning, rather than seeing how on
the contrary it *fills* them with meaning – but of a problematic and even
provocative kind. It is conflict and reactions at this unarticulated hermeneutic level which create the spin off into alienation and self-refutation of
modernity's institutions, and hence the growth of the informal extra-
institutional sector of 'cultural politics'. It is also worth emphasising that
this largely negative hermeneutic dimension must have been strongly
amplified by the enhanced role which social science has played in
environmental and risk policy work, for example in the huge elaboration of
rational-choice economic modelling of environmental choices, of contingent valuation surveys of risk acceptability, and of social-psychological
work on public risk perceptions. All of these, and others, in various ways
impose individualist, instrumental, essentialist and decisionistic models of
the human, in the name of 'neutral' scientific method and observation.
Thus in important respects the intensity of this provocation – and the

growth of the public sense of risk – with respect to its portrayal of the human, must have increased as the role of social science has expanded in these public domains.

Thus whereas Giddens proposes that science contains propositional truths only, my perspective on environment, modernity and risk involves the recognition that it disseminates not only propositional truth claims, but formulaic and hermeneutic ones too. Sociology of science has long since left behind the simplistic rationalistic idea that scientific discourse is one-dimensional and literalistic, and has recognised that scientific discourses contain both propositional and formulaic truth claims, where formulaic means performance-related, even if they are couched overtly only in propositional terms. However, I would go one step further and suggest that scientific discourses contain not only tacit claims to performance in the sense of credibility rituals (like citation practices: Gilbert and Mulkay, 1984), but also hermeneutic truth claims. Thus whilst Giddens can only conceive of possible critical interactions between lay publics and scientific expertise on propositional truth claim grounds (and even then with the public only vicariously involved via dissenting bodies of expertise) since this is all that science supposedly purveys, I propose that critical inter-actions occur on hermeneutic and formulaic grounds too. This is tanta-mount to saying that public critique of science can be, and is, based on more than its propositional contents alone (Wynne, 1994).[5]

An implication of this is that the basis of lay public responses to expert knowledge is always potentially an epistemological conflict with science about the underlying assumed purposes of knowledge, or at least the scope of that epistemic remit, which is wrongly assumed to be just given in nature. This raises questions not only about the basis of the relationships between 'objective' scientific knowledge and 'subjective' lay knowledge, but about the extent to which scientific knowledge is open to substantive criticism and improvement or correction by lay people. In other words, how far might lay people be involved in shaping scientific knowledge, and thus in providing the basis of alternative forms of public knowledge that reflect and sustain different dominant conceptions of the human, and of the social purposes of public knowledge? In the dominant approaches, the answer by default is – not at all. I next examine some cases which provide suggestive if embryonic alternative answers to these questions.

Lay Knowledges and Alternative Orders

The predominant perspectives on the risk society and the transformations of modernity which I have discussed so far, implicitly treat the non-expert world as epistemically vacuous. It may be reflexive, but such reflexivity is implied to have little or no intellectual content in the sense of having cognitive access to nature or society. It has no apparent instrumental value as measured against a scientific world-view, so is assumed to have no real content or authority beyond the parochial, subjective and emotional world of its carriers. This is a diminished view of both science and lay knowledge. It recognises nothing of the fluidity, porosity and constructedness of the boundaries established between them; and, as well as misconceiving the conflicts betweeen public and scientific knowledges, it recognises nothing of the constructive kinds of interaction and mutual inspiration or dependency which may exist between them.

In research on public reception of scientific expertise in a variety of contexts, a very different view has been substantiated, with important implications (Hobart, 1993; Irwin and Wynne, 1995). It is worth examining two such case-studies.

Cumbrian Sheep Farmers and Environmental Radioactivity

Wynne (1992) studied the responses of sheep farmers in Cumbria, a mountain area of north-west England, who had been subjected to administrative restrictions on sheep movements and sales due to radioactive contamination caused by the fallout from the 1986 Chernobyl nuclear accident. The farmers interacted over some years, but most intensely for a year or two, with scientists from a variety of agencies who were responsible for official views of the behaviour of the radioactivity, and of the likely duration of the restrictions. These interactions, between a relatively well defined lay public and a particular, but fairly typical, form of expert system, illuminate several more general points about the social basis of scientific knowledge and its public credibility, and about the nature of lay knowledge.

After initial denials of any problems in the UK from the radioactive fallout, in June 1986 the UK Ministry of Agriculture imposed a sudden blanket ban on the movement and sale of sheep from defined areas in hill regions such as the Lake District of northern England. This was potentially ruinous to what was a marginal and economically fragile sector of British farming, because these farmers depended for almost all of their annual income on being able to sell a large crop of surplus lambs from midsummer onwards. Not only would their income be devastated, but they would be unable to feed this lamb flock if it was forced to remain in their hands, because these hill areas comprise mainly meagre grazing on open mountains and only very limited valley grass, which would 'become a desert in days', as one farmer put it, if the lambs were not moved on. Thus wholesale slaughter of sheep flocks was on the agenda, with long-term ruin of the hill-farming economy and its distinct culture.

These dire threats were alleviated when the Ministry announced that the ban would be only for three weeks, a period which would return the situation to normal well before the annual sales would begin. This reassuring projection was based on prevailing scientific assumptions about the behaviour of radiocaesium in the environment. According to those beliefs the fallout would be washed off the vegetation which sheep grazed, into the soil where it would be adsorbed and 'locked up' chemically, unavailable for any further mobility and possible return to vegetation and the sheep food chain. Thus a once-through model of contamination was involved, and this meant that there would be no further dose to the sheep after the first flush. Thus measured body burdens of radiocaesium in sheep were assumed to be peak levels which would decay according to the biological half-life.[6] Since the biological half-life for caesium in sheep was about 20 days, it was estimated that the contamination levels would fall below levels at which action was required, within three weeks. This view was expressed by the experts with utter confidence unqualified by any hint of uncertainty.

Given the crucial importance of avoiding anything more than such short-term restrictions, the shock announcement in July 1986 that the three-week ban would have to be extended for the indefinite future was a stunning contradiction of previous reassurances and even denials of any problem at all from scientists, officials and ministers. Contrary to scientific beliefs and pronouncements, measured levels had shown no decrease, and an urgent reappraisal of existing understanding was begun. In order to allay rising fears of the imminent collapse of hill farming, the restrictions were altered so as to allow sheep from the contaminated area to be sold, so long as they were marked with a stipulated dye which marked them as unfit for human consumption. Thus they could at least be sold and moved out of the grazing-poor and contaminated hill area, even though they could not be sold for slaughter until deemed clear. It was expected that once the sheep were on uncontaminated land, this would not be long.

It is a point of general importance to observe just how completely controlled by the exercise of scientific interpretation the farmers felt themselves to be. Thus if they sold their marked sheep and avoided their overpopulation and possible starvation, they lost money badly in the markets because these sheep were blighted – indeed so were those that were unmarked but still from the affected area. This social reality was not recognised by the experts until a great deal of upset and loss of credibility had been caused amongst the farmers. Yet if they held on to the sheep, the farmers could only survive by incurring large extra imported-feed costs as well as build-up of disease and other problems. Still believing in their short-term model of the high levels of radiocaesium, the scientists continued to advise the farmers to hold on just a little longer, expecting the restrictions to be removed soon, even if later than originally thought. Caught whichever way they turned, many farmers still followed this advice despite the evidence of expert mistakes; but their hopes were dashed as the early removal of restrictions promised by the experts never materialised.

It gradually became clear that the 'three weeks only' scientific judgement which had been translated into public policy commitments and predictions had been a mistake, but this became evident only over the following years, as more research and debate ensued. The predictions of only a three-week-long problem had been based on the assumed existence of alkaline clay soils (on which much of the original observations had been made). In such soils the behavioural properties of radiocaesium envisaged by the scientists do indeed occur. The problem was that the scientists had overlooked the essentially localised nature of this knowledge, because clay soil was not a universal condition, and in other soils such as those in the hill areas, very different behaviour prevailed. In these areas acid peaty soils predominated, and in such soils radiocaesium remains chemically mobile, hence available for root uptake from the soil, back into the vegetation which the sheep grazed. Thus, because they had assumed that the knowledge drawn from particular conditions was universal knowledge, the scientists did not understand that in these conditions the sheep were exposed to continual recontamination and hence probably much longer-term restrictions.

In the heat of the crisis over the Chernobyl accident and the restrictions, it arose as an issue whether there had been an innocent scientific mistake or a deliberate attempt to cover up knowledge of a longer-term problem, so as to avoid public reaction. Even the admission of a mistake was never made clearly and unambiguously. But in addition a further issue took off from this. At the outset of the restrictions a large area the size of the county of Cumbria was included. Within three months this had been reduced to a small crescent-shaped area in the mountains near the coast, and just downwind from the huge international Sellafield nuclear reprocessing complex. When this area persisted with high levels of contamination, against the confident predictions of the scientists, given its position various people began to ask whether the measured contamination had really been from Sellafield rather than Chernobyl, and had actually existed unnoticed or concealed by the expert authorities. Given Sellafield's notoriety as a discharger of radioactive contamination into the environment (MacGill, 1987; McSorley, 1990) and the history of the world's worst civil nuclear accident in 1957 in a reactor on this site (Arnold, 1992), this was by no means a frivolous suggestion. The 1957 fire was known to have spewed radiocaesium and other radioactive materials over this same area, and had resulted in the banning of milk sales for some weeks afterwards. Some local farmers even argued that the government and the nuclear industry had known all along but had been waiting for a convenient alibi for this environmental contamination; Chernobyl provided it.

Scientists dismissed these suggestions as unfounded, and pointed to what they regarded as unambiguous scientific proof, in the radioactive 'fingerprint' of the radiocaesium samples collected from the environment. The radiocaesium emitted from nuclear fission processes is made up of two isotopes of caesium-134 and caesium-137. The latter has a half-life of about thirty years while the former's is about one year. In nuclear fuel of a given level of burn-up the ratio of caesium-137 to caesium-134 fission products will be the same, but as they age with passage of time, the ratio increases due to the different half-lives. In fresh Chernobyl deposits it was about 2:1, whereas for typical Sellafield emissions (from reprocessed fuel often stored for many years on site before processing) or old 1957 accident emissions, the ratio would be about 12:1. The two isotopes emit gamma radiation of different specific frequencies, thus according to the scientists there was a clear means of distinguishing the two possible sources in the radioactive fingerprints of samples. The scientists asserted – again without any hint of uncertainty – that the origin of the contamination found in the environment was Chernobyl, and not Sellafield. This did not persuade the farmers, and it is worth examining the grounds of their scepticism.

First, they had just experienced the experts as having committed a huge mistake over the predictions of contamination, having expressed that mistaken view unqualified by any sense of uncertainties, and not having admitted any mistake. In this case also there was much more uncertainty in the technical process of discriminating between different sources than the experts' confident assertions implied. Actual soil samples contained mixed deposits, so that measured isotope ratios involved combined isotope intensities and assumptions about the precise ratio from any single source. It was later admitted that sampled deposits typically contained 50% Chernobyl radiocaesium, and 50% from 'other sources', which meant Sellafield and atmospheric weapons testing fallout (Wynne, 1989, 1992). This was quite a significant move in the direction of the sceptical farmers' beliefs, from the initial expert assertion of certainty about Sellafield's innocence.

In addition to direct observation of Sellafield's position and the otherwise unexplained and unanticipated persistent crescent of contamination around it, the lay public also noted various elements of institutional 'body-language' which placed the experts' claims to credibility in question. The exaggerated certainty of official science was one element, but so too was the way that questions about environmental data from the affected area before 1986, which were designed to test the claim that the levels had not been high before that, were deflected to either data from after 1986, or data from other areas. This suggested that either there were data which showed the suspected high levels but which were being covered up, or there were no data at all, in which case there had been gross negligence considering that this was an area that had been affected by the 1957 fire. The choice of judgement of the expert authorities seemed to be either corruption or complacent incompetence.

The historical experience of secrecy and misinformation by official institutions also acted as a direct evidentiary input to the existing risk issue. Effectively recognising that they had to trust the experts and could not independently generate knowledge of the environmental hazards, the public had good reason from past experience of social relationships with what were to them the same institutions, not to invest that trust. This reinforced the evidence from the current issue. Yet feeling mistrustful of the experts, they were nevertheless realistic enough to recognise pervasive dependency on them, and often spoke and behaved *as if* they trusted them. A typical farmer's assessment[7] was: 'The scientists tell us it's all from

Chernobyl. You just have to believe them – if a doctor gave you a jab up the backside for a cold, you wouldn't argue with him, would you?' In other words, we might look as if we trust them, but just because we have no choice but to 'believe' them doesn't mean we don't have our own beliefs.

A further factor involved in the public's evaluation of the scientific knowledge-claims was the way in which the official experts neglected elements of the local situation, including specialist farming knowledge, which were relevant to the understanding and social management of the crisis. Thus the scientists did not understand the implications of the restrictions on hill sheep farming, and appeared not to recognise the need to learn. For example, they assumed that farmers would be able to bring sheep down from the high fells where contamination was highest, to the relatively less contaminated valley grass, and thus reduce levels below the action thresholds. This and other expert misconceptions were scornfully dismissed by the farmers as utterly unrealistic. Outbursts of frustrations at the experts' ignorance occurred often, here in response to their assumption that straw would make up for the drastic shortage of grazing:

> [The experts] don't understand our way of life. They think you stand at the fell bottom and wave a handkerchief and all the sheep come running. . . . I've never heard of a sheep that would even look at straw as a fodder. When you hear things like that it makes your hair stand on end. You just wonder, what the hell are these blokes talking about?

In addition, farmers' specialist knowledge of local environmental conditions and sheep behaviour was ignored by the experts, much to the provocation of the farmers. The scientific knowledge constructed out of field observations began life as highly uncertain and uneven – the farmers watched scientists decide in apparently arbitrary ways where to sample mountainsides or fields with huge variations of readings, and they helped scientists as they changed their recorded monitoring readings of sheep contamination by changing the background reading, or the way the monitor was held to the sheep. Yet these kinds of uncertainty and open-endedness were obliterated by the time the knowledge returned to that same public as formal scientific knowledge in official statements.

Many of the conflicts between lay farmers and scientists centred on the standardisation built into routine structures of scientific knowledge. The quantitative units involved often encompassed several farms and even valleys with one measurement or value, when the farmers knew and could articulate various significant differences in environment, climate factors, management practices, etc., between neighbouring farms, indeed even on a single farm. These variations often reflected substantial elements of skill and specialist identity on the part of the farmers, yet they saw these wiped out in the scientific knowledge and the ignorant or insensitive ways it was deployed. A typical lament indicated this conflicting embryonic epistemo-logical orientation, which was connected to a conflict between central administration and bureaucracy and a more informal, individualist and adaptive culture: 'This is what they can't understand. They think a farm is a farm and a ewe is a ewe. They just think we stamp them off a production line or something.'

In other cases the scientists ignored the farmers' informal expertise when they devised and conducted field experiments which the farmers knew to be unrealistic. An example was an experiment intended to examine the effects of bentonite spread on affected vegetation in reducing sheep contamination. The experiment involved penning sheep in several adjacent pens on similarly contaminated grazing, and spreading different specified amounts of bentonite over each pen area, then measuring contamination levels in the sheep, before and at intervals after. The farmers immediately observed amongst themselves that these experiments would be useless because hill sheep were unused to being penned up, and would 'waste' in such unreal conditions – that is, they would lose condition and their metabolisms be deleteriously affected, thus confounding the experiment. This was a typical arena in which expert knowledge and lay knowledge interacted and directly conflicted over the appropriate design of scientific experiments.

After a few months the scientists' experiments were abandoned, though the farmers' criticisms were never explicitly acknowledged. In this and other cases, also for example over the levels of recognised uncertainty and standardisation, the lay public were involved in substantive judgement of the validity of scientific commitments. Much of this conflict between expert and lay epistemologies centred on the clash between the taken-for-granted scientific culture of prediction and control, and the farmers' culture in which lack of control was taken for granted over many environmental and surrounding social factors in farm management decisions. The farmers assumed predictability to be intrinsically unreliable as an assumption, and therefore valued adaptability and flexibility, as a key part of their cultural identity and practical knowledge. The scientific experts ignored or mis-understood the multidimensional complexity of this lay public's problem-domain, and thus made different assumptions about its controllability. In other words, the two knowledge-cultures expressed different assumptions about agency and control, and there were both empirical and normative dimensions to this.

This example corresponds with many others in which expert and lay knowledge cultures interact, for example Lave's critical examination of the assumptions made by cognitive psychologists and other scientists about the artificial nature of controlled testing of lay people's mathematical reasoning abilities (1988). Dickens (1992) found similar underlying factors involved in conflicts between weather forecasting scientists and lay publics over the prediction of extreme weather events such as hurricanes. Martin (1989) also identified essentially the same cultural dimensions of conflict between the knowledges of working class women and biological scientists about menstruation. These were not a matter of lay public 'cultural' responses to 'meaning-neutral' objective scientific knowledge, but of cultural responses, to a *cultural* form of intervention – that is, one embodying particular normative models of human nature, purposes and relationships.

Many other studies of the interactions between scientific expertise and lay publics support this kind of analysis (for example, Davy et al., 1992; Long and Long, 1992; Hobart, 1993; Watson-Verran and Turnbull, 1994; Irwin and Wynne, 1995). These and other studies show the following common features:

- scientific expert knowledge embodies assumptions and commitments of a human kind, about social relationships, behaviour and values;
- it also embodies problematic 'structural' or epistemic commitments, for example about the proper extent of agency, control and prediction, or of standardisation;
- it neglects and thus denigrates specialist lay knowledges;
- at a secondary level it then defines lay resistances as based on ignorance or irrationality rather than on substantive if unarticulated objections to these inadequate constructions of lay social identity which the expert discourses unwittingly assume and impose;
- thus a further reinforcement takes place, of tacit public ambivalence about being dependent on social actors (experts) who engender such alienation and social control;
- hence the fundamental sense of risk in the 'risk society', is risk to identity engendered by dependency upon expert systems which typically operate with such unreflexive blindness to their own culturally problematic and inadequate models of the human.

It is worth examining the correspondences with a case taken from a very different situation, this time an agricultural development context in South America. The account is drawn from Van der Ploeg, 1993.

Potatoes, Knowledge and Ignorance

Van der Ploeg's (1993) study of Andean potato farmers, their knowledge and interactions with scientific expertise is instructive on a wider scale, illustrating more general issues in the relationships between indigenous knowledges and those which have achieved scientific status. He first notes that such local knowledges are interwoven with practices, in this case craft-based agriculture. These are highly dynamic systems of knowledge involving continuous negotiation between 'mental' and 'manual' labour, and continual interpretation of production experiences. This induces a highly complex and detailed knowledge system and a flexible, adaptive culture which does not lend itself to standardisation or planning. However, because it is so multidimensional and adaptive, experience is rarely expressed in a univocal, clear form. This is frequently mistaken for lack of theoretical content, akin to Bourdieu's (1980) questionable characterisation of this kind of knowledge as going from practice to practice without ever developing an overarching abstract or theoretical discourse.

Van der Ploeg's analysis of potato farmers' knowledge challenges this dismissive modernistic view of indigenous knowledges. He shows that there is indeed systematic theory, even though this is in a syntax linked to the local labour process and does not presuppose a universal and impersonal world. Seen from the epistemological standpoint of modern science it is a highly variable and non-universal knowledge. Seen from the farmers' vantage point this variability is a reflection of the conscious purpose of building diversity into practice, and of adaptively coping with multiple dimensions in the same complex arena. For example, the farmers deliberately seek to increase the variety of ecological conditions of their agricultural plots rather than to standardise them, and they use the variety of conditions and results dynamically to evaluate possible improvements; but they do not assume a singular optimality. Multidimensionality is taken for granted. Furthermore their use of concepts and measures such as hot/ cold or high/low also shows this informal multidimensional sophistication. Van der Ploeg describes the outsider analyst's surprise at understanding that the apparent imprecision of terms such as 'higher' being used to describe fields that are mathematically lower than other fields, reflects the embodiment of further qualifying factors such as exposure to the wind or frost, and interpenetration with other terms such as 'heat', into an interrelated network of meaning.

Certain key properties of these indigenous knowledge systems are noteworthy (Van der Ploeg, 1993: 212):

> These and other concepts are not unequivocal, nor do they lend themselves to precise qualification. They cannot be built into a nomological model of the kind used in applied science and in technology development . . . When one separates these concepts from the people who use them or from their context they indeed become 'inaccurate'. Of course this inaccurate character does not prevent farmers from establishing quite accurately the overall condition of specific plots. They are also quite able to communicate with each other on this topic. The inaccurate nature of the concepts used even seems favourable for such an exact interpretation of a plot's condition and the ensuing dialogue. For interpretation and communication can only be active processes; concepts must be weighed against each other every time a specific plot is being considered. Hence the conceptual overlap becomes strategic. In synthesis: *it is precisely the vagueness or 'imprecise' character that allows for this active process of interpretation and change.* [my emphasis]

A key point here is the observed imprecision in meaning of scientific terms when their use and interpretation amongst specialists in their esoteric, private and local scientific subcultures is examined (Star and Griesemer, 1989; Jordan and Lynch, 1992). This openness is not usually acknowledged when the same science is presented in the public domain, even if that 'imprecision' is functionally valuable within science. This suggests that the difference between science and indigenous knowledges may be more to do with the degree of felt need for social closure around what *appear to be* monovalent publicly agreed meanings than with any measure of intrinsic precision *per se*. In any case, Van der Ploeg's analysis corresponds with that of the Cumbrian sheep farmers in showing the dynamic, complex and sophisticated nature of such local knowledges, and their built-in reflection and sustenance of important cultural and material values. Scientific knowledges are not neutral in this respect but also correspond with particular cultural and epistemic principles – instrumentalism, control and alienation.

Although the epistemology of control has been emphasised as a dominant feature of scientific knowledges, two observations are necessary. First, this epistemic commitment is more of a statement of aspiration or expectation – an orientating prescriptive commitment – than a statement of actual achievement, as all the discussion of the unanticipated nature of modern risks, dangers, accidents and environmental and other 'side-effects' underlines. As in the artificial conditions of the laboratory, science controls only to the extent that it manages to achieve the exclusion of all the factors it does not control, including those of which it is ignorant. It is the achievement of credibility for this implicit promise – or hope – of control, rather than the belief in actual control, which grants whatever authority they have to scientific ways of knowing.

Second, it should be noted that local or lay knowledges do not celebrate some romantic state of lack of control. They too seek control, and this does not exclude forms of social control (Douglas, 1966; Geertz, 1983; Scott, 1985); but it is of a kind which is radically different from that embodied in normal scientific epistemic commitments. This kind of knowledge is manifestly local and contextual rather than decontextual and 'universal' precisely because (Van der Ploeg, 1993: 212): 'it presupposes an active, knowledgeable actor, who actually is the "agent" of the unity and constant interaction of mental and manual work. It can also be defined as local because it allows these actors to obtain a high degree of control and mastership over the highly diversified local situation.'

In other words, this idiom of knowledge allows control, but of a contextually dense and multidimensional reality in which adaptive flexibility towards the uncontrolled is still recognised as a necessary attribute, and where the reductive, decontextualised and alienated 'control' of other situations in the 'universalistic' manner of science is pre-empted. That is, this kind of adaptive 'control' is one which is exercised with personal agency and overt responsibility. It is just this property which, as Beck notes (1992), is missing from modernity's particular discourse of control, namely science; and it is the reintegration of the deleted issues of human agency, responsibility and value which may lead to the democratisation, legitimation and epistemic pluralisation of science.

Van der Ploeg describes the approach to potato farming taken by scientific culture. Whereas indigenous culture selected potato seeds – the genotype – according to the variable environmental conditions of the plots – the phenotypes – (and other changing criteria), and continually monitored and adapted such selection over a long and complex feedback cycle, science took exactly the opposite approach. It was founded on the presumption of an 'ideal genotype' which contains the optimal combination of properties. Note that this assumes a standard and universal definition of the ideal type, even though this implicitly requires a standard specification of environmental growing conditions. These phenotype conditions which will render the ideal genotype effective are then derived, tested, defined and refined in experimental stations.

In other words, scientific culture starts with what is 'standardisable' as if an industrial mass-product, then attempts to reorganise the world to optimise the production of this standard universal ideal type. (Recall the 'production line mentality' lament of the Cumbrian sheep farmer about the scientific experts.) In the farmers' case this meant enforcing standardised environmental conditions where before there had been diversity, complexity and indigenous learning. As Van der Ploeg puts it (1993: 217):

> One of the consequences of this drastic change is that the new genotype will only prove to be an effective and rational innovation in so far as these required conditions can be effectively repeated in the fields . . . to 'innovate' is not just the simple adoption of a recommended object ('a miracle seed') but – as far as the farmer is concerned – a highly complex reorganisation of several farming routines.

And, he might have added, an externally prescribed reorganisation at that – one involving a fundamental transformation of agency. Thus begins the cycle of intensifying dependency, in which for example a specified level of soil nitrogen is demanded; to administer this without burning requires fertiliser spreading to a precise timetable, derived from the particular genotype properties. From this, water regulation requirements arise, 'and so it continues. However the point to note is that these specified requirements must be repeated in the fields, as an integrated whole. Even if all the specified conditions are followed except their exact distribution over time, then the "innovation" fails' (1993: 219).

Furthermore, these new requirements 'initiate the creation of several new dependency patterns' – new artefacts as specified in the scientific design; new procedures; new expertise and training; and new patrons in the banks and markets. This corresponds strikingly with Latour's (1987) account of the development of scientific-technical networks through the reordering of society and nature together, and the achievement of action-at-a-distance in this realignment process by having knowledge and identities pass through 'obligatory points of passage' (here the ideal genotype potato and its necessary phenotype conditions) which impose standardisation on them. Science gains its image of intellectual universality by achieving social control over the standardisation of what are varied situations.

Van der Ploeg's final point about this kind of interaction concerns the logic of destruction of indigenous knowledge and culture when faced with committed 'modernisation' programmes. A crucial feature of the flexible and informal farming knowledge is that it cannot be codified (1993: 220):

the outcome of such methods cannot be exactly predicted. Nor can the necessary methods for reaching pre-established levels be prescribed in detail. For farmers this is no problem whatsoever . . . But regardless of the advantages such methods can offer in a situation managed by local knowledge, in a scientific design they cannot be integrated, simply because they are insufficiently adaptable to the necessary standardisation. Local methods . . . fall outside the scope of scientific design. Consequently farmers as active and knowledgeable actors, capable of improving their own conditions, also fall outside the scope of scientifically managed rural development.

Thus an asymmetrical conflict seems to exist, between a system which is supposed to work in a superior way, so long as the demanding standardised conditions can be repeatedly fulfilled, and a 'local' system which demands too much skill and trust in a non-codified informal and variable craft expertise. The scientific culture brings with it the terms of its own validation, like any other culture. But the sting in the tail is that the scientific culture doesn't work even in its own terms, if one enlarges the scope and extends the timescale of evaluation. Thus the yields from the scientific varieties have degenerated rapidly – 'within three or four years they became incapable of generating even low levels of production' – leading to magical discourses about the scientific varieties 'having no power any more'. The scientific system only 'worked' by socially excluding large parts of the world from its purview – for example ignoring the quite respectable, and *sustainable* observed yields of the indigenous farming system. Thus, it seems (1993: 223), 'ignorance of the local knowledge systems, their dynamics and their scope, is a crucial precondition for the diffusion of the scientific knowledge system'.

Van der Ploeg's conclusion is interesting in respect of the relationships of scientific and lay idioms of knowledge. Reviewing the overall response of the potato farmers to the self-consciously modernising influences of scientific programmes he notes the powerful irony (1993: 222) that:

> In more general terms this implies that the increasing influence of science in the world produces just the opposite effects, at least under the circumstances described: myths, vagueness, poly-interpretability and a certain subjectivity in the relation to nature are not superseded through heavy inputs of applied science, but rather reinforced and extended to farmers' relations to science itself!

If we make explicit the cultural, mythic character of science as well as the readily underlined cultural character of the local knowledges, then this reaction is understandable because the expert system can be seen as a system of myth which is alien and threatening to existing identities and effective knowledges. It is a more cultural or hermeneutic restatement of the self-refutations of modernity described by Beck. However, what Van der Ploeg unfortunately fails to emphasise in his account are the ways in which it points to potential transcendence of the sterile conceptualisation of dichotomy between on the one hand a monolithic culture of rationality and scientific modernity, and on the other a defensive and non-innovative, epistemically closed realm of indigenous 'traditional' cultures. The lay knowledge he describes is complex, reflexive, dynamic and innovative, material and empirical, and yet also theoretical. It is experimental and flexible, not dogmatic and closed. Whatever its ultimate demerits or merits, it is epistemically alive and substantive. It also embodies implicit cultural models, of the human subject, agency and responsibility (just as, I have argued, does the scientific knowledge). It is difficult to see in this kind of non-expert knowledge culture only the defensive, private and epistemically vacuous implicit model of lay knowledge advanced by Giddens, or even the more generous but still expert-dependent version of Beck.

Thus transcending the misleading terms of 'The Great Divide' requires us to address the senses in which modern science is, like all other kinds of knowledge, thoroughly cultural, and the ways in which it conceals its own fundamental indeterminacies by subtly and tacitly building the cultural and institutional terms of its own validation. Latour's (1992) notions of hybridisation and purification offer one such avenue of insight. Science imbues natural categories with culture, and scientific-technical networks are built with a richly heterogeneous hybridisation of the natural, human and artefactual. But then this human achievement is purified of its human content and defined as only natural, to the disorientation of the social world and its concepts of responsibility and agency. These two processes occur side by side. It is difficult to give credence to the ideas of basic epochal transformation, whether from tradition to modernity, or from modernity to postmodernity. Instead, a less constrained examination is called for of the ways in which human responsibility for natural knowledge can be practically reclaimed and redistributed; and exploration of how natural discourses might be able to help stabilise human relationships without at the same time inducing extremes of alienation, exclusion and inflexibility. This will require re-examination of received ideas of the nature of scientific and lay knowledges.

Conclusions

Whilst it shares some of the key elements of Beck's and Giddens's theories of the transformations of modernity, especially about the self-refutations of modern institutions and the rise of 'life-politics' outside of formal institutions, my perspective on expert systems changes quite fundamentally the conceptualisation of the driving forces in those cultural and political transformations, of the basic character of *risk* in the 'risk society', and thus of the possibility of constructing new forms of epistemic and social order which could be seen as enjoying more democratic public identification, legitimation or responsibility. In particular, the potentialities for new forms of political, moral and epistemic order – ones enjoying greater public identification, and reinvigorated democratic grounding – are significantly broadened by introducing the problematisation of 'expert knowledge' which my analysis has done. This approach is founded in the sociology of scientific knowledge, especially in three key tenets:

- its understanding of scientific knowledge as underdetermined by natural evidence and logical decision rules, and of scientific observation and experiment as underdetermined by prevailing theory (for example Latour and Woolgar, 1979; Cartwright, 1983; Collins, 1985);
- its understanding of scientific knowledge as rooted in local (such as specific laboratory) practices, whose claims to universality rest on successful discursive linkages, coordinations and correspondences being made between disparate local practices (for example, standardisation as described in Van der Ploeg's case-study; Latour, 1987; Star, 1989; Pickering, 1992) .
- partly as a function of these properties, the unavoidable embodiment in the constitution of scientific knowledge, of assumptions and commitments directly or indirectly about the human and cultural (Wynne, 1992; Watson-Verran and Turnbull, 1994).

Relating these more directly to the public domain, established concepts of 'good science' which lend politically privileged authority to particular scientific subcultures and exclude others, are not *naturally* given but culturally validated – and the reciprocal validation occurs too. A new domain of debate is therefore opened up, concerning the articulation of different public values and intellectual perspectives, with criteria of 'good science' that come to be institutionalised and exercised in many economic, technological, medical, health, educational and environmental domains. In practice, there is *de facto* reflection of the indeterminacy of such potent normative concepts, for example in the formulation and negotiation of regulatory and risk assessment science and policies (Jasanoff, 1990). But this open-endedness is concealed behind the public scientific rhetoric of objectivity and determinism. By falling into a resultant binary idiom, much of the sociological debate on modernity has crippled itself by an uncritical absorption and reflection of this rhetoric, even whilst affecting a critical orientation.

In identifying the indeterminacies and intrinsically local nature of scientific knowledge construction, my approach also implies recognition of the more substantive intellectual status of lay knowledges than is usually acknowledged (for example by Beck and Giddens). It is important not to misunderstand this as a claim for intellectual superiority or even equivalence for lay knowledges. This question is beside the point in the present context. However, it does imply much greater interdependence than is conventionally recognised between what come to be defined as lay and expert knowledges. Valuable though it is in several important ways, Van der Ploeg's (1993) case-study implies the bleak conclusion that there are categorically distinct epistemological systems, of modern science and indigenous ('cultural') tradition, even if the latter is more dynamic and practically effective than usually seen. He suggests that the two cultures are simply mutually incompatible and that it is either one, or the other. Dealing with identical issues – in their case between Aboriginal knowledge systems and modern scientific ones – Watson-Verran and Turnbull (1994) manage an openness to these very basic categories which is more in basic sympathy with this chapter. In studying the often fraught and conflictual interactions as a matter of practical politics as well as epistemology, they observe:

> What we are producing – practical criticism of past ways of understanding ourselves, and relations between two peoples, and reinterpretation of the political and social processes of those relations – is of course subject to standards of theoretical coherence and empirical adequacy. But its overall adequacy is not solely determined by such criteria. The constructions that we are generating [in these science–Aboriginal knowledge confrontations] are 'verified' also by participants engaging with the newly apparent sets of possibilities for action.

This is remarkably consistent with the sociological views of scientific knowledge validation as being based not in nature *per se*, but (which may of course give nature a large role) in the identification by participants of new possibilities for 'carrying on' the existing culture, not without new elements of practice, relationships and identity emerging.

This more diverse, open-ended and less dichotomised view of where legitimate knowledge and order might come from also of course carries important political implications in terms of potential redistributions of power and recognised authority to subcultures currently marginalised or outside formal institutional processes. It also corresponds with the view of the construction of knowledge as the construction of hybrid (Latour, 1992) or heterogeneous (Law, 1986) networks, necessarily paying no respect to putative boundaries between the natural, the social and the artificial (though constructing and reifying these for legitimation purposes). Thus arises also the challenge to the way in which modernity as such has been conceived, since in the otherwise rewarding perspectives of Beck and Giddens the fundamental divide between nature and culture which is a defining characteristic of Western modernist self-conceptions is ironically not challenged, but uncritically reproduced.

Once one introduces the idea that scientific expert knowledge itself embodies a particular culture – that is, it disseminates and imposes particular and problematic normative versions of the human and the social – then this fundamental divide is no longer tenable. An important strand of sociological and historical work on science has problematised the supposition of an objective boundary between science and the public domain, as if for example knowledge and cognitive influence only flow one way, and as if there were not cultural, epistemic and cognitive commitments that were in principle open, but held in common and mutually reinforcing across the boundary.

The problematisation of scientific knowledge as embodying hermeneutic (and formulaic) and not only propositional truths (as Giddens claims) of necessity also problematises the boundaries established as social constructions between the scientific and the non-scientific. Work to define boundaries between expert and lay as if these were objective categories given in nature becomes critical to the stabilisation of forms of authority. This aspect of science and the public domain has been extensively treated, for example by Gieryn (1983, 1994), Jasanoff (1987), Star and Griesemer (1989) and Shapin and Schaffer (1985). Latour (1983, 1987) has also fundamentally problematised these boundaries. Despite significant differences in other respects, all these perspectives have in common the view that particular epistemic orders or cultures interconstruct and mutually reinforce with particular social or political orders, in a historically contingent way (which is very different from saying that they are subject to subjective whim). However, with few exceptions none of this work has yet been adequately connected with understanding of the nature of 'non-expert', public knowledge (Watson-Verran and Turnbull, 1994). In Giddens's view of reflexive modernity the reflexive processes of lay people seem to have no significant collective intellectual content; it is merely intimate behavioural reflexivity towards 'globalising' expert interventions in personal lives. Thus there is no problematising of a boundary between expert and lay domains of knowledge and epistemology – because the most lay people have to do (or are thought to be capable of) is to choose whom to trust, when experts disagree. If there is no expert contestation, there is apparently no problem anyway, since, it is supposed, only the domain of expert knowledge enjoys any intellectual substance. In Beck's only slightly different view, the problems of whom to trust arise because expert bodies have betrayed trust by not protecting society from the now-pervasive risks 'out-there'. However, in that these 'out-there' risks are identified by counterexperts the problems of trust and risk are only raised by expert contestation, and as in Giddens's account the public is only represented by different expert factions. The human dimensions of such natural knowledges, whether contested or not by other *experts*, is not recognised or problematised as a public issue.

The formal distinction which Giddens emphasises between propositional, formulaic and hermeneutic truth claims, and his assumption that science only deals in propositional claims and commitments, allows him to assert the absolute distinction between expert and lay knowledge. According to this widespread view, expert systems have unmediated access to nature hence peddle only natural knowledge, whilst lay publics are epistemically vacuous, and have only the emotional wellsprings of culture and ephemeral local knowledges. Yet once the picture is complicated in the way that this chapter proposes, science is articulating and imposing not only propositional claims but tacit formulaic and hermeneutic ones too – in other words, symbolic ones about the performance and legitimacy of social institutions, and about the 'naturalness' of particular models of human nature and relationships. Furthermore, once this crucial point is recognised, then lay public responses to scientific expertise can be seen as responses which combine human questioning or rejection of those implicit 'formulaic' and 'hermeneutic' expert system claims, with alternative propositional ones. Indeed it is exposed as problematic to use such categorical distinctions without further qualification, since the basis on human and moral grounds of legitimate non-expert responses to scientific expertise shifts the epistemic framing of the social purposes of knowledge, and hence the criteria by which valid propositional claims would be established. On my perspective, therefore, it is impossible to accommodate the view that non-expert understandings are only represented in public debate and contestation by dissenting expert groups. Yet this is the view both of Beck,[8] as in his model of the sub-politics of reflexive modernity, and of Giddens, with his idea that publics now have to invest trust by deliberate decision and choice between competing experts, and that this reflexive lay awareness has only arisen because of expert conflict. Some sociologists of science have also committed themselves to this unhelpful dichotomous vision. For example, Collins (Collins and Pinch, 1994: 335) asserts that: 'It would be a strange world, and one that I would not welcome, if "the public [had] its own and legitimate interests in the very contents of science" '.

As already indicated, what count as the contents of science can be debated, but here Collins joins common cause with the dichotomous rationalism of Giddens and Beck on modernity and expertise. It is not surprising that his approach within sociology of science has been attacked for, in effect, closing down possible questions about the wider epistemic negotiability of reliable knowledge of nature. This perspective therefore forecloses the open issue of what is to count as 'good science' in public domains, and pre-empts fundamental questions about the indeterminacy of the human and natural orders (Callon and Latour, 1992; Collins and Yearley, 1992).

Because my perspective is vulnerable to such a common misunderstanding, let me utterly disown the reading which takes it as claiming that lay, or 'local' knowledge is to be championed as superior to scientific or universal knowledge. To conclude this from my analysis would be completely to miss the point. Collins again appears to fall foul of this dichotomous thinking when, in response to the suggestion that lay people may have a role to play in the substantive construction of scientific knowledge, he asserts (Collins and Pinch, 1994: 335): 'It would be a weird world in which our desire to avoid elitism stretched democracy to the level of the Chinese Red Guards. When anyone's opinion on a matter, irrespective of their depth of experience, is as good as anyone else's, then society has broken down.'

The public's proper role, according to Collins (Collins and Pinch, 1994: 335), lies only 'in saying how the boiling flux of expertise should be represented and applied to our society'. Thus an absolute boundary between expert knowledge and lay public knowledge is again reinforced, in which the latter only has purchase on local application. Like Giddens he appears to hold the view that when there is no expert conflict, there can be no problem.[9] There is no role for lay publics in evaluating and participating in the redefinition of what is to count as 'expert' knowledge, and no role recognised in renegotiating the proper constitution of scientific knowledge in terms of its normative embodiments of criteria of 'good science' – such as its degree of standardisation and differentiation, its commitment to control and prediction, and the related issue of its treatment of indeterminacy and uncertainty. The separation between these essentially normative-cultural issues and the cognitive issues (which can be abstracted as purely cognitive only by taking for granted a particular cultural framework), is absolute in Collins's view, and in this he is at one with Giddens and Beck.

These are the exact epistemic issues about the proper constitution and scope of modern science as culture, which the modernity issue centralises. The environment and risk debates around which much of modern politics has been shaped[10] are quintessentially tied up with the larger crises of legitimacy of modern economic, scientific-technical and political institutions, and the search for new forms of legitimate order and authority. In this it seems that new forms of emergent political order, with new configurations of global vision and local rootedness, will emerge – are perhaps emerging – in which new imaginations of the relationships between universal knowledge and human values will be vital. In seeking the basis of more legitimate, less alienating forms of public knowledge, and stable authority out of present conditions of incoherence and disorientation, new constitutional norms of valid knowledge may be articulated. Necessary and legitimate involvement of lay publics in this process will also automatically involve them in negotiations, direct or indirect, of the intellectual contents of those new universals. Thus in reflection both of a moral and political impetus towards seeing ourselves as global citizens with corresponding responsibilities and relationships, and of the realities of global interconnections and dependencies, epistemic universals can likewise be expected to enjoy a legitimate and necessary long-term future. The romantic seductions of local knowledges and identities do not come as an *alternative* to modernity's ahuman and alienating universals, but as an inspiration to find the collective self-conceptions which can sustain universals that do not bury the traces of their own human commitment and responsibility.

To relegate the public to the role and identity given in the dichotomous conceptualisations of expert and public which I have criticised here, and to relegate scientific expertise to the associated condition of supposed cultural- and meaning-neutrality, is to commit society to further blind polarisation in the continuing transformations of modernity.[11]

Notes

1. Reflexive processes are implicitly conceived as thoroughly calculative, under the autonomous authorship of an individual subject. This raises an interesting issue as to the extent to which culture is described in terms of its subjects' calculative faculties, implying a deliberative constitution. This deserves more extensive discussion, but in another place than in this chapter.

2. This view is so widespread it is difficult to pick out specific illustrations. See for example the pages of the monthly journal of the UK Atomic Energy Authority, *Atom* (London); and from pro-nuclear and sceptical stances respectively, see Pocock, 1977; and Roger Williams, 1980. See also S. Weart, 1988.

3. Those institutions are unlikely to escape from this constant erosion of the foundations of their own social legitimation if they are encouraged by sociologists into an erroneous view of the public as unreflexive.

4. This could be treated as an instrumental calculation of institutional trustworthiness of the same kind that I attribute to Beck and Giddens. However, I would argue that the process of apprehension and response is more immediate, engaged and less deliberative than this, more captured by describing it as partly an emotional process of identification or otherwise with those organisations and the kinds of human relations and identities which they appear to reflect, uphold or deny. It has to be acknowledged that the choice of descriptive terms here is at least in part a matter of the author's chosen moral engagement with the social world.

5. As the public understanding of science research field shows (Irwin and Wynne, 1995), lay public response to science is frequently – and legitimately – based upon understandings of science's institutional 'body-language' (for example whether it is reproducing private profits or public services) when scientific experts themselves imagine that they are or should be based only on its propositional contents.

6. This is the time taken for a given body burden to decrease to half the original level. It thus depends on the metabolic processes of excretion as well as on the physical radioactive decay rate of the radioisotope concerned. In this case the biological parameter is much the shorter, hence the dominant term.

7. This and the other farmers' quotes are taken from verbatim transcripts of structured interviews conducted during 1987–89 by the author, Peter Williams and Jean Williams as part of a project on public understanding of science funded by the UK Economic and Social Research Council. See Wynne, 1992.

8. It is worth noting that in his accounts of the ways modern expert institutions tacitly construct self-serving and socially disorientating versions of responsibility for the risks of modern science and technology, and in his focus upon the unanticipated, Beck comes closer to avoiding a rationalistic framework than Giddens. However, the mechanisms of self-dissolution or self-refutation, and thus the reflexive transformations of modernity, are still conceived by Beck solely in terms of uncontrolled 'out-there' aspects of the unanticipated – of risks, side-effects, etc. out there in nature or technology. I have explored and emphasised the nature of popular experience and response to science and modernity in the form of concrete interventions and discourses, which are not just about out-there risks, but also about modern expert institutions imposing non-negotiated 'in-here' moral and social identities and relationships. It is for these reasons that I would still characterise Beck's approach as fundamentally rationalist.

9. One of the main contributions of research on public understanding of science (Michael, 1992; Wynne, 1994), and before that on public risk perceptions (Wynne, 1983), has been to explode this simplistic view.

10. Whether or not Beck is correct to call this a historically new organising principle of society akin to the ownership and control of the means of production is a question which can be set aside for the moment. The globalisation of many risk problems does not seem to require the wholesale abandonment of analytical categories to do with capitalist accumulation; but the focus of the present analysis does not need a resolution of those questions.

11. However, to rejoin forces with those whose work I have critically examined here, the thorough lack of any essentialist claims or concepts defining the trajectory of modern social and cultural change is not only consistent with, but is obliged by, a fundamentally relational view of knowledge and ethics (Bernstein, 1983). If the grounding principles of knowledge are to sustain (ethically good) *relationships*, rather than fulfilment of abstract essentialist norms for which relationships are just the functional means, then the orientation of critical analysis such as this is bound to be contextual, as a matter of principle. It may appear to switch sides as one or another gains ascendancy and assumes those unreflexive properties associated with

domination; but this is only an appearance because actually this analysis is committed to no particular 'side', whilst being utterly engaged in their development and interaction.

References

Arnold, L. (1992) *Windscale 1957: Anatomy of a Nuclear Accident*. London: Macmillan.
Bauman, Z. (1991) *Modernity and Ambivalence*. Cambridge: Polity Press.
Beck, U. (1988) 'From industrial society to the risk society: Questions of survival, social structure and ecological enlightenment', *Theory, Culture and Society*, 9: 97–123.
Beck, U. (1992) *Risk Society: Towards a New Modernity*. London: Sage. (Translation of the German version, *Risikogesellschaft: Auf dem Weges einem andere Moderne*. Frankfurt: Suhrkampf, 1986.)
Beck, U. (1994) 'The reinvention of politics: towards a theory of reflexive modernization', in U. Beck, A. Giddens and S. Lash (1994) *Reflexive Modernization*. pp. 1–55.
Beck, U., Giddens, A. and Lash, S. (1994) *Reflexive Modernization: Politics, Tradition and Aesthetics in the Modern Social Order*. Cambridge: Polity.
Bernstein, R. (1983) *Beyond Objectivism and Relativism: Science, Hermeneutics and Praxis*. Oxford: Blackwell.
Black, D. (1984) *An Investigation into Possible Clusters of Childhood Leukemia in West Cumbria*. London, Department of Health: HMSO.
Bourdieu, P. (1980) *Le Sens Pratique*. Paris: Éditions de Minuit.
Brown, J. (ed.) (1989) *Environmental Threats: Analysis, Perception, Management*. London: Belhaven.
Callon, M. and Latour, B. (1992) 'Don't throw the baby out with the Bath School! A reply to Collins and Yearley', in A. Pickering (ed.), *Science as Practice and Culture*. pp. 343–68.
Cartwright, N. (1983) *How the Laws of Physics Lie*. Oxford: Clarendon Press.
Clarke, A. and Fujimura, J. (eds) (1992) *The Right Tools for the Job: At Work in the 20th Century Life Sciences*. Princeton, NJ: Princeton University Press.
Collins, H. (1985) *Natural Order: Replication and Induction in Scientific Practice*. London: Sage.
Collins, H. and Pinch, T. (1994) 'Representativeness and expertise: A response', *Public Understanding of Science*, 3: 331–7.
Collins, H. and Yearley, S. (1992) 'Epistemological chicken', in A. Pickering (ed.), *Science as Practice and Culture*. pp. 301–26.
Conrad, J. (ed.) (1980) *Society, Technology and Risk*. London: Academic Press.
Daly, K. (1970), 'The specters of technicism', *Psychiatry*, 33: 417–31.
Davy, A., Jenkins, E., MacGill, S. and Layton, D. (1992) *Inarticulate Science?* Driffield, UK: Studies in Science Education.
Desmond, A. (1987) 'Artisan resistance and evolution in Britain, 1819–1848', *Osiris*, 3 (2nd series): 77–110.
Dickens, P. (1992) *Society and Nature: Towards a Green Social Theory*. New York and London: Harvester Wheatsheaf.
Douglas, M. (1966) *Purity and Danger*. Harmondsworth: Penguin.
Erickson, K. (1976) *Everything in its Path: The Destruction of a Community in the Buffalo Creek Mining Disaster*. New York: Simon and Schuster.
Garfinkel, H. (1963) 'A conception of and experiment with "trust" as a condition of stable concerted actions', in O.J. Harvey (ed.) *Motivation and Social Interaction*. pp. 187–238.
Geertz, C. (1983) *Local Knowledge*. New York: Basic Books.
Giddens, A. (1990) *The Consequences of Modernity*. Cambridge: Polity Press.
Giddens, A. (1991) *Modernity and Self-Identity: Self and Society in the Late Modern Age*. Cambridge: Polity Press.
Giddens, A. (1994) 'Living in a post-traditional society', in U. Beck, A. Giddens and S. Lash, *Reflexive Modernization*. pp. 56-109.

Gieryn, T. (1983) 'Boundary work and the demarcation of science from non-science: strains and interests in professional ideologies of scientists', *American Sociological Review*, 48: 781–95.

Gieryn, T. (1994) 'Boundaries of science', in Jasanoff et al. (eds), *Handbook of Science and Technology Studies*. pp. 393–443.

Gilbert, N. and Mulkay, M. (1984) *Opening Pandora's Box: A Sociological Analysis of Scientists' Discourse*. Cambridge: Cambridge University Press.

Golinski, J. (1992) *Science as Public Culture: Chemistry and Enlightenment in Britain, 1760–1820*. Cambridge: Cambridge University Press.

Grove-White, R. (1991) 'The emerging shape of environmental conflict in the 1990s', *Royal Society of Arts Journal*, 89 (5419): 437–47.

Harvey, O.J. (ed.) (1963) *Motivation and Social Interaction*. New York: Ronald Press.

Hobart, M. (ed.) (1993) *An Anthropological Critique of Development: The Growth of Ignorance*. London: Routledge.

Irwin, A. and Wynne, B. (eds) (1995) *Misunderstanding Science*. Cambridge: Cambridge University Press.

Jasanoff, S. (1987) 'Contested boundaries in policy-relevant science', *Social Studies of Science*, 17: 195–230.

Jasanoff, S. (1990) *The Fifth Branch: Science Advisers as Policymakers*. Cambridge, MA: Harvard University Press.

Jasanoff, S., Markle, G., Petersen, J. and Pinch, T. (eds) (1994) *Handbook of Science and Technology Studies*. Thousand Oaks CA, London and New Delhi: Sage.

Jordan, K. and Lynch, M. (1992) 'The sociology of a genetic engineering technique: ritual and rationality in the performance of a brain peptide prep', in Clarke and Fujimura (eds), *The Right Tools for the Job*.

Jupp, A. (1989) 'The provision of major accident hazard infomation to the public'. Unpublished M.Sc. thesis, Manchester University.

Krimsky, S. and Golding, D. (eds) (1992) *Social Theories of Risk*. Westport CT, and London: Westview Press.

Kuhn, T.S. (1962) *The Structure of Scientific Revolutions*. Chicago: University of Chicago Press.

Lash, S. (1994a) 'Reflexivity and its doubles: structure, aesthetics, community', in U. Beck, A. Giddens and S. Lash, *Reflexive Modernization*. pp. 110–73.

Lash, S. (1994b) 'Expert systems or situated interpretation? Replies and critiques', in U. Beck, A. Giddens and S. Lash, *Reflexive Modernization*. pp. 198–215.

Latour, B. (1983) 'Give me a laboratory and I will raise the world', in K. Knorr-Cetina and M. Mulkay (eds), *Science Observed: Perspectives on the Social Study of Science*. Beverly Hills, CA: Sage.

Latour, B. (1987) *Science in Action*. Milton Keynes: Open University Press.

Latour, B. (1992) *We Have Never Been Modern*. London: Harvester Wheatsheaf.

Latour, B. and Woolgar, S. (1979) *Laboratory Life*. Beverly Hills, CA: Sage.

Lave, J. (1988) *Cognition in Practice: Mind, Mathematics and Logic in Everyday Life*. Cambridge: Cambridge University Press.

Law, J. (1986) 'On the methods of long-distance control: vessels, navigation and the Portuguese route to India', in J. Law (ed.) *Power, Action, and Belief: A New Sociology of Knowledge? (Sociological Review Monograph 38)*. Keele, UK: Keele University Press. pp. 234–63.

Long, N. and Long, A. (eds) (1992) *Battlefields of Knowledge*. London and New York: Routledge.

McDermott, J. (1974) 'Technology: Opiate of the intellectuals', in E. Mendelsohn (ed.), *Technology and Man's Future*. pp. 107–33.

MacGill, S. (1987) *The Politics of Anxiety: The Black Inquiry and Childhood Leukemias around Sellafield*. London: Pion.

McKechnie, R. and Welsh, I. (1994) in G. Weekes (ed.), *The Lesser Evil and the Greater Good*. pp. 57–78.

McSorley, J. (1990) *Living in the Shadow: The People of West Cumbria and the Nuclear Industry*. London: Pluto.

Martin, E. (1989) *The Woman in the Body*. Milton Keynes: Open University Press.

Mendelsohn, E. (ed.) (1974) *Technology and Man's Future*. New York: St Martin's Press.

Michael, M. (1992) 'Lay discourses of science: science-in-particular, science-in-general, and self', *Science, Technology and Human Values*, 17 (3): 313–33.

Otway, H. (1992) 'Expert fallibility, public wisdom: toward a contextual theory of risk', in S. Krimsky and D. Golding (eds), *Social Theories of Risk*. pp. 215–28.

Pickering, A. (ed.) (1992) *Science as Practice and Culture*. Chicago: University of Chicago Press.

Pocock, R.F. (1977) *Nuclear Power: Its Development in the United Kingdom*. Old Woking, Surrey: Unwin Brothers and the Institution of Nuclear Engineers.

Polanyi, M. (1958) *Personal Knowledge*. London: Routledge and Kegan Paul.

Redclift, M. and Benton, T. (eds) (1994) *Social Theory and the Global Environment*. London: Routledge.

Scott, J.C. (1985) *Weapons of the Weak: Everyday Forms of Peasant Resistance*. New Haven, CT: Yale University Press.

Shapin, S. (1994) *A Social History of Truth*. Chicago: Chicago University Press.

Shapin, S. and Schaffer, S. (1985) *Leviathan and the Air-Pump: Hobbes, Boyle, and the Experimental Life*. Princeton, NJ: Princeton University Press.

Slovic, P. (1992) 'Perception of risk: Reflections on the psychometric paradigm', in S. Krimsky and D. Golding (eds), *Social Theories of Risk*. pp. 117–52.

Star, S.L. (1989) *Regions of Mind: Brain Research and the Quest for Scientific Certainty*. Stanford, CA: Stanford University Press.

Star, S.L. and Griesemer, J. (1989) 'Institutional ecology, "Translations", and boundary-objects: amateurs and professionals in Berkeley's museum of vertebrate zoology 1907–1939', *Social Studies of Science*, 19: 387–420.

Van der Ploeg, J. (1993) 'Potatoes and knowledge', in M. Hobart (ed.), *An Anthropological Critique of Development*. pp. 209–27.

Watson-Verran, H. and Turnbull, D. (1994) 'Science and other indigenous knowledge systems', in S. Jasanoff et al. (eds), *Handbook of Science and Technology Studies*. pp. 115–39.

Weart, S. (1988) *Nuclear Fear: A History of Images*. Cambridge, MA: Harvard University Press.

Weekes, G. (ed.) (1994) *The Lesser Evil and the Greater Good: The Theory and Practice of Democracy*. London: Rivers Oram.

Welsh, I. (1993) 'The NIMBY syndrome and its significance in the history of the nuclear debate in Britain', *British Journal for the History of Science*, 26 (1): 15–32.

Welsh, I. (1995) *Nuclear Power: Generating Dissent*. London: Routledge.

Williams, R. (1980) *The Nuclear Power Decisions*. London: Croom Helm.

Wynne, B. (1980) 'Technology, risk and participation: On the social treatment of uncertainty', in J. Conrad (ed.), *Society, Technology and Risk*. pp. 83–107.

Wynne, B. (1982) *Rationality and Ritual: The Windscale Inquiry and Nuclear Decisions in Britain*. Chalfont St Giles, Bucks, UK: British Society for the History of Science, Monograph 3.

Wynne, B. (1983) 'Redefining the issues of risk and public acceptance: The social viability of technology', *Futures*, 15: 13–32.

Wynne, B. (1987) *Risk Management and Hazardous Wastes: Implementation and the Dialectics of Credibility*. Berlin, New York and London: Springer.

Wynne, B. (1989) 'Building public concern into risk management', in J. Brown (ed.), *Environmental Threats*. pp. 119–32.

Wynne, B. (1990) 'Major hazards communication: Defining the challenges for research and practice', in H.B.F. Gow and H. Otway (eds), *Communicating with the Public about Major Accident Hazards*. London: Elsevier. pp. 599–612.

Wynne, B. (1992) 'Misunderstood misunderstanding: Social identities and the public uptake of science', *Public Understanding of Science*, 1 (3): 281–304.

Wynne, B. (1994) 'Public understanding of science', in S. Jasanoff et al. (eds), *Handbook of Science and Technology Studies*. pp. 361–88.

Wynne, B. (1996) 'The identity parades of SSK: Reflexivity, engagement and politics', *Social Studies of Science*, 26.

Yearley, S. (1992) *The Green Case*. London: Routledge and Kegan Paul.

3

RE-VISION: THE CENTRALITY OF TIME FOR AN ECOLOGICAL SOCIAL SCIENCE PERSPECTIVE

Barbara Adam

Globalised processes and phenomena display features which cannot be grasped with the conceptual tools of the Enlightenment: dualities, objectivity, empiricism and past-based knowledge are widely questioned in the sciences and the arts as adequate conceptual tools for analyses of the local–global connection, the loss of 'the other', invisible threats and unknowable futures (see Capra, 1982; Bohm 1983; Hiley and Peat, 1987; Hekman, 1990; Leggett, 1990; Poster, 1990; Ermarth 1992; Goldsmith 1992). In the social sciences, the analyses of Beck (1992a and b, and this volume) and Giddens (1990, 1991) play a central role in highlighting the distinctiveness of those contemporary features. Their work therefore provides an excellent starting point for the arguments offered in this chapter.

Despite their very different analyses of contemporary social life, Beck and Giddens agree on a wide range of key features which they argue constitute central characteristics of high modernity. Both emphasise risks, threats and existential hazards as unintended and unforeseen yet pervasive consequences of the industrial way of life. They conceptualise uncertainty and unpredictability as by-products of ever-increasing rationalisation, and the loss of temporal and spatial boundaries as a result of interactions between scientific technology and living systems. Both point to processes of globalisation that differ from those of early industrialisation: to the colonisation of the long-term future, to the interpenetration of nature and culture as well as individual, national and global processes, and to a loss of 'the other'. Both argue the need for morals and insist that the question of 'How shall we live?' cannot be avoided. And finally, both stress the centrality of reflexivity: they point to processes folding back upon themselves, to modernity becoming reflexive, to institutional reflexivity and to the reflexive self. As a consequence of their respective analyses both authors are acutely aware that these characteristics of contemporary existence pose problems for understanding and action not only at the level of everyday and political life but also for sociology, a discipline steeped in the Enlightenment tradition and tied to modernist assumptions. To both authors, the conceptual tools of the eighteenth and nineteenth centuries are no longer sufficient for analyses of contemporary life. 'The dangers of highly developed nuclear and chemical productive forces', writes Beck (1992a: 22), 'abolish the foundations and categories according to which we have thought and acted to this point.'

Change at the level of assumptions is, however, not an easy task for social scientists since those conceptualisations are laden with the cultural baggage of modernity. Attempts at reconceptualisation are hampered by conceptual habits and familiarity. On the strength of the former we tend to re-embed new images in existing traditions, transforming and deforming efforts towards theoretical advance, while the latter tends to render assumptions invisible. Habit and familiarity thus constitute serious obstacles to theoretical re-vision. It is for this reason that I want to bring to the fore some of the disattended aspects of social science analyses, since focus on the implicit and untheorised may help us to sidestep existing approaches and begin the urgent task of conceptual renewal.

Next, I want to highlight disjunctures between contemporary phenomena and their analyses and identify necessary points of departure from the classical traditions. Reflexivity is central to this process. Its importance, identified by Beck and Giddens as a key feature of high modernity, is also recognised in the social studies of science approach which stresses the constitutive power of knowledge generally and of scientific knowledge in particular (Knorr-Cetina, 1981; Latour, 1987; Woolgar, 1988; Steier, 1991). These contemporary social scientists accept reflexivity as a feature of their subject matter and of their methodology, as an aspect not just of contemporary social life but of social science practice itself. To impose the reflexive attitude on the self, however, requires that we overcome the powerful belief in an uncontaminated, objective reality and accept the constitutive power of our frames of meaning. In this chapter I therefore want to sidestep the more conventional attention on the *practice* of knowledge generation and focus instead on implicit *assumptions* which normally tend to be considered 'immaterial' and resisted as subjects of reflection. Such reflexivity, I suggest, is necessary not only because knowledge is constitutive but also because (a) the knowledge of self and other interpenetrate, and because (b) we construct 'the other' to the templates of our own theoretical models. Thus, it is neither sufficient to demonstrate the reflexivity of modernity nor adequate to show how researchers do not discover but construct their subject matter; rather we need simultaneously to illuminate the conceptual tools that guide our vision.

Focus on time aids such reflection on assumptions and conceptual tools. A deeply taken-for-granted aspect of daily life and social science, time is a feature which, like an iceberg, is largely submerged and invisible. To highlight implicit temporalities thus facilitates the 'reflexive turn' and makes visible the backcloth upon which our descriptions are drawn. Moreover, it allows us to bracket disciplinary traditions and see existing problems in a new light: the local–global connection, the colonisation of the future, risks and invisible threats, responsibility for the future and life politics – all take on a new hue.

The Local–Global Connection

> Ecological problems highlight the new and accelerating interdependence of global systems and bring home to every one the depth of the connections between personal activity and planetary problems. (Giddens, 1991: 221)

There is much debate about what constitutes globalisation and definitions vary accordingly. For the purpose of this chapter and in agreement with Albrow (1990: 9) I would like to identify globalisation with processes which bind and connect the peoples of this world into a single world society, processes which firmly locate globalisation in the twentieth century. Conceived in this way, globalisation implies social institutions and practices orientated towards global issues. The World Bank, the United Nations, the World Commission on Environment and Development, the Campaign for Nuclear Disarmament and the Organisation of Petroleum Exporting Countries (OPEC), all expressions of this development, dissent from the traditional focus of sociological inquiry, and all transcend society as bounded by the nation state. It is not my objective here to discuss the work of the main protagonists of the debate around globalisation such as Hannerz (1990), Keohane and Nye (1971), Robertson (1991), Sklair (1991) and Wallerstein (1974, 1990, 1991), as well as Beck (1992a) and Giddens (1990, 1991). Rather, I will take those findings as a collective body of thought and use them, where appropriate, as a basis for drawing out temporal features.

Beyond those institutional features, focus on global time points simultaneously to the centrality of technology; it brings into sharp relief the technological influences on social praxis. It demonstrates the importance for twentieth century globalisation of developments in information technology, of the wireless telegraph, telephone, radio and satellite television, to name just a few of the globalising technologies. I will therefore use as my second source of information work which has focused on the impact of technology on contemporary existence (such as McLuhan, 1964/73; Kern, 1983; Rifkin, 1987; Nowotny, 1989; Romanyshyn, 1989; Poster, 1990; Wajcman, 1991; O'Malley, 1992a and b). Global times emerge from those studies in a multitude of expressions. These range from time zones and the global day to standard time and the globalised present, from time-space distantiation to the disembedding of time and space. All in turn provide pertinent clues for the local–global connection.

The invention of the telegraph turned previously invisible events into global news. Thus, the sinking of the *Titanic* in April 1912, for example, became a collectively knowable, global event. It promoted a sense of global connectedness among people who formerly had been isolated by distance. In contrast to the life-saving capacity and the associated sense of a shared present, the telegraph and telephone had a more dubious impact on the diplomatic activities preceding the outbreak of the First World War. Here, the established habits and traditions of diplomacy were not adequate to the new time-compressing tool at their disposal. Kern's (1983) data suggest that the speed of communication afforded by the new technology left no room for the customary time of reflection, consultation and the diplomacy of conciliation. It played havoc with the established art of carefully choreographed diplomatic timing: time and distance lost their established inseparability. Distant events became immediate and decisions were required instantly. Never before had decisions about war and peace been made under such pressure of actuality and immediacy. Never before had diplomacy been conducted 'under circumstances of such extraordinary compression' (Kern, 1983: 278). The material basis for war and peace had changed almost beyond recognition. The collapse of distance connected individuals to global events.

With the development of the wireless telegraph, the sending and receiving of information became almost simultaneous. By the early part of the twentieth century, this technological innovation had become an essential part of a global network of communication that linked the cities of the world as well as land stations and ships at sea. Equally important was the development of the telephone. It too allowed for virtually instantaneous communication across vast distances. Years, months and days of waiting for a reply had been reduced to fractions of seconds, to a gap that was almost imperceptible. Together, these innovations in communication changed the relationship between time and movement across space: succession and duration were replaced by seeming simultaneity and instantaneity. The present was extended spatially to encircle the globe: it became a *global present*. This brought with it an inescapable anomaly. It opened up an unbridgeable gap between the speeds at which information on the one hand and physical bodies on the other could travel across space, a discrepancy ranging from the speed of light to the pace of walking. Today, this gap is routinely incorporated into the anticipations, plans and actions of members of industrial and industrialising societies, whether these involve travel, satellite television, the movement of troops and equipment to the scene of modern warfare or the interaction of people with their computers.

This capacity for global simultaneity thus transformed locally bounded social presents into a unity of local–global presents where the multitude of local differences is simultaneously and inseparably tied to the global present. The existence of such a global present, however, meant not merely that business meetings could take place between people in Bangkok, Bonn and Boston without any of the participants having to leave their desks. It meant also that events in one part of the world could have almost instantaneous effects on the other side of the globe and send ripples through the entire network. Moreover, these processes are largely beyond the control of those involved, since the combination of instantaneity of communication with simultaneity of networked relations no longer functions to the principles of mechanical interaction as characterised by the clock: linear sequences and durations are both extended and supplanted by instantaneously networked connections, one:one relations by those of one:many.

This shift in temporality has a grave effect on the capacity for political control and on the 'tried and tested' practices of socio-economic engineering. Stock markets are a case in point: excitement or problems in one financial centre have inescapable and often unpredictable effects on the rest. 'The new level of interconnectivity', as Poster (1990: 3) points out, 'heightens the fragility of social networks.' Moreover, these changes cannot be confined to action; they are equally relevant for theory. Thus, social scientists need to recognise that the enormous speed coupled with multiple, simultaneous, reflexive connections poses equal problems at the level of perception, understanding and expectation: it constitutes at all these levels an unconquered reality, a reality in need of reconceptualisation. Simultaneity, and instantaneity, the importance of timing, and variable, multiple and incompatible speeds have to become basic assumptions. As such, they have to be incorporated and take equal if not primary position among analyses of linear sequences, duration, and predictable cycles of return.

Not all moves towards global time, however, are of this complex new mode. Some are based on the much more conventional nineteenth century principles of rationalisation. These include the very important developments of standard time and world time, the rationalisation of clock and calendar time across the globe. Yet they too hold clues about the global–local connection. Standard time, for example, brought to an end the myriad of local times and dates traditionally used by the peoples of the world. Although it took many years for this standard time to get adopted on a world-wide basis, its establishment constituted the beginning of the *global day*, a day made up of the same disembedded twelve hours irrespective of context and number of daylight hours.

Closely associated with the globalisation of the day is the development of a globally synchronised, unified time. At 10.00 am on 1 July 1913 the Eiffel Tower transmitted the first time-signal across the globe. Wireless signals travelling at the speed of light displaced local times and established one time for all people on this earth: 1913 is thus the beginning of *world time*. Globalised time in the form of standard time and world time constitutes on essential material condition for the global network of communication in both information and transport. It underpins the planning and organisation of transnational business and global organisations. It is fundamental to an understanding of globalisation as 'all those processes by which the people of the world are incorporated into a single world society' (Albrow, 1990: 9).

This network of information, transport and rationalised time changed the pre-existing global networks of religion, politics and economics. As distances were reduced by the speed of communication so the personal, social, religious, political and economic horizons expanded. Giddens (1990) characterises those processes through the concepts of time-space distantiation and disembedding. Time-space distantiation, which he defines as 'the conditions under which time and space are organised so as to connect presence and absence' (1990: 14) is vastly expanded with electronic communication while disembedding processes, defined as 'the lifting out of social relations from local contexts of interaction and their restructuring across indefinite spans of time-space' (1990: 21), are further advanced by the creation of standard and world time.

World time, the universal day, and the global present, therefore, provided the framework for the development of a global perspective. Such a *global perspective* became a potential reality once the whole world came into reach, in principle at least, at the everyday level. When people can hear on the radio or watch on their TV screens events and tragedies occurring on the other side of the globe, when it takes no more than two days to reach any destination, when, at the press of a button, a personal donation can affect the livelihood or survival of people in another part of the world, then a global perspective becomes part of everyday reality: the famines of the African subcontinent, the massacre at Tiananmen Square, the burning oilfields in Kuwait, the plight of the civilians in the bitter war raging in former Yugoslavia, Norway's decision to lift the ban on hunting certain species of whale, contamination of the seas and shores from stricken oil tankers – all are inescapable, global events, subjects for all to see, pass judgement on and exert pressure. A globalised present inescapably extends responsibility beyond representatives of local and national governments to the individual: it connects the global with the local and personal. As McLuhan (1964/1973: 12) argued 30 years ago, 'it is no longer possible to adopt the aloof and dissociated role of the literate Westerner'. The perspective of the objective observer is no longer appropriate when 'the other' is absorbed into a global *we*.

The Loss of 'The Other'

> With nuclear and chemical contamination we experience the 'end of the other', the end of all our carefully cultivated opportunities for distancing ourselves and retreating behind this category. (Beck, 1992b: 109)

The global *we* has implications for the traditional social science understanding of nature and culture since the globalisation of information, time, and environmental problems destroys boundaries between peoples, species and their physical environments. In the late twentieth century this loss of boundaries and with it the loss of the other is increasingly difficult to ignore. First, there is the inescapable impact of industrial culture on nature which facilitates an 'acculturation' and 'socialisation' of nature (Giddens, 1991: 165). The 'invasion of the natural world by abstract systems', Giddens (1991: 224) argues, 'brings nature to an end as a domain external to human knowledge and involvement'. Recognition of this development enforces acceptance of the inappropriateness of an 'antithesis of nature and society' (Beck, 1992a: 80) as well as the conceptualisation of 'a world of objects existing outside the individual' (Elias, 1992: 28). Technology is centrally implicated in these totalising tendencies. This loss of other has serious consequences for a discipline focused on classes, groups and nation states. It poses conceptual and methodological difficulties for a science established on the irreducible distinction between nature and culture and used to excluding as irrelevant to its concerns the physical and artefactual environment (Benton, 1993).

The problem goes deeper still. Today it is not only traditional dualistic assumptions but even our language which turn out to be inappropriate, since to talk of nature *and* culture or of people's *relation to* their environment still implies that both the artefactual world and nature are *separate and separable* from contemporary cultural activity. Beck and Giddens both demonstrate the difficulty of such conceptualisations by pointing out the interpenetration of nature and culture through the 'internally reflexive systems of modernity' (Giddens, 1991: 165), and they consequently redefine nature as a historical product. 'At the end of the twentieth century', writes Beck (1992a: 80), 'nature is *neither* given *nor* ascribed, but has instead become a historical product, the interior furnishings of the civilisational world destroyed or endangered in the natural conditions of its reproduction.' Closely linked is Beck's suggestion that through the threat to people, animals, plants and the elements that sustain life, Western societies are re-experiencing their interdependence and oneness with nature. They are encountering a knowledge that has been progressively eroded with their Judaeo-Christian religious past and their classical Greek intellectual heritage. Today, fear and helplessness impress on us the realisation of interconnectedness.

> In the threat people have the experience that they breathe like plants, and live *from* water as the fish live *in* water. The toxic threat makes them sense that they participate with their bodies in things – 'a metabolic process with consciousness and morality' – and consequently, that they can be eroded like the stones and the trees in the acid rain. A community among Earth, plant, animal and human beings becomes visible, a *solidarity of living things*, that affects everyone and everything equally in the threat. (Beck, 1992a: 74, referring to the work of Schutz, 1984)

This particular loss of other is the historical product of Western industrial activity which imposes on an earth community of living and inanimate beings the unintended consequences of its actions. The resultant collective *we* forces the social sciences to reconceptualise their strict separation of nature and culture, 'West and the rest', observer and observed, individual and society, local and global realms.

A second and allied argument is presented by feminist scholars who identify the separation of nature and culture with patriarchal social structures and man's ambiguous relationship to nature; de Beauvoir's classic statement is illuminating here.

> Man seeks in woman the Other as Nature and as his fellow being. But we know what ambivalent feelings Nature inspires in man. He exploits her, but she crushes him, he is born of her and dies in her; she is the source of his being and the realm that he subjugates to his will; Nature is a vein of gross material in which the soul is imprisoned, and she is the supreme reality; she is contingence and Idea, the finite and the whole; she is what opposes the Spirit, and the Spirit itself. Now ally, now enemy, she appears as the dark chaos from whence life wells up, as this life itself, and as the over-yonder toward which life tends. Woman sums up Nature as Mother, Wife, and Idea; these forms now mingle and now conflict, and each of them wears a double visage. (de Beauvoir, 1968: 144)

From the twin perspective of eco-feminism our relationship to non-human nature and human liberation are being rethought from women's points of view. This opens the way to develop a new ethics for the usage of, and decision-making about, technology. In these analyses, the 'loss of other' covers not just other species and the universe around us but men and women of different races, different ages and different classes living not just in the present but also in the future. In their reconceptualisation of the human relationship to nature eco-feminists make visible the role of religion and science for our present alienation from living nature as well as for the contemporary efforts to reconstitute nature in artefactual and inanimate form. Moreover, they show the conflictual impulses that underpin the scientific quest for all-embracing knowledge and total control.

> The pursuit of scientific knowledge in our civilisation is beset by an emotional dilemma. In order to control Nature, we must know Nature. But just as we are seeking to know, there is a knowledge we fear. We are afraid to remember what we, in our bodies and in our feelings, still know, but what, in our fragmented, civilised consciousness we have been persuaded to forget. That, like the forests we destroy, or the rivers we try to tame, *we* are Nature. (Griffin, 1989: 10)

Eco-feminists thus present the interpenetration of nature and culture from a different angle of vision. In addition to the impact of culture on nature they impress on us the powerful interpenetration from the direction of nature. They stress cultural dependence on and continuity with nature: their analyses thus complement the historical bias with an emphasis on the biophysical dimension of human being and sensitise us to the earthly status of our being.

An explicit focus on social time supports and deepens those eco-feminist analyses on one hand and work that emphasises the acculturation of nature on the other. Since I have written in detail on this subject elsewhere (Adam, 1988, 1990, 1992a and b), however, I intend to provide here merely a brief summary of those arguments. Traditional approaches to social time define time in purely cultural terms and conceptualise it in distinction to natural time. As social construction, exclusive to the realm of culture, this approach to time mirrors the classical social science conceptualisation of culture as irreducibly separate from nature. Sociological and historical work on social time, however, demonstrates that culture and nature interpenetrate and implicate each other, that they cannot be separated into social and natural time (Luce, 1973; Kern, 1983; Young, 1988; Nowotny, 1989; Elias, 1992). From this research, social time emerges as a seemingly infinite complexity of times, a myriad of aspects, dimensions and meanings, all imbricated in the conditions of existence, in experience, action, transaction, language, social organisation and control, with each containing a multitude of times within. This research shows that social time, in the words of Elias (1992: 8), 'cannot be understood on the basis of a conception of the world split into "subject" and "object". Its preconditions are both physical processes, whether untouched or shaped by human beings, and people capable of mental synthesis, of seeing together what does not happen together.' The separation into natural and cultural time, Elias continues, is an illusion, the 'artificial product of an erroneous development within science'.

This complexity and mutual implication of times from the most physical to the extremely cultural is made visible when we do not predefine time as an exclusively social construction but seek its multiple expressions as they emerge from the breadth of academic disciplines. Such research highlights the intricate interpenetration and interdependence of multiple times which makes it meaningless to speak and write of 'natural' or 'social time' (Adam, 1990: 70–90, 104–26, 149–64). As living beings we *are* time, we *live* time, we *feel* and *perceive* time; as human beings we *know* and *reckon* time, as members of contemporary Western societies we have *externalised* time, *created it in machine form* and now *relate to this time as a resource* to be sold, allocated and controlled. This research shows human beings as activity-matter, as biological clocks that beat in off-beat to the rhythms of this earth, and as beings that get born, grow and die dynamically in interdependence with other systems of change-order. It suggests that we are locked into nature's silent pulse, that our activity and rest alternations, cyclical exchanges and transformations, seasonal and circadian sensitivities are tied to the rhythms of this earth and its solar system. 'We are connected', writes Griffin (1989: 17), 'not only by the fact of our dependency on this biosphere and our participation in one field of matter and energy, in which no boundary exists between my skin and the air and you, but also by what we know and what we feel.' The rhythmic cycles of matter and energy constitute living nature which *includes* human beings and our capacity to experience rhythms and to order impressions, actions and thoughts in a rhythmic fashion.

As human beings we thus express what is separated in academic disciplines: the different realms of being. As rhythmicity and synchronisation, growth and decay, 'natural time' is implicated in human being-becoming, experience and knowledge. As memory and anticipation it constitutes our temporal horizon. As physical measure and source for synchronisation it is integral to social organisation and the regulation of cultural activity. As externalised machine time it is linked to industrial production, to the role as abstract exchange value and to the social control of time. To recognise ourselves as having evolved and thus *being* and *creating* the times of nature allows for the humanly constructed and symbolised aspects of time to become one expression among others.

Once time is constituted symbolically, once it is acculturated, however, it is no longer reducible to its physiological expressions; it is no longer *merely* a sense datum. To have a past and future, to recognise it and to relate to it, entail a representational, symbolically based imagination. Endowed with this capacity, people do not just undergo their presents; they shape and reshape their presents as well as their pasts and futures. Moreover, symbolic meaning makes both the past and the future infinitely flexible. With it, we can not only look back, reflect, contemplate and modify the past to suit our purposes, we can also imagine past futures and future past. As retentions and protentions, memories and anticipations, the past and future are integral to active existence in the present and, from the standpoint of the present, neither past nor future are 'other'. To argue for the irreducibility of the symbolic realm, however, is not to suggest that we should or even could exclude from social science analyses the non-symbolic aspects of temporal existence, be they inorganic, physiological or artefactual: they too are integral to human existence and shape our collective future.

Not choice between 'natural' and 'cultural/symbolic time', therefore, but understanding of the complexity of these times and their multiple inter-relations is the task for social science analyses. Furthermore, even approaches that allow for the interpenetration of nature and culture are not sufficient on their own. Rather, focus on the temporality of being-becoming highlights the inseparability of physical, living and cultural existence, while focus on technologically constituted times emphasises a global present, the standardised day and world time affecting the peoples of this earth. Both document a loss of 'the other': the created time of industrial life demonstrates the global *we* among people whilst the time-generating temporality of life emphasises the global *one* and the intercon-nectedness of all living and non-living things. Both challenge the nature–culture dualism. Together, they enforce a re-vision in accordance with a time-sensitive ecological perspective where an understanding of impli-cation becomes of central importance.

Feminist analyses of Western approaches to human temporality bring to the fore aspects of the nature–culture relation not attended to elsewhere, aspects that shed new light on industrial societies' quest for mastery. They emphasise men's preoccupation with death – the denial of death and the explicit effort to control it – as central to the contemporary condition and the absolute separation of culture from nature (see Brodribb, 1992). 'Patriarchal civilisation', suggests King (1989: 21), 'is about the denial of men's mortality – of which women and nature are incessant reminders.'

Recognition of this link between death and culture is, of course, not new. It has been previously identified by social scientists, notably by Becker (1973). Feminist theorists, however, are highlighting features neglected in those earlier analyses, features that are particularly pertinent to understanding and conceptualising contemporary problems highlighted by work on high and post-modernity.

For writers such as Irigaray (1983) and O'Brien (1989), Heidegger's 'Being unto death' best signifies the masculine approach to time which is rejected by these scholars as an inappropriate perspective on human temporality and the human relationship to nature. It is renounced because it excludes birth and the *time-generating capacity* of procreation. To reintegrate birth as central to human temporality, they argue, is to find a new relationship to continuity. For women, birthing not only takes priority over dying; it is also conceived as a creation, an externalisation without alienation. O'Brien (1981: 32–3) contrasts this female principle of continuity with the masculine one of overcoming finitude by technological and abstract means such as art, artefacts, architecture and machines. Fixed in form and content, these (male) artefactual cultural means of continuity are discontinuous with the principles of life and ecological interconnectedness. Separated from genetic continuity which creates the bond between past and future generations, continuity through artefacts sits uneasily within the transient give and take, the birth and death of living processes. Moreover, in its emphasis on isolated parts it ignores interdependencies and promotes a feeling of control. This sense of control, however, is illusory since emphasis on death without birth signifies the ultimate loss of control. Finally, 'death without birth is not only abstract and unrealistic', as O'Brien (1989: 84) points out, 'but it signals an odd unwillingness to give meaning to species persistence as the material substructure of temporality'. Thus, the *generation* of time and not just its use, *organic continuity* and a tie with past and future generations not just abstract continuity through artefacts, *cooperation* with nature and not just its control, are integral to this feminist perspective on human temporality.

Closely allied to these analyses is the recognition that today's *Dasein* (existence, Being in the world) can be defined no longer in exclusively individual terms. In a world of globalised existence the individualised conception of being-becoming is no longer sufficient. It needs simultaneously to be understood in collective terms: once personal and locally constituted hazards become globalised, *Dasein* loses its individual character. No longer exclusively personal, it has to be reconceptualised to encompass the irreversible shift towards collective being-becoming where 'the other' becomes absorbed in 'the self' and shares communal presents and futures. This general shift towards implication, towards a loss of clear separation between the part and the whole, is intimately tied to a generalised loss of control; it is linked to the stark realisation that despite ever-increasing efforts towards total control we are facing continuously rising levels of uncertainty, a predestined yet unknowable future. Beyond this, it is tied to the realisation that we are not only implicated in but responsible for this collective future.

Blank Cheques to be Honoured

> One can say 'no' to techno-economic progress, but that will not change its course in any way. It is a blank cheque to be honoured – beyond agreement or refusal. (Beck, 1992b: 118)

'Mastery substitutes for morality', writes Giddens (1991: 202) about the technically competent, scientifically inspired social environment. But what is to be done when mastery fails, when scientists and politicians have lost control over their creations, when they are producing today an unknown and unknowable future for the global community of living beings now and hundreds of generations hence? What responses are needed from citizens, politicians and the scientific community? Does it still make sense, for example, to retain the aloof attitude of uninvolved observer and objective researcher in circumstances where people create and share common futures, where consequently blank cheques have to be honoured? Acid rain, ever-increasing levels of harmful radiation, the depletion of ozone, and global warming are *global futures for all*, irrespective of location, nationality and political persuasion. They are an in/visible, uncontrolled reality that permeates and surrounds our earth now and for the foreseeable future.

Nuclear material, for example, is located across the world on land, in the sea and in the air. It is stored deep in the earth, on the bottom of the oceans and it encircles the globe in satellites. Harnessed for both benign and hostile power it affects all life on earth with its potential threat. Its aftermaths may be immediate or take decades, even millennia, to reveal. As invisible hazards, such products of the industrial way of life pose a threat not merely to some distant future, they already permeate our present. In addition to the loss of an absolute distinction between parts and wholes, local and global phenomena, they negate the neat separation between past, present and future. Inclusive of the past, actions now create presents for future generations; they constitute posterity as well as the potential end in the present. Focus on time illuminates those contemporary phenomena and conditions from a number of angles: it offers insights with respect to the prevailing uncertainty and with reference to approaches to the future (see Adam 1993, 1995).

By definition scientific innovation creates unknowable futures. At the turn of the century, for example, it was not only beyond the imagination of ordinary people to think that a system of air transport would connect the cities of the world, that people could watch in their living rooms events that are taking place on the other side of the globe, and that astronauts would take photographs of the earth from outer space. Even scientists could not have predicted those developments, let alone the nuclear attack on

Hiroshima or the depletion of the ozone. Time is centrally implicated in the reasons for that unpredictability. First, true innovations are not predictable on the basis of past knowledge. Past experience, in other words, cannot serve as an indicator for effects of scientific developments. Past experience can only demonstrate the uncertainty of the future for societies wed to the industrial-scientific-technological way of life. Equally problematic are the conceptual models for understanding change, since these too tend to be based on the known past rather than an indeterminate, contingent, fundamentally uncertain future. Change is conceptualised as being caused by the past in a sequential, cumulative way. As such it allows for prediction and measurement on a before-and-after basis: decide on two cut-off points, compare the difference between those two static states and you have the measurement of change. In all these cases the future is irrelevant since the model of change, prediction and the measurement are based on a purely quantitative theory of time; none can encompass the process of creating the unknown, the very essence of scientific innovation and technological 'development'.

A second temporal clue to this unpredictability of the future relates to the scale of change precipitated by those scientific technologies and to the speed and intensity of changes achieved. Globalised hazards as well as cycles of innovation and obsolescence (which have shrunk from centuries to years and even months) create out-of-sync time-frames. They produce mismatches between the time-scales of invention, productivity and periods of waste and pollution, between benefits and hazards, between threats and ameliorative action, between contamination and visible effects, between effects and control (Adam, 1993). Consider the example of a nuclear power 'plant'. By the time such a 'plant' comes into operation it is already out of date: the enormity of the project and the complexity involved in designing and building such a product facilitate its immediate obsolescence. Furthermore, the difficulty and cost of decommissioning the 'plant' and the 'making safe' of its waste products stand in no relation to its productivity and cost-effectiveness (THORP, the British nuclear reprocessing plant at Sellafield is a prime example). With previous technologies, in contrast, the life of a product was always considered in positive terms and did not enter as a cost (even though it should have done). Lastly, safety of this technology cannot be tested but has to be 'established' on the basis of theory and mathematical calculation. The idea of proof takes on a new meaning when it is based not on the verification of observable 'facts' but on confirmation of speculative theories.

A third reason for this unpredictability and uncertainty is to be sought in assumptions underpinning technological designs. Classical science conceived of machines and scientific artefacts as isolated, bounded units and devised them according to their desired functions *without* cognizance of their multiple interrelations and effects. Despite their conception as isolated, bounded inventions, however, these technologies are *not* abstractable from their environment and their functions do *not* conform to simplistic input–output models. Rather, they have effects that become integrated into the complex web of ecological interconnections which in turn impact back on social life: Antarctic penguins suffer from severe lead poisoning, and benign inventions from fertilisers to water pipes turn out to have deadly consequences. Again, aspects of time are illuminating here. The machine time of those designed isolated systems, for example, is constituted on the basis of reversible time. It is based on a conception of time as motion; and motion in Newtonian physics can proceed forwards or backwards which means it is considered symmetrical with respect to past and future. This reversibility, explain Prigogine and Stengers (1984: 61), is a general mathematical property of dynamic equations: 'What one dynamic change has achieved, another change defined by velocity inversion can undo, and in this way exactly restore the original condition.' In real interactions with the environment, however, machine time becomes irreversible: there can be no unmoving, no unpolluting, no reabsorbing the heat and carbons back into the engine from which they emanated (Adam, 1990: 48–91, Prigogine and Stengers, 1984).

Finally, there is a problem with the extensive reliance on materialist/empiricist epistemologies. Our senses are no longer sufficient for dealing with information technologies operating at near the speed of light on the one hand and time-lags between polluting action and visible symptoms lasting for indefinite periods on the other. Moreover, instantaneity and simultaneity, as I pointed out in the first two sections of this chapter, fall outside the designs, plans and actions based on causal analyses and linear, quantitative time. Equally problematic for a materialist/empiricist epistemology are the multiple time-lags and latency periods, so typical of environmental hazards, which tend to mean that the links between causes and effects become invisible and thus are not amenable to scientific certainty and verification. Global warming is a case in point where the relationships between cause and observable effects are neither direct nor visible, where cause is not succeeded by consequence in a simple immediate, linear way. The issue of global warming, in other words, is replete with uncertainties and the prospect of an indeterminate and indeterminable future.

Despite or possibly because of this contemporary prevalence of uncertainty there is a general clamour for proof: insistence on certainty and 'proof' for situations characterised by indeterminacy, unpredictability and multiple time-lags is central to much of the political complacency about environmental problems. Nothing is done until the connections are proven. Yet, proof in the conventional sense of empirical science is impossible to achieve when there is no directly observable link between input and output, when the relation is not one:one but one:many, when we are dealing not with static, isolated phenomena but with interconnected, continuously changing, dynamic situations and parameters, when the reactions are latent and invisible for long periods of time, and when the effects are manifested not in the location of perpetration but disbursed over places both near and distant. This insistence on proof of the unprovable is bound to an exclusively materialist/empiricist conception of life in which the invisible, indeterminate and virtual are denied reality status. Such disregard for the im/material, however, creates a false sense of security. The threats we cannot see, touch, taste, smell or hear, the hazards that operate outside the time of human perception, are ignored at our peril. My argument here, however, takes a different direction from that of Beck when he suggests that

> Many of the newer risks completely escape human powers of direct perception. The focus is more and more on hazards which are neither visible nor perceptible to the victims; hazards that in some cases may not even take effect within the life-spans of those affected, but instead during those of their children; hazards in any case that require the 'sensory organs' of science – theories, experiments, measuring instruments – in order to become visible or interpretable as hazards at all. (Beck 1992a: 27)

I am proposing that the materialist/empiricist epistemology pervades not only our common sense understanding of reality but also the scientific conceptualisation. Science and materialism are inseparably linked and the 'less materialist' assumptions of quantum physics have by no means penetrated to the scientific community at large. That community remains tied to a materialism which can, as Harries-Jones (1989: 7) points out, 'explain some aspects of interaction and communication such as material pathways and adjustments of organisms and machines. But it remains an epistemology of objects without subjects, and of conceptual objects devoid of processes of perception, communication and reflexivity.' It remains impervious, in other words, to the im/materiality of the contemporary condition of its own making. Thus, the fierce materialism of science creates its own negation, conditions that cannot be grasped with the materialist principles of its inception.

It is not surprising, therefore, that the social sciences are silent on issues regarding the future. With their assumptions firmly grounded in the natural sciences and their knowledge fundamentally tied to the past, they cannot take account of a future for which the only certainty is its indeterminacy. As the temporal dimension least amenable to materialist/empiricist analyses the future clearly falls outside their boundaries of inquiry. Yet, when local actions have global effects on contemporaries and their descendants for many generations hence, and when policies of 'making the earth inhabitable' (Beck 1992a: 38) have become standard for industrial and industrialising countries alike, then objective descriptions of the present, of a decontextualised *now*, are as misplaced as they are impossible. When the future is constituted in and constitutive of the social present it is *de facto* the subject matter of the social sciences.

The question then becomes how we are to move from the traditional mode of social science analysis to an explicit cognisance of the future – not the prediction and planning of the future based on knowledge of the past but a mindfulness of the future, a regard for the future which takes responsibility for potential outcomes of present actions and incorporates this into present decisions and actions. Admittedly, taking account of posterity is a difficult task as long as understanding is grounded in Newtonian science and Cartesian philosophy: unknowable futures, the scale and speed of changes, the connectivity and interrelatedness of processes, time-lags and periods of invisibility, all these characteristics of the contemporary global condition elude the Enlightenment vision. The formidability of the task, however, must not detract from the fact that our creations today make us irrevocably responsible for their known and unknown effects. This means that taking account of the futures of successors is not just a laudable aim, but a moral imperative, not a choice but an inescapable duty. *Where mastery fails morals become an imperative.*

If, however, science has no basis upon which to ground values and morals and if it has no answers to the question 'How shall we live?' (Weber, 1919/1985: 143, 152–3; Giddens, 1991: 215, 223; Beck 1992a: 28; Szerszynski, this volume), then science has to be extended and transcended until such questions can be addressed head-on. It has to be surpassed by a system of knowledge and practice that can encompass the im/material and accept the personal as political, ecological and global. This requires far-reaching changes to the taken-for-granted scientific assumptions I have been discussing throughout this chapter: first, it necessitates moving our exclusive trust in materiality to include as central the invisible, virtual and spiritual. Second, it requires a shift in emphasis from the past to the future and from short- to long-term concerns that extend beyond personal interests and those of our immediate offspring to people and beings unknown. Third, it demands an extension beyond individualist, Eurocentric and humanist concerns to an interest in *all* of humanity, *all* of life and the cosmos, *all* time past and future, a move from exclusive to inclusive being. Fourth, it involves recognition that a present which extends into the long-term past and the even longer-term future is no longer bounded by our individual lifetime, that *Dasein* is no longer exclusively individual, that it has become social, public and global. Acknowledgement of the connectivity of being beyond species boundaries, however, has further consequences: it turns the universe from a community of objects which we can observe and control into a community of subjects of which we are an integral part. It transforms our world into a reality that is fundamentally implicated in all present actions and concerns. It shifts our position from outside observers to participants and it acknowledges that the relation between knower and known is not only interactive but *inseparable*. Finally, it recognises all entities in a process of multiple, simultaneous shaping, constructing and inventing so that it becomes meaningless to talk in terms of causes and effects. Moreover, as Ermarth (1992: 23) points out, 'once we begin to see our mental maneuvers as inventions, they become not "neutral" and "natural" ways of behaving but instead modes of exercising responsibility and freedom'. This important insight, though accepted in some quarters of social science, has yet to penetrate to a depth where its full implications will result in a reconceptualisation of the role of values and the social scientist's relation to the future.

Reflection

Once the potential outcome of cultural activity is characterized by globalisation and temporal uncertainty and once the time-lags of cause and effect span from nanoseconds to millennia, socio-political engineering and risk calculation become highly problematic social practices. They pose barriers to effective action because our capacity to predict and control is dependent on processes governed by sequential, linear causality. This means that instantaneity and non-linear, networked processes elude our conventional modes of domination: the simultaneity and instantaneity of global information and environmental effects render our planning, predicting and future-controlling efforts ineffective. Together with the global times associated with the rationalisation of time, communal *Dasein* poses problems for analyses that emphasise the absolute separation of parts and wholes, linear sequences and the measurement of duration: the rationalisation of clock time into global time has brought about its own negation. That is to say, the consequences of this development transcend the principles upon which it was built; namely, the rational development towards simultaneity and instantaneity is no longer graspable by traditional rational means, by causal, quantitative, objective analyses. Similarly, the vast expansion of control over nature brought with it an unprecedented loss of control at every level of socio-political action; it too is badly served by the dualistic separation of culture and nature, self and other, object and subject: the dualisms of traditional social theory are incompatible with *uncertainty and implication*.

If, however, our contemporary reality exhibits global features and is characterised by historically unprecedented characteristics, and if it is marked by a multitude of times that coexist in an embedded and mutually implicating way, then these features must be allowed to permeate not just our everyday, our economic and our political understanding but also our social science assumptions, our theories and our methods. They need to become an integral part of social science in the same way as the key features of the Enlightenment had penetrated the work of the founding fathers and their successors. Such a shift in conceptualisation is crucial if we are to respond more appropriately to the effects of globalisation and the environmental crisis of the late twentieth century.

A focus on time offers new perspectives on these emerging predicaments. It allows us to see previously disattended connections and brings to the surface some of the hidden discrepancies between the subject matter and its tools for analysis. It demonstrates that the principal assumptions of Enlightenment thought are out of sync with some key characteristics of contemporary material existence for which they are employed as conceptual tools. Globalised presents and futures, the construction of impervious posterities, time-spans and time-scales outside the range of human consciousness and perception, the loss of other without the loss of difference, the negation of rationality through the processes of rationalisation, the loss of mastery and the inescapability of morals, and the rise within the materialist culture of the invisible and immaterial, are all expressions of this inadequacy of nineteenth century enlightenment thought. Tradition fails us when the old bounded categories interpenetrate, when past, present and future, time and space, nature and culture, individual and society, local and global, observer and observed, process and structure, material and immaterial, abstraction and embeddedness, epistemology and ontology, implicate each other, when the One implies the whole and when thinking in terms of cause and effect is no longer appropriate.

The reflexive turn, therefore, needs to be extended to those implicit assumptions guiding social science analyses and understanding. Thus, if social science is to become adequate to its subject matter it needs to bring those taken-for-granted presuppositions to the fore and begin to see relations and connections; it needs to grasp their spiralling temporal unfolding, see multiple processes simultaneously, embrace contradictions and paradoxes, the unknowable and unknown. It needs to encompass the latent and the invisible, loosening the dependence on an exclusively materialist/empiricist epistemology. With the loss of clear boundaries, control and certainty, however, social scientists face not just analytical but moral problems; they have to readdress for their discipline the question about the role of values and political engagement. Time is fundamentally implicated in such a re-vision.

References

Adam, B. (1988) 'Social versus natural time: A traditional distinction re-examined'. In M. Young and T. Schuller (eds), *The Rhythms of Society*. London/New York: Routledge. pp. 198–226.

Adam, B. (1990) *Time and Social Theory*. Cambridge: Polity; Philadelphia: Temple University Press.

Adam, B. (1992a) 'Time and health implicated: A conceptual critique', in R. Frankenberg, (ed.) *Time, Health and Medicine*. London: Sage. pp. 153–64.

Adam, B. (1992b) 'Modern times: The technology connection and its implications for social theory', *Time & Society*, 1: 175–92.

Adam, B. (1993) 'Time and environmental crisis: An exploration with special reference to pollution', *Innovation in Social Science Research*, 6: 399–414.

Adam, B. (1995) *Timewatch: The Social Analysis of Time*. Cambridge: Polity; Williston, VT: Blackwell.

Albrow, M. (1990) 'Globalization, knowledge and society. Introduction', in M. Albrow and E. King (eds), *Globalization, Knowledge and Society*. London: Sage. pp. 3–13.

Beck, U. (1992a) *Risk Society; Towards a New Modernity*, trans. Mark Ritter. London: Sage.

Beck, U. (1992b) 'From industrial to risk society: Questions of survival, social structure and ecological enlightenment', *Theory, Culture and Society*, 9: 97–123.

Becker, E. (1973) *The Denial of Death*. New York: Free Press/Macmillan.

Benton, T. (1993) *Natural Relations: Ecology, Animal Rights and Social Injustice*. London: Verso.

Bohm, D. (1983) *Wholeness and the Implicate Order*. London: ARK.

Brodribb, S. (1992) 'The birth of time: Generation(s) and genealogy in Mary O'Brien and Luce Irigaray', *Time & Society*, 1: 257–70.

Capra, F. (1982) *The Turning Point: Science, Society, and the Rising Culture*. London: Wildwood House.

de Beauvoir, S. (1968) *The Second Sex*. New York: Random House.

Elias, N. (1992) *Time: An Essay*, trans. E. Jephcott. Oxford: Blackwell.

Ermarth, E.D. (1992) *Sequel to History: Postmodernism and the Crisis of Representational Time*. Princeton, NJ: Princeton University Press.

Giddens, A. (1990) *The Consequences of Modernity*. Cambridge: Polity.

Giddens, A. (1991) *Modernity and Self-Identity: Self and Society in the Late Modern Age*. Cambridge: Polity.

Goldsmith, E. (1992) *The Way: An Ecological World View*. London: Rider.

Griffin, S. (1989) 'Split culture', in J. Plant (ed.), *Healing the Wounds: The Promise of Eco-Feminism*. Philadelphia: New Society Publishers. pp. 7–17.

Hannerz, U. (1990) 'Cosmopolitans and locals in the world culture', in M. Featherstone (ed.), *Global Culture: Nationalism, Globalization and Modernity*. London: Sage. pp. 237–52.

Harries-Jones, P. (1989) 'Sustainable anthropology: Environmentalism, culture and applied epistemology'. Paper presented to ASA, Anthropology and the Future, Edinburgh.

Hekman, S.J. (1990) *Gender and Knowledge: Elements of a Postmodern Feminism*. Cambridge: Polity.

Hiley, B.J. and Peat, D.F. (1987) *Quantum Implications: Essays in Honour of David Bohm*. London: Routledge.

Irigaray, L. (1983) *L'oubli de l'air. Chez Martin Heidegger*. Paris: Les Éditions de Minuit.

Keohane, R.O. and Nye, J.S. Jr. (eds) (1971) *Transnational Relations and World Politics*. Cambridge, MA: Harvard University Press.

Kern, S. (1983) *The Culture of Time and Space 1880–1919*. London: Weidenfeld & Nicolson.

King, Y. (1989) 'The ecology of feminism and the feminism of ecology', in J. Plant (ed.), *Healing the Wounds: The Promise of Eco-Feminism*. Philadelphia: New Society Publishers. pp. 18–28.

Knorr-Cetina K. (1981) *The Manufacture of Knowledge: An Essay on the Constructivist and Contextual Nature of Science*. Oxford: Pergamon.

Latour, B. (1987) *Science in Action*. Milton Keynes: Open University Press.

Leggett, J. (ed.) (1990) *Global Warming: The Greenpeace Report*. Oxford: Oxford University Press.

Luce, G.G. (1973) *Body Time: The Natural Rhythms of the Body*. St Albans: Paladin.

McLuhan, M. (1964/1973) *Understanding Media*. London: Routledge, Kegan & Paul.

Nowotny, H. (1989) *Eigenzeit*. Frankfurt am Main: Suhrkamp.

O'Brien, M. (1981) *The Politics of Reproduction*. London: Routledge and Kegan Paul.

O'Brien, M. (1989) 'Resolute anticipation: Heidegger and Beckett', in *Reproducing the World: Essays in Feminist Theory*. Boulder, CO: Westview Press. pp. 83–101.

O'Malley, M. (1992a) 'Standard time, narrative film and American progressive politics', *Time & Society*, 1: 193–206.

O'Malley, M. (1992b) 'Time, work and task orientation: A critique of American historiography', *Time & Society*, 1: 341–58.

Poster, M. (1990) *The Mode of Information: Poststructuralism and Social Context*. Cambridge: Polity.

Prigogine, I. and Stengers, I. (1984) *Order out of Chaos: Man's New Dialogue with Nature*. London: Heinemann.

Rifkin, J. (1987) *Time Wars*. New York: Henry Holt.

Robertson, R. (1991) 'Social theory, cultural relativity and the problem of globality', in A. King (ed.), *Culture, Globalization and the World-System*. Basingstoke: Macmillan. pp. 69–90.

Romanyshyn, R.D. (1989) *Technology as Symptom and Dream*. Routledge: London.

Schutz, R. (1984) 'Okologische Aspekte einer naturphilosophischen Ethik'. Unpublished manuscript, Bamberg.

Sklair, L. (1991) *The Sociology of the Global System*. New York / London: Harvester Wheatsheaf.

Steier, F. (ed.) (1991) *Research and Reflexivity*. London: Sage.

Wajcman, J. (1991) *Feminism Confronts Technology*. Cambridge: Polity.

Wallerstein, I. (1974) *The Modern World-System*. New York: Academic Press.

Wallerstein, I. (1990) 'Culture as the ideological battleground of the modern world-system', in M. Featherstone (ed.), *Global Culture: Nationalism, Globalization and Modernity*. London: Sage. pp. 31–56.

Wallerstein, I. (1991) 'The national and the universal: Can there be such a thing as world culture?' in A. King (ed.), *Culture, Globalization and the World-System*. Basingstoke: Macmillan. pp. 91–106.

Weber, M. (1919/1985) 'Science as a vocation', in H.H. Gerth and C. Wright Mills (eds), *From Max Weber: Essays in Sociology*. London: Routledge and Kegan Paul. pp. 129–58.

Woolgar, S. (ed.) (1988) *Knowledge and Reflexivity: New Frontiers in the Sociology of Knowledge*. London: Sage.

Young, M. (1988) *The Metronomic Society: Natural Rhythms and Human Timetables*. London: Thames and Hudson.

4

ON KNOWING WHAT TO DO: ENVIRONMENTALISM AND THE MODERN PROBLEMATIC

Bronislaw Szerszynski

Once, it seems, we knew what to do.[1] Until the early modern period, knowing who we were, and in what practice we were engaged, told us all we needed to know about what we ought to do. That was the nature of moral experience then. There was no distinction, as today, between a world of facts and a world of values – the word 'moral' simply meant 'customary', and to know what a creature or object was was also to know its *telos*, its good. The world was finite, ordered and suffused with meaning and purpose. Our – humanity's – place and role in that world was central and secure.

Then came modernity. Rapid social, economic and cultural change both brought about and were sustained by this epochal shift. The stable, customary character of social relationships was eroded by a rapidly expanding capitalism. Religious authority was fragmented and pitted against itself by schism and sectarianism. Science displaced theology as the highest form of knowledge, and replaced the organic medieval cosmos with an infinite universe of matter in motion. The self-contained medieval world was thus shattered, and we were burdened with the necessity of creating our own meaning and our own projects in an infinite world which no longer told us anything about how we should live, all significance and purpose now being confined to the human mind.

But then came ecology. The shift towards systemic thought in the natural sciences problematised the view of ourselves as being somehow outside of nature – as being able to possess it, to use it and to control it. A growing technical and political awareness of the environmental costs of modern life undermined our Promethean confidence in progress and science. Cultural changes produced a heightened awareness of our profound alienation from nature, and its spiritual cost. In more and more spheres of human existence – politics, consumption, culture, and so on – there is occurring a displacement of the idea of the human subject as sovereign, and as subject to no normative claims which are not derived from what *we*, humans, want. In its place is emerging a recognition that all human projects have to take account of natural limits, and of the intrinsic value of non-human nature. Once again, the world does indeed tell us what to do. Once again an objective ethic has become possible – indeed imperative, since survival itself is contingent on our full embracing of it.

Now, this is a rather tendentious way to present what is, after all, a hugely complex story. Indeed, in many ways the rest of this chapter will serve to challenge parts of it, and to complexify the remainder. Nevertheless, it will serve as a useful starting point for the argument that follows. For what I will be suggesting is that the contemporary turn to nature has to be seen as merely the latest move – or indeed set of moves – within a peculiarly modern problematic, one concerned with how, in a universe stripped of meaning and purpose, we can still ground behaviour and judgements in something more than mere human self-assertion.

Such a claim might seem particularly counterintuitive at a time when the ecological agenda seems to be settling down into middle-aged reasonableness. You are right, an objector might concede, in suggesting that the environmental movement appears to have won the battle to persuade industrialists and governments of the reality of environmental threats. Environmentalist discourse is no longer a closed argot belonging to the margins of society, but a universalised, transferable language of the centre (Douglas and Wildavsky, 1982). We are all environmentalists now. But, they may well continue, this has changed the nature of environmentalist discourse itself. Whereas once environmentalism could indeed claim to burst the bounds of modern politics, with its wild cries of moral outrage, its development of alternative cosmologies, and its counter-systemic utopian experiments, now the coolness of reason and consensus reign. Environmentalism has only been admitted into the central institutions of society in so far as it has been translated into codes that such institutions understand – those of the economy, of planning, of redistribution. Such developments have tamed ecology, giving it little relevance to such questions about epochal shifts in the understanding of humanity's moral condition.

However, this chapter will argue that this account, too, fails to capture the whole story. Firstly, while the moderate, modernistic re-reading of ecology has arguably come to dominate public discourse under such rubrics as sustainable development and ecological modernisation (Eder, this volume; Hajer, this volume), nevertheless there are contexts, often all but invisible to the purview of 'Big Politics', within which quite different, romanticist discourses of environmentalism continue to have purchase and flourish. I will delineate two such discourses below, discourses that can clearly be seen as attempts to solve the modern problematic described in the opening paragraphs. But secondly, even the dominant modernist versions of environmentalism, and even when they take their most technocratic and seemingly morally neutral guises, can themselves be seen as crucially relying on certain moves within this problematic. Assuming as they do particular understandings of the human place in the world, and of the nature of human knowledge, both theoretical and practical, they can only fully be understood if located within the history of such understandings.

But the goal of this chapter goes beyond merely providing descriptions of ecological positions which are historically contextualised. What I want to try to show is how the main currents of environmentalist thought are, however counterintuitively, still circumscribed by the very modern problematic which they might at first seem to transcend. Because they continue to ask the question 'how can we know what to do?' in the terms laid down by modernist thought, however much they might give what appear to be very un-modernist answers to that question, they can never really escape the orbit of the modern problematic and reinscribe human projects within a wider ethical picture.

To do this I will examine the varieties of environmentalist thought under three headings – modernism, expressivism and traditionalism – to indicate their various affinities with the core moral and epistemological tradition of modernity, and with two romanticist traditions that arose in opposition to it. All three of these, in a sense, represent attempts to solve the modern problematic – to find meaning in a meaningless universe – and each has provided resources that have been taken up by environmentalism. But in each case the story is complicated by a further dynamic – that of formalisation. In late modernity each moral tradition has undergone a shift away from content to form – away from substantive moral prescriptions towards a mere description of the formal characteristics or prerequisites of moral knowledge. Environmentalism, too, has been caught up with this dynamic, as the idea of an infallible knowledge of nature which can tell us what to do starts to give way to a concern to specify the merely formal characteristics of an ecological society. And as environmentalism moves in this direction, any hope – however misplaced – that it could deliver us from the modern problematic, and tell us what to do, fades away.

But this is to run ahead of my narrative. First, it is necessary to give a brief account of how the modern ethical problematic came to be – to sketch the diremption of language and reality which underlies our peculiarly modern way of thinking about knowing what to do. Centrally implicated in this account will be the emergence of modern scientific thought. One reason for this lies in the prominent role played by science in environmentalism. But a more fundamental one lies in the fact that modern ethical thought has typically been predicated on the model of the relationship between language and truth which is embodied in scientific discourse. To put this another way, it is only in the context of the model of language epitomised in science that what I have been calling the modern ethical problematic could possibly have emerged. Once, it would have been literally unthinkable.

The Emergence of the Modern Problematic

Modern science, understood as a collective social practice which generates privileged representations of the world which have a universal validity, 'unaffected by changes in social context [and] culture' (Woolgar, 1988: 22), makes its appearance in sixteenth and seventeenth century Europe. Questions about the specificities of that emergence – why then and not earlier or later; why there and not elsewhere; and why in that particular form and not another – have been the subject of much academic controversy. However, one of the preconditions for the development of science seems to have been the emergence of an understanding of language, thought and truth which differed in several respects from the one which had dominated for at least several centuries.[2]

In the classical and medieval eras the dominant understanding of language had been *conjunctive* in nature, with no clear distinction between the world of thoughts and words and the world of things (Reiss, 1982: 59). Words and objects – and indeed objects and other objects – were thought to have natural sympathies and connections which bound them together in a timeless order (Thomas, 1973: 337–8). The world itself was thus treated as a text to be interpreted, rather than a purely material object outside language and to be described using that language. Such a world-view conceptualised knowledge, and how knowledge was acquired, in a very different way than did the scientific world-view that followed. On the one hand, because the human subject was seen as participating in the same symbolic order as whatever they might want to know about, it was unnecessary to look outside to the world of experience for knowledge. Experience in a sense just acted as a reminder of what one already knew. Knowledge was *commemorative*, being the remembrance of innate knowledge (Reiss, 1982: 60; e.g. Plato, 1956: 129–30). But, on the other hand, as this knowledge was not understood as 'the application of an abstract *human* schematization to the concrete', it did not have the appearance of 'clear and distinct' certainty characteristic of modern scientific knowledge. With analogy and metaphor dominating, rather than analysis and induction, classical and medieval forms of knowledge were typically characterised by endless glossing and reinterpretation (Reiss, 1982: 31, 72).

This view of language was gradually displaced between the twelfth and sixteenth centuries by a *disjunctive* one – disjunctive in the sense that it posited a distinction between a descriptive language on the one hand and an extra-discursive reality to which that language referred on the other. It is important not to overstate the abruptness of this change – there having been intimations of this modern view in the Platonic and Aristotelean inheritance of medieval philosophy – or the homogeneity of pre-modern understandings of language (Vickers, 1984). But nevertheless, through the late medieval nominalists such as William of Ockham, who explicitly rejected the idea of an essential conjuction between signs and referents, between words and objects, to the experimental science of Locke and

Boyle which had to assume such a distinction, there is a clear and strengthening notion of language as representational in nature (Reiss, 1982: 91–7; Vickers, 1984: 139).

But this growing conception of signs as arbitrary signifiers, and the resultant detaching of language and thought from any idea of a pre-existing symbolic harmony, did not result in any simple exorbitation of language, an excessive outpouring of abitrary signification.[3] In particular, modern science did not abandon the idea of a harmony between thought and the world, but just replaced the medieval idea that this harmony was *preordained* with the notion that thought and world could be brought into harmony with the use of a ' "neutral" and "objective" scientific discourse'.

So the modern problematic emerges as the question of how that harmony can be brought about. Now that language is seen as a human creation, rather than an aspect of reality itself, there is no automatic guarantee that language and reality coincide (cf. Horton, 1970: 157). This is what Steve Woolgar calls the 'problem of representation', which he poses in the form of a question: 'what grounds provide the warrant for the relationship betwen the objects of study and statements made about those objects?' (1988: 31). All disputants in subsequent debates about epistemology, including rationalists like Descartes and empiricists like Bacon, assume the distinction between language and an extra-linguistic reality, and simply disagree about how that gulf can be bridged.

But all the progenitors of modern science agreed on one thing – that what was crucial for the securing of truth in extra-discursive reality was the purification and formalisation of language. This kind of solution to the modern problematic, a solution which has been influential far beyond the bounds of science itself, is what I will refer to in the rest of this chapter as 'modernism'.[4] The advocates of this perspective argued that knowledge depends on 'Perspicuous words . . . purged from ambiguity', rather than 'Metaphors, and senselesse and ambiguous words', relying upon which 'is wandering amongst innumerable absurdities' (Hobbes, 1914: 22). Some, such as Francis Bacon and John Wilkins, broadly following the classical distinction of logic and rhetoric, distinguished the precise, artificial, universal language required for scientific work from the rhetoric of common speech, ethics and poetry. But others such as John Locke wanted all speech to be purified of ambiguity, part of a trend which at this time saw history and law, and even religion and morality, experiencing new fashions for 'plain speech' (Shapiro, 1983: 242–3). This purification and formalisation of language played a crucial role in the modernist idea of truth which science assumed, a regime whereby '[w]ord and thing are brought to coincide in the sense that the former is a completely adequate and transparent representation of the latter' (Reiss, 1982: 36).

But, as I have hinted above, to call modernism a response or solution to the modern problematic might be misleading. In a sense, the problem and solution emerged together, since it was the idea of knowledge that underpinned modern science – modernism – that created the gulf between language and reality – the modern problematic – in the first place. Before the solution, or at least its outline, had been articulated, even the existence of the problematic could hardly have been expressed. For Timothy Reiss this is most vividly captured in the image of Galileo's telescope, first captured in his *Sidereus Nuncis* of 1610, which, like modern discourse, at once constructs and promises to bridge the distance between the human subject and the material world (1982: 24–5). Once this distance has been opened up, even discourses which arise in reaction to modernism have to work within its terms.

It is this distance which modern ethical thought takes as its starting point. A number of related developments can be pointed to in the emergence of a modernist framework for ethics. Firstly, from the late eighteenth century morality started to be conceived as having its own cultural or discursive space, distinguished from those of theology, law and aesthetics (MacIntyre, 1985: 39). This was part of a general process whereby distinct cultural spheres such as science, politics and aesthetics, each governed by its own internal laws, became separated from each other. This process of differentiation was seen by Max Weber as intrinsic to the processes of rationalisation which produced many of the distinctive features of modern society (Weber, 1946; cf. Brubaker, 1984: 74–5).

Secondly, ethical language, like descriptive language, became disjunctive, in that a new conceptual gulf opened up between context and judgement, between description and prescription. Such a gulf is absent in the moral discourse of the pre-modern era. For example, in heroic societies such as Homeric Greece 'morality and social structure are one and the same', since 'the given rules which assign men their place in the social order and with it their identity also prescribe what they owe and what is owed to them and how they are to be treated and regarded if they fail and how they are to treat and regard others if those others fail' (MacIntyre, 1985: 123). With the modern era, by contrast, morality becomes conceived as being completely detached from the contingencies of historical placement in a given society or role. Whereas the pre-modern coincidence between language and the world which I have been describing as conjunctive brings with it a coincidence of the descriptive and the normative, in the late seventeenth and eighteenth centuries a gulf between fact and value, and between human language and moral realities, comes to seem self-evident, as ethical discourse takes on the disjunctive characteristics of modern science (Hume, 1972; MacIntyre, 1985: 77). Nature – now the world of 'facts' – no longer gives humanity any directions regarding our role in the world (Blumenberg, 1983: 137–43).[5]

Thirdly, ethics understood in this way – as radically autonomous, particularly from religion and from the customary bonds of feudal society, and as disjunctive in character – was seen as a form of universalisable knowledge governed by its own internal laws, and capable of rational, abstract formulation (MacIntyre, 1985: 39). Thus for John Locke, 'morality is capable of demonstration, as well as mathematics; since the precise real essence moral words stand for may be perfectly known, and so the congruity and incongruity of the things themselves be certainly discovered; in which consists perfect knowledge' (1964: 315). The main problem for ethics, mirroring that of science, thus becomes framed in terms of epistemology: how can the human subject, now conceived as an autonomous observer of reality, rather than as implicated in that reality, obtain moral knowledge? The task of moral philosophy, once again like that of science, thus becomes the creation of a neutral, universalisable, abstract moral language (such as utilitarianism or Kantianism) which will perfectly correspond with the morally salient features of any given situation.

But how can that correspondence be achieved? Stephen Crook has identified two related ways in which modern – and particularly modern*ist* – discourse is presented as possessing a privileged truth. The first is with regard to *origin* – where knowledge is seen to be grounded in an extra-discursive reality, or in a primary, indubitable knowledge such as Descartes's *cogito*, or in an epochal break which can insulate 'true' knowledge from a discrediting association with the 'false', such as that separating medieval superstition and modern science (1991: 174–8). The second is in terms of *autonomy*, whereby forms of knowledge are presented as proceeding according to laws internal to themselves, and as insulated from outside influences such as material interests or historical contingency (1991: 179–81).

Using these fundamentally modernist strategies, the ethical theorists of the modern era have attempted to bridge the modern gulf between language and reality, and thus to secure a way of knowing what to do. In all cases, supposedly universally applicable moral languages are grounded in a supposedly extra-discursive reality – utilitarianism in an abstract notion of human happiness, equivalent across different human contexts (Bentham, 1970; Mill, 1979); Kantianism in the rationality of the sovereign individual who, in the face of external authority and received custom, acts in 'bare conformity to universal law as such' (Kant, 1964: 70); rights-based theory in the very concept of 'human being', treated as a transcendent given rather than as culturally contingent (for example Dworkin, 1978; Gewirth, 1978); intuitionism in objective but non-natural properties of situations and actions the perception of which provides self-evident moral truths which neither need nor are capable of further justification (Moore, 1903); and emotivism in supposedly non-discursive preferences and attitudes (Stevenson, 1944).

But claims of an 'origin' for ethical judgements which is in any useful sense outside the flow of culture and discourse remain deeply problematic. MacIntyre, for example, criticises utilitarianism on the basis that it cannot secure this origin – that 'the notion of human happiness is not a unitary, simple notion and cannot provide us with a criterion for making our key choices' (1985: 63–4). Happiness is not an stable, extra-discursive reality which can be used to ground and privilege moral statements. Similar points can be made about attitudes (Potter and Wetherell, 1987), and values

(Crook, 1991: 193), when seen as solid, non-accountable attributes of individuals. Just as the sociology of science has shown that it is impossible to isolate scientific truth claims from cultural and social factors such as theoretical and pre-theoretical commitments, institutional cultures, and the need to negotiate knowledge claims (for example Gilbert and Mulkay, 1984), the putative entities used to ground modern ethical discourse, entities such as 'happiness', 'reason' and 'rights', cannot be isolated from the rhetorical use of language, whereby identities and social relationships are continuously formed and dissolved in the flow of culture.

It is within the context of this modern problematic that ecology makes its appearance. As we have seen, modernity, with its radical disjunction between language and the world, assumes a representational view of language as referring, with more or less accuracy, to an extra-discursive reality. With word and world no longer caught up in an overarching symbolic order, the nature of the world no longer tells us directly what to do, and ethics becomes a purely human project. Nevertheless, we *can* still know what to do, and can thus avoid the nihilism of unconditional freedom, if only we can find an autonomous, purified ethical language, governed strictly by laws internal to itself, and grounded in an extra-discursive reality. Language and reality can thus be brought into corre-spondence, if not coincidence, and we can once more know what to do.

But all such attempts fail, and this for two related reasons. Firstly, the notion of a reality *beyond* language, to which that language refers, is a product of our particular modern understanding of language, and is thus not available as something in which language can itself be grounded. Secondly, the ideal of a formalised language completely abstracted from the social and the cultural is itself impossible to achieve. Ecological thought seems to step into this breach by providing a quite different kind of solution to the problem of knowing what to do. Instead of the impossible project of securing discourse's transparency to moral realities through its purification and formalisation, ethics becomes a recognition of our always already implicatedness in the world. Instead of accepting the gulf between fact and value that accompanies the modern, disjunctive view of language, it insists that nature does indeed tell us what to do. Ethics is no longer merely a human project, concerned with the internal, formal consistency of ethical codes, but is the recognition of laws inscribed within nature itself.

But however much this seems like a radical departure from contempor-ary ethical thought, ecology nevertheless remains firmly implicated within the modern problematic. However much ecology is to be welcomed for its recognition of human limitations and for its refusal of the essentially gnostic notion that we do not really belong in this world, it cannot, after all, tell us what to do. A crucial reason for this is ecology's frequent reliance on the unattainable modernist notion of truth as perfect corre-spondence with reality. But this is not the whole story that can be told here. For the 'strong' modernism which privileges scientific and moral truth through correspondence with an extra-discursive reality has itself been joined over the last century by an attenuated, formalised *neo-modernism* which tries to retain modernism's idea of privileged knowledge while abandoning the idea of truth as perfect correspondence. As we shall see in the next section, in as far as environmentalist thought has taken this neo-modernist route in order to salvage modernism's promise of telling us what to do, it has led itself back to the very nihilistic condition from which it seemed to offer deliverance.

Modernism and Neo-modernism in Ecological Thought

The environmental movement, while in many ways hostile to modern science, has at the same time depended for much its social authority on scientific, seemingly morally neutral, claims about the physical threats produced by present social trajectories (Yearley, 1991). Of course, there is a certain irony in this, but one not without its precursors, since critics of modern society have frequently but unwittingly used the language and categories of the very thing that they were trying to criticise – crudely, accusing society of being, not *too* rational, but not rational *enough* (Reiss, 1982: 37).[6] Modernist environmentalism, in its criticism of the instrumentalism of modern society, is in similar fashion drawn back into the orbit of instrumental reason, criticising modern societies for being insufficiently rational in ignoring the ecological restraints on social action.

For example, discussions of a possible ecological society in harmony with nature have typically assumed the very modernist idea of scientific knowledge as perfect, timeless correspondence with reality. Barry Commoner's famous list of four ecological laws – 'everything is connected to everything else', 'everything must go somewhere', 'nature knows best', and 'there is no such thing as a free lunch' – was a relatively early example of this ultimately technocratic environmentalism, assuming as it did that scientific experts could tell us how to live with nature (Commoner, 1971: 33, 39, 41, 45). For Commoner, director of the Centre for the Study of Natural Systems at Washington University in St. Louis, these are natural laws of which any rational social order would take account. Science can and should 'guide, by objective knowledge, human interactions with the rest of nature' (Commoner, 1963: 128). Ecological survival necessitates not the abandonment of technology, but that 'technology be derived from a scientific analysis that is appropriate to the natural world on which technology intrudes' (Commoner, 1971: 189). Such a rational order, he felt, must necessarily be centrally planned, since the tragic link between production and pollution can only be severed by implementing a social system where production is governed 'according to the rational use-value of the final product rather than by the value added in the course of production' (Commoner, 1971: 287). Such a system would involve the 'rational ideal' of subjecting economics and production to the 'ecological system' and the implementation of a 'rational, thermodynamically sound energy system' (Commoner, 1976: 258; Rubin, 1989: 41). If we were to replace the present, irrational, capitalist economic system by a rational, centrally planned social order, guided by our scientific knowledge of natural systems, we could live in harmony with nature (Commoner, 1971: 287; 1976: 258; cf. Rubin, 1989: 41).

The assumption that scientific knowledge represents a perfect reflection of natural reality and can provide a reliable basis for action is implied by all such modernist aspirations to manage nature, from the computer models of the Club of Rome in the early 1970s to the technocratically conceived sustainable development of the 1990s (Meadows et al., 1972; Worster, 1993; see also Jamison, this volume). But, as we shall see below, even less technocratic attempts to live in harmony with nature can still have the same modernist assumptions at heart – that 'nature' is determinable and describable without reference to human projects and languages, and can thus be something which can tell us what to do. The claim to be able to ground scientific knowledge in a stable extra-discursive nature vitiates all such projects, and simply obscures the political nature of decisions about how we should live (Grove-White and Szerszynski, 1992: 290). Our knowledge of the world is always shaped by pre-theoretical social and cultural commitments, so there is no stable, asocial nature which can tell us what to do (Douglas, 1975; Kwa, 1987).

Of course, there has been no little acknowledgement of the problematic nature of naive modernism amongst those who would otherwise defend many of the features of Enlightenment thought. This is where the story of modernism becomes more complex than is usually recognised in the discussion of our contemporary environmental predicament, because in many respects strong modernism has been overtaken as a model of knowledge by a more qualified version. This weak or *neo*-modernism acknowledges that all forms of knowledge, either empirical or moral, are human and imperfect, but nevertheless defends the idea of a dynamic of progress. Below I will be suggesting that this rather different response to the modern problematic has also found its place in environmentalist thought, but first I want briefly to spell out this distinctive move in the story.

Although I have described a radical shift as having taken place at the end of the medieval era in our understanding of knowledge and truth, one important aspect of that understanding did in fact remain fairly constant from classical times right up to the nineteenth century – the idea that true knowledge is timeless and universal. The only change which the emergence of strong modernism made to this conception was in conceiving of it in a new and particular way – as the situation where language corresponds perfectly with reality (Schnädelbach, 1984: 81–2).

Neo-modernism, by contrast, breaks with this tradition by seeing the idea of static, complete knowledge merely as a determining utopian ideal, rather than as something which could ever actually come about (cf. Mannheim, 1960: 197). History, process and progress are not just accidental and temporary features of the pursuit of knowledge, as if due to an ignorance about to be vanquished, but intrinsic to it. The focus is thus shifted firmly away from a timeless extra-discursive order of facts and onto the procedure for obtaining knowledge itself. In our terms, the truthfulness of knowledge for neo-modernism consists less in its derivation from and correspondence to an extra-discursive *origin* (though such a notion is often retained in attenuated form), and more in the self-legislating, formalistic *autonomy* of the procedure by which it is obtained.

Something of the distinctiveness of this contrast can be indicated by tracing how views about the progress of knowledge changed from Bacon, through Hegel, to the twentieth century. For Bacon the imperfections and contradictions of present knowledge were simply a temporary difficulty, since, given time and a strict adherence to the correct 'method', human knowledge would eventually take on the static qualities of a complete knowledge corresponding to nature (Reiss, 1982: 213, 360). Hegel, too, saw history as an inevitable movement towards the eventual perfect embodiment of reason and truth in human society. But in Hegel there had already been a shift towards conceiving the advancement of knowledge as intrinsically historical (Schnädelbach, 1984: 89). For Hegel, truth emerged from the very (for him dialectical) historical process itself, so that 'philosophy too is its own time comprehended in thoughts' (Hegel, 1942: 11).

This move was taken further as the nineteenth century progressed, with science being conceived less and less as an ultimately static system of knowledge, and more and more as an endless process governed by internal rules. Crucial in this formulation was the Kantian notion, increasingly taken up in the nineteenth century, that the categories by which we understand the world derive not from that world itself, but from the human mind, and thus were the preconditions, rather than the outcome, of knowledge. But whereas Kant had conceived this in static terms, in the nineteenth century this was temporalised, with a shift of emphasis away from systematisation to innovation, and thus from the scholar to the researcher. Increasing emphasis was laid on the procedural and institutional conditions of scientific knowledge, so that what made knowledge 'scientific' was its relationship to such *conditions* rather than its content as such (Schnädelbach, 1984: 81–90). Science was increasingly seen not as an unmediated reflection of reality – the idea of a static, perfect knowledge having been deferred into the infinite future as a merely regulative idea – but as a fallible, human knowledge whose progressive character can be secured by an adherence to the correct method (cf. Popper, 1968).

But accounts of ethics and politics, too, have been developed which fit into this neo-modernist pattern. Like neo-modernist accounts of scientific knowledge, they try to privilege themselves more in terms of autonomy than of origin, focusing as they do on the procedural conditions for valid judgements rather than on the idea of an extra-discursive reality to which such judgements must correspond. Of course, the Kantian turn in ethical thought had already focused attention on the *form* of valid ethical judgements – on features such as universalisability – but had still retained the idea that getting the form right would itself lead to a substantive ethical *content* (Benhabib, 1992: 12, 25). But with neo-modernism this already demoted concern for content is further attenuated, and the historical and social locatedness of moral judgement seen as intrinsic rather than accidental. Such accounts thus typically represent ethico-political knowledge as possible but never certain; give formal accounts of the procedures for settling moral and political disputes rather than attempt to settle such disputes themselves; and represent morality as historically conditioned, yet progressive.

It is here that our narrative converges once again with that of environmentalism, where the neo-modernist conception of truth, too, has found purchase. Scepticism about the possibility of the certain knowledge of nature which would be needed in order for the centralised state to bring about a planned, ecological society has led for some ecological thinkers to an emphasis on the formal, procedural conditions out of which such knowledge – fallible yet still privileged – can emerge. Instead of concentrating on an identifiable desirable end state as something which can be achieved through planning and management, neo-modernist environmentalism focuses on setting up a dynamic, which, it is assumed, will lead in a desirable – if as yet unknown – direction.

Let me clarify what I mean here. It is possible to argue that knowing what to do can only be arrived at through a dialogical process of discussion and debate without being a neo-modernist. One can take the position that there *is* a 'good', that there *are* universally valid moral prescriptions, but also that argument and debate happen to be the best way to discover them (O'Neill, 1993: 92–5). Such a position is entirely compatible with modernist notions of static, timeless truth. But once one moves further down the route of formalisation, so that the process of debate is intrinsically, rather than simply accidentally, necessary for valid judgements to be arrived at, and the 'good' is simply whatever is the outcome of the process, rather than pre-existing and being discovered by that process, we are firmly within the territory of neo-modernism.

Formalisation, then, is not a once-and-for-all process – it is a matter of degree; neither is it a deterministic process which has to take a particular pattern. But, I want to suggest, to the extent that content gives way to form, modernism converges with the very nihilistic world-view to which I presented it as an attempted solution. This will become clear if we consider a number of different contributions to ecological thought in order of their abandonment of content in favour of form and process.

My first example draws on those writers defending a 'deliberative democracy' approach to the environment (Dryzek, 1992; cf. Miller, 1992). To determine what we should do, from such a perspective, we need new political forums, freedom of information and open, rational debate. In a modern, democratic society, such neo-modernists would say, knowing what to do can never arise from the exercise of merely technical expertise –

or, for that matter, from the purified intuitions of deep ecologists – but only from discussion between real, situated actors according to shared rules of sound argument. This is a neo-modernist view because it is procedural in nature, grounding the validity of knowledge claims not in their content but in their purely formal characteristics – that they are the unforced product of open and fair discussion. The outcome is regarded as valid simply because it *is* the outcome.

In this respect, such a view follows Habermas, whose defence of a procedural, discourse ethics attempts to avoid the naive universalisms of strong modernism. But at the same time, it also follows Habermas in its conviction that there are criteria for judging the validity of knowledge claims implicit in the very notion of communication. Just as in neo-modernist understandings of science the idea of timeless, static truth operates only as a determining, unrealisable ideal, so for Habermas the 'ideal-speech-situation' of 'undistorted communication' is a determining ideal which is implied by the very competences necessary for communicative action, and thus can underwrite the possibility of unforced consensus (Habermas, 1979: 64). Whatever result emerges from the debate, for this position, ideally does so not because of its rhetorical power but because of its intrinsic rationality.

For this kind of neo-modernist environmentalism, the shift away from content and towards form manifests as an emphasis on procedures and institutions. Rather than attempting to articulate concrete prescriptions of how we should live with nature, it concerns itself with setting up the social conditions for rational public debate. The environmental movement, for example, is valued by Habermas not because of any substantive ethic of nature it might promote (indeed he denies the possibility of such an ethic (Habermas, 1982: 245)), but because of its defence of such communicative spaces within society from colonisation by the instrumental reason of economics and power politics (Habermas, 1981).

An analogous neo-modernist position is put forward by defenders of what might be broadly called a free market approach to the environment (Anderson and Leal, 1991; Bennett and Block, 1991). Like the proponents of deliberative democracy they insist on a procedural and interactive method of knowing what to do, but in this case this occurs through the medium of market exchange rather than that of rational debate. Following Hayek, they insist that in a pluralistic society the role of the state is not to impose a determinate ethical vision, but simply to maintain the framework for the operation of market mechanisms. In particular, they argue that only the creation of tradeable property rights in environmental 'goods' and 'bads' – involving the privatisation of all commons, and tradeable pollution permits – will solve the environmental crisis (for a summary, see Eckersley, 1993).

Despite their clear political differences, the deliberative-democracy and free market environmentalists occupy a very similar position in the neo-modernist spectrum. Both of them reject the idea of a substantive ethics or technics of nature being arrived at through monological deliberation and 'imposed' on society. For both, the good for society can only be the outcome of an actual interactive process governed by abstract, formal rules. For both, the outcome is good simply *because* it is the outcome of such a process. But also, for both, that process – whether rational debate or market exchange – has an innate rationality that, in principle, will guarantee that the outcome really *is* the best outcome – the good. Both deliberative-democracy and free market environmentalism, then, retain the ghostly presence of a 'real' to which normative statements can and should correspond, even if that 'real' can never be timelessly captured.

Ulrich Beck's notion of 'reflexive modernisation' represents a further point on the retreat from content into form (Beck, this volume). Again, like the other positions considered above, Beck's is a neo-modernist environmentalism in that, instead of advancing a substantive ethics of the environment, it simply specifies the formal social conditions for the solution of the environmental crisis – in this case, reflexive societal self-critique. In a formulation that recalls Habermas's description of his own 'communicative action', Beck's reflexive modernisation is presented as a deepening of the modern project – a radicalisation and generalisation of the principle of doubt immanent in the modernisation process to all dogmatic knowledge claims (Beck, 1992: 166, 223; 1994: 33).

However, Beck does not seem to share Habermas's faith in the idea that reasoned debate (form) can lead us to 'truth' (content), however histori-cally situated. Reflexive modernisation guarantees not that the future is better, or worse, but only that it is different (Beck, this volume, p. 40). Conflicts over risk-definitions, for example, are not settleable *de jure*, by any recourse to objectivity or rationality (pp. 36–7), but only *de facto*, by the reflex of a society riven by epistemic conflicts (pp. 32–3). Beck rejects critical theories of society such as that of Habermas – theories which impose the content of their ethico-political standards onto society in order to make their critiques – in favour of a purely formal account of a society divided by 'sectional rationalities' (p. 33). In so far as reflexivity *is* about 'reflection', rather than just reflex, it is the self-consciousness of a humanity becoming aware of the radical contingency of all knowledge claims. While surely correct in its rejection of strong modernist claims to an 'objective' knowledge of nature which can tell us what to do, Beck's position reveals its capture within the modern problematic in its subsequent all but abandonment of the 'real' as a constraint on human self-definition.

This move is made more explicit in Maarten Hajer's 'cultural politics' version of environmentalism (Hajer, this volume; cf. Thompson et al., 1990). Like the deliberative-democracy environmentalism discussed above it abandons the idea of a single, substantive ethic of nature in favour of a pluralist emphasis on the democratic process itself (pp. 259–60). But by abandoning Habermas's faith in the rationality of open debate in favour of a more agonistic vision of cultural competition between competing dis-courses, it also abandons the last, ghostly vestige of a 'real' which underwrote Habermas's defence of the idea of progress. Here the content of a determinate nature which can act as the *origin* of knowledge has vanished completely, even as the infinitely deferred goal of knowledge. All we can have are 'story-lines' about nature (p. 256). All we are left with is the mere *autonomy* of humanity's task, once stripped of its modernist illusions, of cultural self-definition. As Hajer puts it, the debate should not be on 'the protection of nature but . . . on the choice of what sort of nature and society we want' (p. 259).

Neo-modernism thus comes up against the limits of the modern problematic. Once the project of securing a perfect correspondence between language and the world is abandoned in favour of the pure autonomy of discourse, then modernism becomes a formalisation project. Formalis-ation, once simply the means whereby such correspondence could be guaranteed, is made an end in itself. And, as we can see, the further down this route one goes, and the more that content drops away in favour of pure form, the closer one gets back to what I have presented as the world-picture at the heart of the modern problematic – that of a lonely humanity faced with the task of pure self-assertion in a meaningless world which no longer tells them/us what to do.

What has happened here? How has modernism, apparently humanity's best hand, failed to trump the hollow, nihilistic picture of sheer self-assertion in an alien world? How has the path which seemed to lead so bravely and resolutely away from such a fate led us straight back into its clutches? And how has ecology's attempt to definitively relocate the human story within a larger picture of ethical obligation been vitiated by its having followed this path? To answer this it is necessary to return to the starting point of my narrative, and to retrace our steps. As I suggested at the beginning of this chapter, the transition from the late middle ages to the early modern era consisted, in part, of a gradual but radical shift in ideas about the nature of knowledge. A gulf opened up between language, and a world understood as outside that language, to which it referred. The main significance of this for our purposes is the implications of such a shift for the human moral predicament. Instead of understanding ourselves as existing within a cosmos, full of a meaning which could be glossed and interpreted, and instead of understanding human projects as taking place within the context of a world full of purpose and significance, we passed into an era where our implied condition was the 'secular' one – yet one with its own hidden theology – of a self-identical humanity, burdened with the task of self-definition and self-legislation in a world indifferent to our concerns (Blumenberg, 1983; Funkenstein, 1986; Milbank, 1990).

Modernism, while implicated in the very origins and dominance of this way of understanding the world, can be seen as presenting an escape route from this fate. It offered – paradigmatically through science but also, for example, through modern ethics – the possibility of a reconnection to the 'real', not by a return to the conjunctive, pre-modern experience of the world, but by showing how language could be brought to refer accurately to the 'real' through the former's purification and formalisation. This promise of reconnection seemed to offer an escape from the nihilistic void by once again – although in distinctively modern fashion – allowing us to know what to do. But as this modern project has progressed there has been a gradual abandonment of the hope that the condition of perfect correspondence between language and the world can be achieved. Increasingly, there has been a 'leaning' onto the 'autonomy' pole of modernist epistemology, a shift away from content and towards form. Initially, this was to suggest that the formalisation of discourse and inquiry, while never able to arrive at static, timeless truth, nevertheless could guarantee a progressive dynamic towards that ideal. The content of knowledge was seen as conditional, and as historically conditioned, but the notion of a language which corresponded to the 'real' still stood as the final goal of the formalisation project. Content may have been becoming wholly determined by form – so that scientific or moral truth was whatever was produced by following the formal procedures appropriate to that activity – but at least content still *mattered*, because of the conviction that the formalisation project would lead us ever closer to perfect correspondence.

But, as the modern project has formalised even further, and the last ghostly wraith of a real – or at least a real which can ever be known – has dropped away, we are increasingly left with the impression that our path has led us back, after all, to where we came from. This was surely all but inevitable once the modern disjunctive understanding of the world was accepted. Once the notion of language as reference drives apart language and the world, we seem to be faced with an either–or. Either we believe that language can be made definitively to correspond to the world – that the purification and formalisation of language can lead us to a determinate content – or we believe that it can't. The first option insists that language can, ultimately, be fixed in a static relation to the world; the second abandons such hope – and all we are left with is the 'post-modern' free play of language (Ferrell, 1991: 8–9). So, in fact, the modernist path diverges. Origin (content) and autonomy (form) cannot be held together in the way that it was hoped. For ecology, along one fork lies a technocracy that relies for its legitimacy on a supression of its own contingency; along the other lies the nihilism of a humanity freely creating and asserting its own meanings in a world which has none of its own. On both routes we are shadowed by the spectre of the nihilistic void which modernism at once assumes and suppresses, and from which neither route can ultimately deliver us.

But perhaps this bleak choice is only forced on us because of the path we have taken to try to solve the modern problematic. Are there not other paths that ecology can take, paths that do in fact lead us out of the orbit of that problematic? In the following section I will look at another set of positions within ecological thought, positions which can broadly be characterised as forms of *romanticism*, in order to assess their ability to overcome the modern problematic. Like neo-modernism, they can be seen as reactions to the problems encountered by naively modernist notions of knowledge as the perfect reflection of reality. But whereas neo-modernism reacted to those problems by *accentuating* the gulf between language and reality – so that all propositional knowledge became fallible and historically situated – romanticism reacted by *denying* that gulf – attempting to resituate consciousness within the world itself.

Romantic Ecology: Expressive and Traditionalist

In many ways the oft-noted romanticist strands within contemporary environmentalism might seem a far more promising place to look for an escape from the modern problematic (cf. Harvey, 1993: 15–19, 29–31). Romanticism offers a very different picture of the world and the human place in it to that of modernism. It sees nature as filled with meaning and value, rather than as a neutral backdrop for human projects. It has an emphasis on ethical content, rather than on the formalisation of ethical language. It focuses not on propositional knowledge but on immediate experience – the fusion of knower and known. Surely here, if anywhere, we can find an overcoming of the alienated consciousness that lies at the heart of the modern problematic. Perhaps it is through *this* kind of ecology that we can know what to do.

In fact, of course, romanticism has taken many forms, not least within ecological thought. Here I want to consider two main variants – expressivism and traditionalism. By 'expressivism' I mean to refer to the notion that individuals can reconnect themselves with nature through the recovery of an authentic state of being, one that has been lost due to the artificiality of social existence. This individualistic romanticism is one that runs from Rousseau, through Wordsworth and the American Transcendentals, and manifests itself in contemporary environmentalism in the form of movements such as deep ecology, radical ecofeminism, bioregionalism and neo-primitivism. By 'traditionalism', in contrast, I refer to the belief that unalienated existence is only possible through re-embedding in a concrete community and substantive tradition. This more collectivist romanticism can be found in aspects of Hegel's thought, in the medievalist school of nineteenth century English social criticism that included Carlyle, Ruskin and Morris, and in 'new communitarians' such as MacIntyre, Walzer and Etzioni. In contemporary environmentalism, it manifests in the conviction that vernacular communities, living through traditional forms of knowledge, are by their nature ecologically benign.

Let us consider both of these in turn. Expressivism has at its core the notion of a 'true self', an authentic mode of being from which human beings have been alienated by civilised existence. Thus, whereas modernism offers a narrative of progress, expressivism replaces this with one of decline – a 'fall' from a natural, pre-social existence, in harmony with a providential nature, into our current, artificial existence. But, through rediscovering our natural, true selves – and thus our interconnectedness with everything else – we can overcome this alienation from others and from the natural world. Thus, for expressivism, knowing what to do starts not with propositional knowledge, but with the recovery of unmediated experience. It is only if we purify our consciousness of the alienating influences of artificial social existence that right behaviour will follow. This is not so much a narrative of saving nature but of nature saving us, for only if we abandon modernist notions of control and domination and 'let Being be' (Steiner, 1978: 71) can we know what to do.

Perhaps the most developed version of expressivist environmentalism is that of deep ecology, first outlined in a 1972 lecture by the Norwegian philosopher Arne Naess (Naess, 1973). His ideas have since been widely taken up and developed, particularly by wilderness protection activists in the midwestern United States and in Australia, and by those working in the area of environmental education (such as Seed et al., 1988). Bill Devall and George Sessions describe the two 'ultimate norms' of deep ecology as (i) a Self-realisation (note the capitalisation) which 'goes beyond the modern Western self' by identifying with the rest of nature, and (ii) a biocentric egalitarianism which exhorts us, 'insofar as we perceive things as individual organisms or entities, . . . to respect all human and non-human individuals in their own right as parts of the whole' (Devall and Sessions, 1985: 66–8). This dominant interpretation of deep ecology has been called a 'state of being' as opposed to a 'code of conduct' approach, because of its emphasis on consciousness and experience rather than codified norms, value theories or political strategies (Dobson, 1990: 48). Deep ecology combines 'personal work . . . and political activism', but the 'work of becoming more real' has priority, since it is only from a state of 'ecological consciousness' that right actions (or, for Naess, 'beautiful' actions) can come (Devall and Sessions, 1985: 8–9; Seed et al., 1988: 28). The primary goal of deep ecologists should thus be to cultivate an ecological consciousness which no longer recognises boundaries in the world – between one species and another, or between themselves and the rest of the world – for it is only in such a state that they can know what to do. As Warwick Fox puts it, 'to the extent that we perceive boundaries, we fall short of deep ecological consciousness' (Devall and Sessions, 1985: 66). Through critical work on their own consciousness, 'people can clarify their own intuitions, and act from deep principles', such actions both expressing and deepening a state of ecological consciousness (1985: 8; Fox, 1989: 66).

The first thing to note here is the shift of register from epistemology to ontology – from propositional knowledge to the recovery of authentic existence – as the precondition for knowing what to do. For deep ecologists – as for many ecofeminists (for example Salleh, 1984; Plant 1986–7; cf. Adam, this volume) – the environmental crisis has its roots in the alienated modern consciousness and its dualistic and object-orientated thought. Only if we can reverse the conditioning of modern life and regain a direct, participatory experience of the world can we re-embed our existence in providential nature and truly know what to do. But also it is important to recognise that this is simply a more articulated form of a more general expressivist sensibility in contemporary society. This more diffuse expressivism is evident both in the radical environmental movement – such as in its assumption that community is a natural, pre-social state of unity, rather than being inscribed within concrete social roles and customs (Cheney, 1989b: 132) – and more broadly in society, in the 'romantic gaze' with which modern individuals routinely consume the spectacle of nature (Urry, 1990: 45), and in the widespread ethic of authentic existence (Taylor, 1991).

At first glance the expressivist turn exemplified by deep ecology would seem to fulfil my requirements for an escape from the modern problematic. Its denial of subject–object dualism would certainly seem to place it firmly outside the territory of modernism, and its radical situating of the self within a nature replete with meaning and value seems far from the lonely gnostic vision of a humanity trapped in an alien world. However, at a deeper level expressivism can be seen as subtly following the contours of modernism in the way it tells us what to do. For a start, the path taken by expressivism's quest for re-embedding – towards identification with the *whole* – echoes modernism's own quest for universal propositional truth. The parallels that Jim Cheney has drawn between deep ecology and Stoicism are instructive here. The Stoics responded to the decline of the hegemony of Athens and the emergence of the Alexandrian world of cultural difference with a profound sense of alienation and anomie. But they attempted to overcome this alienation through declaring the cosmos itself to be their city, making them 'cosmopolitans', and thus supposedly disembedded from any particular culture. As such they believed that through their 'cosmopolitan reason' they could participate in the ruling principle of the cosmos, and thus achieve a state of Stoic a-pathy in which their actions would naturally follow the 'grammar of the cosmos'.

The parallels with deep ecology (and with expressivism more generally) are striking. For Cheney, these parallels are to be explained by the similar cultural context in which we find ourselves today – 'the demise of modernism, its shattering into a world of difference, the postmodern world'. In this context deep ecology 'expresses a yearning for embedment coupled with a refusal to forgo the ultimate hegemony so characteristic of modernism' (Cheney, 1989a: 302). For our purposes, we can note that the expressivist belief in a *cosmic* self is ultimately no more a re-embedding than is the universal reason of modernism, both expressing as they do a profound alienation from the situatedness of identity, experience and knowledge in culture, place and history.[7] Expressivism tries to vault over the nihilistic void through identification with the principle of the whole. As such, for expressivism as much as for modernism, the middle ground of our cultural and natural embeddedness is purely accidental and has no meaning in itself; expressivism cannot thematise our 'thrown-ness' in the world. Existence becomes 'hollowed out', with meaning and purpose residing only at the extreme ends of reality – in the self and in the cosmos only. Between, there is just meaningless accident. Stoicism – and deep ecology – turns out to be just another, disguised version of gnostic alienation.

Expressivist ecology does sometimes allow the content of a determinate, middle-range nature to have ethical significance. Bioregionalists, for example, argue that the artificial spatial boundaries of the modern bureaucratic state alienate us from the natural qualities of specific places. They advocate that society should be organised on the basis of natural principles – not just abstract principles of diversity, decentralisation and cooperation, but also in relation to the ecological properties of the biological region in which one resides (Sale, 1985). But when they do so they tend, ironically, to imitate modernists in their reification of a nature that stands outside society, defining it not in terms of use, history, symbol and meaning but just in terms of hard, 'physical' features (Alexander, 1990). This nature may be one that is apprehended through the participatory consciousness of expressivism, rather than through the alienated, objectifying consciousness of modernism, but it is still understood as nature 'out there', uncannily similar to the nature of the physical sciences. The dichotomy of culture and nature is thus not genuinely overcome by expressivism; the cultural, including what are properly ethical and political decisions, is simply subordinated to the natural, as if the very transcendent asociality of nature understood in this way could bypass the need for human judgement and debate (Szerszynski, 1993a: 71–2; 1993b: 252–3).

So expressivist ecological thought tends to reproduce modernism's strategy of *origin*. Whereas modernism invokes an extra-discursive 'reality' in order to underwrite abstract, privileged 'knowledge', with expressivism it is an asocial 'nature' that acts as the final guarantor of abstract, authentic 'being'. As such, expressivism is as vulnerable as modernism to the charge that this strategy can only be carried out at the expense of denying the radical embeddedness of identity and knowledge – as if there is a reality which stands outside culture, history and judgement. But can expressivism not avoid this capture by modernism's influence? Can it not forsake the strategy of origin while still retaining its notion of authenticity? In fact, there have been moves within Western thought which seem to follow such a direction – Neitzsche's repudiation of romanticist notions of the unity and goodness of nature, and Heidegger's displacement of attention away from the perceiving and feeling subject of romanticism, and towards language and Being, for example (cf. Taylor, 1989: 456ff). But, while I will want to return to Heidegger in a more positive vein below, such moves have generally tended to follow the route of formalisation, and thus of proclaiming the pure *autonomy* of human self-assertion in a world without moral signposts. Sartre is a paradigm case here; he argued that it was possible to live in authenticity, in a 'self-recovery of being which was previously corrupted' (Sartre, 1958: 70, n. 9), but that this was only possible if one acknowledged the absurdity of existence and the completely unconditioned nature of the self. One must embrace the imperative to will one's own freedom and simply *choose*. Such a purely formal idea of authenticity, stripped of the 'content' of a providential nature which can guarantee that each individual's spontaneous action will harmonise with each other's, can no longer pretend to tell us what to do. It 'cannot tell one *what* to choose, only *how* to choose' – that is, authentically (Kariuki, 1981: 61). Thus the fate of an expressivism which abandons the 'content' of romanticist nature, and simply asserts the imperative of formal authenticity – of 'doing one's own thing' – is to land back once more in the condition of nihilistic self-assertion.

Let us now turn to traditionalism, the other strand of romanticism which I held up as a possible escape route from the modern problematic. Traditionalism does seem to avoid many of the pitfalls of expressivism that I outlined above. Firstly, instead of denying the embeddedness of identity and experience within culture and convention, it affirms it. Self-consciousness, for traditionalism, 'exists only in being acknowledged', and thus only in relation to other selves (Hegel, 1977: 111). It is only through concrete relations with others that one may become a self – and such concrete relations must assume a set of roles and customs in order that the recognition of the self by others can take place (Kolb, 1986: 24–5). Knowledge too, for traditionalism, is bound up with a particular form of life – with community and tradition. Secondly, while, like expressivism, it counters the progressive narrative of modernism with a narrative of decline, this is one not of alienation from a supposed original pre-social unity, but of the more proximate and concrete erosion of the ties of community and tradition. Thirdly, again like expressivism, it grounds our knowledge of what to do not in the autonomous, individualised reason of modernism but in the intrinsic connectedness of all human beings (or even all *beings*). But whereas expressivism grounds this connectedness in a metaphysical unity which is ontologically and chronologically *prior* to the conventions of human society, for traditionalism it is *through* the particularities of those very conventions that connectedness is secured. For expressivism human beings can only find their true, interconnected nature *outside* society; for traditionalism they can only find it *within* society. Finally, there is no idea within traditionalism of an autonomous, asocial nature with salvific powers – in effect, both nature and humanity have to be 'saved' by being implicated in a substantive tradition.

While this second, more collectivist kind of romanticism has not been developed into articulated ecological positions to the same degree as has the expressivist strand, it has nevertheless clearly informed many aspects of environmentalist thought and behaviour in the Western world, from attitudes to indigenous cultures in the Third World (Reed, 1986; Booth and Jacobs, 1990) to local activism in defence of the familiar vernacular landscape (Szerszynski, 1994). However, the example of one thinker who did develop such a position is instructive – John Ruskin, the nineteenth century English artist and social reformer. Ruskin's fusion of the conservative social philosophy of Thomas Carlyle with the nature mysticism of William Wordsworth created the powerful combination of aesthetics, philosophy and politics which contributed to the distinctively English sense of landscape and, indirectly, brought about institutions such as the National Trust.[8]

In many ways, the medievalist tradition of social criticism to which Ruskin belonged was a reaction to the limitations of expressivist romanticism. In resistance to the latter's preoccupation with subjective experience and the self, Carlyle and Ruskin, and William Morris after them, sought 'to return the quest for paradise from the internal to the external world' (Spear, 1984: 5–6). In doing so they developed a distinctively English style of political romanticism – culturally conservative, aesthetically orientated, medievalist and anti-capitalist. But to this tradition, under the influence of writers like Wordsworth, Ruskin added a passionate aesthetic and moral interest in nature, thus producing a prophetic approach to environmental change which regarded it as a moral indictment on the way that society was developing.

Ruskin railed against the way that Enlightenment rationalism, capitalism and industrialism were dissolving the traditional ties that properly bind society together, creating a world of individuals ruled by market transactions and the myth of 'Mammonism'. Ruskin believed not just that there were virtues in living within a tradition, but that there was an objective moral order from which the increasingly de-traditionalised modern person was being disastrously disengaged. In some ways Ruskin wanted to return to the kind of conjunctive symbolic order which was characteristic of the Middle Ages, with a de-differentiation of the modern cultural spheres of the technical, the moral and the aesthetic (Xenos, 1989: 55–8). But, as he indicated in volume II of his *Modern Painters*, Ruskin was aware that the change in notions of truth and representation between the pre-modern and the modern militated against such a return. For writers such as Dante the landscape had been replete with spiritual significance quite independently of Dante's perception and description of it. For moderns such as Wordsworth, by contrast, the experience of divinity in the landscape was always dependent on the observer's mental and emotional state – they were in that sense subjective (Bate, 1991: 76).

This acknowledgement forced Ruskin to try to fashion a non-subjective ethic from *within* the constraints of this modern problematic. For Ruskin there *was* an eternal sacral and moral reality, but that reality had to be mediated through a language which had become detached from it. How could one secure an accurate correspondence between a language understood as representational and a reality understood as being represented? Ruskin, following Thomas Carlyle, proposed a solution which was literary and artistic in character. For Ruskin, literature and art provided a prism through which eternal moral realities could be discerned (Spear, 1984: 6, 94). The poetry of Wordsworth and the paintings of J.M.W. Turner provided Ruskin with a way of perceiving eternal moral realities in nature which he could use to cast a prophetic judgement over modern, industrialised society (for example Ruskin, 1908). Similarly, his template for a stable and fulfilling social order was inscribed within a particular tradition, that of the chivalric romance, which showed the need for customary ties of loyalty and respect in order to bind society together in relations of mutual obligation and dependence (Spear, 1984: 99; cf. Carlyle, 1899: 34). But for Ruskin, this attempt to 'edit life into literary shape' was not to impose an artificial ideal on society, but to make explicit the timelessly true principles of social organisation which he discerned in the Bible and in romantic literature (Spear, 1984: 6).

So, just as was the case with expressivism, we can see here a reproduction of the modernist strategy of *origin*. Ruskin accepts the terms of the modern problematic – language and reality have been sundered. Like modernists, Ruskin also believes that language and the world can in principle be brought back into correspondence again – that a timeless, 'constant reality' can serve as an anchor to prevent the nihilistic free play of language (Horton, 1970: 157). As is the case with modernism, this would not be a return to the conjunctive, pre-modern experience of the world, since it would assume rather than deny the distinction between words and things; but just as the notion of reference holds word and thing *apart*, it also promises to hold them *together* in a constant relationship. However, while for modernists it is through purification and formalisation that language can be made to refer to that constant reality, for Ruskin it is through a substantive aesthetic *tradition* that reference can be secured. Like modernism, then, Ruskin's traditionalism posits a transcendent reality – now a *moral* reality – lying behind the flow of language and culture. Just as the notion of the 'real' serves for modernism as the ultimate underwriter of its formalisation project, Ruskin's eternal moral reality, lying behind the phenomenal world, grounds his re-traditionalisation project. It is only through the notion of reference to that reality that Ruskin can ground the substantive content of his moral vision.

This use of the notion of reference, whether in modernism, in expressivism or in Ruskin's traditionalism, makes all three positions vulnerable to a number of charges. Firstly, the invocation of a transcendant 'real' (whether the physical reality of science, the providential nature of the expressivists, or the moral realities of Ruskin), to which language refers, can be seen as little more than a ruse to bestow a specious timeless certainty in areas of experience which are properly the domain of judgement, dispute and hermeneutic interpretation. Secondly, the method employed to secure reference (whether through modernism's formalisation of language, expressivism's purification of subjective experience from social influences, or traditionalism's adoption of the 'right' tradition) is one which can never be secured, resting as it does on ideas of autonomy and purity which are unachievable with human culture and experience. Finally, because of their starting point within the modern problematic, and thus from the alienated modern subject, all three positions assume and take up this alienation within themselves, reproducing it in different guises.

At this point we can ask the same question of traditionalism as we did of expressivism. Is it not possible to avoid this strategy of origin? Is there not a traditionalist position which does *not* posit a transcendent ahistorical reality to which the content of a form of life merely corresponds, as the purified language of science, for modernism, corresponds to nature? Would not this be a *real* substantive ethic, one which was not riven by its own internal alienation of content from transcendent reality? In fact, the traditionalist position in Western thought, from Edmund Burke through to new communitarians such as MacIntyre and Walzer, has indeed been dominated by what might be called a non-realist traditionalism, one that does not ground the content of a form of life through the idea of reference to a transcendent moral reality. In this respect, Ruskin can be seen as an unusual figure, even within this tradition of thought. But the thing to note here is that, such is the grip of the modern problematic on thought, that the abandonment of a realist strategy of origin has simply led traditionalists into a formalist one of *autonomy*.

Let me explain what I mean here. I am not denying that traditionalists have been very interested in the content rather than just the mere form of, say, moral judgements. But, nevertheless, if one adopts the perspective of the dominant non-realist, neo-traditionalists such as the new communitarians, it is very difficult to say why the *specificity* of that content should matter at all. For a 'strong' traditionalist like Ruskin, as we saw, it is not just the radical embedding in a form of life that is important, but also that that embedding is in the *right* form of life. For Hegel, the right form of life was the modern state; for Ruskin it was one based on the chivalric literary tradition. For a *neo*-traditionalist, by contrast, it is the embedding *alone* that is important, since there are no universal, decontextualised criteria for determining which tradition should be so privileged. There may be ways of judging one tradition to be *better* than another, but not that it has some correspondence to universal moral realities.

For example, despite all the criticism that new communitarians such as MacIntyre, Michael Walzer, Michael Sandel and Charles Taylor have made of the substanceless formalism of modern, liberal ethics, their work has a curious formalism about it (Sandel, 1982; Walzer, 1983; MacIntyre, 1985; Taylor, 1985). They have criticised modernist ethical and political thought for its refusal to acknowledge the way that personal identity is not specifiable without reference to community and tradition, and its conception of cognitive or practical reason as an 'Archimedean point' outside any given tradition or way of life. In place of the vocabulary of modernist ethics they have offered one where not just personal identity but also any moral or empirical concept is embedded in its social and cultural context.[9] For the new communitarians, community and the traditions it carries are the preconditions for moral existence, and so are proper objects of regard and concern in their own right (for example Taylor, 1979: 57). However, despite all this concern for content, when compared with ethicists such as Martha Nussbaum (1990) the new communitarians seem remarkably indifferent to the actual nature of that content. MacIntyre, for example, for all his disparaging of modern, formalistic ethics, is unable to specify the content of a coherent ethical life. All he can do is insist that it should possess the formally defined characteristic of being based on practice, tradition and virtue. MacIntyre cannot list the virtues which human beings should possess; neither can he say which activities can and which cannot form the basis of ethical practices, beyond the formal requirement that they must involve the pursuit of 'internal goods' (Bernstein, 1986: 131). The new communitarians can only extol the general benefits of community and tradition. Because they have taken the route of formalisation, from their perspective the particular content of any given tradition cannot have any special significance at all.

Let us see how this formalisation of the traditionalist strand of romanticism works itself out in the environmental arena. An instructive example is the work of cultural ecologists such as Roy A. Rappaport, who argue that cultural beliefs can serve ecological functions by maintaining a people in sustainable equilibrium with their environment. Rappaport's study of the Tsembaga of Papua, for example, shows how the complex set of rituals, symbols, and religious beliefs which make up Tsembaga culture shape their interaction with their local ecology to produce a finely balanced whole – a 'ritually regulated ecosystem' (Rappaport, 1979: 41; cf. Rappaport, 1967). 'The operation of ritual among the Tsembaga and other Maring', Rappaport concludes, 'helps to maintain an undegraded environment, limits fighting to frequencies which do not endanger the existence of the regional population, adjusts man–land ratios, facilitates trade, distributes local surpluses of pig throughout the regional population in the form of pork, and assures people of high quality protein when they are most in need of it' (1979: 41). The Tsembaga are indeed an example of a sustainable society, and Rappaport's analysis adds grist to the mill of any traditionalist romantic who wants to argue for the embedding in community and tradition as a prerequisite for an unalienated, ecological existence.

And yet the Tsembaga do not know anything about 'carrying capacity' any more than they express moral concern for nature. They have no awareness of any ecological functions of their rituals which the anthropologist might infer. The 'cognised model' with which they understand the world, with its different categories of spirits and their obligations to them, does seem to keep them in sustainable equilibrium with their environment. But from Rappaport's perspective the truth or otherwise of this model is of no importance. All it has to have is the formal, functional characteristics of regulating the Tsembaga's behaviour in ecologically sustainable ways (1979: 98). The same kind of position is taken by Edward Goldsmith, who has long argued on traditionalist lines that the beliefs, rituals and taboos of traditional societies ensure that they enjoy a high degree of cohesion and organisation, and are adapted to their environment (Goldsmith et al., 1972: 34). For Goldsmith these myths and beliefs can have only a pragmatic truth – they should not be judged as true or false, but simply as functionally adaptive. The function of knowledge 'is not to depict reality in the manner of an encyclopaedia', but just to adapt the behaviour of communities to their environment (Goldsmith, 1992: 60). From such a perspective the content of a form of life is thus arbitrary, just the collective self-assertion of a community creating its own merely human meanings in a world which has none of its own. The knowledge which culture and tradition provide is merely an additional way in which humanity adapts itself to its world – a world it can never objectively know.[10]

So the traditionalist strand of romanticism, too, is caught within the modern problematic. Once it abandons the invocation of a transcendent reality to which the content of a given form of life must correspond, traditionalism falls back into a position from which one can only specify the formal characteristics, and never the content, of the ethical or ecological life. Such a traditionalism cannot tell us what to do, just how to do it – traditionally. Just as was the case with neo-modernism, for neo-traditionalism human knowledge becomes just that – human knowledge, severed from any opportunity of correspondence, simply human calling to human in a world without meaning. Against this background, the end of MacIntyre's *After Virtue*, where he calls for the creation of small communities 'within which civility and the intellectual and moral life can be sustained through the new dark ages which are already upon us' (MacIntyre, 1985: 263), takes on a new and revealing significance. We can read this as an unwitting metaphor for the condition of *all* moral communities from a position such as MacIntyre's – as people huddling together in an alien and hostile world which cannot tell them what to do. With traditionalism, too, we hear the deafening silence of a disenchanted world – this time, beyond the village boundary, indifferent to the arbitrary norms and beliefs that obtain within.

Conclusion

So what options are left for ecology if it wants to tell us what to do? I suggested at the beginning of this chapter that ecology should be seen as an attempt to relocate human projects within a wider framework of obligations and constraints – to overcome the lonely, nihilistic picture of a humanity adrift in a meaningless world to which modernity had consigned us. But as we have seen, all of the candidates for a path away from that picture – modernism itself, and the expressivist and traditionalist versions of romanticism – seem unable finally to leave it behind. Our contemporary moral traditions, from which ecological thought draws its resources, are so shaped by the understanding of language and the world assumed by modernism that they seem unable to help us leave its orbit. Modernist, expressivist and traditionalist ecology all either attempt to secure correspondence to an *origin*, a universal, noumenal 'real' lying behind the phenomenal world, or they abandon this in favour of *autonomy* – the pure, groundless operation of argument, spontaneity or tradition. To the extent that they do the former, they tell us *what* to do, but only in so far as they project a particular, frozen vision of social relations onto that 'real' and then read back off it. To the extent that they do the latter, they cannot tell us *what* to do, only *how* to do it – rationally, authentically, traditionally. Either way, the nihilistic world-picture is always there, either suppressed fearfully in the background, or thrust triumphally forward. Ecology, while seeming to promise a re-embedding of human choices and judgements within a framework which transcends mere human wishes, fails to do so, and always leads us back into the nihilistic condition of groundless self-assertion in a world without purpose or meaning. Ecology, after all, does *not* seem to be able to tell us what to do (Milbank, 1993).

But at this point the reader might legitimately begin to demand that I start to 'come out' in respect of my own position. You have told a bleak story, they might say. But, although you have marshalled the evidence against every other position, it is not clear that this adds up to a coherent alternative. Indeed, they might continue, you have been trying to have your cake *and* eat it, by sliding around from one position to another, thus seeming to demolish all while in fact demolishing none, if consistency is to count for anything. You have sided with the constructionists when discussing the realists, arguing with the former that our knowledge of the world is always and necessarily shaped by culture, history and practice. You have sided with the realists when discussing the constructionists, arguing that the latter's effective abandonment of any notion of the 'real' leads them into nihilism. When conflating the two as various breeds of 'modernist' you have sided with the romantics in your offering of a pre-modern, unmediated, unalienated fusion of consciousness and the world, and an ethics focusing on substantive content. But when discussing the romantics you have sided with the modernists in suggesting that the former can never really bridge the gulf between self and world, so that the content of romantic forms of life are always merely human, with no cosmic groundedness after all. Yours is such a wilfully destructive intellectual project that you have left yourself no stone standing on which to erect an alternative.

My narrative up to now has indeed been bleak – deliberately so, in order to emphasise the depth and complexity of the predicament in which, I would claim, we find ourselves. But in response to a charge of inconsistency I would reply that there has been a constant thread through the preceding discussion of the options that are open to us. Whichever of the paths offered by contemporary ethical and ecological thought we take, and whatever the twists and turns, forks and byways we follow, our journey is always shadowed by the threat of a nihilistic world-picture. It may take many different forms and guises along the way, but, far from providing an escape from nihilism, all of the positions discussed take it along with them. *But* – and this is my defence against the charge of hopelessness – there is not an inevitability to this situation. Indeed, my point is that the nihilistic picture is *not* the timelessly true human condition, but a historically specific understanding of the world thrust on us due, largely, to a shift in our understanding of language, knowledge and reality at the end of the Middle Ages. Thus, for example, the notion that all our understandings of nature are human projections or rhetorics (Harvey, 1993: 14–15, 19–20) or 'story lines' (Hajer, this volume), and that nature itself is mute and unknowable, is *itself* a rhetoric, a story line about nature. As such, we are under no obligation to accept it as an ultimate, timeless truth about our condition as beings in the world. Nevertheless, the question remains: if our contemporary moral traditions cannot provide ecology with the resources for an exit from the modern problematic, what can?

Before setting out a few indications of what an answer to that question might look like, let me first draw a contrast between our modern predicament and that of the gnostics of the early centuries of the present era. Although I have been using gnosticism as a metaphor for the cosmic alienation implicit in the modern problematic, there is one crucial difference between these two orientations to the world. For the gnostics, the human soul was a portion of the divine substance which had fallen into a dark, alien world governed by hostile demonic forces (Jonas, 1963: 44). For moderns, by contrast, the world is not so much hostile as completely indifferent to human meaning and purpose (1963: 338–9).[11] The world does not shout its enmity at us – it is just utterly and unnervingly silent. But is not this silence of the world just the other side of the coin of our modern conception of the human individual as the locus of meaning and purpose, and as the author and controller of language (Manes, 1992)? If we were able to come to a different understanding of the human person, and of language itself, could we not bring this epoch of the world's silence to an end? There is not space here to explore in any depth what such an understanding might look like, but I can perhaps usefully indicate a few pointers in the work of Wittgenstein and Heidegger which indicate the route such a revisioning ought to take. They suggest a way of thinking about our ecological crisis that, while echoing aspects of romanticist thought, emphasises not the alienness but the homeliness of the world.

As I have suggested, crucial to such an understanding would be a radical rethinking of our ideas about language and the world. Firstly, instead of understanding the world as existing outside language, we need to see it as constituted through language and meaning. There is nowhere that interpretation stops, where a hard, extra-discursive reality – one which can fix that language – takes over. The realness of the environmental crisis – its resistance to being dissolved by a mere act of discursive redescription – cannot be grounded in something that stands implacably outside language. If that crisis 'stands fast' in the way that it does, it does so for reasons that cannot be explicated without reference to language and culture.

> [S]ome things stand unshakeably fast and some are more or less liable to shift. What stands fast does so, not because it is intrinsically obvious or convincing; it is rather held fast by what lies around it. (Wittgenstein, 1969: 21e)

When language does stop, this is not because we have found some non-negotiable brute reality. It is simply that our justifications are exhausted – our spade is turned, and we can only say 'This is simply what I do' (Wittgenstein, 1968: 85e).

But, secondly, if reality is language all the way down, reality is also world all the way up (Cheney, 1989b: 118–20). If we should abandon the cold, analytical certainty implied by modernist ideas of truth-as-representation, so too should we shun post-modernist ideas of language-as-endless-free-play. If we want genuinely to overcome the dichotomy between language and the world, we must not simply detach the former from the latter, letting it flap freely in the wind. If language is not to be understood in terms of representations of and correspondence with an extra-discursive reality, neither is it simply a human construction.[12] To take such a stance is simply to adopt the neo-modernist view of language as still representational, but simply denied the privilege of unmediated correspondence with an extra-discursive reality. It may be the case that interpretation never finds a final resting place. It may be that strong modernism is insupportable – that the facts about the damage we do to the environment do not press in on us from a brute reality outside language, and demand our concern. But they *do* press in on us, as the presencing of our very real moral predicament.

So, thirdly, in rethinking language and the world, we are forced to rethink the human. If language is not a medium for the representation of an extra-discursive reality, neither is it simply a human artefact, an instrument for human self-assertion in the world. We cannot own or control language – it is the realm of Being within which the world is disclosed to us. The human subject is not simply a user of language. It is language that speaks; we can only listen, attend and respond (Steiner, 1978: 27, 36). Similarly, if the 'world' is not simply a collection of brute objects that are available for us to use, and to describe, neither is it simply a human construct. The world is rather a 'texture of lived possibilities' in which 'we are involved in action and ongoing purpose'. As human beings, then, we no more use or construct the world than we use or construct language. We inhabit the world, are situated in it. Our actions and choices are not crafted in a space outside the world, and then exercised on that world, but are woven into the texture of that world. We are *involved* in the world; the language of subject and object comes *after*, rather than precedes, that involvement (Kolb, 1986: 132–3). As such, we cannot, after all, be the detached, rational subjects of modernism. But neither can we be the cosmic selves of expressivism, united with an abstract whole, since our identities are inextricably caught up with the specific texture of our thrown-ness in the world. And neither can we be the collectively detached subjects of traditionalism – neither the nature of the world we inhabit, nor of the *way* we inhabit it, is compatible with this vision of bounded, self-contained islands of meaning in a disenchanted world.

I have argued that each of the current positions taken up within contemporary ecological thought has to be located within a much larger complex of positions, all shaped by what I have been calling the modern problematic. This problematic has its roots in the historically specific understanding of language as referring to, rather than being interfused with, the world we inhabit. Their ensnarement by this way of thinking prevents any of these ecological positions from providing a genuine alternative to the alienated consciousness from which the environmental crisis springs. If I am right, then, attempts to think our way forward cannot afford simply to take up one of these positions, but have to engage with the *whole* problematic. If, as Maarten Hajer suggests, we should look at the environmental crisis as simply 'one of the few remaining places where modernity can still be reflected upon' (this volume, p. 265), this reflection has to go deeper than is generally thought. And perhaps, when this has properly begun, we might begin to see what it might *really* mean for ecology to tell us what to do.

Notes

1. I would like to express my thanks to Michael Jacobs, Scott Lash, John O'Neill, Stephen Pumfrey, Mark Toogood, Simon Shackley and Brian Wynne for helpful comments concerning this chapter – and to Paul Morris, who acted as midwife at the birth of the ideas which were to grow into it.

2. The following account, while finding starting points in the work of Timothy Reiss (1982) and Hans Blumenberg (1983), also finds a parallel in Julia Kristeva's account of the replacement of the symbol by the sign as the dominant basis of thought during the late Middle Ages. For Kristeva, during this period '[t]he serenity of the symbol was replaced by the strained ambivalence of the *sign's* connection, which lays claim to resemblance and identification of the elements it holds together, while first postulating their radical difference' (1980: 39).

3. Although such a phenomenon is observable in certain texts, from Rabelais to Montaigne (Cave, 1979).

4. For example, it was all but hegemonic in academic philosophy until the advent of the 'ordinary language' philosophy of Wittgenstein, Gilbert Ryle and J.L. Austin.

5. Apparent exceptions to this, such as nineteenth century evolutionary thought and sociobiology, are still distinctively modern in the *way* that nature tells us what to do, and in the way that they serve to reinforce rather than qualify human self-assertion.

6. Reiss cites Swift's account of the Houyhnhnms in *Gulliver's Travels* as an example of this dynamic. Although widely seen as a vision of a primitivist, conjunctive utopia, the contrast Swift makes with European society is one which accuses the latter as suffering not from a hypertrophy but from a *lack* of reason (1982: 336–9).

7. On the 'cosmic self' of expressivism, see Heelas, 1992. On the situatedness of deep ecological consciousness in concrete social practices, see Luke, 1988: 85–7.

8. Two of the three people responsible for the founding of the National Trust in 1895, Octavia Hill and Canon Hardwicke Rawnsley, were close associates of Ruskin, and in a number of ways the Trust's early history intersected with that of Ruskin's Guild of St George (Spear, 1984: 196–7; Bate, 1991: 47–8).

9. Although the new communitarians differ over exactly how radically the self is embedded in community – cf. Etzioni, 1989; Benhabib, 1992: 76–82.

10. That such communities *do* seem to live in harmony with nature is not, from this neo-traditionalist perspective, an indication that they 'know what to do'. What they 'do' happens

to be ecologically 'right', but only because their myths and rituals ensure this, by the 'invisible hand' of functionalism. However, from the Heideggerian perspective I outline below, which does not reify 'nature' as something outside culture, and which sees a being's environment as always already *for* them, as filled with meanings and possibilities for action, such a harmony takes on a very different significance.

11. Although see Blumenberg, 1983: 142–3.

12. Elizabeth Harlow (1992) can only arrive at such a position from broadly Wittgensteinian premises by assuming the very language–world distinction that Wittgenstein denies (she quotes with approval Rorty's neo-modernist dictum 'the world is out there, but descriptions of the world are not' (Rorty, 1989: 5)).

References

Alexander, Donald (1990) 'Bioregionalism: Science or sensibility?', *Environmental Ethics*, 12 (2): 161–73.

Anderson, Terry L. and Leal, Donald R. (1991) *Free Market Environmentalism*. San Francisco: Pacific Research Institute for Public Policy.

Bate, Jonathan (1991) *Romantic Ecology: Wordsworth and the Environmental Tradition*. London: Routledge.

Beck, Ulrich (1992) *Risk Society: Towards a New Modernity*, trans. Mark Ritter. London: Sage.

Beck, Ulrich (1994) 'The reinvention of politics: Towards a theory of reflexive moderniz-ation', in Ulrich Beck, Anthony Giddens and Scott Lash, *Reflexive Modernization: Politics, Tradition and Aesthetics in the Modern Social Order*. Cambridge: Polity. pp. 1–55.

Benhabib, Seyla (1992) *Situating the Self: Gender, Community and Postmodernism in Contemporary Ethics*. Cambridge: Polity Press.

Bennett, Jeff and Block, Walter (eds) (1991) *Reconciling Economics and the Environment*. Perth: Australian Institute for Public Policy.

Bentham, Jeremy (1970) *An Introduction to the Principles of Morals and Legislation*. London: Athlone Press.

Bernstein, Richard J. (1986) 'Nietzsche or Aristotle? Reflections on Alasdair MacIntyre's *After Virtue*', in *Philosophical Profiles: Essays in a Pragmatic Mode*. Cambridge: Polity Press. pp. 115–40.

Blumenberg, Hans (1983) *The Legitimacy of the Modern Age*, trans. Robert M. Wallace. Cambridge, MA: MIT Press.

Booth, Annie L. and Jacobs, Harvey M. (1990) 'Ties that bind: Native American beliefs as a foundation for environmental consciousness', *Environmental Ethics*, 12 (1): 27–43.

Brubaker, Rogers (1984) *The Limits of Rationality: An Essay on the Social and Moral Thought of Max Weber*. London: George Allen and Unwin.

Carlyle, Thomas (1899) *Past and Present*. London: Chapman and Hall.

Cave, Terence (1979) *The Cornucopian Text: Problems of Writing in the French Renaissance*. Oxford: Oxford University Press.

Cheney, Jim (1989a) 'The Neo-stoicism of radical environmentalism', *Environmental Ethics*, 11 (4): 293–325.

Cheney, Jim (1989b) 'Postmodern environmental ethics: Ethics as bioregional narrative', *Environmental Ethics*, 11 (2): 117–34.

Commoner, Barry (1963) *Science and Survival*. New York: Viking Press.

Commoner, Barry (1971) *The Closing Circle: Nature, Man and Technology*. New York: Alfred A. Knopf.

Commoner, Barry (1976) *The Poverty of Power*. New York: Alfred A. Knopf.

Crook, Stephen (1991) *Modernist Radicalism and its Aftermath: Foundationalism and Anti-Foundationalism in Radical Social Theory*. London: Routledge.

Devall, Bill and Sessions, George (1985) *Deep Ecology: Living as if Nature Mattered*. Layton, UT: Gibbs M. Smith.

Dobson, Andrew (1990) *Green Political Thought: An Introduction*. London: Unwin Hyman.

Douglas, Mary (1975) 'Environments at risk', in *Implicit Meanings: Essays in Anthropology*. London: Routledge and Kegan Paul. pp. 230–48.

Douglas, Mary and Wildavsky, Aaron (1982) *Risk and Culture: An Essay on the Selection of Technical and Environmental Dangers*. Berkeley, CA: University of California Press.

Dryzek, John S. (1992) 'Ecology and discursive democracy: Beyond liberal capitalism and the administrative state', *Capitalism, Nature, Socialism*, 3 (2): 18–42.

Dworkin, Ronald (1978) *Taking Rights Seriously*. London: Duckworth.

Eckersley, Robyn (1993) 'Free market environmentalism: Friend or foe?', *Environmental Politics*, 2 (1): 1–19.

Etzioni, Amitai (1989) 'Toward an I and We paradigm', *Contemporary Sociology*, 18 (2): 171–6.

Ferrell, Robyn (1991) 'Richard Rorty and the poet's utopia', in Rosalyn Diprose and Robyn Ferrell (eds), *Cartographies: Poststructuralism and the Mapping of Bodies and Space*. North Sydney: Allen and Unwin. pp. 3–12.

Fox, Warwick (1989) *Approaching Deep Ecology: A Response to Richard Sylvan's Critique of Deep Ecology*, Environmental Studies Occasional Paper No. 20. Hobart: University of Tasmania.

Funkenstein, Amos (1986) *Theology and the Scientific Imagination: From the Middle Ages to the Seventeenth Century*. Princeton, NJ: Princeton Univerisity Press.

Gewirth, Alan (1978) *Reason and Morality*. Chicago: University of Chicago Press.

Gilbert, G. Nigel and Mulkay, Michael (1984) *Opening Pandora's Box: A Sociological Analysis of Scientists' Discourse*. Cambridge: Cambridge University Press.

Goldsmith, Edward (1992) *The Way: An Ecological World-View*. London: Rider.

Goldsmith, Edward, Allen, Robert, Allaby, Michael, Davoll, John and Lawrence, Sam (1972) 'Blueprint for survival', *The Ecologist*, 2 (1): 1–43.

Grove-White, Robin and Szerszynski, Bronislaw (1992) 'Getting behind environmental ethics', *Environmental Values*, 1 (4): 285–96.

Habermas, Jürgen (1979) *Communication and the Evolution of Society*, trans. T. McCarthy. Boston: Beacon Press.

Habermas, Jürgen (1981) 'New social movements', *Telos*, (49): 33–7.

Habermas, Jürgen (1982) 'Reply to my critics', in John Thompson and David Held (eds), *Habermas: Critical Debates*. Cambridge, MA: MIT Press. pp. 219–83.

Harlow, Elizabeth M. (1992) 'The human face of nature: Environmental values and the limits of anthropocentrism', *Environmental Ethics*, 14 (1): 27–42.

Harvey, David (1993) 'The nature of environment: The dialectics of social and environmental change', *Socialist Register*, 1: 1–51.

Heelas, Paul (1992) 'The sacralisation of the self and new age capitalism', in Nicholas Abercrombie and Alan Warde (eds), *Social Change in Contemporary Britain*. Cambridge: Polity Press. pp. 139–66.

Hegel, Georg Wilhelm Friedrich (1942) *Philosophy of Right*, trans. T.M. Knox. London: Oxford University Press.

Hegel, Georg Wilhelm Friedrich (1977) *Phenomenology of Spirit*, trans. A.V. Miller. Oxford: Oxford University Press.

Hobbes, Thomas (1914) *Leviathan*. London: Dent.

Horton, Robin (1970) 'African traditional thought and modern science,' in B.R. Wilson (ed.), *Rationality*. Oxford: Basil Blackwell. pp. 131–71.

Hume, David (1972) *A Treatise of Human Nature*, vols 2 and 3, ed. Páll S. Ardal. London: Fontana.

Jonas, Hans (1963) *The Gnostic Religion: The Message of the Alien God and the Beginnings of Christianity*. Boston: Beacon Press.

Kant, Immanuel (1964) *Groundwork of the Metaphysic of Morals*, trans. H.J. Paton. New York: Harper and Row.

Kariuki, Joseph (1981) *The Possibility of Universal Moral Judgement in Existential Ethics: A Critical Analysis of the Phenomenology of Moral Experience According to Jean-Paul Sartre*. Berne: Peter Lang.

Kolb, David (1986) *The Critique of Pure Modernity: Hegel, Heidegger and After*. Chicago: Chicago University Press.

Kristeva, Julia (1980) 'The bounded text', in *Desire in Language: A Semiotic Approach to Literature and Art*. Oxford: Blackwell. pp. 36–63.

Kwa, Chunglin (1987) 'Representations of nature mediating between ecology and science policy: The case of the international biological programme', *Social Studies of Science*, 17 (3): 413–42.

Locke, John (1964) *An Essay Concerning Human Understanding*, ed. A.D. Woozley. London: Fontana.

Luke, Tim (1988) 'The dreams of deep ecology,' *Telos*, 76: 65–92.

MacIntyre, Alasdair (1985) *After Virtue: A Study in Moral Theory*, second edition. London: Duckworth.

Manes, Christopher (1992) 'Nature and silence', *Environmental Ethics*, 14 (4): 339–50.

Mannheim, Karl (1960) *Ideology and Utopia: An Introduction to the Sociology of Knowledge*. London: Routledge and Kegan Paul.

Meadows, Donella H., Meadows, Dennis L., Randers, Jorgen and Behrens III, William W. (1972) *The Limits to Growth: A Report for the Club of Rome's Project on the Predicament of Mankind*. London: Earth Island.

Milbank, John (1990) *Theology and Social Theory: Beyond Secular Reason*. Oxford: Blackwell.

Milbank, John (1993) 'Out of the greenhouse', *New Blackfriars*, 74 (867): 4–14.

Mill, John Stuart (1979) *Utilitarianism*. Indianapolis: Hackett.

Miller, David (1992) 'Deliberative democracy and social choice', *Political Studies*, 40 (Special Issue): 54–67.

Moore, G.E. (1903) *Principia Ethica*. Cambridge: Cambridge University Press.

Naess, Arne (1973) 'The shallow and the deep, long-range ecology movement: A summary', *Inquiry*, 16 (1): 95–100.

Nussbaum, Martha (1990) 'Aristotelean social democracy,' in R. Bruce Douglass, Gerald M. Mara and Henry S. Richardson (eds), *Liberalism and the Good*. New York: Routledge. pp. 203–52.

O'Neill, John (1993) *Ecology, Policy and Politics: Human Well-Being and the Natural World*. London: Routledge.

Plant, Judith (1986–7) 'Women and nature', *Green Line*, 48: 13–15.

Plato (1956) 'Meno', in *Protagoras and Meno*. Harmondsworth: Penguin.

Popper, Karl (1968) *Conjectures and Refutations: The Growth of Scientific Knowledge*, second edition. New York: Harper Torchbooks.

Potter, Jonathan and Wetherell, Margaret (1987) *Discourse and Social Psychology: Beyond Attitudes and Behaviour*. London: Sage.

Rappaport, Roy A. (1967) *Pigs for the Ancestors*. New Haven, CT: Yale University Press.

Rappaport, Roy A. (1979) *Ecology, Meaning and Religion*. Richmond, CA: North Atlantic Books.

Reed, Gerard (1986) 'A Native American environmental ethic: A homily on Black Elk', in Eugene C. Hargrove (ed.), *Religion and Environmental Crisis*. Athens, GA: University of Georgia Press. pp. 25–37.

Reiss, Timothy J. (1982) *The Discourse of Modernism*. Ithaca, NY: Cornell University Press.

Rorty, Richard (1989) *Contingency, Irony, and Solidarity*. Cambridge: Cambridge University Press.

Rubin, Charles T. (1989) 'Environmental policy and environmental thought: Ruckelshaus and Commoner', *Environmental Ethics*, 11 (1): 27–51.

Ruskin, John (1908) 'The storm cloud of the nineteenth century', in E.T. Cook and Alexander Wedderburn (eds), *The Works of John Ruskin*, vol. 34. London: Allen. pp. 9–41.

Sale, Kirkpatrick (1985) *Dwellers in the Land: The Bioregional Vision*. San Francisco: Sierra Club Books.

Salleh, Ariel Kay (1984) 'Deeper than deep ecology: The eco-feminist connection', *Environmental Ethics*, 6 (4): 339–45.

Sandel, Michael J. (1982) *Liberalism and the Limits of Justice*. Cambridge: Cambridge University Press.

Sartre, Jean-Paul (1958) *Being and Nothingness: An Essay on Phenomenological Ontology*, trans. Hazel E. Barnes. London: Methuen.

Schnädelbach, Herbert (1984) *Philosophy in Germany 1831–1933*, trans. Eric Matthews. Cambridge: Cambridge University Press.

Seed, John, Macy, Joanna, Fleming, Pat and Naess, Arne (1988) *Thinking Like a Mountain: Towards a Council of All Beings*. London: Heretic Books.

Shapiro, Barbara J. (1983) *Probability and Certainty in Seventeenth-Century England: A Study of the Relationships between Natural Science, Religion, History, Law, and Literature*. Princeton, NJ: Princeton University Press.

Spear, Jeffrey L. (1984) *Dreams of an English Eden: Ruskin and His Tradition in Social Criticism*. New York: Columbia University Press.

Steiner, George (1978) *Heidegger*. London: Fontana.

Stevenson, C.L. (1944) *Ethics and Language*. New Haven, CT: Yale University Press.

Szerszynski, Bronislaw (1993a) 'The metaphysics of environmental concern: A critique of ecotheological anti-dualism', *Studies in Christian Ethics*, 6 (2): 67–78.

Szerszynski, Bronislaw (1993b) 'Uncommon ground: Moral discourse, foundationalism and the environmental movement', Ph.D. thesis, Lancaster University.

Szerszynski, Bronislaw (1994) 'Romantic ecology and the situated self'. Paper presented to the Conference 'Responses to Local Environmental Change', University of Surrey, 19–20 September.

Taylor, Charles (1979) 'Atomism', in Alik Kontos (ed.), *Powers, Possessions and Freedoms: Essays in Honour of C.B. MacPherson*. Toronto: University of Toronto Press. pp. 39–61.

Taylor, Charles (1985) *Philosophy and the Human Sciences: Philosophical Papers, Vol. II*. Cambridge: Cambridge University Press.

Taylor, Charles (1989) *Sources of the Self: The Making of the Modern Identity*. Cambridge: Cambridge University Press.

Taylor, Charles (1991) *The Ethics of Authenticity*. Cambridge, MA: Harvard University Press.

Thomas, Keith (1973) *Religion and the Decline of Magic*. Harmondsworth: Penguin.

Thompson, Michael, Ellis, Richard and Wildavsky, Aaron (1990) *Cultural Theory*. Boulder, CO: Westview Press.

Urry, John (1990) *The Tourist Gaze: Leisure and Travel in Contemporary Societies*. London: Sage.

Vickers, Brian (1984) 'Analogy versus identity: The rejection of occult symbolism, 1580–1680', in Brian Vickers (ed.), *Occult and Scientific Mentalities in the Renaissance*. Cambridge: Cambridge University Press. pp. 95–163.

Walzer, Michael (1983) *Spheres of Justice: A Defence of Pluralism and Equality*. Oxford: Martin Robertson.

Weber, Max (1946) 'Religious rejections of the world and their directions', in *From Max Weber: Essays in Sociology*. New York: Oxford University Press. pp. 323–59.

Wittgenstein, Ludwig (1968) *Philosophical Investigations*, trans. G.E.M. Anscombe. Oxford: Blackwell.

Wittgenstein, Ludwig (1969) *On Certainty*, trans. Denis Paul and G.E.M. Anscombe. Oxford: Blackwell.

Woolgar, Steve (1988) *Science: The Very Idea*. London: Tavistock.

Worster, Donald (1993) 'The shaky ground of sustainability', in Wolfgang Sachs (ed.), *Global Ecology: A New Arena of Political Conflict*. London: Zed Books. pp. 132–45.

Xenos, Nicholas (1989) *Scarcity and Modernity*. London: Routledge.

Yearley, Steven (1991) *The Green Case: A Sociology of Environmental Issues, Arguments and Politics*. London: HarperCollins.

Part II

RISK AND THE SELF: ENCOUNTERS AND RESPONSES

5

LIFE AS A PLANNING PROJECT

Elisabeth Beck-Gernsheim

Translated by Martin Chalmers

'The idea that human life is something that could be designed and planned is by no means self-evident, but has developed in the course of modernisation.'[1] In what follows I want to describe the rise and consequences of this modern planning idea, taking one area – parenthood – as an example. My starting point is the way that spectacular new developments in medicine, biology and genetics are creating ever more possibilities for a deliberate construction of parenthood. 'Programmed heredity'[2] is beginning to be tangible; a 'human being made to measure'[3] is becoming the vision of a possible future. The result may well be the emergence of new tasks for parents, new possibilities as well as new burdens.

The scenario which may be in store for us will be described here in three stages. First of all I will roughly outline certain conditions which characterise the course of a life in modernity. What is of central importance is the tendency towards *planning and rationalisation in the conduct of life*, which is increasingly becoming the task of individuals. Against this background I will then turn attention, secondly, to parenthood in modern society. Here the issue is how the expectations and demands made of parents are rising ever higher. *Upbringing too has become a planning project.* In the third stage I will look at contemporary developments in reproductive medicine and prenatal diagnosis, before going on to ask what the implications for the future of parenthood are. It seems likely – so I shall argue – that the *pressure of planning and expectation on parents is not only growing quantitatively, but also assuming qualitatively new forms.* We may be seeing the emergence of social pressure for the 'genetic optimisation' of genetic lineage.

Individualisation: Life as a Personal Task

Very diverse meanings and contents are associated with the concept of 'individualisation'. Since this has given rise to many misunderstandings and disputes, it is useful to sketch out what individualisation means in the present context.[4]

It refers first of all to a lengthy historical process, which begins with the transition from pre-industrial to industrial society, continues subsequently and has further increased and intensified since the 1960s. In the course of this development people begin to be released from traditional ties, systems of belief and social relationships. On the one hand, that means an expansion of the radius of life, a gain in terms of scope and choice. Life becomes in many respects more open and malleable. But it also means that new demands, controls and obligations fall upon the individual. The labour market, the welfare state and its institutions in particular now develop networks of rules and conditions and claim prerequisites.[5] From pension rights to insurance cover, from child benefit to tax rates – these are all institutional standards, which fix the horizon of our thinking, planning and acting.

Individualisation in this sense therefore very certainly does not mean 'a form of activity carried out skillfully and without constraint in a virtual void',[6] and neither does it mean mere 'subjectivity', leaving out of account the fact that 'behind the surface of the life worlds there is a highly efficient, close-meshed society of institutions'.[7] On the contrary, modern subjects, with their choices, exist in a space in which society is anything but absent. The regulatory density of modern society is well known if not notorious (from MOTs, through tax returns, to refuse classification regulations) – in sum total a highly complex work of art of labyrinthine construction which accompanies us, literally, from the cradle to the grave (for there is no life without certificates of birth and death).

Anyone, however, who does not meet such standards and does not know how to deal with them flexibly, has to bear the consequences in their personal lives. They risk job, income, social position. 'In the individualised society, the individual must therefore learn, on pain of permanent disadvantage, to conceive of himself or herself as the centre of activity, as the planning office with respect to his or her own biography, abilities, orientations, relationships and so on.'[8] In pre-industrial society, life chances were allotted by virtue of birth and station. Against that, the creed of modern society is that life is what you make it. That doesn't necessarily mean that every dish-washer, if he or she only works hard enough, will end up a millionaire. It certainly does mean, however, that one *must do something* to make one's fortune. So be single-minded about your plans! The possibilities must be weighed up and carefully calculated. You've got to know your way around if you want to succeed! You've got to be well informed – about everything from student grants to mortgage schemes to further education courses and pension calculations – and know how to use the information. Anyone who doesn't do it is out in the cold, without a job and without any prospect of work, without a house and garden, without a pension in his or her old age. As Martin Kohli writes, 'Life is no longer . . . a wonderful gift of God, but the property of an individual, which must be permanently defended. More than that, it becomes a task to be carried out, an individual project.'[9]

Health in Individualised Society

An area in which this task is especially evident is the modern approach to health. Certainly, in earlier centuries too, people hoped to be healthy and live without pain. Yet in those days their horizon of meaning was also largely determined by religion, which promised a life after death and deliverance from suffering. In the course of secularisation processes this belief has crumbled as far as large sections of the population are concerned. What remains is the individual in the here and now, his or her individual condition. Hopes and efforts are now focused on it. Where faith in the hereafter is breaking down, health takes on a new significance, increases in value, is turned into an earthly doctrine of salvation. 'What can no longer be expected from the hereafter is now . . . projected onto this life: freedom from cares and wrongs, from sickness and pain – ultimately bliss and immortality.'[10] In short, salvation has been dethroned and replaced by healing.[11]

In recent years, new dimensions to this earthly expectation of salvation have been opened up. From heart transplants and in-vitro fertilisation to prenatal and genetic diagnosis, modern high-tech medicine has had spectacular successes. The biological equipment of human beings is becoming, to an increasing degree, a matter of choice – can be planned, made, corrected. A human being is becoming his or her own project right down to organs, distinguishing features, genes. As Giddens writes, 'The body is becoming a phenomenon of choices and options'.[12] The progress of genetic diagnosis in particular is raising new promises. Its motto goes: someone who knows his or her genetic susceptibilities, his or her particular risk factors, can prepare him or herself for them, perhaps avert fate – prevent the onset of an illness, secure a longer life for him or herself.

In an essay on the future of medicine, published in *Newsweek*, Michael Crichton predicted the future course of this development. Under the symptomatic title 'Greater expectations' he described, among others, the following tendencies:

> The physician as lifestyle expert, as wellness adviser, has already begun to appear. And as genetic profiles and other predictive tools improve, the art of prevention will grow far more sophisticated. Physicians will administer tests and, armed with the results, prescribe measures just as precisely as they now dispense medications . . . Fundamental will be gene-replacement therapy, in which missing or defective genes are supplied by the physician. Such procedures are being developed to treat serious illness, but they will eventually be used to boost enzyme levels and hormone production to retard aging and to increase vigor

. . . What all this means is that our present conception of medicine will disappear . . . Medicine will change its focus from treatment to enhancement, from
repair to improvement, from diminished sickness to increased performance.[13]

This development gains further impetus because looking after one's
health and taking care to remain healthy in future fit perfectly with the
biographical models which individualised society demands and promotes.
Anyone who wants to keep up with the competition, wants to be successful
on the labour market, must demonstrate health, performance and fitness.
('Who can afford to have a cold nowadays? Everybody has to be on top –
day in, day out', runs the advertising slogan for a cold cure.[14]) What
modern medicine has to offer starts with the trend towards the planning
and rationalisation of the conduct of life – and extends it, takes it into new
dimensions. There now exists the possibility of clarifying one's own risk
factors (for example a susceptibility to heart attacks or diabetes) and of
incorporating genetic information as reference points and basic data
of one's own life plan. Preventative protection against injury is an 'element of the "self-management" that is expected of modern individualised
people. If the methodical conduct of life establishes itself, from the
planning of a school career . . . to provision for a "successful old age", then
preventive safeguarding of health will inevitably become very relevant.'[15]
Two pioneers of medical technology put it like this: 'Knowledge of one's
own genome should lead to a more responsible life design.'[16]
  Modern human beings take their fates in their own hands. They plan,
they make provision, they control and optimise. They no longer follow
God and the stars: their genes now tell them how to arrange their lives.

Parenthood in Modern Society: Children as Responsibility and Planning Object

The researches of social historians have shown that for a long time there
was no such thing as bringing up children in the real sense – that is, taking
account of age-group and a child's personal development.[17] Only with the
transition to modern society does the 'discovery of childhood' (Ariès)
begin, soon to be associated with efforts to influence the development of
the child. According to this new doctrine of childhood, parents can make
an essential contribution to the healthy progress of a child, indeed can lay
the foundation for all of its later destiny by appropriate care and education.
  This requirement of support, which begins with the onset of modernity,
is taken much further with the passage of time. In the second half of the
twentieth century certain developments lend it additional weight. These
include advances in medicine, psychology and child education which make
the child malleable to an increasing extent. For example, physical handicaps, which at the beginning of the century still had to be accepted as fate,
can increasingly be treated and corrected. In the 1960s a new school of

research established itself, which emphasises the first years of childhood even more strongly than before, equating the omission of support with lost chances of development. At the same time there has been a significant rise in income, so that possibilities of support, which were once reserved for a small stratum, have now become attainable to large groups. Birth rates are also declining; more and more children are growing up as an only child or with one sibling, and consequently the hopes for the future, ambitions and investments of parents are becoming concentrated. Offspring are a 'scarce resource', whose success must be ensured. Finally, on the political level, a promotion of education has been set in motion which is directed at previously disadvantaged groups.

Cultural pressure is reinforced as a result of this and similar conditions. A child can no longer be accepted as it is, with physical and mental idiosyncrasies, perhaps even flaws. Rather, it becomes the target of a diversity of efforts. All possible flaws must be corrected (no more squinting, stuttering, bedwetting), all possible talents must be stimulated (boom time for piano lessons, language holidays, tennis in summer and ski courses in winter). Countless guides to education and upbringing appear on the book and magazine market. As different as each one is, at bottom they all have a similar message: the success of the child is defined as the private duty and responsibility of the parents/the mother. And the duty reads the same everywhere: the parents must do everything to give the child 'the best start in life'.

As empirical research also shows, most parents – across all social strata – really are trying hard to fulfil this duty.[18] For the message that is conveyed to them has an ever recurring chorus: that inattention to the needs of children leads to irreversible damage, and that lack of support leads to retarded development, if not under-achievement. 'Under-achievement' is a word whose meaning parents understand very well, precisely because in a socially mobile society achievement is a key category. Where the possibility and promise of rising up the social ladder exists – which always implies, as its reverse side, the threat of downward social mobility – then the pressure to secure one's own place in the social hierarchy by way of individual planning, effort and educational endeavours becomes ever more noticeable.

To sum up, one can say that in advanced industrial society the physical maintenance of children has certainly become simpler in many respects, thanks to the mechanisation of the household and to ready-made products like disposable nappies and baby food. But to make up for that, with the discovery of childhood, new themes and duties were increasingly discovered, which became converted into growing demands. Thus a work of research on family sociology concludes: 'the norm of responsible parenting' is ever more dominant, indeed the 'extent of parents' ethical and social responsibility today . . . is historically unprecedented'.[19] The contemporary family 'is under a *pressure to educate* which is without historical parallel'.[20] A child, once a gift of God, sometimes also an unwanted burden, increasingly becomes for parents/mothers 'a difficult object for treatment'.[21]

The Task of the Future: Genetic Optimisation of Offspring

It is at this point – the optimisation of the child's start in life – that reproductive medicine and genetic engineering make their entry today. Care for a child need no longer be restricted to the time after birth; it can begin much more purposefully even before that. A motto for that could be the sentence recently formulated at a congress of human geneticists and specialists in preventive medicine. It went as follows: 'In our time, in which there is such stress on achievement, even slight disorders and handicaps can be of dramatic importance for development, integration, getting on and assertiveness.'[22] What, therefore, will happen under such conditions, when high-tech medicine offers increasing possibilities of intervention? In future, will responsible parents still dare to expect their child to bear the possibility of a handicap? Must they not do everything in their power to avert every impairment?

We can also define concretely what that might mean. Parents who submit to these demands must first of all use the tools of prenatal diagnosis and, in the case of an unfavourable result, terminate the pregnancy – or not allow the embryo to be implanted at all. (The 'checklist for embryo quality',[23] as specialists in reproductive medicine call it, is already being applied today and constantly being refined.) And that is not all. If it is thought out logically, then parents' obligations must begin earlier – that is, at the moment of conception. The responsible parents of the future must ask themselves whether their own 'genetic material' still satisfies the demands of the age, or whether they would not do better to fall back on ovum or sperm donation – carefully selected of course. The moral philosopher Reinhard Löw provocatively imagines the following vision: 'In this brave new world, to have one's own children is to start them out in life with the irresponsible disadvantage of a smaller intelligence and more modest looks than those conceived progressively or combined in a test tube. One can almost foresee a time when children will take their parents to court because of an "inadequate genetic make-up".'[24]

The Scenario of Acceptance

The possibilities which could be in store for us accordingly amount to a conscious 'quality control of reproductive lineage'. No doubt such possibilities still seem distant to us today. Yet the scenario of their acceptance can already be described, since the history of technology has shown that the sequence of events from invention to general dissemination often takes place in similar stages.[25] And the development of reproductive medicine and prenatal diagnosis up to now suggests that similar patterns are also emerging here. The line from the present to the future may then perhaps take the following course.

At present only a few parents are beginning to make use of medical technology. These men and women may individually have quite different motives. Some are infertile and can only come by the desired child with medical assistance. Others belong to groups which according to recent scientific findings are considered to be 'risk groups' – that is, there is an increased probability of a genetic burden on the child. Then there are men who get themselves sterilised, but deposit sperm in a sperm bank beforehand, as a kind of reinsurance. Similarly, women can choose the option of in-vitro fertilisation if they have had themselves sterilised, but later want to have a child after all – for example with a new partner. And finally, the number of those in modern society who are single, but want a child, and turn to the possibilities of artificial conception for that reason, is also growing.

As various as these motives are, they obviously all lead in a similar direction – towards reproductive technology. As this is put into practice and new possibilities are opened up, the desire to have a child can be combined with the desire to influence the nature and constitution of the child. The path is covertly prepared for a new form of the 'wanted child mentality'.[26] And this is not chance but is already predetermined by the process. Reproductive technology does not only make choice possible; it often even makes it necessary. Or as Jeremy Rifkin challengingly puts it, the 'inherent logic of this technology is eugenic'.[27]

A concrete example is first of all provided by those cases where the desire for a child is to be fulfilled via a sperm donor or surrogate mother. In the United States it is common practice for prospective customers to receive a catalogue in which the sperm donors or surrogate mothers are neatly listed according to all the features regarded as relevant. The customers can – no, must – choose from it. But if a choice has to be made – then why not the 'better' choice? Who, if there is a choice to be made between different articles, is consciously going to take the one he or she likes less? And similarly, since a choice must take place in every case, it seems reasonable to decide according to one's own ideal, so as to guide the genetic roulette towards certain characteristics. Accordingly, some clients back intelligence, some health, others blue eyes or athletic achievement.[28]

A further example of the selection processes which are set in motion is prenatal genetic diagnosis. At present, the current legal position in Germany is that an abortion is only allowed if continuation of pregnancy cannot be expected of the woman, because there is a threat of serious, irremediable damage to the child. Social reality looks somewhat different, however. Already today the practice of prenatal selection overwhelms the normative limits which the criminal code tries to set. Abortions are increasingly carried out even if less serious damage, which could, for example, be operated on, is anticipated.[29]

All of these are not visions of a remote future but developments we are already experiencing today. Such developments are an indication of how reproductive medicine and prenatal diagnosis are surreptitiously becoming the gateway for procedures which amount to a 'genetic improvement' of reproductive lineage. Where this is the case, however, the next stage of acceptance can also be anticipated. If some parents begin to make use of biotechnology, then others – it can be assumed – will join them. They will follow suit because they are afraid that otherwise their child will not be able to keep up in competitive, achievement-orientated society.

Women's Changed Life Planning

In addition – and this propels the development even further – there is the fact that at this point not only is the life plan for the child at stake, but that of the mother is simultaneously and very directly affected as well, in a historically completely new way. Until only a few decades ago the imperatives of the individualised achievement society held almost exclusively for men; for women, on the other hand, the socially assigned role was 'to be there for the family'. Meanwhile, however, a distinct transformation of the normal female biography has got under way.[30] More and more women are at last partly freed from the bonds by changes in education, profession, family cycle, legal system etc.; they cannot expect to be maintained by a husband; they are required to be independent and maintain themselves – often under very contradictory conditions. The 'subjective correlate' of such changes is that women are increasingly developing – indeed must develop – desires and life plans which no longer refer to the family alone, but equally to themselves as persons. They can no longer see themselves simply as 'appendages' of the family, but must see themselves also as individual persons with corresponding interests and rights, plans for the future and options.

The compatibility of job and family is, consequently, what is almost always hoped for when young girls and women are asked about their life plans.[31] Social reality, admittedly, looks rather different. The world of work does not show any consideration for family tasks and duties. In education ministries and local authorities there is a lack of money or a lack of willingness to provide sufficient day nurseries, kindergartens and all-day schools (German schools usually finish in early to mid-afternoon) and it is women who are disadvantaged as a result. They experience at many levels every day how difficult it is to combine the demands of the working world with those of bringing up children.[32] Having children is today *the* structural risk of a female wage-earning biography; indeed, it is a handicap, measured by the yardstick of a market society. And this is precisely the reason why many women eagerly accept the offer of prenatal diagnosis. They want such methods so as to 'balance' the risk of age, to be able to forget the fear of a disabled child.[33] As has been pointed out, they have good reason for that. Given the organisation of our working and everyday worlds, women with a healthy child are already handicapped enough.

The connection is explicitly made by women in interview statements: 'Imagine a handicapped child; how terrible and how much work that means. I might as well give up my job right away, then.'[34] Or: 'The main reason for doing the test was that I've got a job I want to keep on doing . . . With a handicapped child I would be tied down for years. I've been working at getting away from the traditional woman's role all these years, and I wouldn't like to slide into it again. The thought of having a Down's Syndrome baby means looking after a child for twenty years or more that will never get past the stage of being an infant; it locks you into a woman's role again.'[35]

Brave New Responsibility

We can see from the above that what first begins with small steps, restricted to exceptional groups, can quickly gain a momentum which overwhelms our previous ways of life. That too is familiar from the history of technology.[36] Where new possibilities of action become available, then standards of behaviour also begin to shift. What was in the past considered impossible, then outrageous, becomes in the present something new, then normal, and in future perhaps the socially expected approach. So much so that the momentum of reproductive technology can also produce a social pressure to conform which parents in future will find difficult to avoid.

From an interview with a pregnant woman: 'I felt I was in an awful dilemma. Everyone was saying to me "Have you had the test yet?" If the possibility's there, after all, you must do it . . . And what if it's a handicapped child? You've already got two children, you must think about them and about your husband!'[37]

What is expressed in such experiences is the creeping change in meaning which the concept of responsibility is undergoing. In earlier decades the slogan 'responsible parenting' was linked to a political movement pressing for the lifting of controls on means of contraception. In that context responsible parenting meant the quantitative restriction of the number of children. There were to be only as many children as one could adequately feed and raise. Today, however, the concept of responsibility is being made to conform to the new possibilities of reproductive medicine and prenatal diagnosis and is thereby also taking on a new aspect. Now it is gradually being drawn in the direction of qualitative selection, of a selection according to genetic characteristics, before birth, perhaps even before conception. Formulations taken from the language of bureaucracy, which avoid expressing aims straightforwardly, are often employed. Words like 'prevention'[38] and 'prophylactic measures'[39] are used. The real intention is to avoid the birth of burdened children. There is already a tendency to praise such behaviour as simply the manifestation of a new responsibility. This, for example, is Hubert Markl, at the time President of the Deutsche Forschungsgemeinschaft (German Research Association), in a lecture on the subject of 'Genetics and Ethics':

> I want to say here very clearly, because sometimes it is put rather differently, that refraining from having children of one's own for such [genetic] reasons deserves to be praised at least as much, perhaps even more than the decision, out of a pitilessly fatalistic piety, at all costs simply to let a cruel fate take its course.[40]

An Unstoppable Development?

Genetic optimisation of offspring – is this the future towards which we are heading? We do not know, because the acceptance of technologies is not a process that follows natural laws, but a *social* process. It is not decided by given determinations, but by social, political, economic conditions. It is dependent on power relationships and group interests, on market shares and career opportunities, on political priorities, legislative regulation and private decisions. It is therefore in principle open, stoppable, controllable. It can – depending on the possibilities – be slowed down.

At the moment, admittedly, the signs point in the other direction. Biotechnology is advanced into even more areas. The reports of successes come thick and fast, and with every new research result new possible applications are constantly presented. The rapid pace with which all this is happening means that this advance is almost uncontrolled – medicine is becoming 'sub-political'.[41]

Yet at the same time a shift has also been developing in recent years. The 'religion of progress' (C. Schmitt) is beginning to crumble, at least in certain fields and among certain groups. The more our lifeworld is determined by technology, by our own interventions and appropriations, and the more the consequences are perceived as potentially problematic, even threatening, the more too a new guiding principle is coming to the fore: 'nature'. The concept of nature becomes a beacon which can be, and is, employed very effectively to mobilise public criticism and resistance. Genetic engineering in particular provides an instructive example of how an increased sensitivity towards interventions regarded as 'unnatural' develops, indeed how it can also be deliberately built up.[42] Apart from all the elements promoting acceptance there also exist (still, perhaps even increasingly) deep-seated cultural obstacles which make the production of legitimation both necessary and at the same time difficult.

If this judgement is accurate, then a curious constellation is emerging here. The guiding values of 'nature' and 'health', at first sight closely interrelated, diverge – in fact become rivals – and are mobilised to support opposing positions. The advocates of genetic engineering attack with the argument 'For the sake of health'; the critics on the other hand proclaim 'For the sake of nature'. A very visible polarisation of viewpoints has taken place, one that splits the established parties and groups, splits the academic world and not least the natural sciences also.

In this context it is interesting to look also at the field of human genetics, particularly in Germany. Differences can clearly be discerned between those involved in pure research, and those, who as human geneticists with consulting practices, deal with clients/patients on a daily basis. Whereas the pure researchers often see genetic engineering as a direct route to a better future,[43] to a world with less injustice and less suffering, the human geneticists who are also practitioners are more likely to see the ambivalences, dilemmas and conflicts between decisions, which are appearing with the rapidly increasing supply of genetic engineering diagnostic procedures.[44] Also of relevance here is the fact that German human geneticists are repeatedly being confronted in public with the history of their profession under National Socialism. The memory of eugenics, of the fatal, indeed murderous, consequences of policies which distinguished between the genetically 'good' and the genetically 'inferior' and carried out selection accordingly, is always present.

Against this background a debate is slowly but perceptibly developing among German geneticists about the future which genetic engineering is opening up. Under discussion are ethical questions and conflicts which affect the value of life and the dignity of human beings. What is being looked for are rules of application and standards on which they can be based. Helmut Baitsch, a prominent representative of this tendency, writes:

> We see ourselves confronted more urgently than ever by the question . . . what our disciplines are doing today, what they will do tomorrow, how we legitimate today our behaviour as scientists . . . Research with and on human beings concerns the dignity of human beings, since basic research quickly leads to application . . . I want the irreducible respect for the personal dignity of our fellow human beings to be the centrepiece of this new paradigm [in human genetics] both for myself and for my discipline.[45]

Whereas genetic engineering in other countries is frequently accepted unquestioningly, in Germany there is a far broader spectrum of positions, viewpoints and assessments. It becomes tangible in the number of committees, commissions, conferences set up on biotechnology, measurable too by the emotional force with which the debates are conducted. Perhaps all this only has an alibi function; perhaps these are the last spasms of a pre-modern culture and form of life. But perhaps not. Perhaps awareness is also spreading that the creativeness which genetic engineering initiates always has two sides, and that the opportunities, which it undoubtedly presents, are always 'risky opportunities'.

Prospects

The tendency towards the individualisation of lives means new opportunities, but simultaneously also new dependencies, controls and pressures. What we can observe today in the area of parenting is a vivid example of that. It is no longer just traditional frameworks like class and station which are losing their capacity to bind, but even the framework of nature itself. Given the possibilities which modern medicine, biology and genetics offer, we are no longer at the mercy of nature, even with regard to the fundamental questions of life, but can take fate itself in our hands. The prospect, according to Christa Hoffmann-Riem, is of 'human control, which alters the concept of parenthood. In accordance with the technological possibilities parental responsibility for the emergent life expands.'[46] If this prediction should prove to be true then the parents of the future will be faced by quite new pressures on decision-making and planning.

It is not only private decisions that are at stake. What is already beginning to emerge today could intensify further, determine conflicts in the public arena and lead to *competition between concepts of risk*. When talking about risk groups, social scientists are used to thinking in terms of social risks and of those groups which are unable to keep up with the imperatives of the individualised achievement society (the unemployed, single parents, the homeless, etc.). In human genetics on the other hand risk groups are considered to be those people who bear a specific genetic risk, an inherited disease or susceptibility to a disease. The displacement of one concept of risk by the other is certainly not theoretically tenable, and represents an inadmissible abbreviation of the relationship of nature and culture. The question is, however, how these things will look in practice – how these two concepts of risk will relate to one another in the competition for public attention, political recognition, financial means, political measures and priorities, whether they are played off against one another and which will dominate in the end.

As an illustration I want to quote a speech that Daniel Koshland, the editor of *Science Magazine* made to a big scientific conference in California. Koshland said:

> In Washington there are people who think it's a better idea to put more money into housing programmes for the homeless than into researching the human genome. Now, I believe that, in the long term the human genome project will contribute more to solving the homeless problem than building houses . . . Many of the homeless are physically or psychically disturbed. So if we are supposed to be fighting the causes and not the symptoms, then we should be investing the money in research into the human gene . . . [47]

Such biological reductionism is certainly not an inevitable consequence of genome analysis. But there is a relationship, as statements by prominent geneticists demonstrate. And even if it proves to be theoretically untenable, it does have consequences. As one of the most famous sentences in sociology, the so-called Thomas Theorem, puts it, 'What men [sic] define as real is real in its consequences'. Wherever a biological determinism emerges, it does not just remain theory, but also contains a practical programme. It contains direct guidelines for political action. Where the determining power of genes is assumed, the demands for equality of opportunity in the educational system lose their force. Where once social reforms appeared necessary, one can then support the genetic improvement of talents. In short, the danger of biological reductionism is that there will be a search for technical solutions alone instead of social ones.

So what will the future look like? Will we see a shift from social to genetic risk? That truly would be the 'path into another modernity',[48] in fact into another risk society. If that is not to happen, social scientists and natural scientists will together have to set about taking up the challenge of biologism and making its errors systematically visible. A decisive question in shaping the future may well be whether it is possible to illuminate the societal and political, the social and psychical dimensions, which disappear from sight when the planning of human life is completely reduced to the technical.

Notes

1. Birgit Geissler and Mechtild Oechsle (1994) 'Lebensplanung als Konstruktion', in Ulrich Beck and Elisabeth Beck-Gernsheim, *Riskante Freiheiten. Individualisierung in modernen Gesellschaften*. Frankfurt am Main. p. 139.

2. Hans Harald Bräutigam and Liselotte Mettler (1985), *Die programmierte Vererbung. Möglichkeiten und Gefahren der Gentechnologie*. Hamburg.

3. Wolfgang van den Daele (1985), *Mensch nach Mass? Ethische Probleme der Genmanipulation und Gentherapie*. Munich.

4. For greater detail see Ulrich Beck and Elisabeth Beck-Gernsheim (1993) 'Nicht Autonomie, sondern Bastelbiographie. Anmerkungen zur Individualisierungsdiskussion am Beispiel des Aufsatzes von Günter Burkart', *Zeitschrift für Soziologie*, June: 178–87; and the Introduction to *Riskante Freiheiten*, op. cit.: 10–39.

5. Karl Ulrich Mayer and Walter Müller, 'Individualisierung und Standardisierung im Strukturwandel der Moderne. Lebensverläufe im Wohlfahrtsstaat', in Beck and Beck-Gernsheim (eds), *Riskante Freiheiten*, pp. 265–95.

6. This is the concept of individualisation assumed by Ilona Ostner and Peter Boy, who then go on to criticise the individualisation thesis. See Ilona Oster and Peter Boy (1991) 'Späte Heirat – Ergebnis biographisch unterschiedlicher Erfahrungen mit "cash" und "care"?' Project proposal to the Deutsche Forschungsgemeinschaft, Bremen. p. 18.

7. This is the concept of individualisation assumed by Karl Ulrich Mayer who also then goes on to criticise the individualisation thesis. See Karl Mayer (1991) 'Soziale Ungleichheit und Lebensverläufe', in Bernd Giesen and Claus Leggewie (eds), *Experiment Vereinigung*. Berlin. p. 88.

8. Ulrich Beck (1992), *Risk Society: Towards a New Modernity*. London. p. 135.

9. Martin Kohli (1986) 'Gesellschaftszeit und Lebenszeit. Der Lebenslauf im Strukturwandel der Moderne', in Johannes Berger (ed.), *Die Moderne – Kontinuitäten und Zäsuren. Soziale Welt, Sonderband 4*. Göttingen. p. 185.

10. Ulrich Mergner, Edeltraut Mönkeberg-Tun and Gerd Ziegler (1990) 'Gesundheit und Interesse. Zur Fremdbestimmung von Selbstbestimmung im Umgang mit Gesundheit', *Psychosozial*, 2: 7–20.

11. Cf. Johann Jürgen Rohde (1974) *Soziologie des Krankenhauses*. Stuttgart. p. 130.

12. Anthony Giddens (1991) *Modernity and Self-Identity: Self and Society in the Late Modern Age*. Cambridge. p. 8.

13. Michael Crichton (1990) 'Greater Expectations', *Newsweek*, 24 September, p. 37.

14. Published in many newspapers, for example *Süddeutsche Zeitung*, 29 November 1990.

15. Wolfgang van den Daele (1989) 'Das zähe Leben des präventiven Zwangs', in Alexander Schuller and Nikolaus Heim (eds), *Der codierte Leib. Zur Zukunft der genetischen Vergangenheit.* Zürich. p. 207; see also Mergner et al. (1990), op. cit.

16. Bräutigam and Mettler (1985), op. cit.: 138.

17. Especially Philippe Ariès (1962) *Centuries of Childhood.* London.

18. For example Regina Becker-Schmidt and Gudrun-Axeli Knapp (1985) *Arbeiterkinder gestern – Arbeiterkinder heute.* Bonn; Klaus Wahl et al. (1980) *Familien sind anders!* Reinbek.

19. Franz-Xaver Kaufmann et al. (1984) *Familienentwicklung in Nordrhein-Westfalen. IBS-Materialien,* no. 17. Universität Bielefeld, Bielefeld. p. 10.

20. Ibid. (1984) 'Familienentwicklung – generatives Verhalten im familialen Kontext', *Zeitschrift für Bevölkerungswissenschaft,* 4: 530.

21. Hartmut von Hentig (1978) Vorwort to Ariès, *Geschichte der Kindheit.* Munich. p. 34 (Foreword to German paperback edition of *Centuries of Childhood*).

22. Quoted in Claudia Roth (1987) 'Hundert Jahre Eugenik: Gebärmütter im Fadenkreuz', in her *Genzeit. Die Industrialisierung von Pflanze, Tier und Mensch.* Zürich. p. 100.

23. Bräutigam and Mettler (1985), op. cit.: 63.

24. Reinhard Löw (1985) *Leben aus dem Labor. Gentechnologie und Verantwortung – Biologie und Moral.* Munich. p. 179.

25. For example Hans Jonas (1985) *Technik, Medizin und Ethik. Zur Praxis des Prinzips Verantwortung.* Frankfurt am Main; see also Daele (1985), op. cit.

26. Wolfgang van den Daele (1986) 'Technische Dynamik und gesellschaftliche Moral. Zur soziologischen Bedeutung der Gentechnologie', *Soziale Welt,* 2 (3): 157.

27. Interview with Jeremy Rifkin in *Natur,* 9, 1987: 54.

28. Empirical evidence of such selection processes can be found in, for example, Linda S. Fidell and Jarislov Marik (1989) 'Paternity by proxy: Artificial insemination with donor sperm', in Joan Offerman-Zuckerberg (ed.), *Gender in Transition: A New Frontier.* New York. pp. 93–110; April Martin (1989) 'Lesbian parenting: A personal odyssey', in Offerman-Zuckerberg (ed.), ibid.: 249–63; Martha A. Field (1988) *Surrogate Motherhood: The Legal and Human Issues.* Cambridge, MA; Jean Renvoize (1985) *Going Solo: Single Mothers by Choice.* London.

29. Daele (1985), op. cit.: 145.

30. Elisabeth Beck-Gernsheim (1983) 'Vom "Dasein für andere" zum Anspruch auf ein Stück "eigenes Leben". Individualisierungsprozesse im weiblichen Lebenszusammenhang', *Soziale Welt,* 3: 307–40.

31. Klaus Allerbeck and Wendy Hoag (1985) *Jugend ohne Zukunft? Einstellungen, Umwelt, Lebensperspektiven.* Munich; Gerlinde Seidenspinner and Angelika Burger (1982) *Mädchen '82. Eine Untersuchung im Auftrag der Zeitschrift 'Brigitte'.* Hamburg.

32. For example Arlie Hochschild and Anne Machung (1990) *The Second Shift: Working Parents and the Revolution in the Home.* London.

33. For example Eva Schindele (1990) *Gläserne Gebär-Mütter. Vorgeburtliche Diagnostik – Fluch oder Segen.* Frankfurt am Main; Maria Reif (1990) *Psychosoziale und ethische Gesichtspunkte.* Stuttgart.

34. Interview extract from Schindele (1990) *Frühe Pränataldiagnostik und gehetische Beratung.* op. cit.: 9.

35. Interview extract from Monika Leuzinger and Bigna Rambert (1987) 'Ich spür es – mein Kind ist gesund', in Claudia Roth (1987), op. cit.: 87.

36. For example Daele (1985), op. cit.; Jonas (1985), op. cit.; Peter Weingart (1989) (ed.), *Technik als sozialer Prozess,* Frankfurt am Main.

37. Interview extract from Leuzinger and Rambert (1987), op. cit.: 70.

38. Werner Schmid (1988) 'Die Prävention des Down-Syndroms (Mongolismus)', *Neue Zürcher Zeitung,* 20 January: 77.

39. 'In families with a genetic risk, human genetic counselling is desirable before conception. If necessary . . . prophylactic measures are to be recommended.' H. Bach et al. (1990) 'Genetische Beratung in der DDR', *Medizinische Genetik,* September: 41.

40. Hubert Markl (1989) 'Genetik und Ethik' (Speech on the occasion of the award of the 1989 Arthur Burkhardt Prize), photocopied manuscript. Stuttgart, 26 April 1989.

41. Beck (1992), op. cit.: 222.

42. Volker Heins (1992) 'Gentechnik aus der Verbraucherperspektive – Symbolische Kämpfe um neue Konsummodelle', *Soziale Welt*, 4.

43. An example is Renato Dulbecco and Riccardo Chiaberge (1991) *Konstrukteure des Lebens. Medizin und Ethik im Zeitalter der Gentechnologie*. Munich, esp. p. 11.

44. Examples are the contributions by Jörg Schmidtke and Gerlinde Sponholz et al., and Walther Vogel, in Elisabeth Beck-Gernsheim (1995) (ed.), *Welche Gesundheit wollen wir? Ambivalenzen des Medizintechnischen Fortschritts*, Frankfurt am Main.

45. Helmut Baitsch (1990) 'Naturwissenschaften und Politik am Beispiel des Faches Anthropologie während des Dritten Reiches', in *Imagines humanae. Festschrift aus Anlass der Emeritierung von Prof. Dr. Dr. Helmut Baitsch, Schriftenreihe der Universität Ulm*, vol. 3. Ulm. p. 182.

46. Christa Hoffmann-Riem (1988) 'Chancen und Risiken der gentechnologisch erweiterten pränatalen Diagnostik. Eine qualitative Studie bei Klienten humangenetischer Beratungsstellen'. Research application, Hamburg (photocopied manuscript).

47. Interview extract from Mathias Greffrath (1990), 'Der lange Arm von Chromosom Nr. 7. Visionen und Ambitionen der Top-Genforscher', *Transatlantik*, December: 17.

48. Cf. Beck (1992), op. cit.

6

INDIVIDUALISATION AT WORK: OFFICE AUTOMATION AND OCCUPATIONAL IDENTITY

Marco Diani

The automation of intellectual work, or office automation, is one of the key areas within which modern subjectivities are being transformed by individualising processes, and yet these changes are little understood. All the social actors involved in the process – scientists and producers, technologists and users – are faced with the 'architecture of complexity' induced by fundamental changes that go beyond traditional understandings of work. What follows, in this chapter, is a schematic analysis of some of these transformations.

One of the most notable qualities of the literature on office automation is the variety of totally conflicting findings reported by various authors. On the one hand office automation is described as a great liberating agent and on the other as a device which will reduce human freedom. The changes in tasks, job profiles, relations among employees, the way the work is supervised, career paths and structure of the organisations, and again about the role of management and of 'designers': the description of all of these varies dramatically according to which authors one reads, bestowing upon the reader a growing confusion, reflected both by the vagueness of the terminology employed in order to define the 'office of the future' and its functions, and by conflicting opinions about its human consequences.

What *is* clear is that, despite any distinction in category and other differences (in salary, company status or career), the centre of gravity in all working practices is shifting towards a series of functions which call for intense mental activity, the actual cognitive mediation of work and of its social and organisational context. Moreover, the stereotyped image of an intelligent, creative and rewarding activity on the one hand, and of a repetitive and intellectually boring job on the other, is now giving way to a vision which is the hybrid product of the information revolution: despite job status and cultural differences, there now exists a series of tasks, both inside and outside the office, which are marked by the same standards, which use the same symbolic mediation, and which create the same sense of loss of identity in dealing with the intelligent processes of the machine.

Today the machine and work procedures require not only a certain amount of mental commitment, which may vary with the complexity of the machines and the operator's knowledge and experience. A new component in the workload seems to have been added – the 'cognitive-organizational load'; that is, the component dealing with the effects of the variables that define the organisation of social relations and work. At the centre of an ever-increasing number of activities (industrial, post-industrial and service orientated) we find the processing, checking and sometimes the analysis of the symbolic data and mediating information produced by information-based systems. The borderline between jobs and their respective cultures now tends to disappear, giving place to a much vaster group of activities in which the work is carried out in similar conditions, with processes of the same kind, content and intelligibility, and above all in similar organizational contexts.

This 'recomposition of work', often presented as one of the promises of automation, carries with it, however, an unforeseen consequence: one's perception of the conditions of work and of the weight of the organization – once its 'mechanical' and material side disappears – vanishes from one's immediate view, while the abstraction inherent in the new conditions of work alters one's psychological sense of the work itself. With the new information technologies the work may indeed recompose, but the meaning of each activity becomes murkier and more inaccessible both for individuals and for the organisation.

Despite the widespread belief underlying much research into the social consequences of automation, the process of symbolic abstraction and mediation of work is not an 'unexpected consequence' but an intrinsic element in information technology. The alteration of the experience, contents and finality of a job takes place independently of the way in which the office system is conceived, planned and introduced. The most dramatic example, perhaps, is the rapidity of access to information and the speed of its processing, which make possible a considerable increase in the number of operations and lead to an intensification of the work tempo.

A brief historical reference is needed in order to gain a perspective on all these issues. Norbert Wiener, in an essay concerned with the moral and technical predicaments of automation with respect to both cybernetic technique, which he discovered and promoted, and the social aftermaths of this technique, suggested that, in advanced industrial societies, automated machines are more ecologically and mentally hazardous than the ones of the industrial past, because they have pervaded the fields of techniques and communication, and the way the human mind works:

> I find myself facing a public which has formed its attitude toward the machine on the basis of an imperfect understanding of the structure and mode of operation of modern machines. It is my thesis that machines *can and do transcend some of the limitations of their designers and that in doing so they may be both effective and dangerous*. . . . [If, as is the case,] machines act far more rapidly than human beings . . . even when machines do not in any way transcend man's intelligence,

they very well may, and often do, transcend man in the performance of tasks. *An intelligent understanding of their mode of performance may be delayed until long after the task which they have been set has been completed.*[1]

Paradoxically, therefore, the intellectual foundations of this chapter were already laid down more than a quarter of a century ago, though Wiener's concept of automation did not then stretch as far as our experience of it today, into the very human relations of organisation. But before analysing some of the more subtle cultural dimensions of office automation, it is necessary to place this present 'information revolution' within the context of the continuous technological transformation of office work since the nineteenth century, of which this is only the latest stage.

What is Office Automation?

In the last 25 years the 'information revolution' has brought about profound changes in the conventional workplaces, and many studies and researches have explored the economic and social consequences of these new technologies.[2] One of the most visible characteristics of these texts is that they have been either lauding or attacking the current trend towards 'office automation' – a term, it needs to be noted, which has been around for at least thirty years, but which has been subjected to several changes over this period, closely following the phases of technological development of office automation.

But the present wave of office automation is not the first technological revolution to take place in the office; indeed, there have been a number of 'office revolutions' since the nineteenth century. Of course, it is important not to represent this development – or any narrative of technological change – as having been linear or necessary. In the first place, there has never existed, in automated work, a definite 'state' to be achieved: 'one never gets home'. This does not mean that automation does not have any direction; though it is certainly not possible to define a condition of 'stability' for it that lasts long enough to become a point of reference for those who live it from within. In the second place, the developmental process of automation is not linear. Given that it has no recognised and consolidated state to arrive at, it proceeds according to a logic of 'discovery,' exploratory in character, that never presents definite objectives from which to derive, hierarchically, intermediate objectives and phases of development. Often moments of repetition can be observed, in which one apparently goes backwards, but which in reality serve to redefine conditions and objectives. This may take place through negotiations that change the relative importance assigned to available technologies and to the consensus of the group; that is, to the capabilities of the machines and to the evaluation of opportunities and options that are offered and that one wants or is able to make use of. It is a radically transformational process, both regarding the use of human resources and concerning the products and services that can be derived from them. In automated work, the objectives of the transformational process can change rapidly. Hence, one cannot define a priori, either as to time or as to kind, the states that automation gradually passes through, much less its final state.

With that qualification in mind, let me summarise the phases through which office automation has passed over the last hundred years or so. In the nineteenth century, 'office' and 'bureaucracy' grew together along similar development paths, moulded as they were on the models of the centralised military states from which they were derived, especially France and Prussia.[3] Someone visiting an office in the early nineteenth century would have seen more or less the same spectacle during the entire century: an all-male system, with strong hierarchical features in which the junior clerks handled both clerical and simple professional and managerial tasks, with the tacit and implicit assumption that they would slowly rise in the hierarchy assuming more seniority and managerial powers. The main technological elements of the office in this period were paper, feathers, ink, pencils and folders. Powerful and detailed literary analyses of this kind of office work were provided by some of the great nineteenth century writers, like Honoré de Balzac and Charles Dickens, but have not been taken up to any degree by social scientists.[4]

But by 1900 a number of mechanical devices had established a place in the office, introducing important modifications. The most notable innovations were Morse's telegraph, Bell's telephone, Edison's dictating machine and, above all, the typewriter. This mechanisation represented a major global change in the nature of office work, not only allowing an increase in the size of the offices and in the quantity of operations performed but also, by separating the mechanical operation of writing from its intellectual content, creating a very rigid separation between clerical and managerial operations. In a very short span of time, the former came to be seen as women's work, and inferior in status. The introduction of the typewriter set the date for the creation of a segregated class of female typists, who were not expected to perform any managerial activities. This was the *first* office revolution.

But all through the first half of the twentieth century, along with the expansion of industrial organisations, the increase in capital and financial resources produced a dramatic rise in the labour force employed in the office and the appearance of an enormous number of innovations and refinements including, among the most important ones, electric typewriters, duplicating machines and photocopiers. More specialised clerks were required and, given the growing importance of the functions performed by the offices in the general economy, a new concern for productivity became a primary preoccupation. Scientific techniques of rationalisation and standardisation, the same as those applied in the factory years before under the name of 'scientific management', landed in the world of the office. This was the *second* office revolution. Thus, the 'functions of thought and planning become concentrated in an even smaller group within the office, and for the mass of those employed there the office became just as much a site of manual labor as the factory floor'.[5]

Office automation, based on what many social scientists call the Information Technology Revolution,[6] is the latest stage of the office revolution, and covers broadly all the current changes provoked by the fusion of several powerful information technologies – computers, telecommunications, and microelectronics – into new computerised systems of office work, symbolised but not entirely represented by the 'visual display terminal' or VDT.[7] It has received a great deal of attention over the last 25 years, but studies have been mainly orientated to: the physical characteristics of new technologies, in particular all the issues arising from long-term use of video display terminals;[8] the effects of office automation on the structure of total employment and the distribution of skills and qualifications;[9] and the elaboration of systematic analysis allowing the redesign of office functions in an automated setting.[10]

One of the unfortunate results of this emphasis on the economic and social consequences of the new technology has been a neglect of the particular characteristics of office work and, consequently, of the modifications introduced in the very structure and nature of one way of working. In doing so, we have repeated, in analysing office automation, the same mistake committed more than 25 years ago, in examining automation and robotics in the area of manual/industrial work: after a wave of 'great fear' and concern about the social and economic consequences, it was found that changes came about much more slowly than predicted or expected, and that the introduction of new technologies proceeded only after long periods of adaptation for each phase of technological development.

This excessive theoretical fear of sudden and radical changes was based in large part on ignorance of the real content and nature of office work and has left, for years now, very little room for the development of more creative undertakings, such as explorations of the social and alternative use of the new technologies. Consequently, the ill-conceived introduction of new systems has tended to encourage the routinisation of job content, a lack of financial incentive, the isolation of workers, and the elimination of jobs – and thus to foster an all-too-rational human resistance to technological change, which in turn prevents any economic advantage.[11]

These 'unexpected consequences' of the diffusion of office automation form the focus of this chapter. The real 'revolution in the office', hitting organisations all over the world, is caused by the problem of operating more and more complex systems, an unprecedented novelty with which our conventional conceptual instruments and methods of social and organisational design are unable to cope.

Participation and Technological Change

How can the numerous conflicts produced by the widespread adoption of information technologies be circumvented? One solution that has been offered has been to encourage a wider worker's participation in technological change. In order to prevent, and to reduce the importance of, these conflictual phenomena, participative methods of technological change have been developed, varying mainly according to the different socio-economic conditions and to the strengths of unions in Europe, the USA and Japan.[12]

The solutions found to prevent the 'unexpected consequences' of office automation can be divided into two categories: procedural and substantive. The first ones consist of a normative set of regulations based on legislation, standards and rules, mostly promoted by unions and concerned with the methods of introducing the new technologies. Substantive issues relate more to operational conditions once office automation has been implemented. The fundamental aim of participative methods is to establish a strong consensus around the new technology and the new organisational setting of the office by promising a democratic decision of implementation of office automation, providing: information to the unions at an early stage of the process; joint union–management bodies to discuss, negotiate and to supervise the changes, with the possibility of consulting independent experts; and users' involvement in the design of future organisation and use of the technology.

Substantive issues are orientated to the protection of existing status, salary and qualifications, typically concerned with: ensuring that the same level of employment existing before the introduction of new technologies will be maintained; restricting in-house displacement to cases associated with important retraining programmes; increasing the quality of working life (QWL); and limiting the time to be spent working on VDTs. However, in spite of important results, in particular a reduction in the number and intensity of actual, visible social conflicts, it appears that the 'participative methods' reveal some new problems, more difficult to solve. An example, drawn from my own research, can illustrate these dynamics.

The National Agency for Production of Energy (OPEN) is a large nationwide bureaucracy in France characterised by a relatively democratic structure of management and decision-making.[13] Before the generalisation of office automation, the organisation relied heavily on a centralised electronic data processing (EDP) system, whose speed, accuracy and performances declined very fast, both for technological reasons and because of the expanded quantity and complexity of the tasks to be performed. The participative introduction of the new system was considered by all the institutional actors involved as the best means to attain an increase in productivity, an improvement in quality of working life (QWL) through the elimination of repetitive and low-skilled tasks, and more autonomy in decision-making processes at all levels. All the standard procedures of participative methods were followed, with a strong emphasis on two points: the preservation of employment, salary and previous qualifications, despite the important modifications created by the new technologies; and the limitation to four hours of daily work on VDTs by the creation of a new pattern of work organisation called 'binomes', with pairs of employees alternating on the same display during the day.

Nevertheless, the process of office automation was not without its problems. Firstly, the division of work created by the binome, based as it was more on health and safety regulations than with the content and the nature of office work, created its own difficulties. In the automated workplace the quantity and the flexibility of the information available is almost beyond the physical limits of the machines. One effect of the binome system was that, paradoxically, operators did not know what to do during the second half of the working day, the most important operations and informations being available only through the VDTs.

Secondly, the job profiles in the organisation were changed by the new technology, but the hierarchical structure of the office was unchanged – largely due to the pledge of the democratic organisation to maintain qualifications and employment. In fact, most of the supervisors' tasks were integrated into the software or decentralised to the operators, with the result that while supervisors and operators are hierarchically differentiated, in fact they do exactly the same job. All the supervisory levels, including the office managers of the Mutual Society, see their task altered by the new computer-based system; in some cases their tasks are completely eliminated.

Thirdly, particularly complex operations required unpredictable quantities of time, and were almost impossible to plan in advance, leading to a very rigid and unbalanced task-allocation between members of the binome. This, and worries about the introduction of standardised criteria of efficiency and individual performance by the machine, led to a reinforced demand for 'peer-group control', further eroding solidary relations.

We can thus see that the introduction of office automation in several territorial branches of a relatively democratic organisation led to unexpected problems that did not seem amenable to the application of participative methods. Indeed, it is likely that the pressure to establish a very broad consensus acted as an organisational constraint, and contributed to the eventual problems. But how should those problems be understood? In the next section I want to explore what has been an overlooked dimension of the consequences of office automation: the implications for occupational and organisational identities. I will do this by exploring five related issues in turn: the transformation of decision-making tasks; the internalisation of the organisational dimension of work; the acceleration of the learning cycle; the 'virtualisation' of work; and the decoupling of individual and organisational goals and identities.

Automation and Individualisation

The Intensification of Decision-making

In automated work several fundamental parameters of decision-making are changed. Firstly, temporal parameters are changed. In the absence of automation, the consequences of a mistaken decision, however disastrous, appear only after a rather long time. One can select an alternative even if one lacks sufficient favourable empirical evidence, since in most cases it is possible to correct the decision, if it turns out to be inappropriate, before it produces any irreparably negative effects. The possibility of 'successive correction' is much less available when one works with automation. The temporal distance between decision and consequence is much reduced and often it is impossible to correct a mistaken decision. Unfortunately, the 'sense of reality' present in the consequences is very low: we are used to longer periods of time and usually we are unable to evaluate appropriately consequences that (we still assume) will occur at a significant temporal distance.

Secondly, the size of the area of influence of a decision, and the severity of its consequences, are both changed. Automation operates as a multiplier on decisions. And once one has broken through the restrictions that automation offers for the control of human errors (in all automatic systems there are modalities of control over human decisions, but they can be disengaged by human operators, or they may not foresee certain kinds of human behaviour), we witness a rapid and intense diffusion of the consequences of mistakes, often in unsuspected areas.

Thirdly, the modalities for communicating a decision are radically changed by the new office revolution. A decision can be made known to several people, may appear very clearly, and is often recorded. It is not concerned with, nor is it regulated by, standard bureaucratic criteria. It involves the assumption of responsibility for situations that are not regulated by known and 'standard' methods of control. It is less 'private,' precisely on account of the conditions of greater risk and lesser familiarity. In the distribution of decision-making functions between humans and automation, of course, what is left to the latter is precisely the 'routine,' as well as the definition of and control over the areas in which human decisions take place. Nonetheless, human decisions are still being scrutinised. Thus one must assume 'responsibility' even in the face of uncertainty.

The Internalization of Organisational Tasks

With computer-based technologies, a component of mental workload that has been insufficiently studied becomes visible: it is represented by all the variables that define the social organisation of aims and the division of work. For instance, given the same conditions, the number of errors varies as a function of the control directly exerted both by the hierarchy or the peer-group: an operator devotes more attention to the 'controller', is less concentrated on the task, and the likelihood of errors increases. Furthermore, the importance of the error itself is immediately enlarged by the organisational dimension created by the social comparison of the two members of the 'binome'.

This organisational workload is relevant for two main reasons. First of all, the market of office automation provides hardware and software that present very little flexibility, based upon analysis of work procedures according importance almost uniquely to structured activities. This technological rigidity of office automation devices makes it difficult for operators to respond to uncertainty, to perform non-structured tasks, and to consolidate every type of informal and learning-by-tasks expertise. Formal negotiations and informal arrangements with the hierarchy and the managers become much more difficult; a number of mental activities shift from accomplishing the tasks to the standardised rules, trying to adapt behaviour to the goals and tasks of the computer-based system.

Once work goals and rules are standardised, less space is left to the bargaining process: the integration of procedures does not increase the richness of tasks and job satisfaction, but leads instead to an increase of attention, concentrated on control, perceived as direct and non-negotiable. Errors are perceived as organisational failures.

In this technological phase of development of office automation, only a low percentage of the organisation of work can be standardised and automated. The rest is composed of coordination, control and integration between the task procedures and the office goals and functions no longer performed by supervisors and managers: an increasing part of individual's attention is then devoted, at the cognitive level, to these organisational tasks.

The Acceleration of the Learning Cycle

When automation is present one always witnesses 'cycles of variation' in cognitive behaviour. These cycles may be shorter or longer (depending on the degree and quality of training, on the possibilities for the 'transfer' of skills, on the design of computer interfaces and their user-friendliness), but they are always typified by a period of decline in performance and by a successive recovery and development in the quality of performance. In essence, each change in the tools and in the modalities of work forces a 'relearning' of skills: that which formerly was accomplished through 'skill-based behaviour' and allowed one to concentrate one's attention on what one was doing, now has to be carried out consciously, with attention to how one is doing it. It is necessary to displace the focus of attention, so to speak, 'from above to below': to pass from concern with the goal of an activity to concern with how to do it.

Later on, when, through practice and learning, the 'how to' is taken care of by a 'skill-based behaviour', attention may be directed towards 'what one is doing' and 'why one is doing it': the focus of interest is once again on the systemic relations between what one is doing and its context. Indeed, since in the meanwhile there has been an enrichment of competence and of knowledge, it is now possible to formulate hypotheses concerning the use and development of these new competences, as well as to spend time and cognitive energy testing and verifying 'what one can do'. This cycle is established every time that one must cope with technological and organisational changes.

Nonetheless, given that in automated work these changes are practically continuous and that they come rapidly one after the other, the cycle too is constantly present. It is not, however, painless. It requires that a price be paid, one which is particularly obvious the first time it is confronted (and in this case one finds the classic negative impact reactions), but which continues to be paid every time the cycle begins anew. Thus, it is obvious that the training process cannot neglect the fact that persons engaged in automated work must deal with continuous 'traumas', and that it is therefore necessary to supply them with tools for foreseeing and managing these situations. It must not be forgotten that continuous change creates conditions unfavourable for the development of 'culture', that is, the tools for reflecting upon and managing innovation. If one is not allowed sufficient time to acquire experience with these 'novelties', it is not possible to manage them, to make them one's own, and thus to place them in an enriched context in which they make sense.

Furthermore, every change in the way one allocates cognitive effort also produces changes in the production of signals of fatigue (in fact, different components of the cognitive system are subjected to stressful events and conditions), and thus the symptoms of fatigue, which inevitably accompany the learning cycle, are followed at a certain temporal distance by adaptations in the conscious mental model of fatigue that serves in the understanding and interpreting of signals of tiredness. With accelerated learning cycles, the mental model which would allow one to put into action coherent strategies of response, and to inhibit in an economical way the signs of fatigue themselves, is far less likely to be able to establish itself.

The Virtualisation of Work and Skills

This description of the internal characteristics of the learning cycles of automated work is not exhaustive: it does not, in fact, indicate in what 'direction' these cycles lead. In reality, even the concept of direction in learning is not completely obvious. We are used to thinking about learning in terms of 'curves', of evidence over time of the quantity of elements learned in relation to a state to be reached. It is known that there are 'phases' in which one learns rapidly and others in which the 'payoff' is much slower. This conceptualisation is valid, however, only as long as one is given a job to learn that remains constant for a sufficient period of time. It is certain, however, that in automated work, new jobs continuously appear and become fundamental points of reference which were previously either almost irrelevant or completely unknown. In fact, it is not possible to establish now in any detailed fashion what characteristics a given job will have within ten years. If this is true, then, what should one learn; in what should one be drilled; towards what goal has one to be trained?

An answer to this question can be found in the way one frames this analysis: it would be a waste of time to try to define precise and detailed situations; better to attempt to produce 'generic' competences. The hypothesis upon which this answer is being formulated is that training, education and professional development should be seen in relation to a 'virtual' or potential work rather than to a predefined task. This 'future' job is a wager (at least up to a certain point), whose contents can only be imagined and which can be seen only if one has the tools to be able to 'wager'. And these tools cannot be verified, except indirectly, because the modalities of competence are vague. They must be measured, however, with respect to whoever is in the process of entering into the wager of undertaking this possible job. A comparison should therefore be developed with the competence of potential competitors in the field – so as, on the one hand, to 'legitimate' one's own competencies, and, on the other, to establish to what degree they are 'up to date'.

The shift from 'fixed' work to 'virtual' work changes the rules of training, destroying the notion of the 'task' as a set of 'concepts to be known' and 'operations to be mastered'. What one must know and be able to do change rapidly over time. It is thus crucial to possess competence for carrying out jobs the details of whose transformation into 'tasks' cannot be completely foreseen. Formal processes of training that are bound to criteria dictated by the current situation would already be out of date in respect of what will soon be needed. It is crucial to know how to manage in unfamiliar situations – and this competence can only be developed through praxis, not 'taught'.

The Disjunction of Occupational and Organisational Identities

The image of the company possessed by those that work in it establishes the foundation for a sense of belonging to it (and, incidentally, is responsible for the loss of individual identity that one observes in those who are expelled from it). Automation destroys this image only at the cost of failure. It has become increasingly clear in the last few years that automation must possess one characteristic: it must guarantee the consistent use of 'survival forms'. In other words, automation must incorporate elements that allow the recognition, in a changing situation, of forms of identity and continuity that prevent any disruption in the mental image that people have of themselves, of the company where they work, and of the work that they do. It should avoid ruptures in personal identity that might produce an underutilisation, or a distorted use, of the technology.

This aspect of automated work has already begun to be taken into consideration in the design of the human–computer interface concerning the organisation of tasks carried out by a single individual. What has been little studied, however, and even less care taken of, is the design of interfaces whose purpose is to support the relationship between, on the one hand, the tasks carried out individually, and, on the other, the organisation.

Conclusion

The main focus of the many sociological studies of the introduction of office automation and related information technologies to organisations has been the 'unintended consequences' of a systems design which has naively proceeded as if organisations function according to formal rules, relationships and organograms. The origins, nature and effects of assumptions of designers about the working practices and capabilities of users, and the ways in which these are built into hardware and software constraints, has been part of this sociological narrative. Yet, despite this quite thorough exposition of such problems and dislocations, and of the organisational remedies that might be introduced to mitigate them, little if any of this extensive work has recognised the fundamental predicament brought by the impact of the new information technologies on subjectivity, identity and relationships within organisations undergoing such cultural revolution.

Let me briefly summarise the basic features of the transformation of subjectivity and identity under conditions of office automation. Firstly, there is an increase and a diffusion in decision-making behaviour. It is therefore crucial that training should broaden and deepen the 'culture of decision-making' understood in the first place as the ability to assume responsibility, but also as the mastery of tools and modalities of decision-making: analysis of error, modalities of discovering and correcting errors, the modalities for recognising, comparing and negotiating values, the use of generic rules of diagnosis and heuristic decision-making, evaluation of the degrees of uncertainty that heuristics introduce, and levels of reliability that they guarantee.

Secondly, both work organisation and social organisation enter into the tasks of individuals. They no longer represent only a context whose management is the responsibility of others. Every job in automation is characterised from within by an organisational component that is increasingly important.

Thirdly, office automation causes an acceleration of learning cycles, to the point at which performance suffers. The phase in the cycles where performance increases gets shorter and shorter, and the time spent mastering purely formal operations, rather than advancing occupational goals, gets proportionately longer. This itself contributes to a decoupling of occupational and organisational goals, as the individual is increasingly concerned with the temporary mastering of purely formal skills. Similarly, the phenomenology of fatigue is constantly transformed, making its recognition and responses to it more and more difficult.

Fourthly, work in automation is not fixed but 'virtual'. Exploration and innovation predominate rather than the execution of the already known. 'What one does' does not at all define 'what one knows how to do', and 'what one does' is always temporary. Occupational identity is thus no longer characterised by an itinerary of formal training (school, university, etc.) followed by an itinerary of on-the-job experience, but is increasingly defined by training (and self-training) experiences in and around the workplace, and through opportunities for professional updating and 'legitimation' in the 'open university' of the professional community to which one belongs.

Finally, there can be a decreased congruence between the individual's mental image of his or her work, profession and company, on the one hand, and the strategies of the company itself, on the other. This can crucially affect the degree to which individuals 'spend' their competence on behalf of the company or outside of it, how they build up this competence, and how they establish criteria for evaluating the 'surplus value' which they produce and the ways that they can maximise it.

A kind of silent revolution is thus producing profound changes in the social life of the office as it affects the identity of individuals, organisations and groups. As I have identified, office automation engenders more isolation rather than less, as work groups become arenas of mutual 'peer review' and competition, more abstracted and less solidary. One of the fundamental bases of the ideology of work, therefore, may become nothing but an empty myth: the community, the work group, which is still absolutely necessary for the efficient running of the organisation, is being detached from the technological base on which office work rests. The form of collective organisation inherited from a developmental phase based on the need to gather in the same space, management, machines and workers, has now been fundamentally compromised by the possibility of office automation. What will happen in the office, then, if for example the employees no longer need or have no chance to intermingle at the workplace, or if they no longer have any control of the deeper significance of both individual and collective work?[14]

The study of the development and generalisation of information techno-logy, and more specifically of computer-based information systems, points at fundamental modification in the meaning and contents of human work. These changes primarily affect operators;[15] but they are also relevant for unions, management and organisations.[16] The office automation process is very often followed by a series of social phenomena. Currently, these phenomena are viewed as *unexpected consequences*, but in fact a better definition would be that of 'predictable unexpected consequences' of office automation. As such, they would more clearly fall within the responsibility of human agents who proceed to engender them, but at present with no responsibility to recognise that they will occur, and that they will have to be dealt with. This causes us explicitly to have to face the challenge of the 'architecture of complexity',[17] the existence of unprecedented novelties that challenge the conventional theoretical tools and methods of design.

Notes

1. Norbert Wiener, 'Some moral and technical consequences of automation', in Morris H. Philipson (ed.) (1962) *Automation: Implications for the Future*. New York: Vintage. pp. 162–73. The quote is from pp. 163–4 (emphasis added).

2. The literature on the subject is immense and growing at a speed which is, by any account, itself out of control. See Tom Forester (ed.) (1980) *The Microelectronics Revolution*. Cambridge, MA: MIT Press and *The Information Technology Revolution*. Cambridge, MA: MIT Press, 1986; and Michael L. Dertouzos and Joel Moses (eds) (1975) *The Computer Age: A Twenty-Year View*. Cambridge, MA: MIT Press.

3. For the more recent theoretical developments, see Eugene Kamenka and Martin Krygier (eds) (1979) *Bureaucracy: The Career of a Concept*. New York: St Martin's Press; and Martin Albrow (1970) *Bureaucracy*. London: The Pall Mall Press. The classical sociological approach can be found in Max Weber (1964) *The Theory of Social and Economic Organization*. New York: Free Press; and Michel Crozier (1964) *The Bureaucratic Phenomenon*. Chicago: University of Chicago Press.

4. See Peter Savage (1965) 'Public administration in literature: A bibliographical essay', *Philippines Journal of Public Administration*, 9: 60–70; Guy Thuillier (1980) *Bureaucratie et Bureaucrates en France au XIX siècle*. Geneva: Droz; I have addressed some of these issues in: 'La "République prêtre": Marx, Balzac et la Bureaucratie', in a special issue of *Milieux* (no. 32, 1988) devoted to the relations between literature, sociology and bureaucracy, and in 'Le lettere della Burocrazia. Analisi letteraria e immaginazione storica, ovvero Balzac e Marx di fronte alla burocrazia', *I sentieri di Erodoto*, 5 (15): 92–121 (1991).

5. Harry Braverman (1974) *Labor and Monopoly Capital*. New York: Monthly Review Press. p. 316.

6. Definitions and interpretations abound: for the sake of simplicity and space, here it is meant as the convergence of electronics, computing and telecommunications which is producing an incessant wave of technological innovations in every field, and in every way we work, live and think, if one is to take seriously the claims of the prophets of 'artificial intelligence'. See, for more information and for extensive bibliographical references, Forester, *The Microelectronic Revolution* and *The Information Technology Revolution*; Shoshana Zuboff (1988) *In the Age of the Smart Machine: The Future of Work and Power*. New York: Basic Books; Federico Butera (1987) *Options for the Future of Work*. Dublin: European Foundation for the Improvement of Living and Working Conditions; and the results of a five-year research programme by Alan Westin et al.: (1985) *The Changing Workplace*. White Plains, NY: Knowledge Industry Publications; and (1984) *The Office Automation Controversy: Technology, People and Social Policy*. White Plains, NY: Knowledge Industry Publications.

7. See Etienne Grandjean and Enrico Vigliani (eds) (1980) *Ergonomic Aspects of Visual Display Terminals*. London: Taylor and Francis; and the extensive bibliographies in Marvin Sirbu (1982) *Understanding the Social and Economic Impacts of Office Automation*. Cambridge, MA: The Japan-Usa Office Automation Forum; and Quentin Newhouse, Jr. (ed.) (1986) *Issues in Human–Computer Interaction*. New York: Garland Publishing.

8. M.J. Smith (1984) 'Health issues in VDT work', in J. Bennet, D. Case, J. Sandelin and M.J. Smith (eds), *Visual Display Terminals*. Englewood Cliffs NJ: Prentice Hall; and M.J. Dainoff (1982) 'Occupational stress factors in VDT operation: A review of empirical literature', *Behaviour and Information Technology*, 1: 141–76; Sebastiano Bagnara (1984) 'Lavorare ai VDT: Fatica o lamentele?', *Scienza e Esperienza*, 38: 45–6.

9. See, in addition to the references already quoted in note 2, the data provided in US Congress, Office of Technology Assessment (1984), *Computerized Manufacturing Automation: Employment, Education, and the Workplace*. Washington DC: US Government Printing Office, passim.

10. See Federico Butera and Jacob Thurman (eds) (1982) *Automation and Work Design: An ILO Project*. Geneva: ILO; Marco Diani (1984) 'Conséquences organisationnelles de l'automation', *Sociologie du travail*, 26 (4): 367–95; and Marco Diani (ed.) (1989) *Le design à la croisée des chemins*. Montreal: Informel.

11. Michael Porter and Victor Millar (1985) 'How information gives you competitive advantage', *Harvard Business Review*, July-August: 150–67; Wassily Leontief (1985) 'The choice of technology', *Scientific American*, 252: 37–45; Tora K. Bikson and B.A. Gutek (1983) *Advanced Office Systems: An Empirical Look at Utilization and Satisfaction*. Santa Monica CA: The Rand Corporation.

12. See the essays in Marco Diani (ed.) (1991) *L'intelligenza dell'automazione*. Milan: Franco Angeli.

13. The names and identifying characteristics of the organisations discussed in this chapter have been changed.

14. See James W. Driscoll (1982) 'How to humanize office automation', *Office: Technology and People*, 1 (2–3): 167–76; and Sebastiano Bagnara (1985) 'From what to how and back to what again: Automatization of mental processes in automation', in E. Basevi (ed.), *Press and New Technologies*. Brussels: Fast.

15. See Grandjean and Vigliani, *Ergonomic Aspects of Visual Display Terminals*, passim.

16. Tora K. Bikson et al. (1985) *Computer-Mediated Work*. Santa Monica CA: The Rand Corporation.

17. See Chapter 4, 'The Architecture of Complexity', in Herbert A. Simon, *The Sciences of the Artificial*. Cambridge, MA: MIT Press. pp. 84–118.

7

THE TEARS INSIDE THE STONE: REFLECTIONS ON THE ECOLOGY OF FEAR

John Maguire

Each day I live, each day the sea of light
Rises, I seem to see
The tears inside the stone
As if my eyes were gazing beneath the earth.[1]

My topic is fear and incoherence. My aim is deconstruction, but only in the positive sense in which archaeology is a deconstruction of a landscape: we need a creative disruption of the weird games played by our world's elites. They are trick-cyclists, keeping upright and steady simply because they move forward so quickly – the Emperor's new bike! As citizens and/or as 'experts' we play our role in this circus-drama: the parcel *must* have a content – because we pass it on! What we do not realise – what we profess not to realise – is that to our elites, problems are not problems: they are solutions, devices of the most basic control. Richard Rorty has given us permission to cease trying to prove and ground what can only be recognised. Our hope is in building on recognition, inventing a world 'founded' in our recognition of each person as a needy narrator.

As a matter of fact, we inhabit/inhibit huge wells of fear and incoherence. If we could utter and express this disturbing richness, then present structures of hierarchy could not endure. I do not try to convince you of the existence or extent of this fear: *it is here*. I feel it and suppress it; I feel it and repress it in others. It is ultimately a fear of creation/creativity/createdness. It fuels the abusive behaviour of adults who in one way or another use children to deny and to distance themselves from their own sense of limitation and mortality. The abusing adult and the hierarch are at one in saying: 'don't make me as yourself, don't land both of us in your enchanting disenchanted world, because my identity can't survive it'. So, vast numbers of us do lead lives of quiet desperation, and indeed the so-called 'democratic deficit' rests upon a more profound psychic loss. I am not a reductionist about our pressing social problems, but I do want to contextualise them and lead us back to the pathological roots of our perceptions.

We are inured to processual and substantive absurdities because absurdity is, as Alice Miller says, the air we breathe in childhood. We learn to live in a weird silent blindness, within which we can make no real use of information about poverty and inequality, child abuse, debt crisis, the bomb, the various ecological threats. Crucially, we cannot even begin to construct the object of our inquiry while we continue to set war and armaments on the margin; economically and – even more crucially – psychoculturally they are at the heart of our world order. They would be neither overlooked nor tolerated without the shared, unspoken psychic legacy which fuels our aggression. All of this has huge implications for the environment and for ecological policy, not only in general terms but also because the environment stands in many ways as the summation of what David Smail has called our failures of care for ourselves, for others and for our world. The unrecognised fear and hurt which fuel our absurd social and political process fuel at the same time both our aggression and our indifference towards the world we inhabit.

A Starting Place: Howls and Decorum

A note of caution is vital here: we need to avoid the specious clarity which peddles pseudo-solutions precisely by editing out all the muddle and incoherence which each of us knows to lie at the roots of our confident, 'adult' discourse. We need radically new ways of talking, of thinking about our predicament. I do not offer a starting *point* – a clear and sharp beginning from which all else logically follows – but offer instead a starting *place*: the long and ragged coastline where discourse encounters silence. Our words are flotsam, thrown up by an inarticulate ocean. We drag these fragments ashore and build with them, heedless of whence they come. Sometimes, however, we need to fashion them into rafts, and face out onto the ocean.

The new forms of discourse which we need to generate require many changes. One at least is the self-involvement of the speaker in what she or he has to say. Too often, we hear the experts calling, each to each. We need to hear what the expert is not telling us, has indeed very likely not told her or himself. We may no longer interrogate the world and others in a discourse that does not interrogate ourselves. The most important things to say are those things too silly, too wild, too embarrassing for normal speech. The root image is best provided by Walt Whitman:

> What living and buried speech is always vibrating here, what howls restrain'd by decorum.[2]

There could hardly be a better image for the pain at once inflicted and neglected by the discourse and process of contemporary society, than 'howls restrained by decorum'. Many decades later, the same theme is addressed by a compatriot of Whitman's:

A naked lunch is natural to us,
We eat reality sandwiches.
But allegories are so much lettuce.
Don't hide the madness.[3]

Whether we recognise it or not, we inhabit the shoreline between discourse and silence, between decorum and howls, between the 'business' and the 'madness'. The only sanity worth having is one which, in a deep sense, is a re-cognition of the madness of contemporary society. A chief consequence of this unrecognised madness is the otherwise baffling inability of societies to tackle problems on which they have strong publicly declared commitments and an abundance of relevant information.

I have argued at some length elsewhere[4] that we often make a mistake when we discuss 'what is to be done' about contemporary problems. We often fall prey to what I call the 'Could Try Harder' syndrome. This is the belief that we are moving along essentially the right lines, and that what we need to tackle our problems is essentially more effort, more application. A specific part of this syndrome is the conviction that what we need is more information. In other words, our priority should be to devote research-energies to the accumulation of more 'hard scientific evidence' to ground policy and action.

I have no quarrel at all with the notion that scientific evidence and argument play a crucial role in the solution of human problems. I have, however, a serious quarrel with the notion that what is crucially lacking in our present predicaments is more technical information as such. Let us take any one of a wide range of recognised problems, from world poverty and underdevelopment, through child welfare, to the threat posed by conventional and nuclear weapons. It is impossible seriously to maintain that in some very important way we do not 'know about' these problems. Of course, were we to decide seriously to understand and tackle them, we would require increased amounts of (differently framed) knowledge. What prevents us, however, from pursuing such action and such knowledge is not plausibly a lack of data. It is much more centrally a failure to integrate those data, a failure to make them real to ourselves, to give them the proper frame.

A crucial ingredient in our failure of response is precisely how we have constructed a public discourse which sets up social issues and problems for what in another context has been called 'nondecisionmaking'. What is required here is not a simple 'call to action', but rather a call to reflection on why so many crucial questions have been posed in such profoundly distorted ways. Not only do we not need to 'try harder' – we should be chary of equally simple-minded instructions to 'look harder' as well. My aim thus is to present some critical reflections on how 'social problems' are set up in ways which guarantee that we do not really address them; this is intended as a contribution to the positive task of inventing a discourse for future policy and action, in ecology and elsewhere.

Howls and Decorum in Contemporary Culture

The decorum of our contemporary social and political order is not immune to relatively frequent – and always apparently surprising – 'outbreaks' of what we regard as 'abnormal behaviour'. These range from the local and personal as in cases of child abuse, murder and so on to the more global and collective as in for example cases of 'terrorism', or an unforeseen rebellion like that of the 'Zapatistas' in Mexico in early 1994. The conventional order of things is also at times interrupted by catastrophic events such as the Gulf War and its attendant mass-slaughter. We are, it seems, more or less accustomed to regarding such events as coming 'out of a clear blue sky', as surprising, perhaps even inexplicable, deviations from normality. In many fields, however, there is mounting evidence that we need to integrate the 'abnormal' into our picture of reality. To E.M. Forster's famous dictum 'only connect' we have to add 'also include'.

The part of the picture which seems at times most glaringly to be overlooked is the prevalence of *fear* within our lives and our social process. It is there, it is corrosive, but it is rarely spoken of. Fear is a much deeper and more pervasive characteristic of our society, culture and personality than we even remotely care to imagine. Fear is the unspoken but crucial subtext of our social normality. I am not trying to quantify here, nor to assert that fear is inescapable in all times and cultures. I am, however – drawing principally on the work of Alice Miller – suggesting that in most of us and in much of our culture there are reservoirs of hurt, anger and fear without which the strange 'decorum' of our everyday being cannot be properly understood.

We have to search wide and deep to find expressions of this fear in how people talk about themselves and their world. One source is in literary fiction, where we find, for example, the author of *Catch 22*, Joseph Heller, speaking through one of his central characters in another novel:

> It is perverse and I try to overcome it. There is this crawling animal flourishing somewhere inside me that I try to keep hidden and that strives to get out, and I don't know what it is or whom it wishes to destroy. I know it is covered with warts. It might be me; it might also be me that it wishes to destroy.[5]

This grotesque image is disturbingly paralleled by a passage from the folk singer Joan Baez in her autobiography:

> What cataclysmic event shook my sunny world so that it was shadowed with unmentionable and unfathomable fright? I don't know. I never will know. Every year, with the first golden chill of fall or the first sudden darkness at suppertime, I am stricken with a deadly melancholy, a sense of hopelessness and doom. I become weighed down, paralysed, and frozen; the hairs on my arms and legs rise up and my bones chill to the marrow. Nothing can warm me. In the eye of this icy turbulence I see, with diamond clarity, that small shining person in the photograph, with slept-on braids and a groggy pout, and a ribbon of worry troubling her black eyes as she sits down with all her small might on the memories of a recurring dream. *I am in the house and something comes in the night and its presence is deathly. . . . I scream and run away, but it comes back at*

my nap time and gets into my bed. Then a voice says angrily, 'Don't look at me!'
as I peer at the face on the pillow next to me, and I feel very ashamed. That's all I
have ever remembered – just that much and no more.[6]

It is rare indeed to hear of such emotional realities in our conventional
news media. This lends even more impact to a very striking passage in the
recent valedictory broadcast by BBC Radio's correspondent in Germany,
Diana Goodman. She attempts to sum up her years in Germany, in which
of course the major event was re-unification. She has reported on and
contrasted the situations and responses of both 'Westerners' and
'Easterners':

> But as I left Berlin, it was a comment from an East German friend which was
> uppermost in my mind. A few days earlier he'd shyly confessed that he still woke
> up at three o'clock in the morning, in a cold sweat, terrified by the realisation
> that he now could – and must – take responsibility for his own life. That is the
> sort of remark that could make a West German recoil in disgust . . . because in
> the West it is not acceptable to admit to such feelings of inadequacy. My friend
> asked me: how long will this fear last? I had no answer . . . nor does anyone else
> in the disunited Germany.[7]

Perhaps the most disturbing claim of all, however, is made by Stephen
M. Joseph:

> Young children are afraid most of the time, so afraid that they find it difficult to
> learn, to think, and to grow. . . . Many adults seem to be constantly fearful, too.
> Did they learn this fear as children? I don't mean the rational fear of touching a
> hot stove, or of running out into the traffic, or of losing one's job, but the
> pervasive, crippling fear of new experiences, of other people as the enemy, of
> punishment for making mistakes or raising questions in taboo areas, and of death
> and punishment, both real and symbolic, fears that haunt our dreams asleep and
> awake.[8]

There is of course a huge amount of work to be done around this topic of
fear, and situating it within our culture. Nevertheless, there seems to be a
great amount of evidence – albeit often off the beaten track – of the
pervasiveness, and hiddenness, of fear within our contemporary culture.
For my present purposes it is sufficient to note that this is to an important
extent the case; my argument relates to the consequences for our
'normality' of this quantum of unrecognised fear within ourselves and our
society.

Childhood, Fear and Power

A vital building-block in the story which I want to tell is provided by the
analysis of Alice Miller. In a large number of books since the late 1970s she
has spelt out the consequences, as she sees them, of adult abuse of the
child. Her own arguments, and parallel arguments by others, are now
much more familiar than they were some fifteen years ago. Nevertheless, I
will try to present the main lines of her picture of fear and power in
contemporary society. Her first book deals with the way in which adults,

particularly parents, can fail to cope with disturbing feelings aroused in them by children. These feelings – of anger, loneliness, shame, fear, dependency, weakness and so on – now stand before the adult, in the child, with an intensity of feeling which threatens the bargain these adults have made with their world. The message, variously conveyed from adult to child, is to deny these feelings, so that the adult may survive and the child may remain loved. This leads to a repertoire of denial and idealisation, where neither adult nor child confronts these subversive feelings. In this way children learn a repertoire of responses based not on their growth-needs but on the negative defence-needs of their adult reference-figures. Children emerge from this process as adults with damaged identities. I use this phrase rather than 'false selves', to avoid the implication of an essentialist 'true self', lurking somewhere beyond and above the whole process. What is centrally involved is our learning a habit of starting out not from our own perceived needs, nor even from the perceived positive needs of others as such, but rather from their negative meta-needs not to be confronted by our needs.

Alice Miller, in her many books, has by now given a large number of examples of the impact of such imprinting on the biographies of many different types of individuals, some of them world-famous literary and artistic figures, some of them ordinary citizens, and some of them political figures such as Hitler, Stalin and Ceausescu. In all of these cases there is at least one common theme: the massive destruction which is brought into the lives of these individuals, and frequently into the lives of many around them, by the 'unfinished business' of their early victimisation. This point is centrally and dramatically grounded by a brief sentence in her very first book:

    . . . und doch, etwas bleibt!
    . . . and yet, something remains![9]

In other words, it is impossible fully to suppress the feelings which have not been allowed in this world of denial and idealisation: no amount of decorum can completely suppress the howl, even if it is never heard as such. In her many books, building on the argument developed in the first, Miller traces out the consequences of this 'etwas' in the lives of many different types of individual: sometimes in the lives of great artists such as Henry Moore, Picasso, Hesse; sometimes in the lives of ordinary individuals, and – most appallingly – in those of dictators such as Ceausescu, Stalin and Hitler. All of these stories have in common the 'repetition compulsion' which draws us back to the scene of the crime, to the hurt which we have not been able to integrate. This compulsion is not some mythical, mystical force. It is the tragic necessity which draws us back to our unfinished business, to the place where our energies are most heavily and most negatively vested. As our efforts to expunge the hurt are fruitless, we are driven to deny it, somehow to create a world from which it is absent or where it is safely and tamely present in a victimised Other. In such ways we strive either to create a surrogate self who is freed from our hurts and limitations, or else to delegate them onto somebody else, in whose suffering we can believe we control what we have failed to master in ourselves.

Miller's analyses of figures such as Stalin, Ceausescu and particularly Hitler are of interest for a number of reasons. One is that they prove the hardest test of her general approach of seeing hatred and destruction as reactive rather than as the products of inbuilt Freudian aggressive drives. More important to us, however, is the fact that even when dealing with such unique 'monsters' as these, Miller is concerned to emphasise the *societal* rather than merely personal or interpersonal nature of the processes involved. In other words, she insists throughout that we must understand not only what produced these individual dictators, but also the cultural 'atmosphere' which made their absurd and destructive behaviour appear acceptable to thousands and indeed millions of their fellow citizens. The general line of her answer to this problem is indicated as early as her first book, where she speaks of the puzzle that Ingmar Bergman, such a sharp observer of cruelty and absurdity, still failed to detect these very realities in the Germany which he visited as a youth:

> When Bergman speaks regretfully of his failure to see through Nazism before 1945, although as an adolescent he often visited Germany during the Hitler period, we may see it as a consequence of his childhood. Cruelty was the familiar air that he had breathed from early on – and so, why should cruelty have caught his attention?[10]

In other words, if we have been inured to cruelty and absurdity in our own upbringing, if we have had to deny our perception of these at a formative stage, we are thereby prepared to accept cruelty and absurdity as the common coin of our later 'mature' political and social dealings.

'Normal' Hierarchy

Alice Miller's work presents us with a challenge, whether our specific concern be with problems of child abuse, militarism, poverty, ecology or the like. The challenge is to integrate into our analysis of the 'normal' status quo the insight into the corrosive effects of fear with which she has presented us. Our world is not populated exclusively by Hitlers and Bluebeards, nor do all our conflicts necessarily result in all-out war. Even though we may miss the 'buzz' of such catastrophic events, we need to find how the reservoir of hurt can also poison our more conventional and routine social interactions and processes. At the same time, of course, we should never forget that our 'stable, normal' new world order seems quite capable of absorbing and sanitising horrors like the recent war in the Gulf, with its hundreds of thousands of deaths. Such 'normal catastrophes' lend urgency to the task of confronting the grotesque in our 'normal routine'.

One could almost say that a study of fear and cruelty which focused mainly on their manifest occurrences amounts to a sick kind of psycho-sociological voyeurism: wringing our hands over 'those dreadful road accidents' when we should be inventing an alternative to the motorways. If we cannot trace the imprint of fear and hurt in the 'banality' of our everyday routines, then we need never evince surprise when they occasionally achieve the critical mass for another catastrophe 'out of the blue'. We need to trace both the complex dynamics which lead some of us to self-select into 'leadership roles', and the equally complex statics whereby the rest of us opt out as 'followers'.

We can trace the consequences of this distorted relationship in many key areas of public policy: the myths of classlessness; the belief that significant inequality of income and wealth is a relic of a past era rather than a corrosive ingredient of our present society; the ritual celebration of improved economic 'fundamentals' in an economy which becomes leaner and fitter by devouring human lives; the invocation of non-violence by societies which 'thrive' on the development and promotion of devices of torture and killing. The US sociologist C. Wright Mills has given us a telling description of the stance of the citizen in this weird world:

> They are not radical, not liberal, not conservative, not reactionary. They are inactionary.[11]

Susie Orbach has recently performed a great service in tracing the lines of what she calls our 'emotional illiteracy'. By this she means our inability to integrate into the reality of our lives, in questions great or small, the emotional impact of our experiences, the emotional springs of our actions:

> where a politics of fear, where a politics of unmetabolised loss rules, then an agenda of denial and cover-up is required. Any alternative is simply too threatening . . . Unless we take these feelings on board we will experience greater disaffection, more alienation. Our undigested hopelessness will incline us to disengagement and we will leave politics to the politicians.[12]

What Orbach is dealing with here are the roots of the 'special, enfeebled vision' of which Jonathan Schell spoke more than a decade ago, 'which is permitted to creep around the edges of the mortal crisis in the life of our species but never to meet it head on'.[13]

When we turn to examining the dynamics of 'leadership', a major contribution is offered by Alasdair MacIntyre in his book *After Virtue*, where he criticises some of the unexamined assumptions of modern managerial culture.[14] One of these assumptions is the claim that there is a world of neutral 'facts', to which somehow those who manage our political and organisational life have a privileged access. Related to this is the further claim that these hierarchs can generate genuinely predictive knowledge of such reality, as a precondition to their promise of successfully manipulating it, given only our loyalty. MacIntyre's deflating of the epistemological and technical pretensions of our leaders is usefully augmented by Gareth Morgan's critique, drawing on the earlier work of Ely

Devons. Morgan focuses on the parallels between much modern decision-making and the kind of 'primitive' magical rituals of 'less developed' societies:

> The myth of rationality helps us to see certain patterns of action as legitimate, credible, and normal, and tends to avoid the wrangling and debate that would arise if we were to recognise the basic uncertainty and ambiguity underlying many of our values and actions.[15]

Perhaps the most significant contemporary instance of such magic is to be found in the thinking behind the current revamping of the European Community into the 'European Union', especially the Single European Market policy. Having already called in question the managerial myth of 'predictive control', we should be careful not to subscribe to it in our own dire warnings, ecological and otherwise. It is, however, safe to say that major changes in the nature and quality of living in 'Europe' and the wider world will follow from this series of policy changes. The main lines of what is promised and planned are spelt out in *The European Challenge: 1992: The Benefits of a Single Market*, otherwise called the 'Cecchini Report' after the chief consultant behind it.[16]

Before briefly criticising this report, it is important to clarify my contention. I am not here arguing that the Single Market is *not* a viable project or a worthwhile one. The point is, rather, that it is not what its boosters present it as: a, more precisely *the*, scientifically and technically landscaped path along which our leaders can assuredly guide us just so long as we have the commitment and the energy to follow their lead. This message is conveyed in a fascinating double-bind: whenever we are tempted to unease about the superficially reassuring array of 'facts and figures', our 'attitude' is fine-tuned by a thinly disguised sermon on the virtue of faith.

The project itself bespeaks a genuine (or assumed) confidence in the fundamentally beneficial consequences of creating 'above all a new and pervasive competitive climate' (p. 73). This will involve among other things 'the removal of market entry barriers (e.g. standards)' (p. 75), as 'the economy's main players – Europe's corporate citizens' (p. 86) change status 'from being "price-takers" to "price-makers" ' (p. 73). We are assured about the 'rises in overall output resultant on lower prices' (p. 82), and given a list of the beneficiaries from this cornucopia – leaner and fitter businesses figure, but not workers as such, who can hope only that all this will provide 'the basis for a durable attack on unemployment' (p. 72). Gains in productivity will mean short-term job losses, but in the long run we can expect the creation of 5.7 million replacement jobs (pp. 97, 101).

The complaint here is not that tens of millions of jobs are not being promised; it is, rather, the sheer vapidity of a document which fails either to take on board the ludicrousness of the future it offers, with millions of our fellow-citizens demobilised without a mention, or to face the challenge of redefining the whole practice of economic life to meet contemporary needs. From no point of view, least of all that of ecological policy, are we consoled in any of this by being told that the project will constitute 'an unqualified bonus' for us all as consumers, in a paradise where each item 'will tend to be produced in the cheapest way' (p. 74).

The Cecchini Report thus provides a salutary text in two respects of relevance to our topic. Specifically, it represents a breathtakingly naive restatement of the most uncritical ideology of 'economic growth' along the lines of an unquestioned faith in 'the market'. The question of needing to rethink the whole nature of work and our interaction with nature is glaringly conspicuous by its absence. More generally, the report constitutes a fascinating instance of the absurdity of contemporary policy rhetoric. It blends apparently precise, quantified predictions with the most staggering assertions that 'the greatest impact is to be expressed qualitatively rather than in figures', and references to 'another reality of immeasurable significance' (pp. 93, 94). At times the language verges on the surreal:

> Chief among the traditional sources of American [sic] business dynamism is the perpetual flux of market entries and exits, providing a steady renewal of market players. This elixir of industrial rejuvenation is at its most potent in the high technology sectors. (p. 88)

The 'psychological', 'qualitative', 'symbolic' character of all this rhetoric points to a sub-text which would be simply funny were it not equally disturbing. This becomes clearer when we read the Cecchini Report in the context of another EC Commission publication, *A Frontier-free Europe*, also issued in 1988.[17] This document presents, in highly psychological language, a Europe suffering from 'Europessimism', symptomised by apathy, unassertiveness and disunity. At the hour of danger along comes the Man of the Moment, Jacques Delors, reflecting on how to remobilise, to galvanise, the patient. The Single European Market, we are told, was chosen as a mobilising project only after a strengthened European central authority, a single currency and a common 'defence' were each considered and rejected as too strong a medicine. One cannot ignore the heavily psychological, indeed psychoanalytical, metaphors used to depict the state of Europe's 'collective unconscious' (p. 20). The two documents, read in conjunction, present a brash technicism which betrays its own unease in its appeals to the psychological dimension: if we are not 'galvanised' by the scientistic rhetoric, this must be because we are sunk too deep in 'Europessimism'; the techno-psychic fix is complete.

The Single European Market may be a good or a bad plan, a sound or a destructive project. What it is not, is what its technocratic proponents represent it to be: 'the' scientific and necessary answer to 'the' problems of the Western European economies. Here, however, it is important to be precise in our criticism. I do not assess the report against an essentialist notion of what *would* be 'the answer'; what we must accept is that 'the answer', in that sense, does not exist even potentially. The authors of the report are not seers but rather story-tellers, and their story may well be worth hearing. The hearing can be worthwhile, however, only if we confront our own irrational dealings with those whom we insist on cruelly canonising as 'leaders'; if we recognise them, in Richard Rorty's words, as our fellow-sufferers in the human predicament.[18]

In attempting to reinterpret our contemporary political and managerial culture along these lines, we would, as has already been made clear, be gravely mistaken in taking a simple reductionist approach. Not only, as is already clear, should we not reduce it all to 'one-to-one' interaction; equally, we must not reduce it all to simply 'phenomena of fear'. There are, of course, many modalities involved in the emergence of structures at the social, economic, cultural, political and ideological levels. The argument here is simply that fear has played a crucial and hitherto unrecognised distorting role in the emergence and shaping of such structures. This is centrally because of the pervasive role of denial in our contemporary identities and culture. In other words, fear of the type which concerns us in this argument will often result not in behaviour which can be reinterpreted straightforwardly as 'fearful', but paradoxically in a form of machismo, cool or hot, whose champions will often convincingly laugh off the imputation of even mild anxiety. As with the incumbents, so also with the roles and processes: we will not 'see' fear in their type of confident assertion. Our task is to discover at one and the same time the unspoken fears which *do* enter into our own contemporary discourse, and the paradoxical imprint of the denial of such fears in the overconfidence of our leaders.

The Valley of Fear

In attempting to make sense of our 'normal madness', then, we need a sophisticated reading of both the dynamics of leadership and the statics of submission. One recent case in Ireland offers rich material for such an exercise, as well as lying squarely in this volume's central area of ecology. This is the case of the Hanrahan family of Co. Tipperary, who had to conduct a prolonged and painful struggle to vindicate their conviction that a nearby factory was poisoning both themselves and the herd on their family farm.

In 1976 the multinational firm of Merck, Sharp and Dohme opened a factory at Ballydine near Carrick-on-Suir. In August 1978, John Hanrahan first noted serious health problems among the cattle herd, and over the next eight or so years many cattle were lost, while the family themselves suffered severe respiratory and other ailments. One major difficulty in sustaining a charge against the adjoining factory was the obviously good health of the workers within the plant, at the same time as the Hanrahans were not only suffering ill-health, but frequently experiencing unpleasant smells and clouds of noxious vapour. Various reports were commissioned, none of which implicated the factory, though the possibility of inadequate combustion, with consequent very brief, but intensely toxic, episodic emissions, was equally never ruled out.

The Hanrahans took their action to the High Court, where they lost in 1985. The basis of the ruling was the failure to establish a causal connection between the damage to humans and animals, and the MSD plant. Now theoretically past the point of financial ruin, they persisted and appealed to the Supreme Court in 1987. Justice Henchy delivered the Court's judgment, reversing the High Court, on the crucial issue of quality of evidence. A vital step in this reversal was the medical evidence of the consultant who had treated John Hanrahan:

> Henchy quoted in detail [Professor Muiris] Fitzgerald's uncontroverted and carefully worded opinion that, on the balance of probabilities, Hanrahan's lung disease was caused by toxic emissions from the factory, because that was the only local source of toxic substances . . . 'I would hold,' Henchy concluded, 'that John Hanrahan is entitled to damages for the ill health he suffered as a result of the nuisance caused by the factory emissions'.[19]

When he turned to the damage to the cattle, Henchy pointed out that MSD was the main source of hydrogen chloride, and of hydrochloric acid mists, in the valley. Such mists were detected and experienced at the time when animals were clearly suffering and deteriorating. The defendants' scientific evidence led Henchy, as O'Callaghan tells us:

> to the conclusion that it only showed what could or should have happened by way of toxic damage. In the light of what did happen, such evidence should not be allowed to prevail . . . 'It would be to allow scientific theorising to dethrone fact to dispose of this claim by saying, as was said in the judgement under appeal, that there was virtually no evidence in this case of injury to human beings or animals which has been scientifically linked to any chemicals emanating from the defendants' factory'.[20]

To follow the twists and turns of this case would lead us through all the various 'dimensions' and 'faces' of power, through manipulation and withholding of information, agenda-control and the various other gambits. One such device is the creation of disabling labels: the Hanrahans were frequently depicted as feckless farmers who had overreached themselves in the agricultural boom years after EEC entry. At one stage, also, the defence came near to accusing John Hanrahan of having poisoned himself with bromine. Hanrahan himself has spoken of his difficulty in not being 'sunk under the weight of science and technology'.[21]

The effects of fear on various parties to the drama are evident. Both the local dairy-processing cooperative, and the Irish Farmers' Association, were reluctant to lend any support to Hanrahan, for fear of the impact of publicity on the reputation of dairy products. We can also see the role of fear in locally isolating and demonising the Hanrahan family. This process is furthered even by the way in which we celebrate the saga in retrospect: the lonely struggle of one man and his family with a problem no one else shared. It is in fact clear that a large number of farms and families experienced everything from discomfort to ill-health; one farmer had died of cancer in 1983, and his wife claimed that all six of his doctors had asked where he had come in contact with chemicals. However, caution or pessimism led others to drop out of the struggle, through the negative learning-process of confronting local and national power-structures. As one farmer whose cattle suffered put it:

> Trying to do anything about it is useless. I see Hanrahan across there trying to fight against them all and I say 'What's the use?'[22]

A major step in this learning-process was the agitation in 1975 against Schering-Plough's proposal to build an antibiotics plant in the same area, while MSD was under construction. After a bitter process of meetings and behind-the-scenes intimidation, the protesters withdrew, stating:

> For the safety of our families and property we individually and collectively bow to the pressure of serious intimidation and threats of violence, which forces us to forgo our rights as citizens of this country. In these circumstances we individually and collectively withdraw our objections to the proposed industry and will take no further action.[23]

Another piece of the picture is the administrative and policymaking culture encountered by such protesters, and by the Hanrahans in their long struggle.

> What did happen in Ballydine brought a curious response from local officials and politicians, local farmers, local professional people, local TDs, the IIRS [Institute for Industrial Research and Standards], the IDA [Industrial Development Authority] and scientists from various institutions; in fact everyone who touched on the case right up to the government responded oddly.[24]

Interestingly, in view of our quotation from eastern Germany on p. 173 above, what we find as a common thread through the Hanrahan's bureaucratic nightmare was the evasion of *responsibility*. Nobody contacted ever seemed to have been around in any of the original decisions when MSD was set up, and everyone was protected by the blanket of 'expertise'. The County Manager put it succinctly: 'You engage consultants because the Council would not have that expertise'.[25]

Both of the studies of the MSD case on which I have drawn make the connection between it and the overall industrialisation policy pursued by the Irish Republic in the last few decades. This has involved an extreme emphasis on Ireland's attractiveness to foreign investment, from the point of view of a skilled workforce, an encouraging tax and grant regime, and – ironically – a clean environment. The roots of this policy, often implemented in a spirit of craven dependency, lie deep and early in that experience of dependence on outside political, economic and cultural forces associated with Ireland's colonial past.

The Hanrahans could not have been isolated and victimised as they were, abandoned by so many individuals, families and institutions, in a political culture which promoted rather than discouraged active citizenship. This is where Alice Miller's analysis of the inheritance of hurt supplies a crucial dimension, as already indicated in her quotation about Bergman and the 'familiar air' of cruelty (see p. 175 above). Not only does Alice Miller's analysis lead us out into society, it also leads us back into history. We need to trace how the silences, evasions and idealisations which characterise our contemporary society and politics have emerged as a decorum masking the howls of class, gender and race attendant on the transition from medieval to modern hierarchy. Whatever our precise theory of social structure and its change, we must allow for that thread whereby over the generations parents, and other significant adults, enforce on the young the 'bargain' which they have made with the world and its pains. Without tracing this thread we can never fully understand, let alone redress, the political failures so neatly parcelled up in the contemporary jargon of 'democratic deficits'.

Howls and Decorum: *Pro Europa Mori?*

It is time briefly to consider the role of aggression in the complex of suppressed emotions which we have been exploring. We have already noted the 'normal' and 'abnormal' horrors which our culture produces and somehow rationalises. It is a measure of how deep this rationalisation goes, that we so often overlook the centrality of war and the arms trade to the contemporary economy. This is as significant for the 'post-Cold-War' world as it was before. We cannot begin to understand, let alone redress, our current situation if we do not take account of the normalisation of aggression, particularly in warfare. It is one of the chief and most destructive manifestations of the 'howl', the unrecognised legacy of hurt and fear.

It is salutary to reflect how the aggressive imagery so often encountered in contemporary economic language – advertising 'campaigns', price 'wars' and so forth – is employed in the Cecchini text already discussed. It speaks of 'the emergence of more telling competitive weaponry' (p. 85) for the 'reconquest of the European market' (p. 75). There is more than a stylistic continuity between such aggressive imagery and another 'pillar' of the new European Union: the so-called 'common European defence policy'. The lines of policy adumbrated in the Maastricht Treaty on this topic are profoundly disturbing for anybody who looks to the evolution of the EEC, EC and EU for a hopeful response to the challenges of human living together in the late twentieth century.

The thinking behind the Treaty reveals none of that auto-critique of European aggression and militarism which would appear to be a necessary precondition for addressing such problems today. Rather, it follows logically from the CEC document's phantastic bombast about:

> the ability of Europeans to rise to a challenge, on that spirit which, down the centuries, has made them great on the international scene. (p. 8)

It would be hard to think of a worse starting point for 'European' policymaking, in the interests of either Europeans ourselves or the various other societies which have experienced our 'greatness' down the ages.

Moreover, the policy envisaged involves a very clear intention of 'defending' so-called 'European interests' at any point around the globe where they are affected, and commits each member of the European Union in the following language:

> The member States shall support the Union's external and security policy actively and unreservedly in a spirit of loyalty and mutual solidarity. They shall refrain from any action which is contrary to the interests of the Union or likely to impair its effectiveness as a cohesive force [sic] in international relations.[26]

The main point of this for our current topic is that it is quite clear that in so far as the emerging European Union embodies a clear project, that project is seen as involving a highly undemocratic war machine as well as the promised land of economic plenty. This is of ecological relevance from many points of view. Contemporary warfare, nuclear and 'conventional', goes to the very heart of the ecological problem. It is not simply that the grotesquely high levels of expenditure on armaments in the contemporary world represent a massive distortion and deflection away from the needs of development, ecological and otherwise. The impact of contemporary warfare is in itself and in its consequences a grievous degradation of the environment; it did not take nuclear weapons to bomb Iraq, in the words of one UN observer, back to the Middle Ages. Moreover, as is all-too-seldom recognised, the very existence of the level and types of armaments with which our world is stocked constitutes a massive and grotesque pollution in every dimension from the 'natural' to the psychological.

We have already adverted, in our discussion of the Hanrahan/MSD case, to the various devices of information-control involved in the Power Debate. One of the key contributions to that debate is the analysis by Bachrach and Baratz of 'agenda-control', whereby certain matters are prevented from becoming issues by those who have control over decision-making bodies.[27] Such strategems, it is clear, apply not only in local and national but also in global politics. In the last couple of decades we have had United Nations conferences on Development, on Disarmament, and on the Environment, in many cases linked to the work of prestigious and worthwhile commissions. There has been very little open discussion of the way in which the agenda of discussion of such issues has been managed. At no conference, in no commission, have the three topics of Disarmament, Development and Ecology been discussed together. The United States government indeed carried its opposition to the linking of even the first two of these concepts to the point of formally withdrawing from the International Conference on the Relationship between Disarmament and Development held in New York in 1987. It is literally vital that any talk of a 'new ecology' should inscribe the interrelations of these three areas – how we live, where we live, how we die – firmly on its agenda.

Such an agenda must of course operate on the highly global level addressed by for example UN commissions. It must, however, never lose sight of the cultural identities, among both 'followers' and 'leaders', which allow such global distortions to emerge and recur. It is the contention of this chapter that a vital dimension of this question is to be found in the shared cultural inheritance of hurt and denial which Alice Miller has done so much to illuminate. Thus if we cannot understand the recent Gulf War as, in one crucial dimension, two boys fighting in the sand, then we cannot understand it at all. We also have much to learn from revelations such as the following, reported by an insider to the Kennedy Administration:

> James Reston who saw Kennedy immediately after the [Vienna 1961] meeting, reports that the President was not fully satisfied with his performance. Kennedy was not prepared for Khruschev's crude and assertive manner, indeed, he said that his meeting with Khruschev was the 'worst thing in my life. He savaged me . . . We have to see what we can do that will restore a feeling in Moscow that we will defend our national interests. I'll have to increase the defense budget. And we have to confront them. The only place we can do that is in Vietnam. We have to send more people there'.[28]

Aggression and Ecology

One cannot help wondering how much the destruction of Vietnam and its populace can thus be laid at the door of threatened masculine identity. We need to trace the roots of the distortion whereby we are governed by leaders, mostly men, whose unresolved insecurities can issue in such destructiveness, and we come to treat it to a mixture of denial and sanitising complacency. This leads us to a consideration of the argument of Stettbacher, who takes up and develops a number of themes from Alice Miller, particularly that of aggression and destructiveness:

> For it is fear, of each other and of the environment, that prevents us from arriving at clear, life-enhancing decisions and acting constructively.[29]

Stettbacher traces this destructiveness to unconscious, unintegrated fear:

> Our unconscious fear that we are deficient, that we are worthless or 'bad' – *this* is the root of all our negative compensations and developments. A person whose primal nature has received support and confirmation will take pleasure in being alive and will not act destructively.[30]

Stettbacher is here summarising the agonies, open or half-suppressed, to which we have already referred on pp. 172–3 above. His language finds an echo in the appalling self-castigation of the novelist Antonia White:

> It is far better to be sans peur than sans reproche. Fear is the real poison of the whole human race . . . Whatever I do I am in terror of losing something. . . . It makes me equally afraid of religion and atheism, success and failure, love and celibacy . . . I wish to heaven I knew who I was – my old eternal cry . . . Until I can get rid of this paralysing fear, I can never have any happiness or be any use.[31]

It is particularly striking how Stettbacher embraces in his analysis both our relations with other humans and our relations to the 'natural environment'. This is the final link in my chain of argument. I have already put forward a case that unrecognised hurt and its consequences play a vital role in the distorted social and political processes which we have considered;

these include such clearly ecological cases as the Hanrahan/MSD one. What remains, however, is to ponder the links between this legacy of hurt and our specific attitudes to and dealings with nature.

Our critique so far, for example in the case of the Cecchini Report, has affinities with both the 'technocratic project' and the 'cultural politics' perspectives discussed by Hajer (this volume): to some extent we deride the failure of hierarchical distortions of 'real' problems, but equally we become aware of how our modern managerial culture is itself the disease to which it claims to be the cure. At stake here is the question of realism. It is of course the case that 'Nature' nowadays is a highly socially mediated category, rather than an out-there objectivity, as Marx gleefully reminds Feuerbach:

> For that matter, nature, the nature that preceded human history, is not by any means the nature in which Feuerbach lives, it is nature which today no longer exists anywhere (except perhaps on a few Australian coral islands of recent origin) and which, therefore, does not exist for Feuerbach either.[32]

Given that 'Nature' is such a highly socialised and mediated concept in the contemporary world, our perceptions and misperceptions of it are, as I have argued here, crucially shaped and distorted by the character of our social process and identities. What Stettbacher is providing, then, is an account of a real process which accounts for the sometimes eerie mediations and blindnesses of our political culture: the insidious working out of our 'unfinished business', the 'etwas' of Alice Miller. As we have already noted, there are many twists and paradoxes in this domain. One of these is the two-facedness of the orientations with which Stettbacher is concerned. On the one hand we have an attitude of aggressiveness towards others and towards our world, which somehow displaces, albeit unavailingly, the burden of suppressed fear and anger. At the same time we are capable of an almost surreal indifference towards the dangers on which our conventional wisdom is so eloquent.

We should not puzzle too long over the apparent 'paradox' of such combined aggression and indifference. As already suggested earlier, they are linked in being two pathological ways of denying our hurt; one, by attempting to displace it, the other by attempting to pretend it never happened. Such an argument not only plausibly accounts for a degree of reckless destructiveness towards physical nature, as an outlet for emotions repressed by the decorum of human society; it also carries psychology a major step towards meeting the deeper challenge recently outlined by Theodore Roszak. Whilst one might quarrel with details of Roszak's own prescriptions on various points, he undoubtedly has put the issue squarely by looking for the link between 'social' and 'ecological' madness. He argues that many of our 'psychological' and our 'ecological' problems have a common root, in the divorcing of in-here/out-there, mind and matter, which characterised the formative period of industrial culture (see Adam, this volume; Szerszynski, this volume). We can properly understand neither ourselves nor our world while maintaining this divorce:

The Earth's cry for rescue from the punishing weight of the industrial system we have created is our own cry for a scale and quality of life that will free each of us to become the complete person we were born to be.[33]

He shares with Alice Miller an appreciation of the positive claims of what is too often described pejoratively as 'narcissism'. He also makes an explicit link between the 'psychological' and 'ecological' agendas:

The modern industrial societies have been reared on a vision of nature that teaches people they are a mere accident in a galactic wilderness: 'strangers and afraid in a world they never made'. What stance in life can they then take but one of fear, anxiety, even hostility towards the natural world? Like children who see their parents as remote, powerful and punishing authorities, they will feel they have no choice but to stand defensively on guard, looking for every opportunity to strike out. Their encounter with nature will not be grounded in trust and security, let alone love.[34]

Clearly, a vital piece in this jigsaw is the notion of *embodiment*; our problems in perceiving and relating to the world as a body arise from and reinforce our problems in recognising our own embodiment. Dorinda Outram has explored one dimension of the emergence of this syndrome, summed up in Elias's notion of *Homo clausus*, the new model citizen who came to centre-stage in the French Revolution. That process, she tells us:

thrust the bourgeoisie into power in a way which did not entail the inclusion in the political nation, except very briefly, of elements in society – the workers, peasants and women – which had been excluded under the old regime.[35]

In the context of a discussion of the importance of the bodily for reconstructing political theory, Outram studies in particular the cruelties of the Terror, and notes 'the terrible ambiguities involved in the adoption of models of Stoic calm'; she is here exploring the early emergence of that modern culture of 'managing' life events which Beck-Gernsheim explores elsewhere in this volume. It is this which grounds Outram's question:

whether through the very ways in which modern people have learned self-control there have also been implanted the seeds of self-destructiveness.[36]

If we accept Outram's argument that aggression, combined with an eerie pretence of indifference, emerges in a peculiarly modern form with *Homo clausus*, we can then perhaps add the dimension of ecology as, along with 'workers, peasants and women', one of the crucial realities excluded by his new decorum. We can then begin to see our distorted relationship with, and perceptions of, nature not simply as the destructive 'payoff' from, but also as grounding, our distorted social and cultural processes.

The contemporary agenda arising from all this is well described by Roszak, with his interweaving of the struggle both for democratic rights and for 'biocentric community':

the endangered species, the imperilled biosphere, cannot speak for themselves. We must be their voice. We speak for them when we speak for the personhood that is endangered by the same forces that endanger the planetary environment. On this historical horizon, the right to self-knowledge parallels the right to self-government . . . It is the brave beginning of a project that both the person and the planet require.[37]

Conclusion

We have traced a lineage of fear and hurt, looking at some of its impact on our contemporary identities and socio-political processes. If my argument here is valid, no amount of effort within our present frames of discourse and policymaking can take us far out of our current predicaments: a straighter frame will not mend a warped landscape. It is only by digging deeper into the magma of hurt that lies beneath the surface that we can learn to cool it where necessary and possible, and release it when and where required. The most crucial damage comes, as we have already seen, not from primary pain as such, but from the various ways in which we deny our pain. This is where fear is central. Not only is it in itself a disturbing emotion, but it can come to function as a second-order custodian of our psychic imprisonment: we cut ourselves off from direct contact with our world and ourselves because we fear the effect on our identity of admitting our negative experiences and their attendant emotions.

This 'state of noncommunication', to use Winnicott's chilling term, involves aggression and/or indifference towards ourselves, towards others and towards our surroundings. Roszak's suggestion is that the environment is crucially implicated here not only because it is a, perhaps the, chief casualty of this syndrome, but that at a deeper level the syndrome may *result from* our alienation from our own and the earth's bodies. Though not yet convinced of this, I recognise a vital extension of our agenda, raising the question of the 'origin' of that fear of creation/createdness/creativity so eloquently diagnosed by Alice Miller. In one sense this 'origin' is no more attainable than the 'origin' of language – though one might hope that the prevalence of such fear is not bound up, as is language, in the very concept of human society. My optimistic guess is that we can learn a new emotional vocabulary where creativity will replace caution, but I am sure that Roszak is correct in suggesting that the way to healing, both 'personal' and 'social', will have to pass through a recognition of our ecological embodiment. This raises the possibility that our reflections towards a new environmental agenda could describe for once a positive 'closing circle', and lead us to a practice of the consciousness which David Smail, echoing so much recent feminist thought, describes in beautiful simplicity:

> We suffer pain because we do damage to each other, and we shall continue to suffer pain as long as we continue to do the damage. The way to alleviate and mitigate distress is for us to *take care of* the world and the other people in it, not to *treat* them.[38]

Notes

1. Robert Bly, from 'Poem against the rich', in R. Ellmann (ed.) (1976) *The Oxford Book of American Verse*. New York: Oxford University Press. p. 941.
2. Walt Whitman, from 'Song of myself' in R. Ellmann (ed.) (1976), op. cit.: 213.

3. Allen Ginsberg, from 'On Burroughs' work', in R. Ellmann (ed.) (1976), op. cit.: 929–30.

4. See Maguire, J. (1990) ' "Could Try Harder"? A Perspective on the Politics of Information', *Administration*, 38 (2): 157–69.

5. Heller, J. (1974) *Something Happened*. London: Cape. pp. 114–15.

6. Baez, J. (1988) *And a Voice to Sing With*. London: Century. pp. 114–15.

7. Goodman, D. in 'From Our Own Correspondent', BBC Radio 4, January 1994, with acknowledgements for her and the BBC's kind help.

8. Joseph, S. (1974) *Children in Fear*. New York: Collier Books. pp. xi–xii.

9. Miller, A. (1978) *The Drama of Being a Child*. London: Virago. p. 26. (See also *For Your Own Good*. London: Virago, 1983; and *Thou Shalt Not Be Aware*. London: Virago, 1985.)

10. Ibid.: 95.

11. Mills, C. Wright (1971) 'The structure of power in American society', in A. Pizzorno (ed.), *Political Sociology*. London: Penguin. pp. 110–25; the quotation is from p. 111.

12. Orbach, S. (1994) *What's Really Going On Here?* London: Virago. p. 19.

13. Schell, J. (1982) *The Fate of the Earth*. New York: Knopf. p. 161.

14. MacIntyre, A. (1982) *After Virtue*. London: Duckworth.

15. Morgan, G. (1986) *Images of Organisation*. London: Sage. p. 135.

16. Cecchini, P. et. al. (1988) *The European Challenge: 1992: The Benefits of a Single Market*. Aldershot: Wildwood House. Page references to this work are given in the text.

17. Commission of the European Communities (1988) *A Frontier-free Europe*. Brussels and Luxembourg: CEC. Page references to this work are given in the text.

18. Rorty, R. (1989) *Contingency, Irony and Solidarity*. Cambridge: Cambridge University Press.

19. O'Callaghan, J. (1992) *The Red Book – The Hanrahan Case against Merck, Sharp and Dohme*. Dublin: Poolberg. p. 194.

20. Ibid.: 195.

21. Ibid.: xi.

22. Allen, R. and Jones, T. (1990) *Guests of the Nation*. London: Earthscan. pp. 37–8.

23. O'Callaghan (1992), op. cit.: xi.

24. Allen and Jones (1990), op. cit.: 33–4.

25. Ibid.: 33.

26. Quoted in Maguire, J and Noonan, J. (1992) *Maastricht and Neutrality – Ireland's Neutrality and the Future of Europe*. Cork: People First/Meitheal. p. 20.

27. For a brief account of this topic, see Maguire (1990), op. cit.

28. Reston, J., quoted in Ball, G. W. (1994) 'Kennedy up close', *New York Review of Books*, 3 February, p. 18. This account is contested by, for example, O'Donnell, K. et al. (1972) *Johnny We Hardly Knew Ye*. Boston: Little, Brown. pp. 297–8; but I believe that there is a significant dimension of the truth in Reston's own first-hand account of his meeting with Kennedy.

29. Stettbacher, J. K. (1991) *Making Sense of Suffering: The Healing Confrontation with Your Own Past*, trans. S. Worrall. New York: Dalton. p. 6.

30. Ibid.: 6–7.

31. White, A., quoted in Hopkinson, L. P. (1993) 'The old demon, fear', in *A Virago Keepsake*. London: Virago. pp. 32–6; the quotation is from p. 33.

32. Marx, K., from 'The German Ideology' in Marx and Engels (1976) *Collected Works*, vol. V. London: Lawrence and Wishart. p. 40.

33. Roszak, T. (1993) *The Voice of the Earth*. London: Bantam. p. 16.

34. Ibid.: 42.

35. Outram, D. (1989) *The Body and the French Revolution*. New Haven CT and London: Yale University Press. p. 154.

36. Outram (1989), op. cit.: 13.

37. Roszak (1993), op. cit.: 282–3.

38. Smail, D. (1987) *Taking Care: An Alternative to Therapy*. London: Dent. p. 1.

8

SOLIDARY INDIVIDUALISM: THE MORAL IMPACT OF CULTURAL MODERNISATION IN LATE MODERNITY

Helmuth Berking

Translated by Paul Knowlton

All that we know indicates that the existence of our world is more than threatened by a deterioration of its own basic environmental conditions. But at the same time it is also the case that at least in most parts of Western capitalist societies a well-founded ecological consciousness has asserted itself down into the last recesses of everyday life. Institutionalised forms of environmental research and a dense network of alternative projects are complementing a social process which nonetheless – and compared with what has yet to be done – conveys the impression that although much is in the offing, nothing much is being accomplished. The dominant rationale of political and economic action orientations continues to stand in crass contrast to the environmental knowledge available, and – this will by no means come as a surprise – the old-fashioned mode of institutionalised decision-making not only favours but appears to guarantee the hegemony of instrumental adjustments more than it fosters the groundwork of creative change.

To be sure, this view of the self-blockades of subsystemic rationality assumptions must not blind us to the fact that dramatic changes have long since taken place in the lifeworlds of empirical subjects. It is here, in this terrain, that will first be decided what innovative ecological solutions a society empowers itself to find. Then there is the fact that both the structural environmental crisis and the successful formation of environ-mental and countercultural social forces constitute elements of one and the same socio-cultural configuration. There is in our culture no outside, no privileged vantage point, and no independent constructions of identity. Crisis, crisis negation, and crisis consciousness form part of one context. They are all grounded in selective patterns of information and perception that stem from the same stocks of cultural knowledge; yet the codings of the individual world-constructions do not meet. The institutionalised forms of political and economic action lack what distinguishes in particular the world-view structures of the social actors and environmental activists: a normative framing; that is, a *moral consciousness*. But how are public-welfare orientation and collective responsibility to be fostered precisely by the dominant cultural self-definitions of utilitarianism and individualism, not the least of the factors responsible for the present ecological dilemma with which we are today confronted?

The Social Effects of Individualisation

In view of the current social circumstances, this thesis of a growing remoralisation of social intercourse must, at least at first glance, appear absurd. For whoever today inquires into the moral economy of modern society will soon find himself in danger either of being relegated to the tradition-laden chorus of a cultural critique attuned to theories of decline, or, indeed, labelled a cynic out to make a virtue of necessity and to sell as a triumph of civilisation the de-moralisation of social semantics. A shrouded future headed in the direction of globicide which, it would seem, can be prevented from taking shape in the present only through fundamental reorientations in the action-structuring triangle of self, society and nature, appears to frame the fundamental perception of our social lifeworlds. The re-emergence of bloodthirsty xenophobic incendiaries, a corruption-prone political personnel that day by day demonstrates to its astonished public the reprivatisation of opportunities of political power in the form of a blithe maximisation of its self-interest, the privatist dissipation of normative self-obligations and institutional ties, unmistakable tendencies toward social closure (Parkin, 1983) and social protectionism as a promising strategy in the competitive struggle for material and symbolic advantage – all of these phenomena conjure up the image of a society whose assets in solidarity and legitimacy are exhausted and whose social-integrative resources appear, at the end of the twentieth century, to have been spent once and for all.

Contemporary diagnoses steeped in capitalism critique and social theory also share the interpretation that the normative, moral and cultural foundations on which, for a protracted period, the implementation of the liberal-capitalist market society was unquestioningly able to build are increasingly crumbling under the encroachment of systemic imperatives on lifeworld practices. Indeed, these societies are drawing parasitically on pre-modern 'systems of meaning and obligation' which they are able neither to regenerate within their own economic and political institutions nor to replace with alternatives (Dubiel, 1991: 126). What has happened instead, the argument goes, is that the logic of sociation has paved the way for the breakthrough of a different cultural pattern, which in the beginnings of civil society was confined to the sphere of economy but which has now, partly because of the removal of the socio-structural constraints on market-related rational behaviour, gained social expression in the form of a utilitarian morality that knows no bounds.

The triumphant advance of utilitarian values, which now seem to oblige the individual to secure and augment his own advantage (see Bellah et al., 1985), is today described, under the heading of detraditionalisation and individualisation, above all as a cumulative effect of the process of cultural modernisation. The basis of the new type of phenomenality of the social is the pluralisation of life-forms typical of Western capitalist societies. This mode of sociation presupposes deep clefts and breaches in the institutionally shaped patterns of life-conduct, stemming on the one hand from growing detraditionalisation, the dissolution of social milieux stabilised in terms of class structure and of collective life-contexts, but on the other hand also deriving from the fact that the identity models unquestioningly centred, even a few years ago, on work, profession and family have lost part of their shaping force.

Ulrich Beck has pointedly formulated the socio-structural effects of modernisation in terms of a second epochal advent of individualisation. 'In the individualised society, the individual must . . . learn, on pain of permanent disadvantage, to conceive of himself or herself as the centre of activity, as the planning office with respect to his/her own biography, abilities, orientations, relationships and so on' (Beck, 1992: 135; cf. Beck-Gernsheim, this volume). For individualisation does not and cannot mean the reinstatement of the old liberal idea of the bourgeois subject, centred on liberty and property. The release of individuals from fixed social frames of reference that have themselves again become tradition for capitalist society, the erosion of life-contexts stabilised in terms of class-specific cultural aspects, of forms of the family, and of vocational ties is, for the first time in the history of this form of sociation, not being reabsorbed by socio-structurally induced processes entailing a reorganisation of social class and group contexts. Utterly dependent on market and state, the social fate of the many is becoming the particular fate of each individual.

But those who are quick to equate the dynamics unfolding in detraditionalisation and individualisation – characteristic for Western capitalist societies and contradictory within itself – with effects stemming from a breakdown of solidarity and a lapse of collective responsibility are at a loss to perceive not only the paradoxical effects but also the possibly quite 'unspectacular civilisational gains' (Ziehe, 1992: 102) which may at present be linked with the – in part attained, in part constrained – individualisation of life conduct and the pluralisation of life-forms.

In this perspective my interest is focused in particular on actual changes in the spheres of cultural reproduction, ideas of personality development, and concepts of subjectivity the conditions of which are in need of sociological clarification. To describe these structural changes of social lifeworlds means in particular to pay close attention to the unintended effects of cultural modernisation both in terms of whether and how it creates both new levels of sociation and collective actors. To be sure, it is not only the transformation of institutional frameworks but also the creative solution found for fundamental ecological dilemmas that will be influenced decisively by the answer given to the question as to what *social-moral potentials* the process of individualisation itself may set free, or at least preserve.

Gift-giving and the Contemporary Self

I therefore wish to direct your attention to a sphere – somewhat neglected in its social-theoretical significance – of entirely commonplace social practices and forms of interaction that have, in essence, one thing in common: namely, the fact that they systematically evade the edicts of exchange value and the logic of the market. If one leaves the level at which assumptions of systemic rationality are most applicable – that is, the locus in which methodological individualism stubbornly asserts its right to existence – and turns to the logics of action of empirical subjects, it is not difficult to discern that our everyday knowledge continues to distinguish strictly between market-governed relations and social relations, between the principles of equivalence and reciprocity, between contract and the non-contractual conditions of any contract. The latter concept includes stocks of traditional cultural knowledge; these are normative and value-related orientations used to initiate and stabilise relationship formulas and recognition-based relations such as love, friendship, trust, solidarity, empathy and compassion, charity, and willingness to make sacrifices. In short, these are cognitive, normlike and emotional competences which anything but reduce interest in the other to the mode of a merely strategic interaction.

True, this two-world theory starts to get really interesting only when it is linked with the provocative thesis that structurally induced individualis-ation processes have successively dried up the social-moral hinterland of our social orders – that, in other words, we more and more see ourselves confronted with that particular form of cold sociation that is regulated solely via money and power.

A brief glance at the homeland of the highly individualised society does, however, tend straight away to blur the contours of this picture. What is to be made of a situation in which, week after week, 80 million Americans, or over 45% of the population above the age of 18, dedicate five hours or more of their time to voluntary relief work and charitable activities, work in crisis centres, civil rights movements and non-profit organisations, organise neighbourhood help projects, build social networks dedicated to geriatric care, maintain women's houses, initiate anti-drug campaigns, etc., thus providing free services which, if their costs were calculated, would amount to far more than $150 million (Wuthnow, 1992: 6f)? Mind you, these figures refer merely to the socially organised, so-called independent sector. They might include donations and benefits, but not the entire sphere of generous giving and helping in informal, but above all private, relationship contexts. Some 4.3% of household incomes – and seen in terms of society as a whole, that is no small figure – also goes into a gift-giving economy centred on family and friends.

Unfortunately, there are no comparable figures available for Germany, a circumstance which may be linked to the fact that, in contrast to the United States, a variety of such activities are covered there by the corporate organisations of welfare capitalism. Still, there, too, there exist a good number of phenomena that signal more an intensification than a diminution of social engagement and collective responsibility. One might think in this context of the furious proliferation of a well-founded ecological crisis consciousness, of the wide variety of civic protest and social movements, which, as early as the mid-1970s, were able to mobilise more members than all of Germany's political parties together. One might also think of the alternative district and neighbourhood structures to be found in all major towns and cities, of the – after all – considerable breadth of the campaigns mobilised against right-wing violence, or of the private initiatives offering hospitality to war refugees and asylum-seekers. Nor are the economic dimensions of voluntary relief and charity any easier to grasp empirically, although the German Central Institute for Social Issues estimates the volume of donations made in 1992 at some DM4 billion.

We also know that the private economy of gift-giving has grown sharply during the last two decades. Like a red thread, this age-old form of interaction pervades the everyday life of modern society, initiating and authenticating relationships, encouraging trust, creating relationships based on reciprocal recognition, and ensuring that generosity and open-handedness continue to enjoy a legitimate, because positively sanctioned, place in the moral vocabulary of a society structurally dedicated to the rationale of utility-maximising activities.

Now, to those who argue that these phenomena illustrate at best the tenacity of traditional cultural resources and in no way concern the dominant logic of capitalist sociation it must be pointed out that their argument is flawed in two particular respects: (1) these are everyday orientations that are *expanding*; (2) they are enacted by persons acting not beyond but *on the basis of universal individualisation experiences*, and they require, despite or precisely because of this fact, solidary social relationships, norms of reciprocity and forms of mutual recognition.

In an impressive study on 'acts of compassion', Robert Wuthnow characterised as the 'American paradox' this complex state of affairs which consists of seemingly exclusive value orientations that can today not only be found in one and the same person but at the same time also call for life-practical expression. If the data can be believed, for over 75% of Americans solidarity, helpfulness and public-interest orientations lay claim to the same prominent relevance that is attributed by them to such motives as self-realisation, vocational success orientations and the expansion of personal freedom. The more a person finds orientation in self-related values, the more he emphasises the importance of altruistic norms for his own lifestyle. 'In other words, people who were the most individualistic were also the most likely to value doing things to help others' (Wuthnow, 1992: 22).

Surprisingly, however, it is narrative structures from the repertory of utilitarian individualism that are used to tie together these contrary motivations to act, and to reconcile the seemingly irreconcilable. In a society so orientated toward competition and success, efforts involving good deeds, personal commitment, energy and sometimes even expense need to be justified less to others than to one's self. Why do I act in such as way as to expend, unproductively, personal resources that could indeed just as well be used to increase my own well-being? Because, thus the popular response, engagement and interest in others entails psychological gratifications which for their part are in turn of particular significance for the point of reference of *self-realisation*: that I feel good, soothe my conscience, perhaps even stabilise feelings of superiority or seek in this way to compensate for experiences of inferiority. There are first of all two noteworthy aspects to the civilisational configuration of altruism and self-interest: the seemingly incontrovertible need to *justify* such actions, preferably with utilitarian figures, and the *normative limitation* of the validity claim of what would usually be seen as a collective obligation. At least in terms of narrative structure and self-perception, it is less with regard to public-interest orientations than in its own personal interest that the individual defines and assumes responsibility. If, however, the non-intended consequences also created by self-referential world-view structures in connection with the dynamics of individualisation are taken into account, the sharp contours of this contradiction between individual and collective responsibility begin to blur.

Solidary Individualism

I therefore wish to invite you to participate in a little thought-experiment, which, taking up a term coined by Robert Musil, will inquire after the 'sense of possibility' of a form of sociation for which I, in accordance with the paradoxical behavioural demands peculiar to it, propose the term *solidary individualism*. Can empirical evidence be found which indicates that utilitarian individualism encourages the shaping of stocks of knowledge and motivational situations which prepare the cultural ground for a solidary individualism?

If, as a cumulative effect of the modernisation process and the modes in which it is cushioned using the means available to the welfare state, a form of social existence beyond 'class and rank' (Beck) gains the power of reality, if the release of individuals out of traditional frames of reference and habitual orientations attains a certain depth of focus, then it may be said that all individuals are responsible for themselves, their own bodies, their relationships and the images that they create of themselves for others. In conjunction with the generalisation of once exclusive stocks of cultural knowledge, altered ideas of subjectivity and personality ideals contour this process in two ways: as favoured self-images which individuals do their very best to live up to, and as base institutions of social control which, in the competitive struggle for social opportunities, seriously endanger those who fail to meet their standards. Interest in the self and interest in the other become at the same time more demanding and more vulnerable.

We have long been confronted with the offshoots of this development. For today individualisation at the same time implies a heightening of the subjective latitudes open to freedom *and* complete dependence on the market, liberation *and* standardisation of expression, heightened self-referentiality *and* external control pushed almost to the limits of what is bearable; it means, in short: learning, at all levels of social intercourse, to deal with paradoxical demands on one's behaviour, controlling one's affects without ceasing to be 'natural', utilising the chances offered by an increasing informalisation without casting conventions to the winds, demanding authenticity, and steering clear of the constraints of depersonalisation.

Regardless of whether they are accentuated as institutionalised behavioural expectations or biographical self-interpretation, as symbolic self-classification or intersubjective self-aspiration (Ziehe, 1992: 102f), what is demanded of the individuals in every case is cognitive, social and affective competences which, the thesis to be developed here goes, practically coerce them to *form and expand reflexive self-relations*. There are fewer and fewer unquestionably given paths of life conduct available. Whoever marries today can and must know that and why he is deciding in favour of a particular relationship form; he likewise can and must know that a tie of this sort may be temporary, happy or catastrophic. Not only the individual but every individual human being finds himself bound to write the scenarios of his own life, to survey the maps of his own social orientations, to direct his own biography, his personality and his self (Hitzler, 1991, 1993), even though he is, in advance, in no way in possession of the resources required to do so. Stocks of cultural knowledge are not only generalised, they are at the same time, in a sort of self-reflexive test behaviour, given a practical turn. Thus, for example, the conviction that individuals create their own inward persona has long been seen as common knowledge, propelling the need for self-justification to undreamed-of heights. My willingness to achieve, my outward appearance, my erotic sense, my psychic make-up – there is hardly anything that could not at any time be drawn into the undertow of a logic of justification (Ziehe, 1989: 20). This logic of justification appears to be at the very heart of our discursive order: it not only permits self-assurance and identification of motives. Self-justification is the dam erected by individuals against contingency and the *polysémie* of signs. Whatever the reasons may be that an individual advances – the universal psychologisation of our everyday knowledge is merely one significant example – justifications are essential, because they, in the first place, evoke for ego and alter ego alike the meaning on which their jointly held situational definition can build.

The belief in the free inward constitution of the individual goes hand in hand with constraints to shape one's outward person – health, good looks, naturalness, elegance – which need to be elaborated and demonstrated bodily, by the sweat of one's brow, so to speak. Unremittingly, work continues on the presentation of the body as the representation of the self; unremittingly, this self is questioned, criticised and compared with the cultural norms of its ideal. Self-reference and perception by others, expressive behaviour and interactional competence proceed along the lines of cultural standards and are saturated with the aspiration levels stemming from stocks of psychosocial knowledge. Working towards the end of intensifying these cultural standards, and holding out promise of subjective relief, a veritable flood of life-counselling and self-help literature has appeared that offers cut-rate expert knowledge for each and every psychosocial disposition.

The sovereign self, the wish-dream of finally being above the vicissitudes of the process of modernisation, nonetheless follows this process to the letter. And yet it is also such that reflexive self-relations provide precisely the motivational and cognitive resources on which the civilisational achievements of cognitive and moral minorities, but also – as can be seen in the emergence of the new social movements – forms of post-traditional community formation, are today based (see Berking and Neckel, 1990; Michailow, 1993).

Reflexive self-relations do, it is true, evoke an additional, seemingly likewise paradoxical effect. They promote an expansion of *instrumental mentalities*, heightening the instrumental access to the self no less than to the other, which can easily be illustrated with reference to the cultural constraints of emotional management. Emotions are generally brought into interaction via expression, whereby the context can be direct and spontaneous, can experience significant shifts via inner action pro-grammes, or can be fully negated via strategic orientations applied directly at the level of expression. What I want to intimate or impart need not necessarily have anything to do with what I experience inwardly. The mechanisms of self-restraint and control over affects that have prevailed in the history of civilisation – and which necessarily constantly heighten the distance between people, render the thresholds of embarrassment and shame ever more vulnerable, and continuously increase the 'inner fear mediated through the eye and through the superego' (Elias, 1978/1982: II, 407; see also Neckel, 1991) – correspond insidiously with the 'face-work' with which self-respect and composure, honour and dignity are demon-strated and socially sanctioned (see Goffmann, 1967: 12.). Self-presentation, that is, implies both an evaluative schema for emotions and a cultural norm for appropriate expressive behaviour. The evaluation of an emotion frequently occurs simultaneously with the emotion concerned. I feel my anger rising and know almost in the same instant that my response is unjustified. I feel anger and feel uneasy about feeling it. Evaluations of emotions are situation-specific applications of feeling rules (Hochschild, 1983: 56), reactions that set off an inner action programme and provide the expressive interest intended with strategic meaning. I will master my fear, conceal my pleasure, so as to be able, calmly and with the soothing feeling of having done justice to my image, to continue plausibly with my interaction sequence.

All emotional management aims at expression; it is always at the same time expressive control that makes use of the body either, depending on the situation, to show emotions or to conceal disagreeable ones. It is this instrumental management of emotions that again heightens aspiration levels and interactional competence, in that it reveals the construction of legitimate expression as a *subjective performance*, while pointing directly to any failure as the consequence of some subjective incompetence. Whoever fails to find the right expression not only knows that he in the end failed to accomplish what he intended, he knows that the others know it too.

It is difficult to resist the temptation to label as deficient, in the vocabulary of theories of decline, the manipulation of emotions, the truthfulness of a gesture or the subjective effort at least to give it the appearance of plausibility. This form of instrumental mentality nonetheless implies terms of recognition: the subjective effort involved in an 'acting-as-if' situation can just as well be interpreted as an effort at bestowing respect and recognition on the other. 'Looking at a bright light to make a tear glisten', writes Arlie Hochschild (1983: 85), 'is a mode of homage, a way of payng respect to those that proclaim that sadness is owed.' An ancient form of interaction that linked the expression of mourning with tears has seemingly remained in force, yet it is no longer a ritually stabilised behavioural programme but interactional knowledge that is now in the position to give to it, or deny it, this power.

The interplay of reflexive self-reference, instrumental mentality and, finally, interactional knowledge culminates in a typical *expressive dilemma* (see Haferland, 1988: 45) which itself undermines the communicative conditions of intersubjective trust. If I, for instance, know that you know that I know that and how compliments are made and gratitude is expressed, I cannot rule out the possibility that you might be assuming that I was acting in this way only because I know that one is expected to act this way in certain situations. To let you know that I am sincere, I try to persuade you, knowing full well that you know that I know what you might be assuming; I thus know that you might attribute my attempt to demonstrate my sincerity solely to the circumstance that I was only pretending to be sincere, because I know . . . etc. Even if the labour of persuasion bears fruit, part of the dilemma will continue; that is, I not only know how to give sincere expression to signs of favour, I also know that I am expected to express gratitude when I am in this situation. But if I only express gratitude because I know this, I am everywhere following a convention, rather than the demands of truthfulness that require me to express gratitude only when I actually experience it. Not the least of the reasons why the problem exists, to follow here the line of reasoning presented by Harald Haferland, is that my knowledge renders the spontaneity of my expressive behaviour obsolete. 'It is difficult for me to distinguish whether or not I am merely feigning my spontaneity, because I of course know that I have to be spontaneous' (1988: 45f).

Spontaneity, as might be said, one of the most powerful culturally sanctioned proofs of individual truthfulness, in this way becomes an option, itself released to be used as a means of instrumental control. Having penetrated into the innermost communicative structures, expanded contingency and heightened abstraction coerce the individual to place highly artificial constructions on recognition-based relations whose intrinsic cultural meaning consists in no longer being able to rely absolutely on the self-assuredness of individual demonstrations of truthfulness.

Post-traditional Communities and the Politics of Lifestyle

Reflexive self-relations, the extension of instrumental mentalities, and the idle motion of demonstrations of truthfulness and sincerity evoked by interactive knowledge are three of the central referential variables from which cultural criticism believes itself able to draw the conclusion that a sound civilisational model has been brought to its catastrophic end by the individualisation of the conduct of life. Too much liberty and too little collective responsibility is the warning call of those who see social order threatened by the individualised lifestyles in which strategic interaction and pure self-interest dominate. There is, however, one other version that appears equally plausible.

The permanent quest for nearness and certainty, the cultural and aesthetic strategies aimed at heightening intensity, self-referential techniques and a sensibility taken at times to extremes in the name of maximising one's own state of well-being lead, together with the compulsion to generalise these self-reflexive potentials, to a situation in which, in the end, they also begin to colour perception and emotional engagement *vis-à-vis* the significant other. More sovereignty over one's own life, heightened attention to the interests of the self, greater care in the closeness of personal relationships, in dealings with the other and the little, supposedly such fine things of life – there is much that indicates that utilitarian individualism is in the process of being subdued by the constellation that gave rise to it in the first place.

To be sure, this still leaves open the dilemma of social integration and collective responsibilities. For where binding frameworks of institutional orders lose their force and institutionalised behavioural expectations are themselves drawn into the pull exerted by 'reflexive modernisation' (Beck, 1996: 57f.), we would be thrown back to a *sectoral schema of normative validity*. We would then have highly integrated, morally overheated zones of nearness, and, as closeness diminishes, increasing indifference. Aside from the fact that this itself would be a formal civilisational achievement – at any rate if empirical subjects were to invent forms of intercourse that raised dealings with and the recognition of difference to the level of a general norm – the personality ideals constituted through reflexive self-reference also open up a view of essential moral orientations which aspire to generalisation and collective responsibility.

The contours of such a new level of sociation based on self-reflexivity and a constraint to universalise can be seen clearly in the emergence of new collective actors and recent group-formation processes. As the type of the individualised individual advances ever further towards a collective life-form, intrasocietal group-formation processes and norms are organised around the post-traditional focus of the *lifestyles* and *lifestyle coalitions* in which collective identities are fashioned in an artificial, 'make-believe' mode.

It is lifestyles that today appear to fill in the blank space left behind by the modernisation process in the exchange between individual and society. Lifestyles can be seen as socially distinctive variants of cultural practices. Lifestyles include the *subjective and group-related constructions of actors* who in this way fashion their reality, invest it with meaning and give this meaning performative expression. Lifestyles thus make it possible to deal non-individually with the exactions of individuality and at the same time permit the socially typified to express the unmistakably individual; in short: they grant the twofold blessing of being someone and not having to be alone in so doing. It need not be recalled that style is an aesthetic category to perceive that 'having style' is the outcome of *conscious and selective acts*. Lifestyles present themselves as relatively homogeneous entities of collective intentions of representation and rules of observation; they constitute a sort of hinge between individuality and group affiliation. If this orientation in terms of lifestyles were to be reduced to a simple formula, it might be said: it is on the one hand the *aestheticisation of everyday life*, the cultural inflation of the commonplace, and on the other hand the *politicisation of the private*, which here form the core of post-traditional communalisation (Berking, 1989). The two forms need not coincide: aestheticisation can be as politically blind as politicisation can be aesthetically indifferent (Berking and Neckel, 1990). In both cultural practices, however, basic demonstrative, reflexive and identificatory patterns of life conduct are dovetailed in such a way that each of them, at least potentially, can open up new intermediary spaces for collective self-relations.

The cultural innovations characteristic of Western societies in the past decades have come about mostly via processes entailing the social generalisation of formerly subcultural and exclusive lifestyle coalitions. The moral investments increasingly crystallising around the problematic of ecology have led to a *lifestyle politics* at odds with the statist discourses of traditional politics. To the extent that expectations are withdrawn from politically administrative systems and concentrated on the inner perspectives of social lifeworlds, political mentalities and collective identities are centred less and less on the idea of the state and more and more on the idea of particularity. The transition from normative dissent assayed in the practice of lifestyle groups to the manifest political protest focused in the new social movements has in this way experienced an enormous acceleration. The path of the individual towards commitment and protest has become shorter and more peremptory. To this extent, the new social movements present merely the visible part of an abiding and persistent form of protest that draws its grounds and its motivational basis from the spheres in which expressive self-relations and alternative life-forms are first of all put to the test and brought on their way towards communalisation.

The politics of lifestyle is above all not without ramifications for institutional order. If the socio-ethical hinterland of institutions is being increasingly undermined by lifestyle coalitions and reflexive knowledge, this does not necessarily imply any pre-eminence of the cold form of sociation that is currently realised via power and money. That an unquestioned acceptance of competences is in decline and loyalties are no longer taken for granted is the prerequisite *for winning back options for action* in, as it were, sub-political spaces. The administrative political system will continue to be at odds with a politics of lifestyles as long as what is prevalent here is an internal communication geared to technocratic, bureaucratic and regulative mechanisms unable to do justice to the self-reflexive orientations of the social sphere. Responses ranging from reflexive disestablishment down to a new institutionalism do point to the problem of state-orientated politics, but not, however, towards a conceivable solution of the problem. It is still the lifestyle coalitions that, as post-traditional communities, are expanding sub-political networks, thus forcing through shifts of meaning within cultural practices, expanding the scope of the expressible and giving new normative impulses to the struggle over the definition of the social. These lifestyle groups have created an entire network of intermediary organisations; they have institutionalised anti-institutions to such an extent that the latter have long since assumed the role of socially acknowledged, institutionally integrated 'normal states of affairs'.

Today it is no longer strident struggles for distinction that dominate the subcultural scenes and lifestyle groups; it is a sort of self-institutionalisation of the countercultural groups, achieving and sustaining their identity and self-awareness no longer via demarcation strategies but by developing culturally productive modes of dealing with such demarcations. Institutionalisable dealings with difference, however, will in the last analysis constitute the decisive criterion of what elements of the sum total of expressive self-relations and normative internal orientations will be generalised in such a way as to enable them, in terms of everyday practice, to be set out as a new form of sociation and turned to advantage as a new civilisational arrangement.

Anthony Giddens (1991: 214f) has characterised as 'life-politics' the self-referential practices of the body, sexual hygiene, etc., and distinguished it from the form of an emancipatory politics dominant up to the 1970s. The former struggled against the constraints and behavioural expectations exacted by tradition and unlegitimated power. The latter focuses its world-view and its political practice on a reflexive self that, from the perspective of a self-constructed identity and in the intention of realising itself, acts towards changing the social world; one of its particular symbolic features consists of realising the necessity of never ceasing to see individual problems in global contexts. If I know what tropical forests or automobile traffic mean for my health; if I know what love and friendship, empathy and compassion can give rise to; if I attribute rights to nature and assign to myself the duty to protect them – what then counts, despite any utilitarian motivations, are extended solidarities that are no longer restricted to my own community of shared values. The moral economy of our society, so it appears, is more and more migrating into the *subjective ecology* of highly individualised individuals.

Subject-centred world-views have this norm-generating power precisely because they are, in their construction, seemingly so unconditionally self-referential. Their action orientations run counter to the logic of the market. In the end it is reciprocity ideals that constitute the core of the new forms of community formation in which not only social relations but also the relationship between self and nature are redefined in terms, as it were, of acknowledgement theory. The ego's identity, its claim to self-realisation, or put more banally, its well-being, is worth not a rap without the care for and attention to the 'others' *and* nature. 'Subjective ecology' is, then, the nutshell version of a motivational situation of our everyday life which is induced by the social modernisation process itself and in which the relationship between self, society and nature is at the same time detraditionalised *and* remoralised through 'life-politics' and 'lifestyle politics' alike.

And solidary individualism? The cognitive conditions for inventing it socially have long since been given in the framework involved in reallocating relevant aspects in the sense of a *subjective ecology*, even if there continues to be some justification in doubting (cf. Maguire, this volume) whether they are securely anchored in affective and emotional terms.

References

Beck, Ulrich (1983) 'Jenseits von Stand und Klasse? Soziale Un-gleichheiten, gesellschaft-liche Individualisierungsprozesse und die Entstehung neuer sozialer Formationen und Identitäten', in Reinhard Kreckel (ed.), *Soziale Ungleichheiten*. Special Issue 2 of *Sozialen Welt*. Göttingen.
Beck, Ulrich (1992) *Risk Society: Towards a New Modernity*. London.

Beck, Ulrich (1996) *The Renaissance of Politics*. Cambridge: Polity.

Bellah, Robert, Masden, R., Sullivan, William M., Swidler, A. and Tipton, Steven N. (1985) *Habits of the Heart: Individualism and Commitment in American Life*. Berkeley: University of California Press.

Berking, Helmuth (1989) 'Kultur-Soziologie: Mode und Methode?', in Helmuth Berking and Richard Faber (eds), *Kultursoziologie: Symptom des Zeitgeistes*. Würzburg.

Berking, Helmuth and Neckel, Sighard (1990) 'Die Politik der Lebensstile in einem Berliner Bezirk. Zu einigen Formen nachtraditionaler Vergemeinschaftung', in Berger and Hradil (eds), *Lebenslagen, Lebensläufe, Lebensstile*. Special Issue 7 of *Soziale Welt*. Göttingen.

Dubiel, Helmut (1991) 'Die Ökologie der gesellschaftlichen Moral', in Stefan Müller-Doohm (ed.), *Jenseits der Utopie*. Frankfurt am Main.

Elias, Norbert (1982) *The Civilizing Process*, Vol. 1: *State Formation and Civilization*. Oxford: Blackwell.

Giddens, Anthony (1991) *Modernity and Self-Identity: Self and Society in the Late Modern Age*. Oxford.

Goffman, Erving (1967) *Interaction Ritual: Essays on Face-to-Face Behavior*. Chicago: Aldine.

Haferland, Harald (1988) *Höfische Interaktion. Interpretationen zur höfischen Epik und Didaktik um 1200*. Munich.

Hitzler, Ronald (1991) 'Der banale Proteus. Eine postmoderne Metapher?', in Helmut Kuzmics and Ingo Mörth (eds), *Der unendliche Prozess der Zivilisation. Zur Kultursoziologie der Moderne nach Norbert Elias*. Frankfurt am Main.

Hitzler, Ronald (1993) 'Sinnbasteln. Zur subjektiven Aneignung von Lebensstilen', in Ingo Mörth and Gerhard Fröhlich (eds.), *Kultur und soziale Ungleichheit*. Frankfurt am Main.

Hochschild, Arlie Russell (1983) *The Managed Heart: Commercialization of Human Feeling*. Berkeley: University of California Press.

Michailow, Matthias (1993) 'Lebensstilsemantik. Soziale Ungleichheit und Formationsbildung in der Kulturgesellschaft', in Ingo Mörth and Gerhard Fröhlich (eds), *Kultur und soziale Ungleichheit. Zur Kultursoziologie der Moderne nach Pierre Bourdieu*. Frankfurt am Main.

Neckel, Sighard (1991) *Status und Scham. Zur symbolischen Reproduktion sozialer Ungleichheit*. Frankfurt am Main.

Parkin, Frank (1983) 'Strategien sozialer Schliessung und Klassenbildung', in Reinhard Kreckel (ed.), *Soziale Ungleichheiten*. Special Issue 2 of *Soziale Welt*. Göttingen.

Wuthnow, Robert (1992) *Acts of Compassion: Caring for Others and Helping Ourselves*. Princeton.

Ziehe, Thomas (1989) 'Die unablässige Suche nach Nähe und Gewissheit kulturelle Modernisierung und subjektive Entzugserscheinungen', in *Ästhetik und Kommunikation*, 18 (70/71).

Ziehe, Thomas (1992) 'Unspektakuläre Zivilisierungsgewinne. Auch Individualisierung kann "kommunitär" sein', in Christel Zahlmann (ed.), *Kommunitarismus in der Diskussion*. Berlin.

Part III

THE POLITICS OF THE ENVIRONMENT: EXHAUSTION OR RENEWAL?

9

THE INSTITUTIONALISATION OF ENVIRONMENTALISM: ECOLOGICAL DISCOURSE AND THE SECOND TRANSFORMATION OF THE PUBLIC SPHERE

Klaus Eder

From Environmentalism to Ecological Discourse

The environmental movement no longer dominates the discourse on the environment. While it was responsible for putting the environment on the public agenda during the 1980s, since then environmentalism has also been appropriated by the movement's opponents.[1] Environmental movements no longer have to struggle for a voice in this discourse: the issue has actually become topical. But there are now so many voices that, ironically, it is difficult to be heard. Can environmental movements now survive this marketplace of communication on the environment? What are the conditions for survival in the emerging discourse on the environment? In the discourse on the environment, I will suggest, a new ideology is developing, in competition with the liberalism, socialism and conservatism inherited from the nineteenth century. This new ideology has become a new discursive medium for political conflicts and public debate. Such claims are linked to two further questions. Does this change the public space as the central political institution of modern societies? Does this lead to more democracy or to a new technocracy in the name of environmental protection?

To support such claims and answer such questions an analysis of the logic and dynamic of public discourse on the environment is needed, for public discourse is the focal point around which communication about the environment is tested for its power and legitimacy. Environmental protest actors are forced by this situation to defend their part in the public discourse on the environment they themselves once launched. In order to survive the public discourse marketplace, they must defend their public image. This image is no longer anchored by their role as the only ones to have sensitised the public to environmental concerns. This 'monopoly' position is increasingly being replaced by a situation in which competitors emerge in the market of producing and communicating 'green' images. Maintaining a public image is bonded to a discourse where interactive strategic moves by competing actors begin to define the discursive field. This is changing the environmental movement's image and forcing it to become a 'cultural pressure group' (Statham, 1995). This term defines a new type of collective actor which has to stabilise its social position within the discourse on the environment. Public discourse is therefore a key to understanding and analysing the rise and fall of environmentalism, taking into account the special role protest actors play in it. Public discourse analysis is therefore what is needed to legitimate such claims and give some answers to the questions raised above.

In order to analyse the effects of environmentalism on public discourse and the public sphere it is necessary to use methods such as *frame analysis* and *discourse analysis*.[2] This is justified on the grounds that the symbolic representation of the environment is the focus of analysis and can be theoretically treated as the specific medium for the reorganisation of the public sphere in advanced modern societies. The key concepts of such a discourse analysis are the concepts of 'frames' and 'symbolic packages' (Snow et al., 1986; Snow and Benford, 1988, 1992; Gamson and Modigliani, 1989). The basic analytical distinction is between *framing devices* which are cognitive rule systems, and *symbolic packages* which organise such framing devices into coherent and consistent *frames*. The social process transforming framing devices into frames is conceptualised as involving *framing strategies*; this allows us to construct conceptually the field of symbolic struggle over an issue. This leads us to the idea of a discourse which extends beyond the context of a specific actor and situates framing strategies in the interaction context of collective actors. Within this context the role of protest actors in environmental discourses can be reassessed. This context will be called *public space*, whereas *public discourse* is seen as the medium for the reproduction of this public space.

The more that environmentalism serves for generating legitimacy, the more it becomes an ideological weapon in political discourse. Environmentalism is becoming a new ideological tradition in addition to the ideological cleavages of advanced modern societies. This new ideological tradition will be analysed as a *masterframe* within which environmentalism gains public consensus. The masterframe constituting this new ideology is 'ecology',[3] and 'ecological discourse' is becoming the common ground on which collective actors meet in today's public discourse and public space. Within this new ideological model a series of practical frames – *ethical (sub)frames* and *identity (sub)frames* – offer new options for legitimising institutions and creating consent. Ecological discourse can thus be seen as the most productive cultural form for generating and mobilising ideological consensus and dissensus in modern societies. Its frames reorganise the discursive field of politics.

Ecological discourse shapes the public space of modern societies through restructuring the ideological cleavages which mobilise social groups and actors.[4] This change is theorised as the 'second structural transformation of the public sphere'. This formula refers to Habermas's analysis of the structural transformation of the public sphere which he locates at the end of the nineteenth century in Europe and the United States (Habermas 1989). This analysis, being rather an analysis of the downfall of the public space, emphasises the decrease in discursive argumentation and the increase in discursive control through the media as the carrier of public debate.

However, this perspective is reversed in the following. The second structural transformation consists in the increasing use of the media and their capacity for discursive control by competing and antagonistic collective actors, and the concomitant rise of public debate.[5] This renaissance is attributed causally to the ascendance of ecological communication in advanced modern societies. The effects of ecological communication are mainly those of fostering the role of collective symbols and beliefs in the organisation of public discourses. 'Nature politics' is not simply one of the many issues that are processed in these discourses. It is an issue which represents the social world, no longer as a collectivity which maximises the wealth of nations and individuals, but as a world which has to protect common goods against the individual utilities that make demands on it. It is an issue which has to defend a collective rationality against the individual rationality. This image of the social as a cooperative undertaking points to the structural importance of the environment as an organising principle of public discourse. The environment is the issue that brings collective rationality back into the theory and practice of modern societies.

Ecology as a Masterframe in Public Discourse

The Social Construction of a Masterframe

In recent years, environmentalism has been successful in providing symbolic representations of the natural environment within which moral, empirical and aesthetic concerns are fused. The preponderance of such 'symbolic packages' in public discourse has even led to the claim that public communication on the environment has marked the beginning of a post-ideological age of discursive noise.[6]

What this claim overlooks is that discursive noise is the symbolic material out of which frames of reality (including major ideological masterframes such as the ones that have been characteristic of the nineteenth century) are constructed. Ideological frames are organised through symbolic packages – among the most famous of these are those of 'the proletariat', 'capitalism', 'communism', 'human rights' and 'national identity'. This holds also for the symbolic packages in ecological communication which form the material for the production of new ideological masterframes. These draw equally on the cognitive framing devices provided by modern culture in the sense of the well-ordered cognitive conceptions of the 'right', the 'real' and the 'meaningful'. What is certainly different is that these new symbolic packages provoke more communication than their predecessors; they are even dependent upon being communicated in order to maintain public attention in a world of mass media and shifting attention cycles. Ecological frames are much more dependent on the marketplace of public communication than the frames connected with the modern ideologies of the nineteenth and the first half of the twentieth centuries. Whether they survive this market will be determined by the resonance of public discourse to the framing strategies employed by consequential collective actors.

In so far as symbolic packages communicated by protest actors have to survive the marketplace, such actors have to compete with opposing collective actors for control of the symbolic packages. This leads to varying discourse coalitions, which in turn are shaped by the opportunity structure of given institutional contexts.[7] The assumption is that in such processes frames emerge that make symbolic packages independent of their carriers and transform them into elements of public discourse. Frames are thus defined as elements of a discourse which is beyond the control of the actors who invented the symbolic packages from which those elements derive. Within the context of an ongoing public discourse on the environment, given frames are reorganised and eventually filled with new meanings, or new frames emerge for old problems.[8]

What follows will address the question of how three symbolic packages of environmental concerns – namely, conservationism, political ecology and deep ecology – resonate in public discourse. While these shaped environmentalism during the last two decades, these packages are today struggling for their survival in public discourse. They have played a vital role in the 'greening' of advanced modern societies, and thus in the transformation of environmentalism into a normal element of public discourse, but they have thereby endangered their own distinctiveness.

Two central hypotheses guide the following discussion. The first is that through this transformation, environmentalism has become more than a mere symbolic package constitutive of a protest actor. It has become a new *masterframe* in public discourse which is addressed by non-protest actors as well. As a masterframe it concerns not only environmental issues in the more narrow sense, but also other policy areas in which 'ecological reasons' can be evolved to mobilise legitimacy for the actions of non-protesters and decisions taken.[9] The second hypothesis is that the political ecology package is gaining in the struggle for survival among competing packages of environmental concerns because it best suits the need for making concern for the environment a constitutive element of modern political discourse. The theory grounding these hypotheses is that political ecology is a discourse which, by separating the heterodox elements of deep ecology and the orthodox elements of conservationism, fosters the conflic-tualisation of environmentalism. It represents a 'doxa' which serves as a referent for conflictual action so that deep ecology (the heterodoxy) and conservationism (the orthodoxy) are not debatable; they have become creeds.

The empirical assumption is that the transformation of the political ecology package, which has emerged in the politicisation of environmental-ism in the last decade,[10] into a masterframe in ecological discourse, is the key to understanding the ecological transformation of the public discourse on the environment.[11] We increasingly find dictionaries of 'ecological thought' (De Roose and van Parijs, 1991). 'Ecology' has become a catchword that can be applied to every element in public discourse on the environment: to ethical questions, scientific theories, and to literary expressions of the relationship of man with nature. The label 'ecological' can be attributed to these phenomena and this makes sense, both from an internal and an external perspective. The increasing dominance of the political ecology package thus leads to a change in the meaning of environmentalism, which is the precondition for transforming environ-mentalism into a conflictual public discourse. The masterframe of this conflictual public discourse is 'ecology' – a symbolic package which contains all the elements necessary for constituting ecological discourse as a major element in the legitimating ideology of advanced modern societies.

Ecology as Ideology

As soon as concern for the environment is taken up by any political group and any traditional ideological current, environmentalism enters a new stage in its development. This stage has been called 'post environmental-ism' (Young, 1990). This, however, does not imply the end of the discourse on the environment; it rather marks the beginning of ecological discourse and the end of environmentalism as a 'counterdiscourse'. The main protagonist in this transformation has been the development of *political ecology* from a variant of environmentalism into a *political ideology*. This has turned the symbolic package of ecology into an ideological master-frame in addition to existing ones. As an ideology, ecology complements the other currents of liberalism and socialism (van Parijs, 1991). It thus takes the place that has never been really filled by conservatism. Conserva-tism has never succeeded in developing its own ideology – it has never been an ideological current. Rather, it reacted to other ideological currents; its

substantive elements were eclectic, taken from the ideological current against which it reacted, without any coherent system of thinking that would have allowed it to develop a coherent and consistent paradigmatic structure; that is, to become an ideology. Thus conservatism never became an ideological current (notwithstanding neo-conservatism which is more of a heterodox tradition of liberalism). An ideology that is modern and at the same time orientated towards conserving something in the world has so far not developed. This open position in the field of ideological currents is going to be filled for the first time in modern history. Since nature is an endless good, the ideology dealing with the relation of man to it has – by definition – a conservative logic. This conservatism is no longer pre-modern, looking back into a past, and trying to restore it. It is a modern conservatism (and probably the first modern conservatism), based on the principles of keeping a lifeworld threatened by man's use of nature, defending the lifeworld against the bureaucratic and technocratic rationality of organised systems, and defending people against the risks the environment poses for them.[12]

The main effect of environmentalism in modern ideological discourse, then, consists in the emergence and stabilisation of an ideological current beyond liberalism and socialism; it favours an ideological position that represents the first really modern version of conservatism. To what extent this ideological position can be stabilised depends on social and institutional factors which are intricately linked to the success and failure of the ecological movement. There are some obvious conditions that are favourable to this type of ideologisation. A comparative look at the rise and fall of welfare cultures shows that the development towards the political ecology paradigm is strongest where welfare capitalism has evolved the most. The precondition for its emergence is the existence of a well-developed frame of just distribution. The more questions of social distribution are settled (in the sense of distributing the given resources in a collectively accepted way), the more this frame becomes part of everyday culture. Thus it is likely that environmentalism would develop further in countries with a strong welfare tradition. The preponderance of communist states would account for a temporary fixation on traditional forms of claims for distributive justice, namely the remuneration of workers. Giving way to social-democratic forms of political culture will certainly push the environmental question towards the political ecology paradigm.[13]

A possible effect of this ideologisation is a convergence of environmental concerns in countries where different cultural traditions shape the representation of man's relationship with nature. Another effect is the changing role of social movements. The institutionalisation of environmentalism transgresses the symbolic space created by environmental movements in a double sense: it extends into the public space as it is no longer restricted to its role as a constituency of a movement, and it creates a symbolic universe which can no longer be controlled and claimed as movement property.[14] Environmentalism leaves its generating context and becomes part of modern society, thereby exposing itself to the dynamics of modern discourses which also make environmentalism the object of processes of rationalisation and disenchantment. A Weberian perspective would thus seem better suited to explain changes in environmentalism than theories which emphasise the image of society as a self-generating system.

Frames in Ecological Discourse

The Masterframe and its Derivatives

The effects of the ecological reconstruction of environmentalism can be observed in two different dimensions. The first concerns *ethical (sub)-frames*, the second *identity (sub)frames* which emerge in ecological discourse. For the ethical dimension, this claim is based on the observation that ethical commitments and ethical theories have become a central concern in legitimating the relationship between modern political institutions and environmental issues. In terms of the identity dimension it is based on the observation that to have a 'green identity' has become a central symbolic asset that contributes to the further individualisation of the self in modern society. It argues against the traditional idea that factual frames, the 'pure information' on the state of the environment, will accomplish anything. Without packaging information on the environment, nothing will be achieved: not legitimacy for the political institution, mobilisation for the environment, or rational attitudes (or even behaviour patterns) in the public as a whole. This claim is based on the assumption that it is the methods of communicating environmental conditions and ideas, and not the state of environmental deterioration itself, which explains the emergence of a public discourse on the environment, 'ecological discourse'. The theory underlying this analytical perspective is that ethical frames and identity frames emerging within ecological discourse explain the framing and communicating of environmental issues in present-day societies. Thus the moralisation of environmental issues through ethical and identity frames becomes a strategic element of ecological discourse when knowledge about the environment has increased significantly. The knowledge we have and produce might even be the reason for this moralisation of the environmental issue.[15] To give an idea of the frames emerging in ecological discourse, two frames will be discussed: frames linked to an environmental ethics legitimating science and politics in modern society, and frames linked to the 'greening' of the identity formations which create basic consensus in modern societies.

Legitimating Institutions: Ethical Frames in Ecological Discourse

Environmentalism has been an attack on the legitimacy of political institutions dealing with the relationship between modern society and nature, thus leading to a legitimation crisis among those institutions.

Simultaneously, its transformation into a new ideological masterframe provides the possibility of a way out, legitimating social institutions by means of environment-related ethical frames. This solution is examined in the rest of this section, which looks at the formal properties and the content of the ethical frames mobilised in ecological discourse.

On the level of formal properties, the ethical conception underlying ecology as a masterframe in modern culture is competing with a 'proceduralization' (Eder, 1990b; Habermas, 1992) of ethical conceptions. Ethical notions by which environmental issues are cognitively validated are based on a substantive ethics which has led to competing formulations of an ethics for an ecologically responsible society.[16] This substantivism, however, does not solve the problem of how to formulate an environmental ethics. Its cognitive reputation has fallen short of the minimal requirements for a modern ethics as defined in procedural notions of a modern ethics since Kant (see Szerszynski, this volume). One way out of this situation is to return to a pre-modern or anti-modern or non-modern ethics which has seduced the construction of an environmental ethics to a large extent. Modern ethical proceduralism, however, remains a challenge to the ethical self-understanding and self-justification of environmentalism, which has certainly been a major factor in pushing the transformation of environmentalism into an ecological discourse.[17]

In this transformation environmentalism has redefined its ethical basis and entered the debate about the ethical foundations of politics, so far dominated by liberalism and socialism.[18] Because of the extent to which environmentalism has turned towards a rather pragmatic philosophy that has left behind academic discussions of environmental ethics, and because of the cleavage between preservationist and conservationist points of view, the ethical bases of environmentalist beliefs have been opened up to debate. The rise of the idea of sustainable development has intensified this discussion,[19] not least because of the controversy concerning the criteria of what sustainability means in terms of provisions for future generations, or distribution among present generations that start with different chances (Barry, 1983). Such an ethics is no longer based on substantive notions of the value of nature, but on the notion of a fair distribution of nature's resources. Nature, defined and valued as a *collective good*, forces moral discourses to relate the problem of distributive justice (for example, the distribution of rights to pollute) to the problem of distributing collective goods. Assuming that there is a consensus about nature as a collective good, the question that arises is the price that people will pay for the protection of this good, the protection of nature. This is a special case of distributive justice, special in the sense of introducing external limits to the distribution of goods which guarantee the availability of the collective good 'nature' for all existing and future generations. This argument shows that too strong a distinction between the problem of nature and the problem of distributive justice should not be made. The idea that environmentalism has led to a shift from a distributional logic to a non-distributional logic in modern culture is not warranted.[20] What changes is the context within which we have to solve distributional problems. When nature becomes a scarce good, the use of natural resources has to be regulated by using some criteria of distributive justice. What makes the difference is the definition of scarcity in nature. Some claim that nature has become a zero-sum object: her resources are limited. This is controversial; natural scientists will show us how inventive nature can be and that destruction of parts of nature is not necessarily a destruction of nature as such. It can, on the contrary, trigger evolutionary processes. Whatever the assumption is, it is no longer possible to use nature without taking into account the effects of our action upon nature which have repercussions upon the fair share of the resources nature offers.[21]

But no society developing an environmentalist culture escapes the problem of how to relate the principle of minimising· environmental damage to the principle of the just distribution of the restrictions imposed upon the behaviour of everyone. Since this balancing does not regulate itself, a balancer is needed. Traditionally, the state has provided the balancing rationale. In environmental matters, however, the state no longer has the ultimate control over the processes of environmental decision-making. Informal networks of concerned actors have challenged and still challenge the way in which distributional questions in environmental matters are being solved. They do this by referring to an intrinsic value of nature, by valuing the collective good 'nature' differently. This is where the really interesting ethical questions start, because a consensus has emerged, a consensus that nature is a collective good.

However, the value of this collective good is contested. This has given to environmental ethics its specific role in shaping and legitimating political institutions. The value of nature is seen as a political question, to be defended by those who claim a special value to nature. The state cannot do it because of its engagement in social policy matters. Functionally specified as the organ of social cohesion, defending society against inner and outer violence as well as against the disruptive consequences of market processes, the state has to take nature as a second-class collective good. But nature needs an advocate beyond the state and the economy. This advocate is to be found in a social sphere which is neither public nor private, but their negation (van Parijs, 1991: 139ff). If there is anything new in the ethical discussions in environmental discourse, it is the *defence of an autonomous sphere*, necessary for defending the value of nature as a collective good. Who else could defend this collective good beyond a mere instrumentalist notion but those who want to see nature as a spiritual inspiration, as a source of emotional experience, as an object of aesthetic judgement? Thus the needs tied to the collective good 'nature' play a central role, and they have to be organised beyond the state and the economy. To politicise such needs requires them to be communicated – they have to be *made* political. The conceptualisation and justification of a collective actor anchored outside state and economy[22] is therefore the central problem that could explain political ecology as an ethical endeavour.

This ethical discussion has also affected *science* as an institution. The ecological influence can be felt in the social sciences, above all in economics. The idea of a green economics (Porritt, 1984: 126–44) is not an alternative economics, but is a flourishing field in economics as a social science. It analyses nature no longer as a given asset to economic action, but as something interacting with man. It gives science an ethical dimension. Science's often discussed 'credibility gaps' (Wynne, 1988) disappear within political ecology, since it generates an idea of science which does not make its methods, but its goals and aims accessible to the personal wisdom and experience of people.[23] The effects go even deeper when considering the basis of science as an institution, namely its reliance upon facts. Science has not only an ethical context which limits the range of scientific curiosity, but its construction of facts is also socially constituted, which means that ethical perspectives can – indeed necessarily do – enter the construction of scientific facts themselves.

Contrary to the fundamentalist quest for an alternative science or even anti-science,[24] ecology provides a frame for the use of scientific expertise and the communication of scientific certainties in an area where certainties are rare and expertise fallible. The ecological critique of science has led to a generalisation of the factual frame in the sense of extending its range to all spheres of life.[25] The ecological attack on the concept of facts has contributed to their rethinking in terms of their social constitution. Measuring problems in the environmental sciences has highlighted the problem that the measurement of facts also defines what the facts are.[26] Thus the idea of an interactive relationship between observer and object belongs to the structuring features of ecologically orientated science. The ecological attack has – and this is implied in the former argument – contributed to a change in the mechanistic conception of nature that is the heritage of early modern science (Lovelock, 1989). Systemic thinking is the basic characteristic of the ecological claim to interdisciplinary and boundary-crossing approaches to analysing reality.

Creating Consent: Identity Frames in Ecological Discourse

A second effect of the emergence of ecology as a masterframe in modern public discourse refers to the emergence of identity frames. Environmentalism is also humanity's search for their place in nature, a quasi-anthropological situation that has served as a medium for posing the question of identity. This quest for identity has traditionally been satisfied by religious belief systems. Religion contains cognitive, moral and aesthetic framing devices which permit a 'counterfactual' solution to the problem of personal identity.[27] The religious solution to the problem of personal identity also characterises modern societies. Modern societies had once thought to find personal identity in material equality and in the absence of alienation from work. This, however, is no longer the case. The socialist ideology (from its welfare version to its real socialist version) has lost any appeal with regard to its capacity to give an answer to this problem. It no longer contains a cognitive frame capable of defining what the problem of personal identity is and what the ways are to resolve it. In its dissolution we rather observe new religious ideologies. The 'new religious movements' as the carriers of these ideologies are probably a temporary (and perhaps even necessary) regression in this transition (Beckford, 1986). They manifest free-floating cultural ideas without a centre which crystallise ideals of personal identity around a collective experience. This upsurge of religious movements has given a final blow to the model of secularisation as the basic trend of modernisation.[28] Thus the return of religion is not necessarily a regression. It can be also a reformulation of the need to ground the construction of personal identity in a cognitive frame that is collective.[29]

Life histories of environmental movement activists clearly show that religious motivations have in fact played a major role in the engagement of caring for 'nature'.[30] Members of the traditional Christian churches have played a major role in the environmentalist movement.[31] Attitudes and everyday practices show the strong influence of ecological argumentation which goes beyond the effects of other 'new' social movements[32] (including the peace movement as the one that mobilised the largest number of people) in shaping identity patterns in large groups of the population (especially middle-class groups). Accepting the claim that the notion of personal identity is today still tied to religious beliefs does not imply that these belief systems still rely upon the idea of a religious community of believers. To the extent that religious organisation has lost its pervasive force in everyday life, personal identity is no longer the privilege of the believers. The substitute has been the idea of an associational community, where the notion of 'community' is the secularised version of the community of believers that has been characteristic of traditional religions. This secular community replaces the traditional religious group.[33] The reference to the associational community among human beings becomes the major force in the cognitive framing of personal identity. This associational community can be defined in a rather flexible way. It can be religious or secular, in either national or multicultural forms.

The connection between ecology and identity has been established in recent theoretical discussions on modernity and the idea of the modern self, where ecology appears as a strategy for the reorganisation of self and identity in modern society.[34] It gives a coherent interpretation to a series of new religious movements that lay emphasis on the expressive side of personal existence. They include meditation groups, personal growth movements and New Age groups, and relate to different types of green religiosity. In large part shaped by deep ecology, these movements are becoming the target of more ecologically minded groups such as the WWF, seeking (as its Mission Statement says) to develop its '4th leg', which is to develop its grasp on the personal ideas and experiences that influence everyday practices (Grove-White et al., 1991). It is an attempt to give to the idea of sustainable development, a key concept of present-day ecological discourse, a new quasi-religious basis. To what extent the infusion of spiritual feelings into more secular beliefs will succeed has yet to be seen.

For environmentalism as a movement such developments will certainly imply a strong backlash from deep ecology groups, and ideological struggles internal to environmentalism are to be expected. The important point, however, is that deep ecology no longer occupies the terrain of identity and self-realisation. Modern society has already entered a 'post-narcissistic' phase in which exclusive environmentalist identities will no longer be able to survive the identity markets which transform the public space of advanced modern societies. Competition in the field of identity construction is deadly for deep ecology beliefs, for they cannot coexist with other gods. Conservationist claims are more able to adapt to identity markets, and political ecology is a form of environmentalism which is explicitly orientated towards such identity markets. The ecological discourse emerging in today's public discourse has started to modernise these identity claims of environmentalism, has secularised its assumptions and ideas, and has made them part of public debate. Thus the identity markets engendered by environmentalism, in conjunction with new institutional ideologies, are transforming the public sphere of advanced modern societies – a state of affairs that is contrary to the image of a closed and radically hegemonic public space.

Towards Post-environmentalism

Is the age of environmentalism vanishing? The increasing communication of environmental issues has caught the environmental movement in a paradox: the movement that created the green public agenda can no longer rely on remaining high on that agenda. It is bonded to this public agenda, which in turn is bonded to the once resonant symbols of environmental dangers that created the culture of environmentalism. On the other hand, the media agenda that increasingly influences the policy agenda has developed its own dynamic with the tendency to exclude environmental movements from the agenda-setting process.

This has led to the constitution of movements as cultural pressure groups (Statham, 1995), because in order to survive they had to invest in public discourse. However, they could do so only by mobilising frames, thus creating a market of frames open to competing framing actors. The question of whether they will survive in this marketplace cannot yet be answered; it depends on what kind of survival is sought. Environmental movements will certainly not survive as movements of mass mobilisation.

Their repertoire of action will change fundamentally, and with it the relationship between movements and their constituencies. They will survive as a collective actor, concerned with needs and risks not covered by traditional pressure groups such as trade unions. Such a survival depends on their capacity to keep control of their stake in public discourse, since survival in this market is contingent upon the successful communication of symbolic packages that resonate with the respective constituency.

Under such conditions protest discourses will continue to play an important role in the further development of ecology as a *public-good issue*. Such development can take place in two ways. It can simply mean a variation of the symbolic packages of frames, variously emphasised depending on economic, political or cultural circumstances. This outcome would see the current dominance of the ecology package as a temporary phenomenon in actual public discourse, due to fashion cycles. It can also mean transforming the public discourse into something *new*, integrating *new meanings* into it. When such a transformative process occurs and the framing devices underlying public discourse change, then a cyclical explanation will no longer be sufficient. In such case a development has taken place that cannot be reversed without creating profound legitimatory problems. The industrialist discourse on nature has been such a master-frame, having dominated the traditional discourse on modernity. This has given a secondary meaning to the notion of moral responsibility towards nature and to nature's expressive side, and has privileged a view of nature which made it the subject of objectifying knowledge. This traditional masterframe in modern public discourse, based on the belief in progress through subduing nature, has undergone a *paradigmatic* change through the mobilisation of environmentalism. *Ecology* provides the new master-frame that offers a new symbolic package for the cognitive framing devices through which we experience and perceive social reality. Making nature not only the subject of empirical knowledge, but equally the subject of aesthetic and moral perspectives, is exactly what this new ecological masterframe of ecology has brought about.

The claim that something 'new' is emerging in modern culture has been made by environmentalism itself. Its philosophical and ideological discussions confer the self-description of something 'new', but this claim has been neutralised by the paradigmatic change of public discourse. In assimilating environmentalism, public discourse has succeeded in reorganising moral, empirical and aesthetic framing devices in a 'reflexive' way: framing devices are packed into coherent frames which have left the limits of the everyday lifeworld. Environmentalism has been the lifeworld discourse *par excellence* and has even been euphemised in this respect.[35] The symbolic packages of environmentalism have taken on a format that enables their use in public communication and debate: they have become cognitively well-organised packages, systems of thought detached from the concrete lifeworld, reflexively organised packages for using cognitive framing devices. An indicator of this is the fact that these discourses and related communications are described as 'ecological communication' (Luhmann, 1989) or 'ecological discourse' (Kitschelt, 1984), without much reflection on the choice of terminology. The 'ecological discourse' of the last two decades thus seems to be a historically and ideologically specific form of environmentalism, a reflexively organised symbolic packaging of environmental issues that is detached from the lifeworld.[36] It has neutralised the competing deep ecological and conservationist packages by integrating them, has succeeded in dominating public discourse, and has led to a masterframe which has allowed the integration of environmentalism into a full-blown ideology capable of redefining the rationality claims of modern public discourse.

The 'modernisation' of identity formations that have so far been considered to be romantic backlashes or pathological regressions provides another – and perhaps even more important – effect of ecology as a masterframe in modern public discourse. The ideological systems of the nineteenth century are still functioning, but the public discourses centred on these elements never solved the problem of identity construction. Liberalism and socialism have failed in this task; ecology seems to be the experiment of carrying out the overdue modernisation of one of the most consequential aspects of social life.[37]

However, the significance of ecology goes further. While entering public discourse, it has also started to restructure the public space, having opened it up and contributed to its emancipation from the lifeworld. Institutional changes have contributed to channelling these mobilisations. Participation in public discourse can no longer be conceived as the mere extension of the lifeworld into public life. Ecology as masterframe defines specific selective conditions for taking part in public discourse: namely, the reflexive use of framing devices in the discourse on nature. This also means that the age of environmentalism, the collective mobilisation for a cause, is over. The age of post-environmentalism begins when ecology is established as a masterframe that can be referred to by all actors, thus laying the ground for a further development of the public space which is the genuine modern condition for guaranteeing the cognitive, moral and aesthetic rationality inherent in the culture of modernity.

Notes

1. An excellent empirical analysis of environmentalism is found in Milbrath (1984). Its presence on the public agenda is indicated by the high rankings that environmental questions have reached in social surveys over the last decade (Hofrichter and Reif 1990). Comparing Milbrath (1984) and Milbrath (1989) gives an interesting idea of the direction of change which environmentalism has undergone in the late 1980s.

2. We use the term 'discourse analysis' in the sense that van Dijk (1985, 1988) uses it. Discourse analysis is simultaneously the analysis of the semantics of texts and the analysis of discursive strategies of actors. This duality of discourse analysis is its most interesting contribution to sociological analysis, because it allows one to relate textual representations of social reality to the social processes generating them. For early uses of discourse analysis see

Bennett, 1980; Cicourel, 1980; Corsaro, 1981. Further explications of discourse analysis as sociological method are found in Brown and Yule, 1983; Potter and Wetherell, 1987; Wetherell and Potter, 1988; Fairclough, 1989, 1992, with different emphases on linguistic, social-psychological or sociological perspectives. The term 'public sphere' relates to the social context of public discourse, i.e. the social-structural properties of the discursive space and the actors engaged in it. Here we follow the early idea Habermas (1989) developed by 1962. See also the further development of this sociological concept of a public space in Eder, 1985, 1992.

3. Ecology is used here in a strict sense: it is a way of looking at nature in which scientific expertise, ethical concerns and aesthetic judgements have been integrated into a coherent ideological framework that provides a common ground for collective actors. An analogous status in modern history could be attributed to the concept of 'welfare' which combines elements of social justice, economic efficiency and a kind of 'New Deal culture'. Both masterframes, ecology and welfare, refer to basic codes of modern culture – above all its coding of progress (Eder, 1990b). Masterframes are therefore frames that are located on the level of modernity as a culture. The theoretically defined meaning of 'ecology' will be made more clear in the course of the following discussion.

4. This argument goes beyond the argument that the modern public space is shaped by technological changes in communication facilities and the new power structures which are the result of the economics of communication. Public spaces also have a symbolic dimension, and it is this dimension which is crucial in ecological communication.

5. This renaissance is also of a 'reflexive' nature in so far as collective actors have learned to understand the way in which public communication works.

6. This is the main point of Luhmann's essay on 'ecological communication' (Luhmann, 1989). Ecological communication, he declares, creates noise – sometimes even too much, with the effect that people no longer want to listen. Although the latter part of his argument may be idiosyncratic, it nevertheless points out that ecological communication has significantly increased communication in modern societies.

7. In other words, they are socially 'embedded'. This expression is taken from Granovetter (1985), who argues in similar way with regard to economic action.

8. The empirical referents of such a discourse analysis can be found in the well-defined corpus of literature on agenda-setting. The classics are McCombs and Shaw, 1972, 1977; and McCombs, 1981. Further important contributions are found in Erbring et al., 1980; Cook et al., 1983; and Brosius and Kepplinger, 1990. Overviews of the literature are found in Rogers and Dearing, 1988; and Reese, 1991. An interesting piece of research showing the importance of print media for the attraction of public attention to environmental issues is Atwater et al., 1985.

9. The most obvious reference is that of 'sustainable development', which affects all modern policy areas, including social policy.

10. Political ecology in France is 'écologie politique' (Deléage, 1992), in Germany 'grüner Realismus' (Wiesenthal, 1993) and in Great Britain 'green politics' (Porritt, 1984; Porritt and Winner, 1988). Ultimately, even Beck's position (1992, and this volume) has its roots in political ecology; he, however, goes further and generalises this position into a general 'ecological' position.

11. This is an empirical claim which has to be nuanced for different countries. Methodologically, this package can be taken as a reference package (an 'ideal type') to understand these variations.

12. The idea of a risk society is a fundamentally conservative idea – it implies the distancing from what makes life risky, back to a lifeworld that avoids dangers. See Beck, 1992.

13. These hypotheses have been tested in a comparative research project on environmental cultures in Europe (Eder, 1995).

14. In the early 1980s envinronmental movements made the 'environment' an issue. They have since been joined by others who have also contributed to the social construction of this issue. As a result, there has been a basic change in the relationship between the movement and its action environment, in that it no longer dominates the discourse using the action

repertoires of exposure and scandal. The conditions for the survival of environmental movements and their discourse have therefore become dependent upon their capacity to define a specific action space and to develop an ideology that justifies such political claims.

15. Moralisation can be packaged in different ways: it can be an application of ethical principles to the normative relationship of man with nature, or a search for individual and collective identity. Thus moralisation crosscuts any institutional boundaries that might be defined by normative arrangements or identity formations.

16. There is a growing literature on an environmental ethics. See, among many others, Barbour, 1973; Attfield, 1983; Jonas, 1984; Stone, 1987; Dower, 1989; Hargrove, 1989. These approaches are empirical proof of moral pluralism in the discourse of environmental ethics. See also the critical discussion in Grove-White et al., 1991; and Grove-White and Szerszynski, 1992.

17. See also my discussion on the notion of practical reason in environmentalism and its critique in Eder, 1988 (English translation 1996).

18. An indicator for this change is the 1992 special issue of *Critical Review*, which is concerned with the debate between liberalism/socialism and the environmental ethical mood. A good example is the discussion of classical liberalism applied to environmentalism by Weale, 1992.

19. See as an example the discussion of the use of this concept by free-market environmentalism in Daly, 1992. The turn the ethical discussion takes through such debates is well explicated in Daly and Cobb, 1989.

20. This has often been taken as an indicator of cultural change, by the proponents of a post-materialist value change as well as in the discussion of the 'newness' of the new social movements.

21. The idea of a distributive justice concerned with collective goods can be elucidated by counterfactual constructions of optimal solutions to the problem of distributing collective risks in society. These topics are the subject of an extensive discussion in economics and philosophy. For further references see Pearce et al., 1989. An early statement is found in Baumol and Oates, 1975; a first examination of the new ecological paradigm of 'sustainable development' can be found in Redclift, 1990.

22. Social movements are a possible candidate, but their centrality has been overemphasised in the period of high collective mobilisation in Western countries. Attempts at an ethics of collective responsibility can no longer be based solely upon these collective actors. Mobilisation is no guarantee of a rationality that will give to nature a value as a collective good. The internal social organisation of this collective actor and its organising principle as a social sphere have to be clarified. The discussion on the classic notion of a 'public sphere' that has revived in recent years points in the necessary direction. This argument will be expanded below.

23. The discussion of the increasing orientation of scientific theorising and research towards social goals has been an early version of this kind of approach to science. See Böhme et al., 1972, 1978. See also van den Daele, 1987, for a critical evaluation of this early attempt.

24. Van den Daele (1987) speaks of the 'dream of an alternative science' which is necessarily unrealisable.

25. An interesting effect of this can be found in the newspaper reporting on ecology which has become coextensive with reports on science as such. The rubrics 'science, environment, ecology' have gained – in this or similar combinations – a stable representation in public communication.

26. This is true for natural as well as of social facts. Within the social sciences this phenomenon falls under the heading of 'reflexivity'. It is sufficient to note that one of the most influential books on environmental problems, Beck's *Risk Society* (Beck, 1992) relates the notion of an emerging risk society and the notion of societal reflexivity.

27. This counterfactual solution has been made a factual solution only among the 'religious virtuosi' analysed by Max Weber in his sociology of religion. In Protestantism even these virtuosi no longer succeeded in realising the counterfactual ideal of personal identity. Instead, they were those most terrified about the impossibility of realising it.

28. The rise of what has been called 'Political Islam' (Ayubi, 1991) is pertinent here. This phenomenon can be seen as a mere religious movement trying to restore an idealised past, but this is true for only a fraction of those subsumed under this concept. Its main role is rather to serve as a cognitive frame within which people can redefine their personal identity. The collective identity of being part of Islam is therefore basically a cognitive frame that allows a solution to the problem of personal identity.

29. The problem of determining criteria which can distinguish between regressive and non-regressive forms of religious revival implies a theory of rationality that is applicable to the idea of identity. Since identity is a concept that has much to do with emotions and affective behaviour, it is unavoidable that a cognitivistic theory would have some difficulties in dealing with it – see Habermas's discussion of post-conventional identity in modern society (Habermas, 1979). This discussion has been revived by the upsurge of religious and nationalist conflicts since the late 1980s.

30. Good sources for this are the autobiographies of German Greens collected in Hesse and Wiebe, 1988. Even if German environmentalism is considered to have stronger fundamentalist leanings than that of other European countries, this religious motivation is nevertheless an important indicator for the role which questions of personal identity, and their anchorage in religious frames, play in environmental discourse.

31. An interesting discussion on the 'greening of religion' is found in Nash, 1989: 87ff. There is evidence of the same paradox with regard to religion as there is with regard to science. The anti-religious feeling is strong, arguing against an incorporation of religion into a green 'philosophy'. The attack of Lynn White on Christian religion, referring to it as the most anthropocentric religion the world has ever seen, has become famous. See this 1967 seminal essay, as well as some of the critiques of it, in Barbour, 1973. Generally, it is not the established Church, but a minority movement within the traditional churches, that are involved in environmentalism. Heterodox traditions in Christian religion have always tended to move towards this kind of philosophy – Saint Francis being only one, and the most famous, example. See also the review of this discussion by Sessions (1987), and my discussion on counterculture movements in Eder, 1993: 119ff.

32. A good review of the literature on 'green' attitudes is Lowe and Rüdig, 1986. Inglehart, 1982, 1990, is perhaps the most famous example.

33. The return to 'community' is not only to be felt in philosophical discourse (MacIntyre, 1985, 1988), but also in real life in the form of the resurgence of the quest for ethnic and national identity.

34. This is one of the main motivations in Beck's analysis of the 'risk society' which, leaving behind traditional class society with its well-established class cultures, produces the problem of socially contingent identities. Giddens (1991) argues in a similar way.

35. This euphemisation has found its concrete expressions in frames such as 'the politics of the I', or 'science for the people', or any kind of psychologising adaptation of environmentalism to everyday world-views. But closeness to spontaneous or ritualistic forms of everyday life is not a value in itself. On the contrary, such euphemisation is open to any use in public discourse, and is easily amenable to non-intended consequences.

36. Here we enter, through an analysis of environmental discourse, the debate about the logic of the development of modernity, launched by Habermas and carried on by Giddens and others who put emphasis upon its inbuilt reflexivity.

37. This claim is again in line with the recent emphasis on the expressive side of the human existence and its role in the production and reproduction of society. See the classic Elias, 1978, 1982; for an overview of recent discussions, see Lash and Friedman, 1992.

References

Attfield, R. (1983) *The Ethics of Environmental Concern*. Oxford: Blackwell.
Atwater, T., Salwen, M.B. and Anderson, R.B. (1985) 'Media agenda-setting with environmental issues', *Journalism Quarterly*, 62: 393–7.

Ayubi, N. (1991) *Political Islam: Religion and Politics in the Arab World*. London: Routledge.

Barbour, I. (ed.) (1973) *Western Man and Environmental Ethics*. Reading, MA: Addison-Wesley Publishing Company.

Barry, B. (1983) 'Intergenerational justice in energy policy', in D. MacLean and P.G. Brown (eds), *Energy and the Future*. Totowa, NJ: Rowman and Littlefield. pp. 15–30.

Baumol, W.J. and Oates, W.E. (1975) *The Theory of Environmental Policy* (new edition 1988) Cambridge: Cambridge University Press.

Beck, U. (1992) *Risk Society: Towards a New Modernity*. London: Sage.

Beckford, J.A. (1986) *New Religious Movements and Rapid Social Change*. London: Sage.

Bennett, W.L. (1980) 'The paradox of public discourse: A framework for the analysis of political accounts', *The Journal of Politics*, 42: 792–817.

Böhme, G., van den Daele, W., Hohlfeld, R., Krohn, W., Schäfer, W. and Spengler, T. (1978) *Die gesellschaftliche Orientierung des wissenschaftlichen Fortschritts*. Frankfurt: Suhrkamp.

Böhme, G., van den Daele, W. and Krohn, W. (1972) 'Alternativen in der Wissenschaft', *Zeitschrift für Soziologie*, 1: 302–16.

Brosius, H.B. and Kepplinger, H.M. (1990) 'The agenda-setting function of television news: Static and dynamic views', *Comunication Research*, 17: 183–211.

Brown, G. and Yule, G. (1983) *Discourse Analysis*. Cambridge: Cambridge University Press.

Cicourel, A.V. (1980) 'Three models of discourse analysis: The role of social structure', *Discourse Processes*, 3: 101–32.

Cook, F.L., Taylor, T.R., Goetz, E.G., Gordon, M.T., Protess, D., Leff, D.R. and Molotch, H.L. (1983) 'Media and agenda setting: Effects on the public, interest group leaders, policy makers, and policy', *Public Opinion Quarterly*, 47: 16–35.

Corsaro, W.A. (1981) 'Communicative processes in studies of social organisation: Sociological approaches to discourse analysis', *Text*, 1: 5–63.

Daly, H.E. (1992) 'Free-market environmentalism: Turning a good servant into a bad master', *Critical Review*, 6: 171–83.

Daly, H.E. and Cobb, J.B. (Jr.) (1989) *For the Common Good*. Boston, MA: Beacon Press.

De Roose, F. and van Parijs, P. (1991) *La pensée écologiste: Essai d'inventaire à l'usage de ceux qui la pratiquent comme de ceux qui la craignent*. Bruxelles: De Boeck Université.

Deléage, J.P. (1992) 'Ecologie: Les nouvelles exigences théoriques', *Ecologie Politique*, 1: 1–12.

Dower, N. (ed.) (1989) *Ethics and Environmental Responsibility*. Aldershot: Avebury.

Eder, K. (1985) *Geschichte als Lernprozess? Zur Pathogenese politischer Modernität in Deutschland*. Frankfurt: Suhrkamp.

Eder, K. (1988) *Die Vergesellschaftung der Natur: Studien zur sozialen Evolution der praktischen Vernunft*. Frankfurt: Suhrkamp (English translation forthcoming, Sage Publications).

Eder, K. (1990a) 'Prozedurales Recht und Prozeduralisierung des Rechts: Einige begriffliche Klärungen', in D. Grimm (ed.), *Wachsende Staatsaufgaben – sinkende Steuerungsfähigkeit des Rechts*. Baden-Baden: Nomos. pp. 155–86.

Eder, K. (1990b) 'The cultural code of modernity and the problem of nature: A critique of the naturalistic notion of progress', in J. Alexander and P. Sztompka (eds), *Rethinking Progress: Movements, Forces and Ideas at the End of the Twentieth Century*. London: Unwin Hyman. pp. 67–87.

Eder, K. (1992) 'Politics and culture: On the sociocultural analysis of political participation', in A. Honneth, T. McCarthy, C. Offe and A. Wellmer (eds), *Cultural-Political Interventions in the Unfinished Project of Enlightenment*. Cambridge, MA: MIT Press. pp. 95–120.

Eder, K. (1993) *The New Politics of Class: Social Movements and Cultural Dynamics in Advanced Societies*. London: Sage.

Eder, K. (1995) 'Environmental cultures and environmental politics in Europe: A comparative analysis'. Final Research Report. Unpublished manuscript, Florence: European University Institute.

Eder, K. (1996) *Die Vergesellschaftung der Natur*. Translation forthcoming, 1996. London: Sage.

Elias, N. (1978) *The Civilising Process. Vol. I: The History of Manners*. Oxford: Blackwell.

Elias, N. (1982) *The Civilising Process. Vol. II: State Formation and Civilisation* (USA: *Power and Civility*). Oxford: Blackwell.

Erbring, L., Goldenberg, E.N. and Miller, A.H. (1980) 'Front-page news and real-world cues: A new look at agenda-setting by the media', *American Journal of Political Science*, 24: 16–49.

Fairclough, N. (1989) *Language and Power*. London: Longman.

Fairclough, N. (1992) *Discourse and Social Change*. Cambridge: Polity Press.

Gamson, W.A. (1992) *Talking Politics*. Cambridge: Cambridge University Press.

Gamson, W.A. and Modigliani, A. (1989) 'Media discourse and public opinion on nuclear power: A constructionist approach', *American Journal of Sociology*, 95: 1–38.

Giddens, A. (1991) *Modernity and Self-Identity: Self and Society in the Late Modern Age*. Cambridge: Polity Press.

Granovetter, M.S. (1985) 'Economic action and social structure: The problem of embeddedness', *American Journal of Sociology*, 91, 481–510.

Grove-White, R., Morris, P. and Szerszynski, B. (1991) *The Emerging Ethical Mood on Environmental Issues in Britain* (Report to the World Wide Fund for Nature (UK)). Lancaster: Lancaster University, Centre for the Study of Environmental Change.

Grove-White, R. and Szerszynski, B. (1992) 'Getting behind environmental ethics', *Environmental Values*, 1: 285–96.

Habermas, J. (1979) *Communication and the Evolution of Society*. London: Heinemann.

Habermas, J. (1989) *The Structural Transformation of the Public Sphere: An Inquiry into a Category of Bourgeois Society*. Cambridge, MA: MIT Press.

Habermas, J. (1992) *Faktizität und Geltung. Beiträge zur Diskurstheorie des Rechts und des demokratischen Rechtsstaats*. Frankfurt: Suhrkamp.

Hargrove, E.C. (1989) *Foundations of Environmental Ethics*. Englewood Cliffs, NJ: Prentice-Hall.

Hesse, G. and Wiebe, H.H. (eds) (1988) *Die Grünen und die Religion*. Frankfurt: Athenäum.

Hofrichter, J. and Reif, K. (1990) 'Evolution of environmental attitudes in the European Community', *Scandinavian Political Studies*, 13: 119–46.

Inglehart, R. (1982) *Changing Values and the Rise of Environmentalism in Western Societies*. Berlin: International Institute for Environment and Society, Science Centre Berlin.

Inglehart, R. (1990) 'Values, ideology, and cognitive mobilisation in new social movements', in R.J. Dalton and M. Kuechler (eds), *Challenging the Political Order: New Social and Political Movements in Western Democracies*. Cambridge: Polity Press. pp. 43–66.

Jonas, H. (1984) *The Imperative of Responsibility: In Search of an Ethics for the Technological Age*. Chicago: University of Chicago Press.

Kitschelt, H. (1984) *Der ökologische Diskurs: Eine Analyse von Gesellschaftskonzeptionen in der Energiedebatte*. Frankfurt: Campus.

Lash, S. and Friedman, J. (eds) (1992) *Modernity and Identity*. London: Blackwell.

Lovelock, J. (1989) *The Ages of Gaia: A Biography of Our Living Earth*. Oxford: Oxford University Press.

Lowe, P.D. and Rüdig, W. (1986) Review article: 'Political ecology and the social sciences – the state of the art', *British Journal of Sociology*, 16: 513–50.

Luhmann, N. (1989) *Ecological Communication*. Chicago: University of Chicago Press.

McCombs, M.E. (1981) 'The agenda-setting approach', in D.D. Nimmo and K.R. Sanders (eds), *Handbook of Political Communication*. Beverly Hills CA: Sage. pp. 121–40.

McCombs, M.E. and Shaw, D.L. (1972) 'The agenda-setting function of mass media', *Public Opinion Quarterly*, 36: 176–87.

McCombs, M.E. and Shaw, D.L. (1977) 'The agenda-setting function of the press', in D.L. Shaw and M.E. McCombs (eds), *The Emergence of American Political Issues: The Agenda-Setting Function of the Press*. St Paul MN: West Publishing Company. pp. 1–18.

MacIntyre, A. (1985) *After Virtue: A Study in Moral Theory*, second edition (first edition 1981). London: Duckworth.

MacIntyre, A. (1988) *Whose Justice? Which Rationality?* London: Duckworth.

Milbrath, L.W. (1984) *Environmentalists: Vanguard for a New Society*. Albany NY: State University of New York Press.

Milbrath, L.W. (1989) *Envisioning a Sustainable Society: Learning Our Way Out*. Buffalo NY: State University of New York Press.

Nash, R.F. (1989) *The Rights of Nature: A History of Environmental Ethics*. Madison WI: University of Wisconsin Press.

Pearce, D. et al. (1989) *Blueprint for a Green Economy*. London: Earthscan.

Porritt, J. (1984) *Seeing Green: The Politics of Ecology Explained*. Oxford: Basil Blackwell.

Porritt, J. and Winner, D. (1988) *The Coming of the Greens*. London: Fontana.

Potter, J. and Wetherell, M. (1987) *Discourse and Social Psychology: Beyond Attitudes and Behaviour*. London: Sage.

Redclift, M. (1990) 'Economic models and environmental values: A discourse on theory', in R.K. Turner (ed.), *Sustainable Environmental Management: Principles and Practice*. London / Boulder CO: Belhaven Press / Westview Press. pp. 51–66.

Reese, S.D. (1991) 'Setting the media's agenda: A power balance perspective', in J.A. Anderson (ed.), *Communication Yearbook*, Vol. 14. Newbury Park CA: Sage. pp. 309–40.

Rogers, E.M. and Dearing, J.W. (1988) 'Agenda-setting research: Where has it been, where it is going?', in J. Anderson (ed.), *Communication Yearbook 11*. Newbury Park CA: Sage. pp. 555–93.

Sessions, G. (1987) 'The deep ecology movement: A review', *Environmental Ethics*, 8: 105–25.

Snow, D.A. and Benford, R.D. (1988) 'Ideology, frame resonance, and participant mobilisation', in B. Klandermans, H. Kriesi and S. Tarrow (eds), *International Social Movement Research*. Vol 1: *From Structure to Action: Comparing Social Movement Research across Cultures*. Greenwich CT: JAI Press. pp. 197–217.

Snow, D.A. and Benford, R.D. (1992) 'Master frames and cycles of protest', in A.D. Morris and C.M. Clurgh Mueller (eds), *Frontiers in Social Movement Theory*. New Haven CT: Yale University Press. pp. 133–55.

Snow, D.A., Rochford, E.B., Worden, S.K. and Benford, R.D. (1986) 'Frame alignment processes, micromobilization and movements participation', *American Sociological Review*, 51: 464–81.

Statham, P. (1995) 'Political pressure or cultural communication? An analysis of the significance of environmental action in public discourse'. Unpublished manuscript, Florence: European University Institute.

Stone, C. (1987) *Earth and Other Ethics: The Case for Moral Pluralism*. New York: Harper and Row.

van den Daele, W. (1987) 'Der Traum von der "alternativen" Wissenschaft', *Zeitschrift für Soziologie*, 16: 403–18.

van Dijk, T.A. (1985) 'Structure of news in the press', in T. van Dijk (ed.), *Discourse and Communication: New Approaches to the Analysis of Mass Media Discourse and Communication*. Berlin: de Gruyter. pp. 69–93.

van Dijk, T.A. (1988) *News as Discourse*. Hillsdale NJ: Lawrence Erlbaum Associates.

van Parijs, P. (1991) 'Epilogue: les deux écologismes', in F. de Roose and P. van Parijs (eds), *La pensée écologiste. Essai d'inventaire à l'usage de ceux qui la pratiquent comme ceux qui la craignent*. Bruxelles: De Boeck Université. pp. 135–55.

Weale, A. (1992) 'Nature versus the state? Markets, state, and environmental protection', *Critical Review*, 6: 153–70.

Wetherell, M. and Potter, J. (1988) 'Discourse analysis and the identification of interpretative repertoires', in C. Anataki (ed.), *Analysing Everyday Explanation. A Casebook of Methods*. London: Sage. pp. 168–83.

Wiesenthal, H. (1993) *Realism in Green Politics: Social Movements and Ecological Reform in Germany*. Manchester: Manchester University Press.

Wynne, B. (1988) 'Technology as cultural process', in E. Baark and U. Svedin (eds), *Man, Nature and Technology. Essays on the Role of Ideological Perceptions*. London: Macmillan. pp. 80–104.

Young, J. (1990) *Post Environmentalism*. London: Belhaven Press.

10

THE SHAPING OF THE GLOBAL ENVIRONMENTAL AGENDA: THE ROLE OF NON-GOVERNMENTAL ORGANISATIONS

Andrew Jamison

The contemporary concern with global environmental problems is due to scientific research: the hole in the ozone layer, the projections of global warming, and the implications of decreasing biodiversity have all been brought to light by scientists. Indeed, it seems fair to say that scientists have *constructed* these problems, and not just any scientists, but particular cadres of well-supported and highly technified natural scientific researchers. Global environmental problems require some of the most sophisticated instrumental techniques available to technoscience for their disclosure. We simply wouldn't know about global warming or the hole in the ozone layer if complicated instruments had not been devised to 'see' these previously invisible phenomena. Like many, if not all, scientific facts, global environmental problems are not really out there in nature present-ing themselves for all to see; they are rather the products of a collective, instrumentally dependent and institutionally circumscribed professional activity that we call science or scientific research.[1]

In order for global environmental problems to become politically important, however, something more than scientific construction is required. It is not sufficient that facts and concepts are created by scientists in relation to 'natural' phenomena; global environmental problems also require intermediary actors with the ability to translate the calculations, simulations and projections of the oceanographers, biochemists and meteorologists into issues of public concern. The public awareness of global environmental problems is inconceivable without a range of middle-men organisations serving as information conduits between scientists, the media and the public, translating expert discourses into politics, and also recombining specialised expert knowledges into policy-orientated pack-ages. In these respects, the global environmental discourse can be seen as having been shaped, in significant ways, by a new kind of transnational or multinational environmental 'movement'; or to put it more provocatively, the global environmental discourse represents the environmental movement's coming in from the cold, its incorporation into established political routines and, as such, its demise, at least temporarily, as an activist, outsider movement.[2]

In most sociological discussions of the ecological problematique, the movement – whether thought of as ideas, organisational entities, or cognitive/intellectual activities – is seldom examined explicitly. Indeed, there is a remarkable lack of interaction between those sociologists who, in recent years, have followed Ulrich Beck into the elucidation of the risk society and those sociologists who have studied the developmental trajectory of environmentalism as a social movement. At work is the familiar fragmentation of the social sciences – the 'to each his/her own specialisation niche' syndrome – but there is, I suggest, something else going on, as well. The academic discussion of the risk society apparently assumes that knowledge generation is the province of professionally legitimated experts, and, even more seriously perhaps, that social movements, because of their status as non-experts, do not produce knowledge that is important (see Wynne, this volume). My claim, however, is that much of the environmental problematique – and indeed the idea of the risk society itself – can be seen as the product of the 'cognitive praxis'; that is, the intellectual, or knowledge-generating activity, of environmental movements. It might thus be of some significance to examine specifically the role that non-experts have played in framing the environmental discourse. A closer look at the contours of the movement discourse that pre-dated and contributed to the formation of many of the contemporary expert discourses might even provide some assistance in generating a meaningful critique of the dominant frameworks – both intellectual and institutional – of what has been termed ecological modernisation (see Hajer, this volume).

The concern over global environmental issues can be seen as the most recent phase in the development of post-war environmentalism, a phase marked by the dominance of powerful and influential transnational organisations such as Greenpeace International, the Worldwatch Institute and World Resources Institute and the Worldwide Fund for Nature. In recent years, these well financed and highly professionalised environmental NGOs (non-governmental organisations) have largely supplanted the more activist groups that dominated environmentalism in the 1970s as the main articulators of the environmentalist message. Furthermore, they have tended to steal the stage of global concern from the local environmental groups that have emerged in the Southern or developing countries, and which are increasingly vocal in their opposition to Northern definitions of global environmental problems.[3] At the same time, they have served to redefine environmentalism, in the Northern countries themselves, as an international movement, and to direct attention away from the more local issues that inspired so much of the original activism.

The role of transnational environmentalism in the shaping of the global environmental problematique raises important questions about how scientific knowledge is framed by 'external' social forces. Large environmental NGOs, as expert consultants, publicists and problem formulators, and knowledge producers are directly involved in the initiation and the implementation of major programmes of scientific research and technological development, often funded by development assistance agencies and/or multinational development banks. They are also the most active informants of the public of the new environmental issues, through their books, magazines, reports and museum exhibitions. The NGOs have developed highly effective media strategies, which have helped to give their activities and their definitions of the problems a broad public visibility which less professional organisations have difficulty achieving. The ways that these organisations have defined global environmental problems and their solutions has been extremely influential in the design of international scientific research programmes and in framing the environmental agendas of many developing country governments.[4]

The 'international regimes' that are being shaped in environmental politics – the intergovernmental treaties and agreements on global resource use and protection – are seen by some commentators as indicative of an important new political trend, namely the transcendence of national boundaries as meaningful political lines of demarcation. In many ways, these issues provide transnational NGOs with a political significance that they previously have not had, at least not to the same extent. In the transnational arenas where agreements are negotiated over the exploitation of the 'global commons' NGOs have come to play a particularly crucial role.[5] Their perceptions of environmental problems form the basis for policy measures, and their studies and expertise produce a good deal of the knowledge that is used in the global environmental discourse.

In this chapter I want to do three things. First I want to trace briefly the development of post-war environmentalism, and indicate the main phases through which environmentalism has come to be organised as a social and cognitive actor. I want to show something of the social dynamics by which popular, grass-roots activism and locally based critical movements have been transformed into a transnational political actor-network dominated by professional organisations. Then I want to look at some of the ways in which this transnational actor-network is shaping the global environmental policy agenda. Finally, I will contrast the new transnational environmentalist 'cognitive praxis' with that of the movements that emerged in the 1970s. In my perspective, environmentalism was originally constituted by the articulation of a set of new 'knowledge interests' and it is those interests that are currently being reformulated by both corporate and non-governmental actors. An interesting transformation of the original environmentalist message is thus taking place. While the movement has changed into something quite different than it was originally, the nature of the problems as well as the proposed solutions are also changing. Here I merely want to give some preliminary indications about what is happening and raise some questions about the political and scientific implications of these transformations.

A Processual View of Environmentalism

In order to get a handle on how these transformations have taken place, it can be helpful to think of post-war environmentalism in a processual way, and briefly characterise some of the main phases in that process (Table 10.1). These phases can be thought of in two main ways – as changes in strategic orientation and 'collective identity' on the part of already established organisations, and in the emergence of new groups, campaigns or organisations which identify new issues and new forms of activism (cf. Jamison et al., 1990).

It was in the immediate post-war period that the more traditional concern with nature and resource conservation began to change into a new kind of environmental consciousness. It has become customary to think of this consciousness emerging in the 1960s, inspired primarily by Rachel Carson's *Silent Spring*, but we can actually see it articulated and acted upon much earlier by some of the leading figures in the older conservation 'movement', particularly in the United States and Britain. Julian Huxley, a naturalist and the first director of Unesco, played an important role in bringing environmental issues into the United Nations system, and helped establish IUPN, the International Union for the Protection of Nature which, in 1956, would become IUCN, the International Union for the Conservation of Nature. Meetings arranged by both organisations were extremely important as forums for the articulation of a new environmental perspective to supersede the somewhat more limited and traditional nature-protection perspective that had characterised conservation circles since the late nineteenth century (cf. McCormick, 1991).

Fairfield Osborn, director of the New York Zoological Society and founder of the Conservation Foundation, was one of the first to put this perspective into print in his book, *Our Plundered Planet*, which came out in 1948 and was translated into 13 languages. In 1953, Osborn published *Limits of the Earth*, and continued throughout the 1950s to foster a more

Table 10.1   *Phases of post-war environmentalism*

Period		Emphasis
pre-1968	awakening	public education
1969–74	organisation	institution building
1975–80	social movement	political controversy
1981–86	professionalisation	environmental assessment
1987–	internationalisation	incorporation/integration

international and ecological perspective among nature-lovers and biologists. He was perhaps the most successful of the conservation movement's new 'organisation men', people who arranged meetings and research projects, lobbied for funds, and gradually altered the agendas in nature societies and natural history institutions (see Jamison and Eyerman, 1994). In the United States, the transformation of conservationism into environmentalism was a gradual process that was brought to a head and to a larger public primarily through the eloquent prose of Rachel Carson. But there were others in the post-war period – writers like Joseph Wood Krutch, activists like David Brower of the Sierra Club, established figures like the American Supreme Court justice William Douglas, and even the nature photographer Ansel Adams – whose activities helped pave the way (see Fox, 1985). Particularly with the development of a 'mass culture' of television and popular science, nature was brought into the home, and with it, the need to 'save nature' from further degradation reached a mass audience. In 1961, the World Wildlife Fund was established to give this new conservation message a more professional form in terms of fund-raising, public relations and dissemination. The WWF was started with the expressed purpose of bringing more financial resources into the hands of the nature organisations. Aristocrats, industrialists and bankers were brought onto its board of directors in order to attract funding for programmes of international wildlife protection. The WWF, with its international headquarters in Switzerland, and a number of national organisations throughout the world, represented a more explicitly international focus and organisational framework for environmental issues. With the founding of the WWF 'family' of organisations, the looser – and poorer – networks of international environmentalism were given a more powerful and effective structure.

In the late 1960s, a new range of environmental problems were identified – industrial pollution, atomic radiation, urban sprawl – that tended to supplant conservation issues from most national political agendas. As these problems came to be discussed in popular books and the mass media, a new socio-economic developmental perspective gradually came to be articulated: an ecological paradigm in contrast to the industrial paradigm that had guided post-war development (Cotgrove, 1982). As more books were written, the awareness grew, and the diagnoses of the problems grew more alarmist, so that by the late 1960s when Paul Ehrlich published *The Population Bomb*, which was an even bigger best-seller than *Silent Spring*, a kind of doomsday, or at least crisis, mentality had emerged, giving the problems an urgency that they had not previously had. When combined with the more philosophical critique of modern technology of Herbert Marcuse and Lewis Mumford, as well as the spiritual journeys to the east and beyond by the beat poets and their hippie disciples, environmentalism became a broad movement of social and political opposition.

We can think of this period – from the late 1940s to the late 1960s, with a rather long period of latent interest in the boom years of the 1950s – as a period of awakening. It was primarily a time of public education and it took place almost exclusively in the industrialised countries. What was involved was the enunciation, by biologists, nature-lovers and writers, of a new range of issues and eventually a new ecological perspective on social development. On a macro level of social discourse, the environment was being re-cognised as an arena for public dispute and state policy intervention. Nature was no longer to be conceived in oppositional contrast to society, as a refuge from society as had been characteristic of conservationism; with the concept of the environment and the related concept of the biosphere, the focus was shifted to the interactions between nature and society, their mutual dependencies and interrelationships. In the course of the 1960s, this shift in focus took on an ever more 'scientific' coloration, as the systems approach to ecology spread through scientific circles, challenging the previously dominant evolutionary approaches to ecology (Worster, 1979). This conceptualisation was, in the first phase, more implicit than explicit. It would be in the early 1970s, in a second brief and intensive phase, that ecology would be presented as a new holistic world-view to steer society in an alternative direction.

The second phase of environmentalism was inspired by the general questioning of industrial society that came in the wake of the student revolts and can be called the age of ecology. It was also a period of active institution building. It was from about 1968 to 1973 that almost every industrialised country established an agency or governmental department to deal with environmental protection, and at the same time environmental research, education, and even technological development were organised in new institutional forms. Many countries passed stronger environmental legislation, and set up new kinds of courts to decide over cases of environmental pollution. The period also saw the organisation of environmental activism in local and national action groups and federations, many of which broke away from the older conservation societies which were now seen as being too conservative to take on the new environmental issues. This was also a period when environmentalists, in many countries, formulated a more explicit collective identity, or to put it differently, when the environmental debate developed into an environmental movement. The influential environmentalist writings of the early 1970s – *A Blueprint for Survival, The Closing Circle, Tools for Conviviality, Small Is Beautiful, Only One Earth* – articulated a positive programme of social ecology, rather than a depiction of doom and crisis. And they explicitly translated the internal scientific language of ecology into social or political philosophy. In this activity, some ecologists took part, like the American brothers Howard and Eugene Odum, the creators of much of the terminology of systems ecology; but the lead was taken by scientists and especially science students of a more activist bent, many of whom left the academic setting to establish identities for themselves in a new kind of environmental movement space (see Cramer et al., 1987).

Another dimension of the organisational phase was the creation of UNEP, the United Nations Environment Programme, in 1972, as an outgrowth of the UN Conference on the Environment in Stockholm. UNEP provided an institutional base for international environmental activities; but it has had little impact on the UN system as a whole, nor has it, until recently, been able to exercise much influence over developing country governments: it has been primarily a sectoral organisation that has carried out specific educational, information and research programmes.

All these organisational efforts of the early 1970s – both governmental and non-governmental – did not eliminate the environmental crisis. The new agencies and laws did encourage certain developments in pollution control, but the efforts soon took on the character of a specialised state policy sector, separated from the other areas of public policy and thus with little impact on economic development priorities. We can say that in the cyclical pattern of movement critique and institutional reaction, the main effect of the first wave of environmental activism was to create an environmental 'sector' in government and academia.

When many countries came to experience economic downswings in relation to the oil price increases in 1974, environmental protection tended to be downgraded. What had been a concern with the quality of life and with controlling pollution was transformed into a massive concern with energy. Here again reactions were different in the United States and Europe; but generally we can refer to a third phase of environmentalism from the first oil crisis until about 1980. We can think of this period in two ways: on the one hand, it was a time when environmentalism had a major impact on national political agendas, especially in relation to energy policy, and on the other, it was a time when the environmental organisations turned into full-scale bureaucracies.

An important result of the energy debates of the 1970s was a profession-alisation of environmental consciousness and a related incorporation by the established political cultures of what had originally been a somewhat delimited, even marginal political concern. As a result, there was a specialisation of knowledge production, as experts moved in to dominate the discourse initiated by 'movement intellectuals'; and, on the cosmologi-cal or world-view level, the systemic holism of the early 1970s gave way to a more instrumental and fragmented energy research. This meant that there was a separation of cognitive praxis into different specialised levels; and while 'deep ecology' emerged to delve further into the philosophical ramifications of the ecological world-view, energy analysts and some large corporations turned alternative technological criteria into new profitable innovations in energy conservation and alternative production systems. For our purposes, however, what was most important about the energy debates was that they brought about a politicisation of the environmental movements, forcing the previously sectoralised and specialised groups and individuals to think about political strategy and even political theory and analysis much more directly than they had done before. It also meant that more politically conscious people joined in the fray as well as in the expert advising.

The effect was that, when nuclear energy was removed from many national political agendas in the early 1980s, either by pricing itself out of the competitive marketplace or by being voted upon in referendums or parliaments, there was a domain and a range of expertise that had previously not existed. In almost every country, as well as internationally, there were activist organisations, university departments and substantial state bureaucracies that had, as it were, an institutional interest in new environmental problems. This is not to say that the professionalisation of energy created the new global environmental problems, but it certainly was a necessary condition for the spate of initiatives that have been taken over the past four or five years.

In any case, in the early 1980s one can identify a fourth phase of environmentalism in both industrialised and developing countries, inspired by the new international economic context as well as by the new high-technology culture. On the one hand, there was a growing parliamentary interest through new green parties, as well as through the adoption of the environmental issue by other political parties. In Europe, of course, the green parties have been quite visible; while in other countries it has been particular politicians who have brought environmental issues to parliamentary attention. In the United States, with its system of parliamentary hearings and consultations, a new kind of organisation, the environmental 'think tank' emerged in the guise of the World Resources Institute to produce expert advice and develop more constructive solutions to international environmental problems. Started by James Gustave Speth, who had been the director of President Carter's Council of Environmental Quality, the WRI has grown into an important producer of environmental knowledge. Located close to the halls of American government, its reports have served as the basis for both legislation and government policy, even during the ascendancy of conservative presidential administrations.[6] In the American system, the WRI has helped the Congress play an active role in the shaping of environmental policy. Working with other international organisations, the WRI has also been instrumental in shaping the global environmental agenda. It was a WRI study that first proposed the GEF, the Global Environmental Facility; and WRI studies have been used as the basis for many of the negotiations on ozone depletion, climate change, and biodiversity.

On the other hand, the 1980s have been marked by the resurgence of more established or mainstream environmental organisations; in many countries, the older conservation societies have experienced a new lease of life with substantial increases in membership and influence, while newer organisations such as Greenpeace have pioneered what might be called multinational environmentalism. Greenpeace succeeded in channelling the activism of the 1970s into more effective, professional directions. By streamlining the organisation, and limiting membership to the paying of

dues, activism was itself transformed into a profession, organised strategically and orientated to mass media that had grown increasingly interested
in sensational environmental 'disasters'. Greenpeace, in many ways, can
be thought of as a more radical version of the WWF; it emerged as a
trouble-making group, willing and eager to grab headlines with dramatic
escapades. Both Greenpeace and the WWF, however, have served to take
environmental activism out of the hands of amateurs and place its funding,
its management, and the articulation of its message into the hands of
professional advertising men, media and management consultants, and
policy experts. In order to increase its international range, its effectiveness
and its level of expertise, the environmental movement had largely been
transformed into transnational NGOs (Eyerman and Jamison, 1989).

By this, I mean that organisations such as Greenpeace and the World-
wide Fund for Nature function in much the same manner as multinational
corporations, with sophisticated communications and information
networks, effective and professionally managed media strategies, and well-
organised fund-raising and research activities. It is these new powerful
environmental lobbies, or NGOs as they are most commonly labelled,
which have been among the most active forces during the past five years in
constructing the global environmental discourse which led to the Rio
Summit in June 1992. It is largely their conceptions of global environmental problems that have influenced the programmes of the United
Nations agencies and the World Bank, and it is their conceptions, as well,
that have helped set environmental policy agendas in many developing
countries. In this latter respect, the active collaboration between the WWF
and IUCN, which led, in 1980, to the formulation of the World Conservation Strategy, with its articulation of the idea of 'sustainable development', has been an important force.

In the intervening years, WWF/IUCN have continued to provide expert
advice, as well as training and actual research cooperation, to many
developing countries, as they have sought to bring environmental protection into their developmental activities (see Adams, 1990). From the mid-
1980s, these efforts have been encouraged by both the World Bank and the
various UN agencies. The recent creation of the Global Environmental
Facility (GEF) in 1990 by UNEP, UNDP and the World Bank represents a
new set of opportunities, as well as a new focus of attention, for this
multinational environmentalism. Interestingly enough, the new international activity has also led to a split between the WWF and IUCN, and to
a strengthening of the WWF's own policy and projects in areas outside of
the traditional wildlife preservation focus. The change is reflected in the
new name, Worldwide Fund for Nature, which the international body, but
not the American national organisation, has adopted. Another element of
the change is the creation of an international institutions programme
within the WWF 'family', with offices at international headquarters in
Switzerland, near EC headquarters in Brussels and near World Bank
headquarters in Washington. David Reed, the director of the new

programme, has taken the lead in outlining a new 'NGO role' in international environmental activities, particularly within the GEF.[7] NGOs can no longer afford to stand on the sidelines and refuse to take part in such major programmes, Reed contends; rather, their participation is essential in ensuring transparency and in increasing the chances that the programmes actually contribute to sustainable development.[8] Reed, a development expert with little previous experience in wildlife issues, represents a new kind of environmental expert in the large NGOs, which parallels the emergence of environmental divisions and the hiring of environmental economists in the World Bank and the regional development banks. Obviously, the WWF, WRI and Greenpeace do not speak with one voice, but they do represent a similar kind of professional, expert-steered and politically delimited environmentalism which has tended to marginalise less media-orientated environmentalists, particularly those from action groups in developing countries.

From the mid-1980s, as the lobbying and public relations activities of the new environmental professionals have begun to be felt, we can legitimately speak of a fifth, or international, phase of environmentalism, in which the so-called global environmental problems have taken over from local problems as the main areas of concern. Ozone depletion, climate change and biodiversity preservation have become the fundamental issues of concern; and the solution to these problems has been characterised, since the report of the World Commission on Environment and Development in 1987, as 'sustainable development'. At the same time, many large corporations have begun to adopt new methods of clean, or cleaner, production, including environmental auditing, recycling of waste products, and more efficient uses of resources and energy supplies in production processes. For some, the shift is seen as a change in production paradigm; increasingly, environmental concern is being integrated into corporate planning and innovation strategies, while management schools are beginning to provide training in environmental economics as well as in the new methods of production. In the words of Christopher Flavin and John E. Young, writing in the influential *State of the World* report of the Worldwatch Institute, 'Once seen as a distraction to the real business of business, environmental concerns are becoming an engine of the next Industrial Revolution. . . . Businesses are likely to prosper in the future not by selling massive quantities of identical products – the traditional route to economic success – but by meeting consumer needs in the most efficient way possible: supplying energy "services" rather than electricity, "information" rather than a newspaper, and crop protection rather than pesticides.'[9]

The so-called 'greening of industry' is, of course, a multifaceted process that involves both changes in production and consumption as well as in government regulation, and it is not my intention to analyse the new paradigm in any detail here; I merely want to indicate that environmentalism has recently begun to take on a new importance for many industrial corporations, which has thus affected the political agenda of environmental discourse. In many respects, this shift in agenda can be seen as a convergence of interests between environmental NGOs and multinational corporations. It is in the interests of both types of actors to construct a global environmental problematique; the new global message helps provide new audiences and research tasks for the NGOs, and new markets and profitable product lines for the corporations. For that matter, the promulgation of programmes to encourage 'cleaner production' in industrial firms is also of benefit for universities and engineering schools, and, in many European countries, new departments of environmental management, economics and engineering are being established to provide the professional experts who are to direct the greening of industry (see Fischer and Schot, 1993).

The Global Environmental Message

The global environmental message is often presented as one of interdependence and cooperation. The adversarial relationships of the previous phases – when environmentalists criticised corporations for their pollution and environmentally destructive behaviour – are now seen by many NGOs and businessmen as anachronistic. Now, corporations and environmentalists are asked to collaborate in the development of the so-called sustainable society. As such, the problems and their solutions are redefined in ways that lead to new technological fixes for industry and new opportunities for environmental organisations. An analysis of some advertisements from the two types of actors which were disseminated at the time of the UN Conference on Environment and Development in 1992 might better indicate the kind of convergence that I have in mind.

Firstly, the business, or corporate, culture used the image of a global environment to legitimate its own global reach, as well as its new-found green soul. Asea Brown Boveri's ad in the special Rio Summit issue of *Newsweek* is particularly illustrative of this new trend, with a picture of the globe placed over the rhetorical question: 'Can you provide the energy the world needs today and preserve the earth for the generations to come? Yes, you [i.e. ABB] can.' The world needs energy – as the smaller text tells us, 'Mankind needs energy to fuel the processes that create light, heat, shelter, transportation and goods – the basis of our modern civilisation.' But energy resources are not inexhaustible, we are told. That's why ABB is committed to the principle of sustainable development. 'The balance between mankind's needs and the conservation of the natural resources of the planet depends on clean and efficient technology in the fields of electrical engineering, industry and transportation.'

Then look at a recent Greenpeace ad (Figure 10.1). 'Goodbye Sunshine', it says, with a picture of a little child being blinded by the strong rays of the sun coming through the hole in the ozone layer. Greepeace aims to stop the production of chemicals that destroy the ozone layer. As the ad

Figure 10.1

puts it, 'We want to encourage the use of environmentally safe alternatives so that the ozone layer will be able to recover as soon as possible.' To convince governments and industries to change their ways is 'not easy'. 'We need your help, too,' the ad says, asking for our support. But what are we being asked to support? In both cases we are being urged to buy something, the clean and efficient products of ABB or the costly campaigning activities of Greenpeace. And we are given very little indication that what we are buying will actually help future generations. What has happened is that the problems of environmental destruction have been framed – or constructed – in such a way as to lend themselves to mass media advertisements. This means simplification, exaggeration and, perhaps more to the point, linear causality. The assumption, never discussed and certainly never questioned, is that global environmental problems can be solved through new technologies and/or committed professional activists with the global reach of Greenpeace. Of course, that is not all that is being said in the global environmental discourse; but it is the point at which the interests of the NGOs and the corporations converge. Once again, we are being asked, by ABB as well as by Greenpeace, to put our faith in technology and experts – in the case of Greenpeace, experts in activism.

In this respect, the environmentalist message has been significantly transformed from the holism that was so characteristic of the early 1970s. Then environmentalism represented, among other things, a new world-view, a new ecological way of organising society, and not merely a new set of products or production processes. Then, we were asked not merely to buy new products or support clever advertising campaigns, but to take part in changing society, to get involved. Something of that participatory approach can be seen in a recent WWF ad, but the democracy that was so central to the 1970s environmental movement is here transformed into support for a new environmental aristocracy. It is the Duke of Edinburgh himself (Figure 10.2) who wants our support to 'look after this planet'. That takes money, we are told, money for the WWF, as well as people, and there is something for each of us to do to change our attitudes towards nature. But, most importantly, there is a great deal that the WWF and its experts can do, if they are given our support.

The global environmental message that is being projected by environmental organisations and large corporations is seen by critics in developing countries as a new form of imperialism. In the words of Vandana Shiva (1992):

> The 'global' in the dominant discourse is the political space in which the dominant local seeks global control, and frees itself of local, national and global control. . . . The way 'global environmental problems' have been constructed hides the role and responsibility of the globalising local in the destruction of the environment which supports the subjugated locals. . . . Through a shift from the present to the future, the North gains a new political space to control the South. The 'global' thus creates the moral base for green imperialism.

A Cognitive Approach to Social Movements

One way to think about the social construction of the new global environmental message – and its scientific/technical knowledge – is to view the

Figure 10.2

process in terms of closure. It is customary to think of closure in scientific controversies as resulting from a convergence of interpretations, and the resolution of underlying conceptual and cognitive conflict (see Engelhardt and Caplan, 1987). In the case of the global environmental agenda, the

concept of closure needs to be extended to include the dynamic transformations of social movements. Indeed, it can be argued that without
extending the range of analysis to include critical actors and social
movements, it is difficult to explain the closure of even apparently internal
scientific controversies. Political debates over scientific and technological
issues are an important mechanism in the processes through which new
scientific ideas and technical innovations are assimilated into societies. This
assimilation process, at least since the late eighteenth century, can be
thought of as a periodic opening and closing of political debate. In this
perspective, social movements often play the role of 'early warners',
identifying problems, mobilising critical opposition and pointing to the
need for cognitive and institutional adjustments and transformations (see
Jamison, 1988). Far from being merely passive reactors to the development
of knowledge, social movements are often active contributors to the new
disciplines and orders of knowledge production that emerge after controversies have been temporarily closed.

The role of social movements in cognitive change has tended to be
ignored by students of social movements as well as by students of science
and technology. It is as if knowledge production only becomes interesting
for science studies when it has become professionalised and entered the
confines of authorised knowledge-producing institutions. Controversies
within science are sometimes given attention, but when they extend out
into broader and typically messier social and political arenas, students of
science tend to lose interest. Social movements have thus come to be seen
as peripheral to the main concerns of science studies. As a result, there is
as yet little understanding about how social issues come to be 'translated'
into scientific problems; we also know precious little about the cognitive
and institutional channels through which new science-based problems are
brought into national and international policy agendas. While increasingly
sophisticated network models are being applied to our understanding of
the construction of scientific knowledge and technical artefacts themselves,
the larger society is unwittingly reduced to playing a bit part in the
drama.[10]

Social movements for their part have been of far more interest to
sociologists and historians as political, rather than cognitive, actors. They
have been studied primarily as 'mobilisers' of political resources or as
vehicles of political campaigns, and not as knowledge-producers. While
some attention is given to their role in political and social change, their
own processes of intellectual development and issue articulation are
seldom subjected to detailed scrutiny. Important dimensions of the
collective construction of social – and natural – reality thus remain
curiously unexamined, even though social movements have come to
interest a growing number of historians and social scientists as objects of
study.[11]

This dual blindness has created a rather serious gap in our understanding
of cognitive change. The interaction between social movements, however

defined, and accredited knowledge-producing institutions has, with few exceptions, not attracted the interest of either the movements themselves or of academic analysts. As a result, there has been little attempt, either by activists or by students of science, to develop ways to grasp or even conceptualise this interaction. We thus know very little about the role that 'external' actors play in the shaping or construction of knowledge. Looking at social movements as knowledge-producers can therefore be expected to fill in some of the holes in our understanding of where new ideas come from.

The approach that I have developed together with Ron Eyerman conceives of social movements as carving out temporary public spaces in which ideas are combined and articulated in new ways. We discuss the importance of new types of intellectual roles which are practised in social movements, and of new organisational forms that are developed for both the production and dissemination of knowledge (Eyerman and Jamison, 1991). Social movements, for us, are conceptualised as 'cognitive praxis'; and this cognitive praxis is an integrative activity, bringing together new world-view assumptions, or ideas about reality, with the identification of new problems or issues in innovative organisational settings. We refer to three dimensions of 'knowledge interests' – cosmological, technological and organisational – and our argument has been that social movements become cognitive actors when the three dimensions are integrated into a cohesive cognitive praxis. What is often involved is a translation of more narrowly defined concepts and problems into social issues.

Such integrative praxis exists only for short periods; other social actors eventually grow interested and try to incorporate the various component parts of the social movement's knowledge interests into their own cognitive praxis. The strong claim, at least for environmentalism, however, is that the formation of a relatively autonomous movement space was a necessary condition for new environmental sciences, technologies, institutions and professional roles to emerge. The movement provided both a breeding ground, as well as a new social context, within which ideas could be shaped or constructed. In the case of environmentalism, what was especially important was the translation of an internal, or natural science, terminology – the language of systems ecology – into a social or political programme. During the 1960s, ecological ideas, which had mainly been confined to biological scientists or professional conservationists, were transformed into social or political ecologies.

In our terminology, environmental movements articulated a new set of knowledge interests that consisted of three levels, or dimensions: (1) an ecological or holistic world-view, drawing on the conceptualisations of systems ecology but also bringing social and human factors into the ecological perspective (for example Commoner, 1971); (2) an alternative set of criteria and principles for technological development: small-scale, renewable, locally appropriate, environmentally friendly and resource conserving (for example Dickson, 1974); and (3) a new, more democratic mode of producing and disseminating knowledge, a convivial or radical kind of participatory knowledge-production that drew on some of the practices of the student movement as well as the purported experiences of the Chinese and Vietnamese revolutions (for example Harper et al., 1976). For us, it was the active combination of these three dimensions – the cosmological, technological and organisational – into a movement cognitive praxis that transformed environmentalism, for a time, into a social movement (Jamison et al., 1990). It was through its cognitive praxis that environmentalism became social; the movement provided new audiences, new contexts and new areas of application for what had previously been an internal scientific discourse. It is the social and political ecologies that were articulated in the environmental movement of the early 1970s which have been deconstructed in the 1980s, and are now being incorporated into the activity of somewhat more powerful and more established actors than the people and groups who originally articulated them.

The Fragmentation of Environmental Knowledge Interests

It is helpful to try to remember the original environmentalist message of the early 1970s, and contrast the ideas and practices that were then articulated with the message that is now being projected by the large environmental NGOs. The knowledge interests of the environmental movement at that time can be thought of in three main ways: as a social cosmology, a set of technological criteria, and a way of organising the production and dissemination of environmental knowledge. All three dimensions have been significantly transformed, as environmentalism itself has been transformed from a critical social movement into an influential international science and technology network of actors (see Table 10.2).

On the one hand, there was the technical or technological interest; environmental movements first emerged by criticising certain technologies, like nuclear energy and hydroelectric dams, petrochemicals and large-scale projects in general. And they proposed alternative criteria for technological development – resource conservation, recycling of wastes, use of renewable energy, small scale, etc. The phrase 'small is beautiful' generally sums up the environmental movement's technological interest. Secondly, there is what we can call the organisational interest: environmental movements opposed the rule of expert elites, and favoured traditional

Table 10.2 *Environmentalist knowledge interests*

Dimension	1970s	1990s
cosmological	systemic holism/'ecologism'	globalism/'sustainable development'
technological	appropriate/small-scale	'clean production'
organisational	participatory/anti-elitist	professional/expert-dominated

approaches to science and technology and grass-roots initiatives. Even more importantly, they challenged the way science is divided up into faculties and specialised disciplines; their approach to knowledge has continued to be interdisciplinary, and has attempted to combine natural science and social science into various kinds of 'human ecology'. Finally, environmental movements have brought with them a new world-view. From the early 1970s, environmentalists argued that nature is a whole, the earth is one, and that natural processes that take place in one part of the world have an impact on the environment thousands of miles away. The book that was written for the 1972 United Nations Conference in Stockholm, *Only One Earth*, by Rene Dubos and Barbara Ward, presents this environmental world-view very well. But a number of other books that came out around that time – a time when the environmental movement was on the rise in its period of organisation – also articulated this new, systemic world-view. As we see it, the environmental movement took ideas that scientists had been developing – the holistic ideas of systems ecology – and carried them into the larger society.

In the 1970s it was the combination of these three knowledge interests – the holistic cosmology, the alternative or small-scale technology and the anti-elitist organisational practice – that made environmentalism a social movement. In the course of the 1980s, those interests or dimensions have been split apart, removed from a movement space or context and institutionalised in corporate or at least established settings. The movement itself, or rather the grass-roots organisations that still exist, have been marginalised, while the message of the movement has been deconstructed or decomposed into its various component parts. ABB singles out the technological dimension, because it makes good economic sense. The wave of clean technology that has descended upon us and that ABB epitomises can best be seen, I think, as a translation of alternative technological criteria – and an alternative technological praxis – into new product criteria. The WWF singles out the world-view or cosmological dimension, but makes it a nature-loving holism that can appeal to everyone. The WWF has helped transform the political and social ecologies of the early 1970s into the ambiguous programme of 'sustainable development'. Meanwhile, Greenpeace singles out the organisational dimension, but has transformed the movement's anti-elitist organisational ideal into a radical – and rather problematic – populism that is now separated from any underlying political goal or programme. As such, the message of environmentalism has been diffused and spread, but what was once a radical, even revolutionary, system-transcendent message has now been transformed into the different and institutionally separated aspects of multinational environmentalism.

Conclusions

In this chapter I have tried to disclose some of the personal and organisational paths through which the environmental movement of the

1970s has been transformed into the science and technology policy actor of the 1990s. My effort is only a beginning, and makes no claims of having identified all, or, for that matter, even the most important, linkages between environmental non-governmental organisations and the global environmental agenda. I have merely tried to point to a new range of actors and a series of processes of science–society interaction that are seldom focused upon in either the science studies or the broader social scientific literature. NGOs are becoming significant in the social shaping of science and technology, particularly in the environmental field. Organisations like the World Resources Institute and Worldwatch Institute have become highly effective in their production and dissemination of environmental information, and their various publications are widely read by other actors, as well as by the general public. They have become, in my terms, crucial 'translators' of academic research findings into the discourse of science and technology policy. Nor should this surprise us; this is the very task for which they were established. What should surprise us, however, is that their role in the contemporary world of technoscience is so unexamined.

My intention has not been to disparage the work of these and the other, more professionally activist, NGOs. They are certainly no better or worse than the other actors in the system. Rather, I have wanted to focus attention on two aspects of their operations that, I feel, are ripe with implications, the one having to do with their actual cognitive praxis – its epistemological status, we might say – and the other having to do with their political legitimacy – who or what do these NGOs actually represent? Much of what NGOs actually do lies somewhere between what we usually think of as science, on the one hand, and politics, on the other. The work of organisations like the WWF and WRI is largely a new form of 'applied' science, defined not so much from an externally motivated interest but from an internal, organisational interest. It most resembles industrial research, in that it is generated by the developmental needs of the 'firm' rather than by curiosity or broader goals of social enlightenment. The activities of the WWF, Greenpeace and the others are governed by a concern for global survival and sustainable development, and these goals have become operationalised in ways that have led to profitable avenues of organisational growth. The NGOs have emerged, we might say, to fill, or carve out, certain niches in the global ecosystem of knowledge production. The problem is not that these organisations are not accountable to their members or peers – on the contrary, by being so market orientated, they are more directly accountable to their users, members and/or the consumers of their products than academic scientists, corporations or government agencies. The problem is rather that, by being so commercially successful, the interests of the NGOs will continue to converge with the interests of the large multinational corporations, thus seriously weakening the critical role that NGOs, or the environmental movement, for all its constructive value, still should play. By becoming established actors in the global environmental discourse, the environmental movement may have lost an important part of its (critical) identity. The question then can be raised as to what kind of actor, or movement, is to assume the mantle of critical assessment in an age of environmentally friendly production.

It will be crucial for new alliances to be formed between environmental activists and critical social scientists. In some manner, it will be necessary to reinvent the kind of 'partisan' intellectual activity that Rachel Carson, Barry Commoner and other environmentalists represented in the 1960s. Along with more theoretically minded writers such as Herbert Marcuse and Lewis Mumford it can be claimed that Carson and Commoner practised a form of intellectual partisanship, using their scientific competence and their writing skills to identify a new social problem and range of issues. Something similar is needed today; but now it is imperative to reconceptualise the environmental problematique in terms of the emerging configurations of economic and political power. The global environmental agenda, as Vandana Shiva and others have been arguing for several years, cannot be separated from the conflict between the Northern industrial nations and the Southern so-called developing countries. Social conflict, at the global, national and local levels, must be brought into the environmental discourse; and, in that mission, partisan social scientists have a key role to play.[12]

Notes

This chapter has been written as part of a research project on global warming and the UN system, financed by DANIDA, the Danish development assistance agency. A Swedish version was published in *VEST* 3, 1993, and a Danish version in *Den Ny Verden* 1, 1995. I would like to thank my colleagues in the project, Erik Baark and Gan Lin, for their comments, as well as Brian Wynne, Sheila Jasanoff, Vandana Shiva and other participants at the session at the 4S/EASST conference in Gothenburg, August 1992, where the paper was first presented.

1. The sociological understanding of scientific knowledge – the claim that science is a social, or collective, construction of knowledge – is still not generally accepted. Even today, over 30 years after Thomas Kuhn's influential *The Structure of Scientific Revolutions*, 'realist' epistemologies continue to dominate, or at least flourish, in the philosophy of science. For a recent introduction to the sociology of science, which might well improve matters, see Collins and Pinch, 1993. In this chapter, I take the sociological construction of science for granted; I want to argue, however, that the sociology of scientific knowledge has, as it were, been insufficiently sociological. In directing so much of its intellectual and polemic effort toward philosophers in what seems to be a never-ending battle of epistemological positions, insufficient effort has been given to integrating work in other sociological sub-fields into the sociology of scientific knowledge. As a result, it has been difficult, if not impossible, to bring other 'actors' into the construction process. My intention here is to suggest that one important actor, or cluster of actors, at least when it comes to environmental knowledges, are the range of organisations which are customarily referred to as the environmental movement.

2. For a readable introduction to the development of the global environment movement, see McCormick, 1991.

3. For a presentation of some of the most important NGOs, see Porter and Brown, 1991: 56ff. In their book, which is meant to be a textbook in political science and international

relations, Porter and Brown divide NGOs into three main categories: (1) large, membership organisations in one country (such as the Sierra Club in the USA), (2) international organisations (such as the WWF and Greenpeace), and (3) non-membership expert organisations, or 'think tanks'. It should be noted that Porter and Brown are themselves employed by NGOs of the third type, Porter at the Environment and Energy Study Institute and Brown at the World Resources Institute, which indicates that NGOs are influential even in the social scientific study of environmental politics. A particularly outspoken critique of some of the WRI studies is Agarwal and Narain, 1991.

4. A number of cases are discussed in Adams, 1990. In Vietnam, the 'National Conservation Strategy', which was first drafted in 1986, and has guided environmental policy ever since, was written with the advice of consultants from WWF/IUCN. Like many other such strategy documents in developing countries, the Vietnamese plan is based on the 'World Conservation Strategy', produced by WWF/IUCN in 1980, in which the idea of 'sustainable development', later to be popularised by the Brundtland report, *Our Common Future* (1987), was first enunciated.

5. See Porter and Brown, 1991: 69ff for a discussion of the main international environmental issues and regimes.

6. Speth has recently (1994) been appointed director of the United Nations Environment Programme (UNEP).

7. See David Reed (ed.) (1992) *Structural Adjustment and the Environment*, Westview, and David Reed (1993) *The Global Enviromental Facility: Sharing Responsibility for the Biosphere*, WWF. The International Institutions Programme has received funding from several European governments to provide analytical assessments of World Bank and other development assistance programmes.

8. Interview with Reed, Washington DC, 17 March, 1993.

9. Christopher Flavin and John E. Young, 'Shaping the next industrial revolution', in Brown et al., 1993: 181–2.

10. Social movements appear in science studies primarily as participants in scientific controversies; but even there the tendency has been to focus largely on controversies among scientists themselves, placing movements and non-scientific groups in the surrounding landscape, rather than actually on the stage of controversy itself (see Wynne, this volume). The exceptions are the treatments of the anti-nuclear energy movements (see Rüdig, 1991) where anti-nuclear groups are seen as having an influence on the formation of energy policy. These works generally fall outside of the central canon of science studies, however, which remains steadfastly concentrated on deconstructing the 'science and technology' that is practised by authorised scientists and engineers.

11. See Eyerman and Jamison, 1991: 24ff, for detailed discussion of these studies.

12. Vandana Shiva and Anil Agarwal, as well as other Southern environmentalists, continue to provide 'role models' for those of us in the West who see a need for a critical assessment activity within the environmental movement. Agarwal's Centre for Science and Environment (CSE) in Delhi remains, after more than a decade, a good example of an organisation that bridges some of the gap between academic and activist work. The CSE has recently begun to publish a journal, *Down to Earth*. In the North, the British publication, the *Ecologist*, in spite of frequent rhetorical exaggeration, is perhaps the best example that comes to mind of critical environmentalism. For examples of a more academic critical environmentalism, see the articles collected in Lipschutz and Conca, 1993. This is a topic that deserves its own article, however. I have discussed partisan intellectuals of the 1960s in Jamison and Eyerman, 1994.

References

Adams, W. (1990) *Green Development*. London: Routledge.
Agarwal, A. and Narain, S. (1991) *Global Warming in an Unequal World: A Case of Environmental Colonialism*. Delhi: Centre for Science and Environment.
Brown, L. et al. (1993) *State of the World 1993*. New York: Norton.

Collins, H. and Pinch, T. (1993) *The Golem: What Everyone Should Know about Science*. Cambridge: Cambridge University Press.

Commoner, B. (1971) *The Closing Circle*. New York: Knopf.

Cotgrove, S. (1982) *Catastrophe or Cornucopia*. Chichester: Wiley.

Cramer, J., Eyerman, R. and Jamison, A. (1987) 'The knowledge interests of the environmental movement and its potential for influencing the development of science', in S. Blume, J. Bunders, L. Leydesdorff and R. Whitley (eds), *The Social Direction of the Public Sciences*. Dordrecht: Reidel. pp. 89–115.

Dickson, D. (1974) *Alternative Technology and the Politics of Technical Change*. Glasgow: Fontana.

Engelhardt, H. and Caplan, A. (eds) (1987) *Scientific Controversies: Case Studies in the Resolution and Closure of Disputes in Science and Technology*. Cambridge: Cambridge University Press.

Eyerman, R. and Jamison, A. (1989) 'Environmental knowledge as an organisational weapon: The case of Greenpeace', *Social Science Information*, 28 (2): 99–119.

Eyerman, R. and Jamison, A. (1991) *Social Movements: A Cognitive Approach*. Cambridge: Polity.

Fischer, K. and Schot, J. (eds) (1993) *Environmental Strategies for Industry*. Washington DC: Island Press.

Fox, S. (1985) *The American Conservation Movement*. Madison: University of Wisconsin Press.

Harper, P., Boyle, G. and the editors of *Undercurrents* (1976) *Radical Technology*. London: Wildwood House.

Jamison, A. (1988) 'Social movements and the politicisation of science', in J. Annerstedt and A. Jamison (eds), *From Research Policy to Social Intelligence*. London: Macmillan. pp. 69–86.

Jamison, A., Eyerman, R., Cramer, J. and Læssøe, J. (1990) *The Making of the New Environmental Consciousness*. Edinburgh: Edinburgh University Press.

Jamison, A. and Eyerman, R. (1994) *Seeds of the Sixties*. Berkeley: University of California Press.

Lipschutz, R. and Conca, K. (eds) (1993) *The State and Social Power in Global Environmental Politics*. New York: Columbia University Press.

McCormick, J. (1991) *Reclaiming Paradise: The Global Environmental Movement*. Bloomington: Indiana University Press.

Porter, G. and Brown, J. (1991) *Global Environmental Politics*. Boulder CO: Westview.

Rüdig, W. (1991) *Anti-nuclear Movements: A Global Survey*. London: Longman.

Shiva, V. (1992) 'Science, technology and 500 years of colonisation'. Address given at the 4S/EASST conference, Gothenburg, August.

Worster, D. (1979) *Nature's Economy: The Roots of Ecology*. Garden City NY: Anchor Books.

11

ECOLOGICAL MODERNISATION AS CULTURAL POLITICS

Maarten A. Hajer

In his celebrated study of the US conservation movement around the turn of the century, Samuel Hays (1979) describes how the popular moral crusade for conservation of American wilderness paved the way for a group of experts that, under the veil of working for conservation, advanced their own particular programme. These 'apostles of efficiency' did not share the somewhat sentimental attitude towards wilderness that was typical of the predominantly urban movement for conservation. Above all, they were interested in applying new techniques of efficient resource management in introducing new forestry practices or in constructing and experimenting with the latest hydroelectric dams. For the American urbanites wilderness had a deeply symbolic meaning. Trees and mighty rivers were the icons of the alleged moral superiority of nature that stood in sharp contrast to the bitter reality of a rapidly industrialising society. For experts like Gifford Pinchot and his colleagues, in contrast, wilderness was a nuisance and nature was a resource: trees were merely crops and rivers were to be tamed and tapped. For the urbanites nature had to be preserved; for the experts nature had to be developed.

The story is instructive in several respects. Firstly, it shows that 'our' ecological 'problematique' most certainly is not new. The negative effects of industrialisation for nature have been thematised time and again over the last 150 years. Yet characteristically the public outcry focuses on specific 'emblems': issues of great symbolic potential that dominate environmental discourse. Examples of emblems are deforestation in the mid-nineteenth century, wilderness conservation (USA) and countryside protection (UK) at the turn of the century, soil erosion in the 1930s, urban smog in the 1950s, proliferation of chemicals in the early 1960s, resource depletion in the early 1970s, nuclear power in the late 1970s, acid rain in the early 1980s, followed by a set of global ecological issues like ozone depletion or the 'greenhouse effect' that dominate our consciousness right now. Given this sequence of issues it is better to refrain from speaking of today's predicament in terms of 'our ecological crisis' (which suggests it is time and space specific) and to speak of the *ecological dilemma* of industrial society instead.

Secondly, if we accept the thesis that environmental discourse is organised around changing emblems, we should investigate the repercussions of these subsequent orientations of the debate. After all, emblems mobilise bias in and out of environmental politics. They can be seen as specific discursive constructions or 'story lines' that dominate the perception of the nature of the ecological dilemma at a specific moment in time. Here the framing of the problem also governs the debate on necessary changes. In the case of the US conservation issue the prevailing story line framed the environmental threat as a case of 'big companies' that tried to destroy the American wilderness and rob 'the American people' of something that was constitutive of its national identity. This then paved the way for the state-controlled technocrats who established 'national parks', and seized control over rivers and pastures in the name of the common good. Hays's reinterpretation of the history of the conservation movement illuminates the often disregarded fact that technocrats subsequently used their brief to implement a comprehensive scheme of 'scientific resource management' in which wildlife and nature were largely made subordinate to their concern about achieving optimal yields, thus directly going against the original intentions of the popular movement. The word 'conservation' remained central, yet its institutional meaning changed radically. Ergo: ecological discourse is not about the environment alone. Indeed, the key question is about which social projects are furthered under the flag of environmental protection.

Thirdly, the story of the US conservation movement illustrates the complex nature of what is so often easily labelled the 'environmental movement'. Here the term 'movement' leads astray. Hays's narrative is in fact about not so much a movement as a bizarre coalition that comprised at least two rather distinct tendencies: a popular tendency that was morally motivated, and a technocratic tendency organised around a relatively confined group of experts, administrators and politicians. The important thing is that both had their own understanding of what the problem 'really' was and what sort of interventions could or should be considered as solutions. Nevertheless, together they constituted the social force behind the changes that were made. Hence, instead of speaking of a movement, we would be better to think in terms of 'coalitions'. And, as the above indicates, these coalitions are not necessarily based on shared interests, let alone shared goals, but much more on shared concepts and terms. We therefore call them 'discourse-coalitions' (see Hajer, 1995).

Fourthly, in environmental debates we can often identify implicit ideas about the appropriate role and relationship of nature, technology and society that structure implicit future scenarios. Hays sees a dialectical relation between the public outcry over the destruction of the American wilderness and the implicit critique of industrial society. Nature symbolised the unspoiled, the uncorrupted or the harmonious which was the mirror-image of the everyday reality of Chicago, Detroit or Baltimore at that time. The popular movement wanted to save nature from the effects of industrialisation but did not address the practices of industrial society head on, focusing instead on the effects on nature. In the end it thus paved the way for a programme that focused on the application of new technologies and scientific management techniques to 'conserve nature'. Here the concern about the immorality of society was matched by a renewed appeal to forms of techno-scientific management that were very similar to those industrialistic practices that had motivated the moral outcry in the first place.

This chapter investigates some similar dynamics in contemporary environmental politics. It argues that environmental politics is now dominated by a discourse that might be labelled ecological modernisation. It presents an outline of this policy- or regulation-orientated programme and gives a brief account of its history. Subsequently the chapter presents three ideal-typical interpretations of what ecological modernisation is about. In the fourth section this chapter then discusses the social dynamics of ecological modernisation. Extrapolating from the developments in some countries where ecological modernisation is now put into action, it tries to ·grasp the socio-political tendencies in the environmental domain in the years to come.

What is Meant by Ecological Modernisation?

Ecological modernisation is a discourse that started to dominate environmental politics from about 1984 onwards.[1] Behind the text we can distinguish a complex social project. At its centre stands the politico-administrative response to the latest manifestation of the ecological dilemma. Global ecological threats such as ozone layer depletion and global warming are met by a regulatory approach that starts from the assumption that economic growth and the resolution of ecological problems can, in principle, be reconciled. In this sense, it constitutes a break with the past. In the 1970s environmental discourse comprised a wide spectrum of – often antagonistic – views. On one side there was a radical environmentalist tendency that thought that the 'ecological crisis' could be remedied only through radical social change. Its paradigmatic example was nuclear power. On the other side of the spectrum was a very pragmatic legal-administrative response. The 'Departments for the Environment', erected all over the Western world in the early 1970s, worked on the basis that pollution *as such* was not the problem; the real issue was to guarantee a certain environmental quality. Its paradigmatic example was the end-of-pipe solution. Where ecological damage was proven and shown to be socially unacceptable, 'pollution ceilings' were introduced and scrubbers and filters were installed as the appropriate solution. Moderate NGOs or liberal politicians would subsequently quarrel about the definition of the height of ceilings and whether 'enough' was being done, but they shared with the state the conviction that ecological needs set clear limits to economic growth.

Ecological modernisation stands for a political project that breaks with both tendencies. On the one hand it recognises the structural character of the environmental problematic, while on the other ecological modernisation differs essentially from a radical green perspective. Radical greens or deep ecologists will argue that the 'ecological crisis' cannot be overcome unless society breaks away from industrial modernity. They might maintain that what is needed is a new 'place-bound' society with a high degree of self-sufficiency. This stands in contrast to ecological modernisation which starts from the conviction that the ecological crisis can be overcome by technical and procedural innovation. What is more, it makes the 'ecological deficiency' of industrial society into the driving force for a new round of industrial innovation. As before, society has to modernise itself out of the crisis. Remedying environmental damage is seen as a 'positive sum game': environmental damage is not an impediment for growth; quite the contrary, it is the new impetus for growth. In ecomodernist discourse environmental pollution is framed as a matter of inefficiency, and producing 'clean technologies' (clean cars, waste incinerators, new combustion processes) and 'environmentally sound' technical systems (traffic management, road pricing, cyclical product management, etc.), it is argued, will stimulate innovation in the methods of industrial production and distribution. In this sense ecological modernisation is orientated precisely towards those forces that Schumpeter once identified as producing the 'fundamental impulse that sets and keeps the capitalist engine in motion' (Schumpeter, 1961: 83).

The paradigmatic examples of ecological modernisation are Japan's response to its notorious air pollution problem in the 1970s, the 'pollution prevention pays' schemes introduced by the American company 3M, and the U-turn made by the German government after the discovery of acid rain or *Waldsterben* in the early 1980s. Ecological modernisation started to emerge in Western countries and international organisations around 1980. Around 1984 it was generally recognised as a promising policy alternative, and with the global endorsement of the Brundtland report *Our Common Future* and the general acceptance of Agenda 21 at the United Nations Conference of Environment and Development held at Rio de Janeiro in June 1992 this approach can now be said to be dominant in political debates on ecological affairs.

Making Sense of Ecological Modernisation

How should we interpret ecological modernisation? Is it just rhetoric, 'greenspeak' devoid of any relationship with the 'material' reality of ongoing pollution and ecological destruction? Here we have to differentiate. The empirical evidence of the developments in environmental policymaking and product-innovation in Germany and Japan, the experience of the Dutch 'environmental policy planning' approach, or the emergence of Clinton's and Gore's 'win-win' strategy in environmental and conservation issues (see for example Cockburn, 1993), shows that the least we can say is that ecological modernisation has produced a real change in *thinking* about nature and society and in the *conceptualisation* of environmental problems in the circles of government and industry. This is what I call the condition of discourse structuration. One of the core ideas of ecological modernisation, 'integrating ecological concerns into the first conceptualisation of products and policies', was an abstract notion in the early 1980s but is by now a reality in many industrial practices. Especially in OECD countries, ecomodernist concepts and story lines can now be seen to act as powerful structuring principles of administration and industrial decision-making from the global down to the local levels.[2] It has produced a new ethics, since straightforward exploitation of nature (without giving thought to the ecological consequences) is, more than ever before, seen as illegitimate.

Yet one should also assess the extent to which the discourse has produced non-discursive social effects (the condition of discourse institutionalisation). Here one has to define a way to assess social change. There seems to be a consensus that in terms of classical indicators (such as energy consumption, pollution levels) one cannot come to a straightforward conclusion. There have been marked successes in some realms (say, curbing SO_2 emissions), but mostly they have been cancelled out by other developments (such as rising NO_x levels). Likewise, where energy consumption has gone down one may legitimately wonder whether these changes are the result of the new discourse or whether the 'achievements' should be attributed to some other processes (such as economic restructuring). Hence in terms of *ecological* indicators it is difficult to come to an assessment.

The question that we focus on here is the sort of *social* change that ecological modernisation has produced, a question that is neglected only too often in social-scientific research on environmental matters. Is ecological modernisation 'mercantilism with a green twist'? Has it led to a new form of 'state-managerialism'? Does ecological modernisation produce a break with previous discourses on technology and nature, or is it precisely the extension of the established technology-led social project? Or should the 'ecological question' be understood as the successor of the 'social question', and ecological modernisation as the new manifestation of progressive politics in the era of the 'risk society'?

My approach here is to first sketch three different interpretations of ecological modernisation. They are ideal-typical interpretations in the sense that one will not find them in real life in this pure form. Almost inevitably all three of them draw on certain social-scientific notions. In this respect it is important to see them merely as heuristic devices that should help us define the challenges that the social dominance of the discourse of ecological modernisation produces. Each ideal-type has its own structuring principles, its own historical narrative, its own definition of what the problem 'really' is and its own preferred socio-political arrangements.

Ecological Modernisation as Institutional Learning

The most widespread reading of the developments in environmental discourse interprets the course of events as a process of institutional learning and societal convergence. The structuring principle of the institutional learning interpretation of ecological modernisation is that nature is 'out of control'. The historical account is framed around the sudden recognition of nature's fragility and the subsequent quasi-religious wish to 'return' to a balanced relationship with nature. Retrospectively, *Limits to Growth* here appears as the historical starting point. *Limits to Growth* first argued that we cannot endlessly exploit nature. Of course, the report was based on false premises but now we can see that the Club of Rome had a point: we should take nature seriously. Global environmental problems like global warming or the diminishing ozone layer call for decisive political interventions.

Typically, the political conflict is also seen as a learning process. 'We owe the greens something', it is argued. The dyed-in-the-wool radicals of the 1970s had a point but failed to get it through. This was partly due to the rather unqualified nature of their *Totalkritik*. The new consensus on ecological modernisation is here attributed to a process of maturation of the environmental movement: after a radical phase the issue was taken off the streets and the movement became institutionalised as so many social movements before it. With the adoption of the discourse of ecological modernisation its protagonists now speak the proper language and have been integrated in the advisory boards where they fulfil a 'tremendously important' role showing how we can design new institutional forms to come to terms with environmental problems. Likewise, the new consensus around ecological modernisation has made it possible that the arguments of individual scientists that found themselves shouting in the dark during the 1970s are now channelled into the policymaking process.

The central assumption of this paradigm is that the dominant institutions indeed *can* learn and that their learning can produce meaningful change. Following that postulate the ecological crisis comes to be seen as a primarily *conceptual* problem. Essentially, environmental degradation is seen as an 'externality' problem, and 'integration' is the conceptual solution: as economists we have too long regarded nature as a 'sink' or as a free good; as (national) politicians we have not paid enough attention to the repercussions of collective action and have failed to devise the political arrangements that could deal with 'our' global crisis. Likewise, scientists have for too long sought to understand nature in a reductionist way; what we need now is an integrated perspective. Time and again nature was defined 'outside' society, but further degradation can be prevented if we integrate nature into our conceptual apparatus. Fortunately, the sciences provide us with the tools needed: systems theory and the science of ecology show us the way. This understanding of the ecological crisis is supported by what the institutional learning perspective sees as the 'key problems' – collective action problems like the greenhouse effect, acid rain or the diminishing ozone layer. Basically, the institutional learning perspective would define ecological modernisation as the perception of nature as a new and essential subsystem and the integration of ecological rationality as a key variable in social decision-making. The hardware can be kept but the software should be changed.

The preferred socio-political arrangements in essence follow its reading of the history of ecological modernisation and its definition of the problem. Its historical narrative illustrates the strength of pluralist social arrangements. After all, ecological modernisation is the historical product of the critical interplay of opposing social forces. The fact that the World Bank has now adopted an ecomodernist stand is the best example of the radical power of rational argument: even the big institutions will change if arguments are phrased convincingly and correspond with the scientific evidence available. The institutional learning perspective would insist that we have to consider which alterations in scale and organisation we have to make to the existing institutional arrangements to improve 'communication' and make ecological concerns an 'integral part' of their thinking. On the one hand, that implies changes on the level of the firm and the nation state (that is, the stimulation of so-called 'autopoetic' or self-organising effects – for instance mineral or energy accounting in the firm, or the 'greening' of GNP and taxes on the national level). On the other hand, the need for integration finds its political translation in an increased demand for coordination which results in a preference for 'centralisation' of decision-making. Global ecological problems have to be brought under political jurisdiction so what we need, above all, are new forms of global management. On the local level, ecological modernisation implies that the scenarios that have been devised to further the ecologisation of society have to be protected against the – inevitable – attacks from particular interest groups. Hence the possibilities for essentially selfish NIMBY (Not In My Back Yard) protests might have to be restricted.

The sciences should in this perspective search for the conceptual apparatus that can facilitate instrumental control over nature and minimise social disturbances. They should, first and foremost, devise a language that makes ecological decision-making possible. What is required is a specific set of social, economic and scientific concepts that make environmental issues calculable and facilitate rational social choice. Hence the natural sciences are called upon to determine 'critical loads' of how much (pollution) nature can take, and should devise 'optimal exploitation rates', as well as come up with ratings of ecological value to assist drawing up of development plans. Engineering sciences are called upon to devise the technological equipment necessary to achieve the necessary ecological quality standards respecting existing social patterns. In a similar vein, the social sciences' role in solving the puzzle of ecologisation is to come up with ideas of how behavioural patterns might be changed and to help understand how 'anti-ecological' cultural patterns might be modified.

In all, in this interpretation ecological modernisation appears as a moderate social project. It assumes that the existing political institutions can internalise ecological concerns or can at least give birth to new supranational forms of management that can deal with the relevant issues. Hence it is a sign of the strength and scope of ecological modernisation that the World Bank has become the manager of the Green Fund – it assumes that national governments can rethink their sectoral policies and that the network of corporatist interest groups can be altered in such a way that it becomes sensitive to ecological matters.

Ecological Modernisation as a Technocratic Project

The interpretation of ecological modernisation as a technocratic project holds that the ecological crisis requires more than social learning by existing social organisations. Its structuring principle is that not nature but technology[3] is out of control. In this context it draws upon the dichotomies dominant–peripheral and material–symbolic. It holds that ecological modernisation is propelled by an elite of policymakers, experts and scientists that imposes its definition of problems and solutions on the debate. An empirical example is the UN Brundtland Report. It is a 'nice try' but, as the Rio Conference and its aftermath show so dramatically, it falters because it is only able to generate global support by going along with the main institutional interests of national and international elites as expressed by nation states, global managerial organisations like the World Bank or the IMF, and the various industrial interests that hide behind these actors. Hence ecological modernisation is a case of 'real problems' and 'false solutions'. The material–symbolic dichotomy surfaces in the conviction that there is a deeper reality behind all the window dressing. Behind the official 'rhetoric' of ecological modernisation one can discern the silhouette of technocracy in a new disguise that stands in the way of implementing 'real solutions' for what are very 'real problems'.

Its historical narrative starts with the emergence of the 'counterculture' in the 1960s. The environmental movement is essentially seen as an offspring of that broader wave of social criticism. Environmentalism was driven by a critique of the social institutions that produced environmental degradation. Important icons are the culture of consumerism that forces people to live according to the dictum 'I shop, therefore I am', or nuclear power that would not only create a demand for more energy consumption but would also enhance the tendency towards further centralisation of power in society. Certainly, *Limits to Growth* is also seen as a milestone, but not for the environmental movement. Yet what *Limits to Growth* was for social elites and governments, so were *Small Is Beautiful* and *Blueprint for Survival* for the counterculture. While in *Limits* the environmentally sound alternative was largely left implicit, the latter publications showed the way towards a truly sustainable society. In this world there would be no place for the 'big government', 'big industry' or 'big science' that, incidently, dominated the Club of Rome that published *Limits to Growth*.

The technocracy critique also has a different interpretation of the significance of the environmental movement of the 1970s. The social movements of the 1970s were not ineffective 'interest groups' that shouted loud but achieved little because they did not know the nitty-gritty of lobbying and strategic action. Quite the contrary, they were embryonic examples of new alternative democratic and ecologically benign social structures and lifestyles (Cohen, 1985). In this movement one found not only 'young well-educated middle class radicals' as some analysts would have it. It also included many scientists who were disturbed by the centralist culture that penetrated the realm of scientific inquiry but who did not necessarily share the radical political agenda of some of the activists. Likewise, it attracted many housewives and farmers who again had their own motives for participating and their own understandings of what the problem 'really' was (see the by now classic article by Offe (1985)). Many a social critic looked upon the environmental movements as one of the forerunners of a new non-technocratic society. Yet rather than learn from these movements 'the state' repressed the alternative movement, either by brute force on the squares of the cities and near nuclear power plants or by 'repressive tolerance', inviting the movements to participate in its judicial inquiries where their political message was inevitably lost in the strait-jackets of legalism (see for example Wynne, 1982). Consequently, in this perspective the emergence of ecological modernisation is not seen as product of the 'maturation' of the social movements. Ecological modern-isation is much more the repressive answer to radical environmental discourse than its product. Now the ecological issue has been 'taken up by the apparatuses of power, it becomes a pretext and a means for tightening their grip on daily life and the social environment' (Gorz, 1993: 57). In this context it is not seen as a coincidence that nuclear power is conspicuously absent in the main text of the Brundtland Report. The debate has shifted from this politically explosive issue to global ecological issues that after all suggest that 'our common future' is at stake, thus obliterating old dichotomies and social alternatives.

In this perspective the ecological crisis is basically depicted as an *institutional* problem. The technocracy critique fiercely challenges the assumption that the dominant institutions can learn. How can it be that we try to resolve the ecological crisis drawing on precisely those institutional principles that brought the mess about in the first place: efficiency, technological innovation, techno-scientific management, procedural integration and coordinated management? Who believes that growth can solve the problems caused by growth? Incidently, which institutional learning processes followed the Green Revolution? Is sustainable development not the next 'top-down' model destined to bring evil while in name it intends to do good?

This interpretation would also point at the 'structural' aspects of the problem that are left unaddressed in the discourse of ecological modernisation. What ecological modernisation fails to address are those immanent features of capitalism that make waste, instability and insecurity inherent aspects of capitalist development. Surely ecological modernisation will not end the 'leapfrog' movement of capitalist innovation whereby production equipments, generations of workers or geographical areas are 'written off' periodically? In this perspective the fact that the World Bank is now in charge of the Green Fund is not seen as a sign of strength of the 'ecological turn' but precisely as evidence of the fact that ecological modernisation is really about the further advancement of technocracy. Clearly, eco-software will not save the planet if capitalist expansionism remains the name of the game.

This interpretation opens the black box of society and argues that the emergence of ecological modernisation was to be seen in the context of the increasing domination of humanity by technology, where technology refers not merely to technical 'artefacts' or machines but to social techniques as well. Consequently, the *real* problem at issue is how to stop the 'growth machine'. Only then can one set about trying to remedy the very real environmental problems.

The technocracy critique argues that the sciences have in fact to a large degree been incorporated in this technocratic project. The institutional history of the discipline of systems ecology is used as a case in point (see Kwa, 1987). As historians of science have shown, it was a paradigm on its way out that during the 1960s suddenly got new institutional momentum as NASA engineers and politicians showed an interest in the science that could be integrated in the context of a wider cybernetic perspective. Likewise, the consequence of the prevailing institutional framework is that engineers develop only those technologies that enhance control over nature and society rather than achieve ecological effects while making society more humane. The social sciences are similarly implicated and are called upon as 'social engineers' who only work to help achieve preconceived policy goals. Alternatively, new institutional arrangements in academia and 'science for policy' should be developed. 'Counterexperts' should be able to illuminate the 'technocratic bias' in the official scientific reports. Likewise, more attention, credit and space should be given to those engineers who have been working on 'soft energy paths' that would show the viability of decentralised alternatives. Finally, the social sciences should not work on puzzle-solving activities like changing individual consumer patterns but on the analysis of the immanent forces that keep the juggernaut running towards the apocalypse, so that it might be possible to steer it, or preferably to stop and dismantle it.

The preferred socio-political arrangements of this technocracy critique are those that can correct the prevailing bias towards hierarchisation and centralisation. Its initiatives to further a more democratic social choice centre on 'civil society' rather than on the state. Social movements and local initiatives need protection and attention. New political institutions that would facilitate this correction are the introduction of 'right-to-know' schemes (in Europe), the widespread use of referendums, and, above all, the decentralisation of decision-making and the right to self-determination. Here the differences with the institutional learning perspective come out clearly. The fight to circumvent local NIMBY protests through centralisation and 'increased procedural efficiency', indeed the mere construction of complaints as 'NIMBY' protests, are now seen as illustrations of the tendency to take away democratic rights under the veil of environmental care. Here NIMBY protests are recognised as a building stone for an anti-technocratic coalition. After all, protests that are initially motivated by self-interest often lead to a increased awareness of the ecological problematique. Hence NIMBYs may become NIABYs (Not In Anybody's Back Yard) (see Schwarz and Thompson, 1990).

In all, ecological modernisation as a technocratic project is a critical interpretation that extends Habermas's argument of modernisation as the 'colonisation of the lifeworld' to include Galtung's concern over the colonisation of the future. With the demise of the radical environmental movement its hope is set on the 'triggering effect' of a few ecological disasters.

Ecological Modernisation as Cultural Politics

The interpretation of ecological modernisation as cultural politics takes the contextualisation of the practices of ecological modernisation one step further. Here one is reminded of Mary Douglas's classic definition of pollution as 'matter out of place'. Her point was that debates on pollution are essentially to be understood as debates on the preferred social order. In the definition of certain aspects of reality as pollution, in defining 'nature', or in defining certain installations as solutions, one seeks to either maintain or change the social order. So the cultural politics perspective asks why certain aspects of reality are now singled out as 'our common problems' and wonders what sort of society is being created in the name of protecting 'nature'.

Ecological modernisation here appears as a set of claims about what the problem 'really' is. The cultural politics approach argues that some of the main political issues are hidden in these discursive constructs and it seeks to illuminate the feeble basis on which the choice for one particular scenario of development is presently made. The structuring principle in this third interpretation is that there is no coherent ecological crisis, but only story lines problematising various aspects of a changing physical and social reality. Ecological modernisation is understood as the routinisation of a new set of story lines (images, causal understandings, priorities, etc.) that provides the cognitive maps and incentives for social action. In so doing ecological modernisation 'freezes' or excludes some aspects of reality while manipulating others. Of course, reductions are inevitable for any effort to create meaningful political action in a complex society. The point is that one should be aware that this coherence is necessarily an artificial one and that the creation of discursive realities are in fact moments at which cultural politics is being made. Whether or not the actors *themselves* are aware of this is not the point. Implicitly, metaphors, categorisations, or definition of solutions always structure reality, making certain framings of reality seem plausible and closing off certain possible future scenarios while making other scenarios 'thinkable'.

To be sure, in this third interpretation there is no implicit assumption of a grand cultural design. Quite the contrary, environmental discourse is made up of 'historically constituted sets of claims' (John Forester) uttered by a variety of actors. Yet in interaction these claims 'somehow' produce new social orders. Foucault speaks in this respect of the 'polymorphous interweaving of correlations'. The analytical aim of this approach is, firstly, to reconstruct the social construction of the reductions, exclusions and choices. Secondly, it tries to come to a historical and cultural understanding of these dispositions. Hence it tries to reconstruct the social forces behind ecomodernist discourse, for instance by studying discourse-coalitions. Subsequently, this approach tries to facilitate the discussion on the various probabilities, possibilities and, above all, on the various alternative scenarios for development that could be constructed.

The historical narrative of this third perspective takes up the themes touched upon at the beginning of this chapter. It emphasises that the ecological problem is not new. It observes that the ecological dilemma of industrial society is almost constantly under discussion, be it through different emblems. What these discussions are about, it argues, are in fact the social relationships between nature, society and technology. For that reason this perspective calls attention to the 'secondary discursive reality' of environmental politics: there is a layer of mediating principles that determines our understanding of ecological problems and implicitly directs our discussion on social change. Hence it would investigate what image of nature, technology and society can be recognised in the 'story lines' that dominated environmental discourse at the time of *Limits to Growth*, or during the confrontation between the state and radical social movements in the 1970s, or in the consensual story lines that dominate ecological modernisation in the 1990s. What is the cultural meaning of the biospheric orientation that is central to present-day environmental discourse? In this respect it argues that ecological modernisation is based on objectivist, physicalist and realist assumptions, all of which are highly arbitrary. Story lines on global warming, biodiversity or the ozone layer suggest the presence of the threat of biological extinction and assert that these problems should be taken as the absolute basis for an ecological modernisation of society. But do these story lines really have the same meaning and implications for all regions? Are they as relevant for the farmers of the Himalaya as for the sunbathers of the coasts of Australia? Should we not understand the global environmental story lines as the product of 'global-ised local definitions', as intellectuals from the South have suggested, since the problems have mainly been caused by the North while the solutions apparently have to come mainly from the South (Shiva, 1993)?

Rather than suggesting that there is an unequivocal (set of) ecological problem(s) the third interpretation would argue that there are only implicit future scenarios. The point here is not to doubt whether environmental change occurs. Neither would this social constructivism lead to a position in which each account is equally true or plausible. The point is primarily anti-objectivist and criticises the uncritical acceptance of certain scientific constructs as the starting point of politics. Bird (1987: 256) summarised this position most succinctly, writing that

> scientific paradigms are socio-historical constructs – not given by the character of nature, but created out of social experience, cultural values, and political-economic structures. . . . the actual objects of inquiry, the formulation of questions and definitions, and the mythic structures of scientific theories are social constructs. Every aspect of scientific theory and practice expresses socio-political interests, cultural themes and metaphors, personal interactions, and professional negotiations for the power to name the world.

Here it departs from the more traditional understandings of social action that are implicit in the previous two interpretations. To suggest that the developments in environmental discourse between the publication of *Limits* in 1972 and Rio in 1992 should be interpreted as a process of social learning does not appreciate the cultural bias of the process nor the contingency of the present definitions. But the technocracy critique has omissions too: its proponents might also reject the naive notion of social learning, but their differentiation between the material and the symbolic indicates that they too work with a naturalist understanding of what the problems 'really' are.

Whereas the previous two interpretations in fact shared a clear idea of the ecological problem, and both had their own idea about a possible remedial strategy (respectively conceptual or institutional change, and more coordination or more decentralisation), the third interpretation holds that there can be no recourse to an 'objective' truth. It suggests that the ecological crisis is first and foremost a discursive reality which is the outcome of intricate social processes. It is aware of the ambivalences of environmental discourse and would, in the first instance, not try to get 'behind' the metaphors of ecological discourse. It would try to encircle them to be able to challenge them scientifically, and to enhance conscious-ness of the contingency of knowledge about ecological matters. What is more, it would investigate the cultural consequences of prevailing story lines and would seek to find out which social forces propel this ecomodern-ist discourse-coalition. Once the implicit future scenarios have been exposed, they might lead to a more reflective attitude towards certain environmental constructs and perhaps even to the formulation of alterna-tive scenarios, the socio-political consequences of which would present a more attractive, more fair, or more responsible package. Hence the central concern of this third interpretation is with *cognitive reflectivity, argumentation* and *negotiated social choice*.

The role of academia follows from this commitment to choice and open debate. They have to help to open the black boxes of society, technology and nature. The cultural politics perspective would resist the suggestion that nature can be understood and managed by framing it in a new 'ecological' language, as for instance by giving priority to economics and systems ecology, on the basis that a pure language does not exist. Its aim would rather be to pit different languages and knowledges (for example expert knowledge versus lay knowledge) against one another to get to a higher understanding of what ecological problems could be about. Here it would assume that this interplay would lead to the recognition of the wide diversity of perspectives.

A more radical consequence of the cultural politics perspective for science would be that the ecological crisis would, potentially, be put upside down: the debate would no longer be on the protection of nature but would focus on the choice of what sort of nature and society we want. After all, once the deconstruction of, say, the biospheric discourse has exposed its naturalist and realist assumptions, the debate might take a different turn. If people have become aware of the political and economic motivations behind biospheric discourse,[4] and have come to grips with the backgrounds of their own naturalism,[5] they might become intrigued by the 'myriad ways in which we make, unmake, and remake "nature" and "human nature" ' (Bennett, 1993: 256). If technology is no longer seen as inherently problematic but also as a potential force to reconstitute the social relationships between nature, technology and society according to one's own needs and preferences, the debate might lose its simplistic modern/anti-modern format and a debate on the re-creation of society might result. The consequence would, of course, be that the debate would no longer necessarily focus on environmental matters: the re-creation of society might often focus more explicitly on the conceptualisation of technologies, on the conditions of application of certain techniques, and on the preferred 'socialisation of nature' (rather than the mere protection of nature as it is – see the next section).

The preferred socio-political arrangements of this third interpretation follow from this analysis and focus on facilitating the discussion of implicit future scenarios. It should be emphasised that in terms of concrete ideas of how this might be organised this perspective is still searching. The most conventional suggestions follow the tracks of the republican tradition, emphasising the need for explicit choice, defence and argument, for the (re)legitimation and/or rejection of certain interventions. Like the technocracy critics it would like to bring society back in. Here we should locate the idea of a 'Societal Inquiry' which would give citizens the right of initiative – for example to re-examine the policy towards acid rain that failed to bring about results.[6] The suggestion is that this initiative would be qualitatively different from the new democratic forms that were introduced as part of the technocracy critique. A societal inquiry does not assume a clearly defined subject matter: the point of the exercise is precisely to explore and expose the contradictions, the reductions and exclusions and to bring into the discussion the implicit understandings of technology, nature and society as well as the implicit future scenarios. Subsequently the societal inquiry would try to create the basis for focused rhetorics, for defence and argument, for relegitimation and/or rejection, and for the reorientation of political action in the light of social debate. This would also hold true for the procedures of 'symbolic law'. The idea here is that the law should no longer be seen as a conclusive statement of dos and don'ts. It would rather have to be a set of normative arguments the meaning and consequences of which should constantly be rethought in the context of concrete cases. The role of government would thus be one of defending the operationalisation it has given to the normative commitments that were the outcomes of societal debates (although one may wonder whether these suggestions are not again based on a traditional understanding of politics).

A more radical version of the cultural politics perspective would break with the traditional understanding of politics as a centralised process. It would take the very process of the creation of discursive realities as its object. Rather than seek to develop arrangements that allow to 'get behind' the metaphors it would explore how new perspectives on society can be created. The issue would not be to 'free' the natural human identity that now suffocates under the hegemony of technological applications; its aim would rather be to explore the unintended potentials of new technologies to create new identities and facilitate the awareness of affinities between various distinct identities.[7]

In all, ecological modernisation as cultural politics starts off by opening up the three black boxes of society, technology and nature and seeks to illuminate the principal openness of ecological discourse. Indeed, it would go so far as to inquire what the meaning could be of the present *ecologisation* of the risks of modernisation.

The Social Dynamics of Ecological Modernisation

In sociological theory the ecological crisis is interpreted as the confrontation of industrial society with its own latent side-effects. Zygmunt Bauman speaks about post-modernity as 'modernity coming of age'. We are, says Bauman, now able to see modernity as a 'project'. We have acquired the ability to reflect on what brought us the unprecedented wealth and we now see the (ecological) risks and dangers that we have created in the process of modernisation (see Bauman, 1991). The theory of reflexive modernisation as proposed by Ulrich Beck suggests that it is the unintentional self-dissolution or self-endangerment which he calls 'reflexivity' which has produced the ecological crisis. Reflexivity here relates to modernity as a social formation that constantly and immanently *undercuts* itself (see Beck et al., 1994; Beck, this volume). He distinguishes this 'reflexivity' from 'reflection', which relates to the knowledge we may have of the social processes taking place. Beck holds that as the modernisation of society unfolds, agents increasingly acquire the ability to reflect on the social conditions of their existence. Yet whether or not the self-endangerment of society leads to reflection remains an empirical question.

The question is of course to what extent this reflection can be shown to be present in the present discourse on ecological modernisation. Furthermore, we should assess what forms of reflexivity we can discern in the project of ecological modernisation. Which processes of deinstitutionalisation and reinstitutionalisation take place in the context of the process of ecological modernisation? Which social projects are furthered under the flag of environmental protection? Actors might now broadly share the concepts and terms of ecological modernisation but which implicit future scenarios can we discern?

It is instructive in this respect to have a look at the regulatory efforts of some of the countries that are internationally seen as the most advanced examples of ecological modernisation, such as Germany, or The Netherlands with its comprehensive policy planning approach.[8] In these Western European countries we now see a broad societal coalition working on the institutionalisation of ecomodernist ideas. By and large this institutionalisation is based on the premises of the institutional learning interpretation of ecological modernisation that was sketched above. Yet the social dynamics of ecological modernisation come out to be not as predictable as that ideal-type might suggest. We can in fact observe at least four distinct lines of development.

There can be no doubt about the fact that the main *direct* effect of ecological modernisation is the *rationalisation of ecology*, through the conceptual and institutional amendment of existing bureaucratic structures and the creation of new ones, be it by the state or by new ecocorporatist associations. There seem to be good grounds to argue that there are certain parallels between the history of the US conservation movement in the Progressive Era and the development of the discourse-coalition of ecological modernisation. What started in the late 1960s and early 1970s as a concern about the lack of care for nature seems, over the years, to have given way to a coalition of forces that produces social effects that are at odds with the original intentions of the environmental movement. This tendency towards rationalisation is well known and is in fact implicitly described in the discussion in the previous section, while its dynamics have been analysed elsewhere (Fischer, 1990; Paehlke and Torgerson, 1990; Hajer, 1995).

One should observe, however, that the attempt to rationalise ecological issues according to the prescriptions of the institutional learning paradigm does *not necessarily* produce a rationalisation of ecology. It may also produce a critical form of cultural politics. Take for instance the effects of the national political commitment to sustainable development on policy-makers at the local level. They are confronted with the need to translate 'sustainable development' into new planning procedures, conservation strategies, etc. By directive they are ordered to make sustainable development their new 'cognitive map'. Yet here they are confronted with all sorts of interpretative difficulties. After all, sustainable development is merely a 'story line' that generated its global support precisely because of its ambivalence. So what happens in actual practice? Policymakers are left to themselves when it comes to the operationalisation of the notion of sustainable development. Here they have a great freedom. They can either make a few aesthetic alterations but basically continue with business as usual, or they can use sustainable development as a crowbar to break with previous commitments. In that case institutional learning produces cultural politics and opens the possibility for a more broadly defined reflection on the sort of problem the ecological crisis 'really' is.

Another interesting development in this respect are the quarrels that are beginning to erupt over the first ecomodernist practices, most notably the waste recycling programme. Whereas waste-reduction programmes have so far not proved to be successful, waste-recycling schemes are threatened precisely because of their success. This causes similar difficulties in Germany, The Netherlands and Austria. The unexpected quantity of materials (glass, plastics, metals) that consumers manage to bring together for recycling now exceeds the capacity of the recycling facilities. On the one hand this causes a renewed resistance of industrial firms to the waste-recycling schemes. On the other hand it is a case where the pragmatic solutions themselves produce the evidence that waste might require more fundamental changes, thus – potentially – enhancing the reflection on the meaning and consequence of the 'ecological crisis'.

A second tendency we can discern is the *technicisation of ecology*. Perhaps the most significant development is taking place behind the scenes in the leading ecomodernist countries – the striking but little discussed reorientation that has taken place in the strategic planning of big multi-national firms such as Siemens, DASA and BMW. They are central in the ecomodernist discourse-coalition. They strive towards a set of clearly defined ecoindustrial innovations, they have a new idea of what the relevant actors are, and they carefully work towards a set of new institutional arrangements. They too can be seen using the threats of potential ecological disaster or climate catastrophes as a crowbar, but this time it is used to fulfil the promise of 'intelligent' traffic systems, 'smart' highways, 'intelligent' energy savings technologies, renewable energies, and socially engineered behavioural changes. NGOs like Greenpeace, trade unions and politicians can, albeit for varying reasons, all be seen to help push ecological modernisation in this direction. Similar developments are well under way in the United States, where the 'Big Three' car producers work together with firms like IBM, AT&T and the Federal government on multi-billion dollar plans to create this new 'intelligent' transport system. What this in fact amounts to is the amendment and extension of existing large technical systems, a tendency which will prove to be extremely powerful.

From the perspective of the technocracy critique the danger of this technicisation of ecology is that ecological modernisation short-circuits a superficial understanding of some emblematic ecological problems with a new technological commitment. Essentially, microelectronic technologies are presented as the solution for the 'juggernaut effect'. The cultural politics perspective observes that the discussion on alternative future scenarios is thus strangled in a double way: both the debates on information technology and on the ecological crisis are shifted aside to make way for 'efficient' and 'positive sum game' solutions.

Other examples of this tendency towards the technicisation of ecology are not difficult to find. Compared to the 1970s the ecomodernist policy-discourse has also caused a huge shift in the conceptualisation of environmental problems by the NGOs. The shift in thinking about strategic solutions is of such an extent that an NGO like Greenpeace that once started off opposing nuclear tests, and is well known for its protection of endangered species, could recently announce its backing of the development of a 'green car' as well as its own plan to construct a tunnel under the Öresund, creating a rail link between Sweden and Denmark. The idea behind this latter initiative is to provide a readily available solution as an alternative to the longstanding plans of the Danish and Swedish governments to build a bridge for car traffic. Similarly, efforts are now being made in Japan to apply the latest freezing techniques to conserve species that are threatened with extinction, and, as a final example, German social scientists have found that in the debate on biotechnology ecology is now used as a justification for continued development in this area. Unlike in the early days, when biotechnology was still proposed as the 'Eighth day of the Creation', it is now constructed as an 'ecologically benign' technology because it would require radically less resources (see Lau et al., 1993).

This technicisation of ecology receives its social strength of course not primarily from its beneficial effects in terms of ecological improvements. The technicisation of ecology is the translation of a social and moral issue into a market issue. It is based on the conviction that ecology is, potentially, a new – and huge – market which is to be created and, subsequently, to be conquered. Traditionally, sociologists would perhaps argue that this tendency is based on a great faith in the capacity to control side-effects in advance. Yet it is questionable whether that belief really was constitutive of this tendency in the first place.

A third line of development that ecological modernisation has produced is the tendency towards the *ecologisation of the social*. This tendency is not so much part of ecological modernisation as a response to it. Ecological modernisation is a strategy that believes in further rationalisation, and in creating and maintaining the society-wide coalitions to 'fight' environmental degradation. Despite all the critique that one might advance of the Brundtland process, the fact remains that this was conceived as an essentially social-democratic and Western European project. Brundtland was in fact the third Western European social-democratic leader to head a UN commission on global integration (after the Brandt Commission on development and the Palme Commission on disarmament) (Ekins, 1992: chapter 2). The principle of international solidarity, and the social-democratic belief in modernist productionist solutions, therefore always figured prominently.

Inherent in the positive sum game format is the commitment to conceptualise solutions within the existing social system. That means going along with the further integration of world markets, and trying to *add* the social or, more recently, the ecological dimension. Hence *add* a 'social chapter' to the Maastricht Treaty, *add* an ecological paragraph to GATT, *add* the Green Fund to the World Bank. The contradictions that are inherent in this integrative thinking now clearly also produce their reactive counterparts. And here the alliance with the 'big institutions' and existing discourses of power backfires.

Here I would point to the important role of the ecological issue in what various others have called the new regionalism, the new localism, the new tribalism or the 'politics of place'. Those concerned about environmental degradation can rejoice in great interest from the circles of the German new right, which is pasting together a 'place'-orientated ideology. Here the economic and political uncertainties are interpreted as being the product of globalism. This is then subsequently used to recreate a new national sense of order based on a renewed appreciation of 'place' versus 'space'.

In this discourse the national environment becomes the basis for a new national identity, and care for the environment is put forward as an argument to try to regain an allegedly natural social ecology:

> Ecology opens our eyes and shows that nations are not simply human complexes, based on shared language, attitudes, culture and history. Their evolution and their inexchangable identity is also to be understood as the product of the soil from which these complexes grew, the space in which that happened and with which they are connected.[9]

Environmental problems are here seen as the product of a global political project in which a diffuse array of various 'insensitive' actors including the EC bureaucracy, multinational industries and democratic politicians participate. In this context the 'problem' of asylum seekers is drawn into the ecological debate. On the one hand they do not share concern for the regional environment (they do not 'feel' it); on the other hand it is argued that they are extra mouths to feed and people to house, which will require an increase in industrial production and hence cause more environmental destruction (see Jahn and Wehling, 1991, 1993). As Jahn and Wehling have shown for Germany, this new ecologisation of the social should not be seen as a clearly defined ideology that is confined to the new right. It is much more an 'argumentative formula' that can be found much more widely (see also Eder, this volume). Indeed, it is a formula that can be found in mainstream politics in other countries too.

The fourth line of development is the *socialisation of ecology*. Here the debate on the ecological crisis is simply recognised as being one of the few remaining places where modernity can still be reflected upon. It is in the context of environmental problems that we can discuss the new problems concerning social justice, democracy, responsibility, the preferred relation of man and nature, the role of technology in society, or indeed, what it means to be human. This gives ecological discourse a great political importance. In a way it is completely irrelevant whether emblematic problems like global warming constitute the dangers that some people argue they present. Global warming should simply be seen as one of the few possible issues in the context of which one can now legitimately raise the issue of a 'No' to further growth. Here the philosophical imperative of responsibility can be introduced in centre-stage political decision-making through a plea for a 'No regrets' scenario on global warming targets for low energy consumption.

At the same time, the socialisation of ecology perspective would hold that the 'ecological crisis' is by no means unique. Here it elaborates on the cultural politics perspective. Indeed, there is much to be said for the integration of the debates on new technologies that are generally kept separate. If one would break with the conception that nature should be understood as something 'out there', and with the idea that nature stands for the 'authentic', the pure and the good, one might create the possibility of a more vibrant sort of debate. If technology is no longer simply seen as what threatens 'nature' (and hence society) but is also seen as something which creates, at least potentially, new opportunities and new social arrangements, one might be willing to go along and take one more step and discuss the introduction of *in vitro* fertilisation, experiments on embryos or man–animal transplants as essentially ecological issues. This socialisation perspective reflects on 'nature in the age of its technical reproducibility' as the eloquent German philosopher Gernot Böhme (1992) has put it. Rather than mourn over the end of nature we might start to think about what kind of nature we really want. The struggle to protect nature 'as it is' often brings barbed wire into the prairie while the ever more frequent attempts to bring back 'nature as it was' lead to the most bizarre engineering exercises. So rather than leave modernist commitments as they are, it seeks to save Enlightenment thought from the attempts to interpret the ecological crisis as the basis for a further centralisation of power (as in the prevailing global discourses) and from the attempts to use the ecological crisis as the basis for a new intolerant regionalism.

This challenges the boundaries of what is normally understood to be the subject-matter of ecological discourse. That is precisely the point. Ecology would here become the keyword under which society discusses the issues of 'life politics' (Giddens) in a way that allows for a rethinking of existing social arrangements. The rhetorical strength of the ecological crisis would be used to reflect on the nature of modernity.

Conclusion

It will be clear that the four lines of the development sketched above are by no means equal in strength. The rationalisation and technicisation of ecology are well under way while the popular critique drifts more and more in the direction of the ecologisation of the social. The issue really seems to be how to improve the strength of the fourth perspective. Yet how would one increase the reflective awareness of the possibilities of ecological modernisation? How would we arrive at a position where reflection means more than awareness of the 'ecological crisis' alone? How would we get it to include awareness of the necessary openness of the definition of problems and solutions and, finally, how would we achieve an increased awareness of the fact that ecological modernisation should be based on a debate on the recreation of the relationships between nature, technology and society?

It should be said at the outset that there can be no naive idea about the possibilities of bringing about this discussion on 'the nature we really want'. The sociology of technology literature has given us ample evidence of how large technical systems have their own logic of development. Nevertheless, the critical task now is to devise the discursive stages where these patterns can be discussed and democratically renegotiated. In the context of the prevailing tendencies towards a rationalisation and technicisation of ecology, and in an awareness of the dangers of a ecologisation of the social, one should seriously reflect on the need to reinvent democracy. As Bauman (1991: 276) writes:

> What is left outside the confines of rational discourse is the very issue that stands a chance of making the discourse rational and perhaps even practically effective: the *political* issue of democratic control over technology and expertise, their purposes and their desirable limits – the issue of politics as self-management and collectively made choices.

Exploring the ambivalences of ecological modernisation and trying to come to institutional forms that could accommodate the increase of cognitive reflectivity, argumentation and negotiated social choice seems one of the key issues that could reconstitute the basis and meaning of environmental politics.

Notes

1. For a more elaborate analysis of ecological modernisation, see von Prittwitz, 1993; Hajer 1995.

2. This interpretation is now more widely supported. See for example Weale, 1992; Spaargaren and Mol, 1992; von Prittwitz, 1993; Harvey, 1993; Liefferink et al., 1993; Healey and Shaw, 1993; Teubner, 1994.

3. Whereby technology is conceptualised in the Schelskyan sense of the term – that is, including both technology as artefacts and 'social technologies'. See Schelsky, 1965.
4. See the various contributions in Sachs, 1992, and Sachs, 1993.
5. For this aspect compare the discussions in Harvey, 1993, and in Beck, 1995.
6. For an elaborate discussion of these ideas and others, see Hajer, 1995: chapter 6; also Zillessen et al., 1993.
7. The best examples of this can be found in Haraway, 1991; and Bennett and Chaloupka, 1993.
8. For a discussion of the development in environmental policy in these countries, see Weale, 1992.
9. Professor W.G. Haverbeck, quoted in Maegerle, 1993: 6.

References

Bauman, Zygmunt (1991) *Modernity and Ambivalence*. Cambridge: Polity Press.
Beck, Ulrich (1995) *Ecological Politics in an Age of Risk*. Cambridge: Polity Press.
Beck, Ulrich, Giddens, Anthony and Lash, Scott (1994) *Reflexive Modernization: Politics, Tradition and Aesthetics in the Modern Social Order*. Cambridge: Polity Press.
Bennett, Jane (1993) 'Primate visions and alter-tales', in Jane Bennett and William Chaloupka (eds) *In the Nature of Things*, pp. 250–66.
Bennett, Jane and William Chaloupka (eds) (1993) *In the Nature of Things: Language, Politics, and the Environment*. Minneapolis: University of Minnesota Press.
Bird, Elisabeth Ann R. (1987) 'The social construction of nature: Theoretical approaches to the history of environmental problems', *Environmental Review*, 11 (4): 255–64.
Böhme, Gernot (1992) *Natürlich Natur – Die Natur im Zeitalter ihrer technischen Reproduzierbarkeit*. Frankfurt am Main: Suhrkamp.
Cockburn, Alexander (1993) ' "Win/Win" with Bruce Babbitt: The Clinton administration meets the environment', *New Left Review*, 201: 46–59.
Cohen, Jean A. (1985) 'Strategy or identity: New theoretical paradigms and contemporary social movements', *Social Research*, 52 (4): 663–716.
Ekins, Paul (1992) *A New World Order: Grassroots Movements for Global Change*. London: Routledge.
Fischer, Frank (1990) *Technocracy and the Politics of Expertise*. London: Sage.
Gorz, André (1993) 'Political ecology: Expertocracy versus self-limitation', *New Left Review*, 202: 55–67.
Hajer, Maarten A. (1995) *The Politics of Environmental Discourse: Ecological Modernisation and the Policy Process*. Oxford: Clarendon Press.
Haraway, Donna (1991) *Simians, Cyborgs, and Women: The Reinvention of Nature*. London: Free Association Books.
Harvey, David (1993) 'The nature of environment: Dialectics of social and environmental change', in Ralph Miliband and Leo Panitch (eds) *Socialist Register 1993*. London: Merlin Press. pp. 1–51.
Hays, Samuel P. (1979 (1959)) *Conservation and the Gospel of Efficiency: The Progressive Conservation Movement, 1890–1920*. New York: Atheneum.
Healey, P. and Shaw, T. (1993) *The Treatment of 'Environment' by Planners: Evolving Concepts and Policies in Development Plans*. Working Paper no. 31, Department of Town and Country Planning, University of Newcastle upon Tyne.
Jahn, Thomas and Wehling, Peter (1991) *Ökologie von Rechts – Nationalismus und Umweltschutz bei der Neuen Rechten und den Republikanern*. Frankfurt am Main: Campus.
Jahn, Thomas and Wehling, Peter (1993) 'Ausweg Öko-Diktatur? Umweltschütz, Demokratie und die Neue Rechte', in *Politische Ökologie*, 34: 2–6.
Kwa, C. (1987) 'Representations of nature mediating between ecology and science policy: The case of the international biological programme', *Social Studies of Science*, 17: 413–42.

Lau, Christoph et al., (1993) *Risikodiskurse-Gesellschaftliche Auseinandersetzungen um die Definition von Risiken und Gefahren*. Report to the German Federal Minister for Research and Technology.

Liefferink, J.D., Lowe, P. and Mol, A.P.J. (eds) (1993) *European Integration and Environmental Policy*. London: Belhaven.

Maegerle, Anton (1993) 'Wie das Thema Umwelt zur Modernisierung des rechtsextremen Denkens missbraucht wird', *Frankfurther Rundschau*, 21 December, p. 6.

Offe, Claus (1985) 'New social movements: Challenging the boundaries of institutional politics', *Social Research*, 52 (4): 817–68.

Paehlke, R.C. and Torgerson, D. (eds) (1990) *Managing Leviathan: Environmental Politics and the Administrative State*. Peterborough (Ontario): Broadview.

Sachs, W. (ed.) (1992) *The Development Dictionary: A Guide to Knowledge as Power*. London: Zed Books.

Sachs, W. (ed.) (1993) *Global Ecology: A New Arena of Political Conflict*. London: Zed Books.

Schelsky, H. (1965) 'Der Mensch in der wissenschaftliche Zivilisation', in *Auf der Suche nach Wirklichkeit*. Düsseldorf/Köln. pp. 439–80.

Schumpeter, J.A. (1961 (1943)) *Capitalism, Socialism and Democracy*. London: George Allen and Unwin.

Schwarz, M. and Thompson, M. (1990) *Divided We Stand: Redefining Politics, Technology and Social Choice*. London: Harvester Wheatsheaf.

Shiva, Vandana (1993) 'The greening of the global reach', in W. Sachs (ed.), *Global Ecology*, pp. 149–56.

Spaargaren, G. and Mol, A.P.J. (1992) 'Sociology, environment, and modernity: ecological modernisation as a theory of social change', in *Society and Natural Resources*, 5: 323–44.

Teubner, Gunther (ed.) (1994) *Ecological Responsibility*. London: Wiley & Sons.

von Prittwitz, V. (ed.) (1993) *Umweltpolitik als Modernisierungsprozess*. Opladen: Leske & Budrich.

Weale, Albert (1992) *The New Politics of Pollution*. Manchester: Manchester University Press.

Wynne, Brian (1982) *Rationality and Ritual: The Windscale Inquiry and Nuclear Decisions in Britain*. Chalfont St Giles: The British Society for the History of Science.

Zillessen, Horst et al. (eds) (1993) *Modernisierung der Demokratie – Internationale Ansätze*. Opladen: Westdeutscher Verlag.

12

ENVIRONMENTAL KNOWLEDGE AND PUBLIC POLICY NEEDS: ON HUMANISING THE RESEARCH AGENDA

Robin Grove-White

What sorts of new knowledge does the world *need* these days? How can the research community, particularly in the social sciences and humanities, contribute best, in the bewildering circumstances in which societies like ours now find themselves?

Behind such questions lies a more specific, and still more contentious issue: are the presently dominant forms of academic research in countries like Britain able to generate insights of the kind society now needs in order to help address environmental problems and enhance social equity, in a period of immense turbulence in many parts of an ever more industrialised world? This chapter argues that new approaches to research may now be necessary in the public domain.

With different emphases, the various contributors to the present volume have pointed to the range and depth of new cultural configurations affecting late twentieth century industrial societies – characteristically involving tensions in the domain of the citizen's relations with 'the state'. In response to the fact of ever-ramifying technological change and specialisation, of intensifying globalisation of trade and competition, and of the insistence of governments that the continuation of such ratcheting processes is an inescapable necessary condition for increased human welfare, unfamiliar cultural tensions and new imbalances of power and authority are now being generated in countries like Britain. Not simply individuals, but also governments the world over, are struggling to cope with the implications of these processes of change for social stability.

The strains are such that it is small wonder the credibility of politicians and political institutions in the Western world has been shrinking. Numerous recent polls and surveys suggest that, even in historically stable countries like Britain, there is mounting fatalism and cynicism about the capacity of institutions which formerly commanded public identification (Parliament, political parties, trades unions, churches, even local 'communities'), to shield us from the increasingly unsettling impacts of continuing processes of change. To the strong, such new uncertainties may be bracing, even exhilarating. To the less fortunate – amongst whom more and more of us are now to be counted – they are disturbing, indeed hugely unsettling.

This has significance for the machinery of politics itself. There are few clues as to how its erosion of public respect and authority might be remedied. Yet whatever the inadequacies, or even the mounting irrelevance, of governing elites in the public mind, the need for institutions of government is still indisputable. In 'risk society', there is still a need – indeed, a greater need than ever – for processes of communal public decision, for the definition and making of choices about the deployment of public resources, for the updating and sustaining of common frameworks of regulation and law, for advancing the welfare of the disadvantaged, and for maintaining common infrastructures (networks of communication, defence, and the like).

However, most of the analyses in this book imply that some of the most important implications of the whirligig economic forces now transforming societies around the world are poorly appreciated by our public institutions. For example, Beck and Adam (both this volume) argue that the unfamiliar character of such changes is now making them increasingly impossible for our institutions to control, or even to anticipate; whilst Maguire and Berking (both this volume) suggest that the transformations are now such as to reach into – indeed directly to challenge – people's very sense of their own identities, at the most personal levels. Yet for the most part, governments, with their armies of subordinate regulators and bureaucracies reaching into every nook and cranny of contemporary life, appear to be driving blind, when it comes to understanding such novel cultural dynamics, now being produced in the circumstances of (let us call it) 'late modernity'.

So what potential new role might this imply for research? Over the past three decades, the relationship between governments and independent research communities (universities, think tanks, research consultancies) has become an increasingly instrumental one. In countries as different as Britain, the USA and Japan, governments have used researchers to produce short-term 'policy-useful' knowledge. The dominant disciplines have been those which have been seen as able to meet such requirements – the hard natural sciences, adapted to the requirements of public administration, and the harder of the social sciences, particularly economics and social statistics.

Officially funded research, therefore, has tended to be designed to provide the analyses and data which can underpin politically driven policy initiatives. But when voices in the research community raise questions about the implied normative assumptions concerning people and human motivation made by the official bodies commissioning such research, or the adequacy of established institutional frameworks for addressing them, the answer (in the UK at least) has generally been that such fundamental matters are *political* questions, most appropriately to be resolved through prior arguments amongst politicians themselves, rather than to be regarded as legitimate issues for research by outsiders. We can see such tensions, for example, in recent debates in the sphere of environmental risk assessment (Wynne, this volume), between decision analysts who favour numerical, mathematical representations of risk probabilities – accepting as given the official positivistic definitions of risks, and therefore in continuing demand as advisers to government – and sociologists who argue that conflicts between 'expert' and 'public' perceptions of risk may actually be pointers to an absence of public trust in the very institutional frameworks by which the risks are claimed to be addressed, or even defined (Royal Society, 1992: chapter 5), and whose expertise is in rather less call from public institutions. Thus the issue of the legitimate terrain of academic researchers in politically sensitive areas of public policy – a source of recurrent dispute over the years – is returning in new guises, as the increasingly opaque interactions between research and policy worlds blur the boundaries between the two domains (Wynne, this volume).

More specifically, the question now arises: How are we to respond to such a required distinction between the normative axioms of 'politicians' and the supposedly neutral intellectual processes of data-gathering by researchers, *in circumstances like those of the present*, when politicians show increasing signs of losing touch with the human implications of accelerating cultural change and confusion of the kind discussed through-out this volume? The fact is, insistence on such a distinction may now be a dangerous irrelevance, when cultural change on the scale implied by the preceding chapters is under way.

There is a clear challenge. Social scientists need to begin exploring fresh ways of generating 'intelligence' on these matters at a human level – intelligence which might assist public bodies towards developing more sensitive awareness of the ways in which individuals, singly and collec-tively, are responding to these accelerating processes of change in society. Equipped with such enhanced sensitivity, such bodies might then be better placed to begin approaching new initiatives or issues of institutional reform in ways which could maximise their benign influences, and minimise their more damaging ones.

What might this mean in practice? There are clues all around us. In the next section, I outline three major issues, all of them of considerable contemporary environmental significance. Each one illustrates the tenacity of dominant positivistic research understandings in present-day Britain, and the urgent need for a richer understanding of the phenomena at issue. The first example – the controversies surrounding the process of estimating the future capital costs of Nuclear Power – has been a live problem for more than two decades. The other two issues – the social impacts of biotechnology, and public understanding of 'sustainability' – are more recent, but no less charged with significance for society as a whole. Through such examples, it is possible to see that currently dominant forms of social-scientific understanding are tending to confuse and mislead us all, including government, in areas of mounting social and political significance. Each provides grounds for speculating that more 'culturalist' research perspectives, of the kind towards which this book has been pointing, could provide new and helpful insights, to assist the redesign of public institutions in modern complex societies over the period ahead.

Three Illustrations

The Capital Costs of Nuclear Power

Controversies surrounding civil nuclear power have been an arena in which radically different understandings of social reality have found expression in industrialised countries over the past twenty years. The currently dominant research approaches have failed adequately to unravel their implications, both for future official approaches to energy policy, and for society's broader processes of self-understanding. This can be illustrated by the landmark case of the Sizewell B PWR in Britain, over the period 1982–1994.

A key technical issue at the heart of this particular case concerned the fact that the immense cost of *building* a nuclear power station constitutes the dominant element (the other being the cost of fuel) in the lifetime cost of the electricity generated by such a station. Indeed, for a pressurised water reactor (PWR) of the kind now favoured by Britain's nuclear industry, as much as two-thirds of the unit cost of all the electricity such a station will generate is attributable to the initial costs of its materials and construction. Since a nuclear station usually takes anything from six to ten years to build, this makes the advance estimation of its likely capital cost a critically important exercise in crystal ball gazing.

In the late 1970s and early 1980s, environmental and consumer groups critical of the expansion of civil nuclear power in Britain, and aware of the Central Electricity Generating Board's (CEGB) poor track record on such cost projections, mobilised a serious intellectual challenge to them. At the 1982–84 public inquiry into the proposed 'Sizewell B' PWR – proclaimed by the government and nuclear industry as a test case for the future of nuclear power – the Council for the Protection of Rural England (CPRE) advanced detailed expert evidence disputing the Board's capital cost projection, stressing particularly that this neglected the likelihood of future social and cultural 'feedbacks' arising from public concerns about nuclear safety, feedbacks which would be likely to translate during the post-inquiry and construction periods into substantial extra costs directly attributable to the station (HMG, 1986: paras 67.7–67.8). Whilst CEGB offered an overall central capital cost projection of £2,010 million (1993 prices), CPRE argued with its own expert evidence that a central figure more than £700 million higher – £2,778 million, with an upper sensitivity bound of

£3,502 million (1993 prices) – would turn out to be more realistic. Had this alternative been accepted at the time by the Inquiry Inspector (which it was not), it would have undermined totally CEGB's overall economic justification for the station (HMG 1986: paras 67.74–67.75).

In the context of this chapter's concern about research paradigms, the important point to note is that the CEGB's figure was based on the officially accepted economic appraisal methodology, used by public utilities and ratified as valid by the government's own economists, according to which only costs seen as *directly within CEGB's control* were regarded as legitimate elements for inclusion in the projected capital cost estimate figure. Possible unforeseen eventualities were to be catered for simply by a standard 20% 'start-to-finish allowance' built into the estimate.

By contrast, CPRE extended its rival cost projection to embrace wider-ranging social and cultural judgements. These rested in part on an evaluation of the real-world experience of the regulatory pressures encountered previously by PWRs around the world, and of the ways in which these pressures had tended to reflect a social dynamic, which in turn had stimulated the progressive imposition of *additional* cost burdens by the nuclear regulatory authorities, in response to intensifying public safety concerns. CPRE speculated that, given the political likelihood of further regulatory constraints in the face of continuing public anxieties, the Sizewell PWR could also be expected to experience comparable processes during the post-inquiry and construction periods. It argued that such social realities, intrinsic to nuclear technology itself, should not be sidelined in the estimate, as CEGB was proposing; any extra costs that might flow subsequently from them would be as directly part of a proposed PWR in Britain as the bricks, mortar and pipework from which the station was to be constructed.

As we have noted already above, these contrasting approaches of CEGB and CPRE yielded dramatically different projections of the likely final cost. Nevertheless, authorisation for the station was granted by the government, and CEGB proceeded with the scheme.

The construction of Sizewell B was completed in 1994. The actual cost turned out to be £2,980 million (1993 prices), upwards of *£900 million* more than CEGB had predicted at the opening of the 1982 public inquiry. By contrast, CPRE's rival 1982 projection of £2,778 million, offered to the inquiry in the same year (to CEGB's scorn, and the Inquiry Inspector's scepticism – HMG, 1986: paras 2.137–2.152), appeared almost excessively conservative, after an interval of 12 years (COLA, 1994).

What are the implications of this extraordinary outcome? Analysis from the standpoint of 1995 vindicates emphatically CPRE's case at the Sizewell inquiry that CEGB's officially sanctioned methodology was both reductionist and profoundly inadequate. In calculating its capital cost estimate for the station, the Board focused only on those elements of cost that lent themselves to unambiguous measurement based on its own (selective) historical experience. Social or cultural realities deemed to be *outside* its direct control formed no part of this picture. They were seen by CEGB's officials, and by the Whitehall civil servants monitoring them, to be 'irrational' uncertainties, exogenous to the design of the station, and not relevant to an assessment of its 'true' economic efficacy. CPRE, on the other hand, was in touch with, and sought to reflect in *its* estimate, both the social reality of escalating world-wide public concern about growing reliance on civil nuclear technology, and the ways in which such concern might be expected to ripple through the thinking and responses of official bodies in Britain in the late 1980s and early 1990s. With such cultural realities in mind, it argued that there were massive indeterminacies in any cost projection for a new nuclear station, and that these should be reflected in far wider economic contingency margins than CEGB (and the government) contended were appropriate.

In the nature of things, CPRE could not predict what the precise contingencies likely to give rise to further cost increases would actually be. It could only point to social dynamics inherent in the development of the technology itself in a relatively open society like Britain, and speculate intelligently on the orders of magnitude of extra cost that might be entailed. However, in due course, the late 1980s saw a range of developments with almost precisely the impacts on cost that CPRE had argued were probable. The most striking of these was the 1986 Chernobyl disaster in the Soviet Union, which led to major slowdowns and reappraisals of nuclear programmes around the world, and contributed to further tightening of the regulatory climate in Britain. This and other shifts in official safety-related thinking and practice – the most recent of them Greenpeace's 1994 High Court judgment *vis-à-vis* BNFL – played the major role in pushing the final total cost of Sizewell B to £900+ million more in real terms than the Government had originally authorised – a fact which went brazenly unacknowledged when the completed station was launched by CEGB's successor body, Nuclear Electric, in early 1995.

Remarkably, Nuclear Electric has continued to show little sign of having learnt from this saga. In 1994, in its submission to the government's Review of the nuclear industry, its proposed methodology for estimating nuclear capital costs remained essentially that which had proved so inadequate in the Sizewell B case. This failure of adjustment, in the face of the patent inadequacy of the methodology in the Sizewell case, suggests the depth of the intellectual – indeed, ontological – commitment in energy policy circles to a view of the world in which cultural forces, however significant, lying outside the direct control of engineers continue to be understood as largely irrelevant to their thinking.

Two further observations should be made. First, the critique outlined above suggests that the official nuclear cost estimation methodologies constitute, *de facto*, an evasion of responsibility for understanding the full implications of continuing to advance a socially contentious technology like nuclear power in a country like Britain, an evasion endorsed implicitly by the government. By treating 'culturally' induced escalations of capital cost as simply anomalous and irrelevant, the methodology obscures – indeed, implicitly denies – social tensions and dynamics of the greatest importance not only for society's own self-understanding, but also, more immediately, for the prudent development of future national energy policy, with the immense political, industrial and economic commitments that entails. The 'culturalist' perspective implicit in embryonic form in the critique by CPRE, whilst advanced in this particular case from a partisan 'environmental' perspective, suggests the scope and the need for far richer descriptions of the human and institutional dynamics in play. Such descriptions could vastly improve society's 'intelligence' on such matters, and, in the process, assist the evolution of more prudent deployment of the nation's resources on major matters of public policy.

The second point is a corollary. Much of CPRE's documentation of these specific Sizewell B processes interacted with that of independent academic economists at the Science Policy Research Unit (SPRU) of Sussex University (ECC, 1982; CPRE, 1989; COLA, 1994). SPRU's tenacious and path-breaking economic analyses have been crucial to the opening-up of these issues. They have built on a largely quantitative style of analysis, to unravel the *facts* of the cost escalations and the methodological limitations giving rise to them, rather than exploring the human and institutional dynamics driving the persistence of the processes themselves.

The scope and need for new research approaches, building out from the work of SPRU and CPRE to enlarge general understanding of complex human realities in cases like this, is thus clear. Such research, aimed at excavating the critically important normative assumptions about human behaviour embedded in the methodologies of technical 'experts', could contribute to the emergence of new political perspectives on technological development which would respect more fully the indeterminacies inherent in knowledge in spheres like this.

Social Impacts of Biotechnology

The issues in the case of biotechnology have generic similarities with those in the nuclear case above. They too concern the ways in which restrictive definitions of public concerns are tending to be built, *ab initio*, into processes of political appraisal – in this case, concerning new techniques of genetic modification of plants and animals.

The vast economic potential of the biotechnology industries (Ernst & Young, 1994) has led to acute anxiety within the European Union (EU) that member states should not be hampered by excessive regulation from competing effectively with the USA and Pacific Rim economies in this sphere (CEC, 1993). This anxiety is all the more acute because of public apprehension – particularly in Germany but also in other member states such as Britain – about the speed of deployment of new biotechnological 'artefacts'.

In a well-intended attempt to anticipate and address public concerns, as required by an EU Directive, the British government created in 1990 the

Advisory Committee on Release to the Environment (ACRE), with the role of advising the Department of the Environment (DoE) on the granting of consents for the release of particular new genetically modified organisms (GMOs) into the environment, and on necessary research. The members of ACRE are stated to be people with relevant scientific knowledge, including individuals representing particular 'interests', such as the industry, workers and environmentalists.

What is striking about the ACRE initiative, and more generally about the terms within which wider public concerns about GMO developments have tended to be debated in British public institutions and research bodies (including the new research funding body, the Biotechnology and Biological Sciences Research Council (BBSRC)), is the extent to which the key issues have tended to be identified almost exclusively in terms of *physical* environmental risks. With the exception of the 1994 BBSRC-sponsored National Consensus Conference on Plant Biotechnology (of which more below), this has been as true for official and industry bodies as it has been for ACRE and for those few UK environmental groups, such as the Green Alliance (Green Alliance, 1994) and Greenpeace (Greenpeace UK, 1994), who have concerned themselves with the issues.

Important as these dimensions are, however, they are far from embracing the full spectrum of social and ethical concerns to which the advent of the new technologies has already given rise. These include not only legal and political concerns about the principle of patenting of new life-forms, but also, more fundamentally, hostility on ethical grounds to the very principle of tampering with existing life-forms in order to reap commercial (or even wider social) benefits. Such deeper social concerns have strong resonances with recent, increasingly intense pro-life/anti-life controversies, manifested in abortion and new IVF politics, on both sides of the Atlantic. It need hardly be added that the polarisations involved in such debates are themselves linking to other mounting social tensions between religious fundamentalists and libertarians in certain Western countries – all in all, a dangerously potent set of issues.

Paralleling these social realities are observations from recent research, within a sociology of knowledge perspective, in the fields of public risk perceptions and public understanding of science (Martin and Tait, 1992; Wynne, 1992; Levidow, 1994). A growing body of this work tends to point to the crucial role played by *mistrust* of regulatory institutions, and by the fatalism that members of the public feel towards decisions they judge they cannot influence, in public anxieties (frequently represented in official contexts as 'irrational') about the relative severity of different forms of risk.

Applied to the sphere of biotechnology, such findings make sobering reading. When seen in the context of wider controversies about expert manipulation of life-forms, they suggest two disturbing possibilities. First, since people appear from such research not to be motivated to *articulate* strong concerns on matters in relation to which they do not feel significant 'agency', it may well be that there are substantial latent tensions within the public at large surrounding biotechnology, tensions which could well emerge in strong and passionate form should a genuine political opportunity present itself at some point in the future. (An analogy might be the recent mass protests in early 1995 about veal calf exports at ports in southern England; arguably, the intensity of such protests was a reflection of precisely the fatalistic, pent-up character of public resentment noted by Wynne (this volume) and others, on this occasion focused on the industrialised treatment of farm animals, and presented at last with an opportunity to have an impact on political events, however specific.)

The second issue concerns the dangerously distorting impact of the way in which such public concerns about biotechnology are now represented within government overwhelmingly in physical *environmental* terms. Like other Ministerial Advisory Committees under the British system, ACRE is composed largely of scientists (albeit a number of them of high calibre) and operates within terms of reference which restrict its concerns to the potential *physical* risks of releases of particular GMOs into the environment. Ironically, this 'physical' focus may arise in part from the recent success of environmental perspectives in becoming established as a mainstream political preoccupation in Britain. However, it is argued (Grove-White and Szerszynski, 1992; Grove-White, 1993) that the discourses of physical environmentalism may have tended to act frequently as surrogates for wider social and cultural anxieties, simply because of the relative digestibility of their 'realist' idioms to established political institutions. This adds weight to the suggestion that the positivistic environmental 'realism' of ACRE's terms of reference is acting inadvertently to obscure latent social tensions about GMO possibilities, tensions which might be expected to flare up, apparently unaccountably, when provided with some suitable trigger in the future.

As in the case of the earlier controversy about nuclear costs, the problem with speculations of this kind is that, *ex hypothesi*, it is impossible to specify in advance the precise future events that might constitute 'proof' of the validity of the observations. Indeed a powerful range of forces combine in present circumstances to thwart the emergence of an institutional framework within which such approaches might be explored with official seriousness. Such forces include both the intellectual interests of the currently powerful molecular biology research community, and the political/industrial axis anxious to advance the EU's relative standing and competitiveness in the field.

Nevertheless, there continues to be a danger of an adverse public reaction towards major GMO commitments at some point in the near future – a possibility which carries significant economic as well as social costs. With such concerns in mind, the Science Museum and BBSRC mounted, in March 1994, a 'UK National Consensus Conference on Plant Biotechnology' (Science Museum, 1994) – an initiative which built (albeit without regulatory force) on recent Danish and Dutch precedents, in seeking to crystallise opinions of the lay public on the issues. It was striking that, whilst a cautious endorsement of plant biotechnology emerged, the potential for future conflicts on moral and 'risk perception' grounds was also acknowledged. Such pointers reinforce the need for the social-scientific research community to build on the embryonic work of Rifkin, Roy and others (for example Rifkin, 1984; Roy et al., 1990) in developing richer and better-informed *cultural* 'maps' of this important field. The potential importance of biotechnology for society is as great as its keenest advocates are suggesting. A denser understanding of its social and cultural dynamics in real-world situations is urgently needed.

Public Understanding of 'Sustainability'

My third illustrative example concerns the issue of 'sustainable development' (or 'sustainability'), and the potentially perverse impacts of certain restrictive ways in which this concept is tending to be used and represented in current political discourse.

Although the arrival of the term in mainstream politics dates from the Brundtland Commission's report, *Our Common Future* (WCED, 1987), 'sustainability' in its present 'environmental' sense has its provenance in the 'Limits to Growth' debates of the early 1970s, and in the subsequent *World Conservation Strategy* (IUCN/UNEP/WWF, 1980; Jamison, this volume). Linked to biological concepts of 'carrying capacity' and 'eco-system', the term has overwhelmingly *physical* connotations, implying the necessity for human societies to respect the physical *limits* to the biosphere – in sharp reaction to the espousal by governments of the notion of undifferentiated *growth*, as the previous lodestar of industrial societies' aspirations. Since the Brundtland Report and the 1992 United Nations Conference on Environment and Development, the notion of sustainable development has drawn together an impressive coalition of governments, NGOs, industry and local authorities (via Agenda 21), committed to finding ways of moving economic and social development onto more *sustainable* trajectories, in this essentially physical sense (Hajer, this volume). There are growing networks of national and local government officials and other political actors seeking to innovate creatively within what some now see as a new collectivist agenda (LGMB, 1993; Jacobs, 1995a, 1995b). Crucially, however, the tacit model of sustainability on which most of this activity appears to rest continues to be one defined by expert (principally natural scientific) knowledge, purportedly able to be implemented by harnessing 'stakeholders' and the wider public, through education and exhortation, leading in turn to public 'participation' in the refinement and ultimate achievement of sustainability goals.

However, indications are emerging that such a discourse of sustainability lacks appropriate public resonance, a state of affairs which may be jeopardising its ability to encourage the wider participation sought (Worcester, 1994; Harrison et al., 1994). One explanatory hypothesis is that such a weakness reflects the alienating character of the tacit models of human nature and needs embedded in epistemologically 'realist' representations of sustainability (Grove-White, 1993; Wynne, 1994). Inadvertently, these may be reinforcing the damaging idea that the 'human' and 'cultural' are related to the 'environmental' only in an instrumental sense. If this is so, the admirable and open-ended 'public participation' aspirations of the new Agenda 21 community may be in growing tension with the overwhelmingly 'realist' and 'expert' terms in which sustainability goals are tending to be articulated by those most enthusiastically in favour (for example as targets for decreased per capita energy consumption, reductions in private personal mobility, more waste recycling, water savings, etc.).

Such problems of communication are being compounded in countries like Britain by the recent growth of public mistrust towards, and perceived disconnection from, policymaking bodies at all levels (Gallup, 1993; Macnaghten et al., 1995). There is increasing evidence of the fragmentation of public loyalties towards many of the mainstream 'traditional' institutions in society such as political parties, Parliament, local government, trades unions, churches and the like. The implications of such social trends for the achievement of 'sustainability' objectives have so far received minimal attention from the research community (though note Macnaghten et al., 1995; Jacobs, 1995b). For the most part, non-natural scientific research in this domain has tended to focus on economic tools for 'achieving' specified sustainability goals (Pearce, 1994), and sociological, political and philosophical discussion of the concept itself (Worster, 1993), largely within a framework of the same 'realist' physicalist assumptions (though note Redclift, 1993).

Equally neglected in the dominant research culture has been the potentially positive significance of a range of relevant new grass-roots cultural configurations in various EU countries. Arguably, these new networks carry within them the seeds of new collective social values consistent with the idea of sustainability – for example, the cultural networks and groupings around preoccupations as diverse as complementary medicine, gender, local 'place', animal rights and vegetarianism, personal therapies, disability and self-help, food quality, and new spiritual practices (Szerszynski, 1995). Notwithstanding the pioneering work on new social movements by sociologists in the 1980s (Touraine et al., 1983; Melucci, 1989; Eyerman and Jamison, 1991), social scientists and governments alike are tending now to concentrate only on the 'given' agenda of physical sustainability challenges and their policy corollaries (changes to transport, energy and agricultural policies, for example), and in an overwhelmingly instrumental fashion.

It appears that in countries like Britain many people are enthusiastic about the social values they sense to be latent in the notion of sustainability (Worcester, 1994; Macnaghten et al., 1995). Yet so far they have appeared unwilling or unable to realise such enthusiasm by actions along the lines which governments and NGOs have been advocating. Indeed, the gulf between people's everyday experience of official institutions and the claims now being made for achieving sustainability *through* such bodies is great enough to risk constituting a serious impediment to progress. For local authorities seeking to advance the admirable public participation aspirations of Agenda 21, these tensions are especially significant. Indeed, it is through their initiatives that the limitations of the dominant physicalist vocabulary are beginning to become apparent (Macnaghten et al., 1995).

How might the research community become more useful in this context? It appears that the tensions surrounding Agenda 21 may need to be understood in the context of the wider processes of transformation with which 'late modern' industrial societies are now struggling. Public identification with established forms of public life and civic engagement – embodied in political parties, trades unions, urban associations, established churches and the like – has been on the wane for at least the past two decades (Sennett, 1974; Lasch, 1979). Now, barely noticed, new forms of relationality and interdependence are being forged, albeit disguised behind the apparently atomising practices and vocabularies of 'individualism', 'consumption' and 'the market' (Jacques, 1993; Szerszynski, 1994).

This suggests that an urgent present requirement for progress towards 'sustainable development' is for better *intelligence* about these dynamics – a richer, more sensitive understanding of the moral and cultural mutations now taking place in the sinews of society. These have the potential to harmonise with the coalitions for change now beginning to emerge, but which are currently in danger of becoming becalmed. Instead of simply cataloguing or seeking to reverse the apparent 'decline' of inherited models of citizenship and civic-mindedness, social researchers should enter this new arena, and consider the question: What may now be the true human potentialities, and the positive wider significance for sustainable development, of the transformations taking place in countries like Britain concerning the boundaries between individual and collective identity, behaviour and values?

Moving Forward

The three domains from which the above examples have been drawn – energy policy, the development of biotechnology, and sustainable development – are all of immense significance for modern industrial polities. But what general point might they be taken collectively to illustrate?

At the most obvious level, each of the three encapsulates a problem for current research understandings and methodologies. Relevant social and cultural realities are being neglected, in a fashion ultimately counterproductive to the aims of policy. Such an emphasis might be taken to point to an urgent need in each case for corrective, supplementary measures, aimed at grafting on the absent research dimensions to the knowledge cultures of the key institutions affected. Adaptive processes on broadly such lines can be seen in their early stages in the UK in the parallel domain of 'probabilistic risk assessment', in which the Health and Safety Executive and others (HSE, 1988, 1992; Royal Society, 1992) have begun to show signs of responsiveness towards new sociological insights about the 'cultural' and 'institutional' dimensions of public risk perceptions (Douglas, 1986; Wynne, 1989; Thompson et al., 1990). On the face of it, adjustments analogous to these might be sought to the research cultures underpinning the three domains from which the examples in the previous section have been drawn.

However, such 'whiggish' prescriptions for *ad hoc* adjustment of research programmes would risk obscuring the deeper implications of what is now truly at stake in cases like these. Adjustments of research perspective might conceivably be possible in each individual sphere, but recent precedent suggests that this would almost certainly be on terms which sidelined key elements of the underlying critique.

Consider the parallel sphere of 'the environment' over the past few years. Recently, government institutions and industry have apparently embraced many of the concerns and perspectives advanced by grass-roots environmental movements around the world (crystallised by non-government organisations (NGOs) and Green parties) in the 1970s and 1980s (Eder, Jamison, Hajer, all this volume). At varying rates, in all EU countries, official practices and regulatory regimes have been adapting. The new political vocabulary of 'sustainable development', discussed above, has been one significant manifestation of these processes. Another has been the mounting mainstream political significance of some of the key emblematic NGO issues of the 1970s, such as excessive social dependence on the car, and the wider impacts (for the global climate, for example) of mounting energy dependency. However, the processes of growing incorporation of such environmental issues into the core of public policy, on terms *apparently* similar to those urged by 'radical' NGOs and Green parties over the past 25 years, has nevertheless sidelined key dimensions of the messages of the 'social movement' of environmentalism. Whilst a variety of specific issues (some of them very major) have been incorporated, much of the fuller 'meaning' of the environment movement as a culturally significant phenomenon in its own right has been firmly excluded (Jamison, this volume). Modern environmentalism needs to be seen as having evolved not only as a response to the damaging impacts of specific industrial and social practices, but also, more fundamentally, as a social expression of cultural tensions surrounding the underlying ontologies and epistemologies which have led to such trajectories in modern societies (Melucci, 1989; Beck, 1992; Grove-White, 1993). Modern polities, in responding to public concerns about the adverse *physical* impacts of these trajectories, have found the wider critique largely unpalatable. Indeed, as a reading of almost any official statement of environmental policy will confirm, the very *definitions* by government and industry of how 'environmental' issues are to be understood exclude, deliberately, any sense of that critique. One result is that, over the past decade, NGOs and Green parties have found themselves drawn uneluctably to become part of the body politic – but (for the most part 'innocently') on terms which have largely neutralised the wider important messages their original emergence implied for society, about the chronic cultural tensions of 'late modernity' (Beck, Adam, this volume).

The dangers of a 'neutralising' dynamic similar to this are obvious in the three spheres from which the examples in the previous section have been taken. Such dangers are all the more acute in the light of recent developments surrounding the relationships between governments and research communities in countries like Britain, developments which are tending to make still more difficult the emergence and full acknowledge-ment of new culturally relevant perspectives. It is appropriate, before moving to a final reflection on a possibly appropriate way forward for social researchers, to comment briefly on these tendencies in the recent 'politics of research'.

Three tendencies are especially striking. The first concerns continuing official anxieties – for example in the UK and within the institutions of the EU – about the appropriate relationship between 'science' and the policy world. Over the past 25 years, for example, the UK has seen a succession of official reports (such as HMG, 1971, 1993), resulting in adjustments of research funding aimed at inducing a more 'responsive' and 'useful' national research community in the universities and independent research institutes. The most recent manifestation, the 1993 White Paper on Science Policy (HMG, 1993), has reorganised the research councils (the official arm's-length research funding bodies), and sought to bring the new priority of contributing to 'wealth creation' and 'the quality of life' into the centre of future research practice. Such official *dirigisme* links to a second major concern of governments in EU member states – that future international competitiveness in trade will be driven by skills in new forms of specialist knowledge, and hence that universities should be pressed to help equip society accordingly. This is tending to reinforce the importance of 'user' needs in helping shape and determine publicly funded research priorities. Such a 'user' emphasis may well have certain important positive dimen-sions; it may undermine the tendency of disciplinary peer hegemonies to maintain restrictive notions of 'sound knowledge' in their domains, and in the process may encourage a more genuine pluralisation of research avenues and approaches (Gibbons et al., 1994). But it also interacts with a third dynamic within the research world itself – namely, the expanding preoccupation of researchers in both the natural and the social sciences with increasingly complex *computerised modelling* of complex systems. This syndrome, far too extensive to be documented here, can be under-stood, in part at least, as the product of a marriage between the opportunities offered by new information technologies, and the dominant quantitative, reductionist disciplines in the natural and social sciences.

Because of the apparent ability of such models to *synthesise* and *integrate* knowledges across disparate domains, in ways which appear to capture real (policy) users' problems, they have rapidly become almost synonymous with the very idea of interdisciplinary, user-orientated scientific research. The resultant explosion of modelling, within and across disciplines, is a new cultural phenomenon in its own right, and one which lends itself increasingly to interaction with public agencies wishing to plan their priorities on flexible, if still overwhelmingly deterministic, lines. Its effect is to move research, including social research in such dominant disciplines as economics, social statistics and geography, progressively into the meta-world of the laboratory and of 'integrated' computerised simulations.

Collectively, these various dynamics are generating a growing momentum, which universities and other research establishments across the EU see themselves as having an interest in following. But the risk is that they will encourage an ever greater technicisation of knowledge – a new twist in 'late modernity' to processes against which a succession of social prophets over the past century have warned (Ellul, 1964; Schumacher, 1973; Winner, 1977). These are processes which, however sophisticated or benignly intended, threaten to generate decreasing sensitivity in the research world to the warp and woof of everyday moral, social and cultural experience, both that of ordinary people in daily life and that of officials and regulators in their work in public institutions – at the very time when what is most needed by society is *increased* research sensitivity in relation to such matters.

Let us reflect finally on the three examples in the previous section in this context. Far from being individual aberrations, each one of them can be seen to embody a striking common syndrome. In each case, *embedded* in the relevant institutions is a knowledge culture which embodies a truncated and inadequate conception of the human subject – that is, of what real people are like and what their relational and communal needs may be, in the circumstances of modern complex societies. In the nuclear power case, the key methodologies have been used to absolve engineers and economists in powerful bodies from responsibility for understanding the perverse social dynamics their initiatives tend to unlock. In the biotechnology case, the knowledge culture in which even benign regulators are embedded makes the tacit assumption that people care predominantly about narrowly defined, highly specific physical hazards, rather than the broader social relations surrounding the manipulation and marketing of life-forms. In the sustainability case, similarly reductionist ideas about the relationship between 'the human' and 'the environmental', within an otherwise enlightened and pioneering policy community, risk generating perverse grass-roots antipathy towards some of their most valuable aspirations. The common syndrome appears to be an obstinately embedded reliance, in modern bureaucracies, on operationally useful but nevertheless seriously limited notions of human nature, the provenance of

which may be traced in the scientific reductionism and atomistic individualism criticised elsewhere in this volume. As Beck and Adam (both this
volume) point out in their different ways, the 'myths' of modernity – of
planning, control, and the individual in control of his/her destiny – are now
being undermined by the very social and technological dynamics they have
set in motion. The tensions triggered by restrictive knowledge cultures in
the three case studies I have cited provide pointers to the depth of the
current difficulties.

But perhaps they also point to some possible ways forward for the
research community. My suggestion is a modest one, consistent with other
essays in the present volume. The public domain needs greater sensitivity
to what is going on in the everyday world of human interaction, and to the
increasingly perverse consequences of many of its present tacit assumptions about what people are like, how they behave, and what they need
from one another, in the real-world circumstances of 'late modernity'.
Intensifying present trajectories of research in pursuit of more and more
instrumental knowledge, as most of our currently dominant disciplinary
cultures aim to do (the natural sciences, economics, social statistics), may
be important in its own terms, but it risks compounding society's present
confusions. Huge institutional blockages are developing, with the result
that we and those who 'govern' and regulate us understand one another
and our real-world day-to-day relationships less and less well. This in turn
is contributing to the spiralling of public disrespect for those official
institutions whose very legitimacy rests on their claims to be in control, and
on whom we all have to rely in present circumstances.

All of this suggests a new and urgent need from the research world – for
what Iris Murdoch, echoing Simone Weil, calls simply 'attention', the
humble, empathetic entering into people's felt, lived experience, with 'the
patient eye of love' (Murdoch, 1970). This is an ancient and deeply
honourable 'research' tradition, kept alive these days in academia for the
most part only in the humanities (though even there now under great
pressure from the deconstructive energies of the social sciences). It calls for
pretensions, practices and methods radically different from those involved
in the increasingly dominant quantitative sciences (natural and social). It
implies a growing focus on the human, the cultural and the relational, on
the significance of context and of place. It requires attention to the
particularities of experience, and also to lessons for the general latent
within the specific. Its implications in present circumstances are beginning
to be explored by individuals and groups like some of those whose work
has been represented in the present volume.

Such approaches offer no guarantees of grand solutions. But they are
better than driving blind, at increasing speed – which is what we are being
pressed to do, more and more. Out of research aspirations rooted in such
greater modesty can emerge, perhaps, significant fresh enlightenment – the
beginnings of what could prove in time to be indeed *a new ecology*.

Acknowledgements

My thanks to Lancaster colleagues, particularly Bronislaw Szerszynski and Brian Wynne, for their comments and continued stimulus at the Centre for the Study of Environmental Change, with ESRC's support.

References

Beck, U. (1992) *Risk Society: Towards a New Modernity*. London: Sage.
CEC (1993) *White Paper on Growth, Competitiveness and Employment*. Brussels: Commission of the European Communities.
COLA (1994) *The Capital Costs of Sizewell C*. Submission to the Nuclear Review by the Coalition of Local Authorities, by Gordon MacKerron (SPRU), September. Taunton: Somerset County Council.
CPRE (1989) *Nuclear Capital Costs*. Proofs of Evidence CPRE P/5 and CPRE 5/3 to the Hinkley C Public Inquiry, by Robin Grove-White and Gordon MacKerron (SPRU). London: Council for the Protection of Rural England.
Douglas, M. (1986) *Risk Acceptability According to the Social Sciences*. London: Routledge and Kegan Paul.
ECC (1982) *Construction Times and Costs*. Proof of Evidence ECC P/2 to the Sizewell B Public Inquiry, by Gordon MacKerron. London: Electricity Consumers Council.
Ellul, J. (1964) *The Technological Society*. New York: Vintage.
Ernst & Young (1994) *Biotechnology's Economic Impact in Europe: A Survey of its Future Role in Competitiveness*. London: Ernst & Young.
Eyerman, R. and Jamison, A. (1991) *Social Movements: A Cognitive Approach*. Cambridge: Polity Press.
Gallup (1993) 'Confidence in institutions', in *Gallup Political and Economic Index*, 390 (February): 39–40.
Gibbons, M., Limoges, C., Nowotny, H., Schwartzman, S., Scott, P. and Trow, M. (1994) *The New Production of Knowledge: The Dynamics of Science and Research in Contemporary Societies*. London: Sage.
Green Alliance (1994) *Why Are Environmental Groups Concerned about Release of Genetically Modified Organisms into the Environment?* London: Green Alliance.
Greenpeace UK (1994) Unpublished letter to ACRE, 11 April.
Grove-White, R. (1993) 'Environmentalism: A new moral discourse for technological society?', in K. Milton (ed.), *Environmentalism: The View From Anthropology*. London: Routledge. pp. 18–30.
Grove-White, R. and Szerszynski, B. (1992) 'Getting behind environmental ethics', in *Environmental Values*, 1 (4): 285–96.
Harrison, C., Burgess, J. and Filius, P. (1994) *From Environmental Awareness to Environmental Action*. London: UCL Working Paper.
HMG (1971) *A Framework for Government Research and Development* (Cmnd. 4814). London: HMSO.
HMG (1986) *Sizewell B Public Inquiry Report*. London: HMSO.
HMG (1993) *Realising Our Potential: A Strategy for Science, Engineering and Technology* (Cm. 2250). London: HMSO.
HSE (Health and Safety Executive) (1988), (1992) *The Tolerability of Risk from Nuclear Power Stations* (1st and 2nd editions). London: HMSO.
IUCN/UNEP/WWF (1980) *World Conservation Strategy*. International Union for the Conservation of Nature and Natural Resources, United Nations Environment Programme and World Wildlife Fund, Switzerland: Gland.
Jacobs, M. (1995a) *Sustainability and Socialism*. London: SERA.

Jacobs, M. (1995b) *Reflections on the Discourse and Politics of Sustainable Development (Part II)*. Working Paper. CSEC, Lancaster University.

Jacques, M. (1993) 'The end of politics', *Sunday Times*, 18 July: section 9, pp. 8–10.

Lasch, C. (1979) *The Culture of Narcissism*. New York: W.W. Norton.

Levidow, L. (1994) 'Biotechnology regulations as symbolic normalisation', *Technology Analysis and Strategic Management*, 6 (3): 273–88.

LGMB (1993) *A Framework for Local Sustainability*. London: Local Government Management Board.

Macnaghten, P., Grove-White, R., Jacobs, M. and Wynne, B. (1995) *Public Perceptions and Sustainability in Lancashire*. Preston: Lancaster County Council.

Martin, S. and Tait, J. (1992) *Biotechnology: Cognitive Structures of Public Groups*. Milton Keynes: Centre for Technology Strategy, Open University.

Melucci, A. (1989) *Nomads of the Present: Social Movements and Individual Needs in Contemporary Society*. London: Hutchinson Radius.

Murdoch, I. (1970) *The Sovereignty of Good*. London: Routledge and Kegan Paul.

Pearce, D. (1994) *Blueprint 3: Measuring Sustainable Development*. London: Earthscan.

Redclift, M. (1993) 'Sustainable development: Needs, values, rights', *Environmental Values*, 2 (1): 3–20.

Rifkin, J. (1984) *Algeny: A New Word – A New World*. Harmondsworth: Penguin.

Roy, D., Wynne, B. and Old, R. (eds) (1990) *Bioscience⇌Society*. Report of the Schering Workshop on Bioscience⇌Society, Berlin, 25–30 November. Chichester: John Wiley and Sons.

Royal Society (1992) *Risk: Analysis, Perception, Management*. London: Royal Society.

Schumacher, E.F. (1973) *Small Is Beautiful*. London: Blond & Briggs.

Science Museum (1994) *Report on UK National Consensus Conference on Plant Biotechnology*. London: Science Museum.

Sennett, R. (1974) *The Fall of Public Man*. Cambridge: Cambridge University Press.

Szerszynski, B. (1994) *The Politics of Dependence: The Self and Contemporary Cultural Movements*. Working Paper. CSEC, Lancaster University.

Szerszynski, B. (1995) *The Politics of Cultural Change*. Report. CSEC, Lancaster University.

Thompson M., Ellis, R. and Wildavsky, A. (1990) *Cultural Theory*. Boulder CO: Westview Press.

Touraine, A., Hegedus, Z., Dubet, F. and Wieviorka, M. (1983) *Anti-Nuclear Protest: The Opposition to Nuclear Energy in France*, trans. P. Fawcett. Cambridge: Cambridge University Press.

WCED (World Commission on Environment and Development) (1987) *Our Common Future*. Oxford: Oxford University Press.

Winner, L. (1977) *Autonomous Technology: Technics out of Control as a Theme in Political Thought*. Boston: MIT Press.

Worcester, R. (1994) 'The sustainable society: What we know about what people think and do'. Paper presented to Values for a Sustainable Future, World Environment Day Symposium, London, 2 June.

Worster, D. (1993) 'The shaky ground of sustainability', in W. Sachs (ed.), *Global Ecology*. London: Zed Books. pp. 132–45.

Wynne, B. (1989) 'Frameworks of rationality in risk management: Towards the testing of naive sociology', in J. Brown (ed.), *Environmental Threats: Perception, Analysis and Management*. London: Belhaven. pp. 33–47.

Wynne, B. (1992) 'Risk and social learning: Reification to engagement', in S. Krimsky and D. Golding (eds), *Social Theories of Risk*. New York: Praeger. pp. 275–97.

Wynne, B. (1994) 'Scientific knowledge and the global environment', in M. Redclift and T. Benton (eds), *Social Theory and the Global Environment*. London: Routledge. pp. 169–89.

INDEX